Form and Style in
Early English Literature

Form and Style in
Early English Literature

Pamela Gradon

Methuen & Co Ltd
LONDON

First published 1971
by Methuen & Co Ltd
11 New Fetter Lane, London E.C.4
© 1971 Pamela Gradon
Printed in Great Britain by
Butler & Tanner Ltd, Frome and London

SBN 416 12270 1

Distributed in the U.S.A.
by Barnes & Noble Inc.

Contents

Contents

Preface

The time is not yet ripe for a definitive book on the relationship between language and literature in the medieval period. That this is so is to some extent due to a misunderstanding of the task involved; to some extent due to the magnitude of the task itself. This book cannot hope, therefore, to be more than an exploratory and experimental work in this kind. The book has not been provided with a bibliography, since the range of material would make a bibliography difficult to compile and not very useful to consult. For the same reason, the references in the footnotes do not aim at completeness in every case. They attempt, when they are not purely referential, to indicate various aspects of the topic under discussion, with something of a bias towards more recent books and articles. It should perhaps also be noted here that, in a few cases, the punctuation of texts has been tacitly modified to help the modern reader. Virgules, for example, have usually been replaced by commas, turned points by stops, and punctuation has sometimes been amplified.

I have to thank many people for kind assistance in the writing of this book. My thanks are due, as always, to the staff of the British Museum and the Bodleian Libraries. I am indebted also to Professor C. Grayson for references to books and articles on Italian literature; to Mr. C. Talbot D'Alessandro for kindly advising me about points of translation in Italian and to Mr. B. E. Harbert for advice about points arising from the numerous quotations in Latin. Miss Elspeth Kennedy has kindly given me advice about Old French. I am indebted also to the following scholars for permission to consult their unpublished theses: Miss Gay Clifford (*Techniques of Description in some Manuscripts containing Personification Allegory*); Mrs. Twycross (*The Represen-*

tation of the Major Classical Divinities in the Works of Chaucer, Gower, Lydgate and Henryson); Mr. D. J. Williams (A *Literary Study of the Middle English Poems* 'Purity' *and* 'Patience'). I am particularly grateful to Dr. Anne Hudson for reading the whole manuscript and for supplying me with microfilms of Juliana of Norwich and the Middle English *Stimulus Amoris*. But, above all, I am grateful to her for stimulating suggestions and criticism.

Abbreviations

A.N.T.S.	Anglo-Norman Text Society
E.E.T.S.	Early English Text Society, Original Series
E.E.T.S. (ES)	Early English Text Society, Extra Series
E.E.T.S. (SS)	Early English Text Society, Supplementary Series
ELH	(*Journal of*) *English Literary History*
JEGP	*Journal of English and Germanic Philology*
JWCI	*Journal of the Warburg and Courtauld Institutes*
MED	*Middle English Dictionary*, edited by H. Kurath and S. M. Kuhn *et al.*
MLN	*Modern Language Notes*
MLQ	*Modern Language Quarterly*
MLR	*Modern Language Review*
MP	*Modern Philology*
NQ	*Notes and Queries*
OED	*Oxford English Dictionary*, edited by J. A. H. Murray, etc.
OS	Old Series
PBA	*Proceedings of the British Academy*
PL	Patrologia Latina, edited by J. Migne
PMLA	*Publications of the Modern Language Association of America*

PQ	*Philological Quarterly*
RES	*Review of English Studies*
S.A.T.F.	Société des anciens textes français
SP	*Studies in Philology*
S.T.S.	Scottish text Society
TRHS	*Transactions of the Royal Historical Society*
ZfDA	*Zeitschrift für deutsches Alterthum*
ZfDP	*Zeitschrift für deutsche Philologie*

Footnotes A complete reference is given at the first citation. Thereafter the Bibliographical Index must be consulted for full particulars.

INTRODUCTION

The Chequered Sky

'Strictly speaking, we might divide the art of Christian times into two great masses – Symbolic and Imitative – the symbolic, reaching from the earliest periods down to the close of the fourteenth century, and the imitative from that close, to the present time.' Thus wrote John Ruskin in 1856.[1] He illustrated the essential difference between these types of art by comparing two illustrations from MS. Additional 11, 639, one of which has a plain blue background, the other a chequered sky, the chequered sky which we have adopted as the heading of this chapter. A similar dichotomy has been observed by later students of medieval art. Otto Pächt, for example, to name only one, has commented thus on the Egerton *Genesis*:

> the relationship between the various persons of a scene is no longer, as in the early Gothic, regulated by abstract and general rhythmic principles; nor is the pictorial order an equivalent to the spiritual order which our mind projects into the subject. The aesthetic order and unity now come from within the picture, from the actors themselves, their actions and psychological relations.[2]

So we have, to use Ruskin's own term, a *crisis*, precipitated by Giotto, which was to prove significant for the whole of later medieval art. But the naturalism which the discovery of perspective in the later medieval period made possible, is not reflected only in the increasing autonomy of the artistic form.

[1] John Ruskin, *Modern Painters*, ed. E. T. Cook and A. Wedderburn (London, 1904), III, 262.
[2] Otto Pächt, 'A Giottesque Episode in English Mediaeval Art', *JWCI*, vi (1943), 67.

It necessitated, in the opinion of another art historian, a change in the manner of using symbolism also. Panofsky, in his discussion of symbolism in early Flemish painting, has worked out these implications in some detail. For example, he cites a crucifixion scene in the Psalter of Yolande of Soissons, of about 1275, in which are assembled beneath the cross, not only the Virgin, St. John and the Centurion, but also such witnesses to the divinity of Christ as could not have been present at Mount Golgotha; Moses, Balaam, Caiaphas and, in a literal rendering of the words of Simeon, a huge sword protrudes from the bosom of Our Lady. In order to bring out the identity of the cross with the Tree of Life, the cross is depicted as a twelve-branched, richly foliated tree and on its top can be seen the familiar symbol of Christ's sacrifice, the pelican. Panofsky comments:

> We can easily see that such a blend of present, past and future, of things real and things symbolic, proved to be less and less compatible with a style which, with the introduction of perspective, had begun to commit itself to naturalism. The application of perspective, we remember, implies that the painting surface is understood as a 'window' through which we look out into a section of space . . . on the other hand, the world of art could not at once become a world of things devoid of meaning. There could be no direct transition from St. Bonaventure's definition of a picture as that which 'instructs, arouses pious emotions and awakens memories', to Zola's definition of a picture as 'un coin de la nature vu à travers un tempérament'.[1]

The attempt to reconcile these two procedures and these two viewpoints resulted in what Panofsky terms 'disguised symbolism'. He points out that whereas when the illuminator of about 1275 wished to represent prophets of the Old Testament as witnesses to the crucifixion, he simply placed them beneath the cross and identified them by suitable attributes and scrolls, Broederlam, wishing to introduce similar figures as witnesses to the Annunciation, did so by representing them as statues attached to an apparently real *tempietto*. Or again, when the

---

[1] E. Panofsky, *Early Netherlandish Painting* (Cambridge, Mass., 1953), I, 140–1. Cp. R. L. Montgomery, 'Allegory and the Incredible Fable', *PMLA*, lxxxi (1966), 45–55.

thirteenth-century illuminator wished to refer to Simeon's prophecy, he represented its fulfilment by showing the Mater Dolorosa with her heart transfixed by a sword; but when Dürer wished to allude to the same prophecy, he showed her 'in the happiness of her motherhood, overshadowed by a big iris the ancient name of which was gladiolus, or "sword lily" '.[1] Panofsky continues,

> The principle of disguising symbols under the cloak of real things, is, however, not a new invention of the great Flemings, nor does its application begin with Melchior Broederlam. It emerged, as a concomitant of the perspective interpretation of space, in the Italian Trecento.[2]

This judgement broadly coincides, it may be noted, with that of Ruskin:

> For the great medieval art lies in a cluster about the culminating point, including symbolism on one side, and imitation on the other, and extending like a radiant cloud upon the mountain peak of ages, partly down both sides of it, from the year 1200 to 1500, the brightest part of the cloud leaning a little backwards, and poising itself between 1250 and 1350.[3]

Whatever may emerge from our study of medieval literature, this distinction between a symbolic and an imitative mode of writing is the starting point; not because it is an absolute but because the apparent disregard of naturalism is something which the modern reader first remarks in reading medieval literature or looking at medieval art. To the unsophisticated reader, or spectator, it is what marks medieval art as naïve, and inferior to the art of later ages.

If the distinction is not a critical absolute, however, neither is it a chronological one. It may be, as Worringer has suggested, that 'the urge to abstraction stands at the beginning of every art and in the case of certain peoples at a high level of culture remains the dominant tendency, whereas with the Greeks and other Occidental peoples, for example, it slowly recedes,

---

[1] Panofsky, I, 141.
[2] Panofsky, I, 141.
[3] Ruskin, *Modern Painters*, III, 263.

making way for the urge to empathy'.[1] But it is evidently true
that symbolic modes of expression are not a purely medieval
phenomenon. The same kind of disregard for spatial and
chronological probability which Panofsky and others have
noted in early medieval art, can be observed in the emblems of
the early modern period.[2] And how 'unmodern' are those
wonderful baroque churches of Southern Germany! How surprising and improbable is it to the modern mind that the famous
Birnau *Honigschlecker*, at first sight a charmingly natural *jeu
d'esprit*, is symbolic of the sweetness of the rhetoric of St.
Bernard beside whom he stands! John Bourke has drawn
attention to the extension of such symbolism even to the structure of these churches; the number three, representing the
Trinity, the number five for the five wounds of Christ, the
number seven recalling the words from the cross and the
sorrows of Mary, the number twelve for the twelve apostles, all
are represented in the structure itself. Ornament and furnishing,
also, use traditional symbols, the lily of the Annunciation, the
sword of Mary's sorrow, the pelican or the lamb as symbols of
Christ's sacrifice and many more. A notable example is the
ship-pulpit symbolising the Church.[3] Here, as in medieval art,
we have the sacramental patterns of the Church. And patently
the art of symbolic writing has notable exponents in the post-
medieval period such as Spenser and Bunyan to name only
two. An opposition, not unlike that posited by Panofsky for the
late medieval period, has even been assumed for a later period.
For Honig has compared Kafka with Spenser in the following
terms:

> The structure of oppositional relationships (in Kafka's *Meta-
> morphosis*) is not more complex than in *The Faerie Queene*. It is
> conditioned differently; that is, by a realistic milieu instead of a
> mythicised fairyland. Yet Kafka's localisation is significantly

---

[1] W. Worringer, *Abstraction and Empathy*, translated by M. Bullock (London, 1953), p.15.

[2] Cp. M. Praz, *Studies in Seventeenth-Century Imagery* (2nd edn., Rome, 1964);
R. Freeman, *English Emblem Books* (London, 1948).

[3] John Bourke, *Baroque Churches of Central Europe* (London, 1958), pp.47–8,
58, 124.

deceptive, for it is really an emanation of the hero's own disabled consciousness. Only through this inward focus are the scene and characters realised, although the objective tone of the narrative, emphasising the exigent event and the action of others, makes the focus and relationship appear to be outward.[1]

On the other hand, medieval theorists were, as we shall see, by no means unaware of the concept of 'imitation' nor of art as 'creation'.[2] The distinction between symbolism and imitation is thus not a chronological absolute, nor intended to be. It is rather a critical distinction with some chronological correlates. For I think it would be generally agreed that the similarities between medieval and contemporary art lie in the region of the disregard of naturalism, indifference to the creation of a surface image recognisably congruent with our sense experience. It would be hard indeed to deny that a painting of a lady by Picasso or Modigliano is radically different from such a painting by Lawrence or Reynolds, or that *Las Meninas* of Velasquez is radically altered when presented in the style of Picasso.

Yet this seemingly obvious distinction between a naturalistic and a non-naturalistic art is not without difficulties. For it has led to other dichotomies; art as autonomous form, and art as dualistic, matter and theme; art as a window on life and art as a window on morality; in other words, 'mechanic' and 'organic' form, the teasing but critically pervasive distinction between symbolism and allegory. The following passages offer a simple illustration of the point. The first is from Felix's *Life of St. Guthlac* written about 730-40:

> Itaque cum supradictus vir beatae memoriae Guthlac inter dubios volventis temporis eventus et atras caliginosae vitae nebulas, fluctuantes inter saeculi gurgites iactaretur, quadam nocte, dum fessa membra solitae quieti dimitteret et adsueto more vagabunda mente sollicitus curas mortales intenta meditatione cogitaret, mirum dictu! extimplo velut perculsus pectore, spiritalis flamma omnia praecordia supra memorati viri incendere coepit.[3]

---

[1] E. Honig, *Dark Conceit* (London, 1959), pp.63-4.

[2] Cp. E. De Bruyne, *Études d'esthétique médiévale* (Brugge, 1946), especially III, 114-15, 151, 316-17.

[3] Felix, *Life of St. Guthlac*, edited by B. Colgrave (Cambridge, 1956), p.80.

[*And so when this same man of blessed memory, Guthlac, was being storm-tossed amid the uncertain events of passing years, amid the gloomy clouds of life's darkness, and amid the whirling waves of the world, he abandoned his weary limbs one night to their accustomed rest; his wandering thoughts were as usual anxiously contemplating mortal affairs in earnest meditation, when suddenly, marvellous to tell, a spiritual flame, as though it had pierced his breast, began to burn in this man's heart.*][1]

The second passage is from *Dombey and Son*:

Sister and brother wound their arms around each other, and the golden light came streaming in, and fell upon them, locked together. 'How fast the river runs, between its green banks and the rushes, Floy! But it's very near the sea. I hear the waves! They always said so!' Presently he told her that the motion of the boat upon the stream was lulling him to rest. How green the banks were now, how bright the flowers growing on them, and how tall the rushes! Now the boat was out at sea, but gliding smoothly on. And now there was a shore before him. Who stood on the bank? . . . Oh, thank God, all who see it, for that older fashion yet, of Immortality! And look upon us, angels of young children, with regards not quite estranged, when the swift river bears us to the ocean![2]

In the first passage we have a pure metaphor, an *allegoria* in which the sea, representing the turbulence and sorrow of the world, is no part of the saint's experience on the night of his conversion. So understood it would make nonsense of the narrative. In the passage from Dickens, on the other hand, we assume that the river and the sea, although having metaphorical implications of transitoriness (as elsewhere in the book), are also part of the actual experience of the dying child, as they were part of his brief experience of life. Now I intend to cut across the abundant critical discussion occasioned by such contrasting techniques by referring in all discussion of texts to 'image' and 'meaning'. By the 'image' I mean the object of apperception; by the 'meaning' the perceived relationships and

[1] Felix, *Life of St. Guthlac*, p.81.

[2] Charles Dickens, *Dombey and Son*, edited by H. W. Garrod (London, 1950), pp.225–6.

structure of the text.[1] And I shall assume this to be equally valid for metaphor, allegory and the kind of symbolic narrative represented by the passage from Dickens. I shall thus, in a sense, be abandoning the distinction between monistic and dualistic literary modes such as symbolism and allegory, and falling perhaps into the intellectualist error;[2] but this is not to return to an old-fashioned dualism. Rather, as Hjelmslev has said in regard to his distinction between 'expression' and 'content': 'They are defined only by their mutual solidarity, and neither of them can be identified otherwise. They are each defined only oppositively and relatively, as mutually opposed functives of one and the same function.'[3] For this reason I have not used the term 'form', since the form is the meaning. The distinction between a naturalistic and non-naturalistic art with which we began I shall therefore regard not as a difference between monistic and dualistic literary modes but between different kinds of structure or, put less exactly, different relationships between image and meaning. Such a view is by no means without its problems, as will appear later in this chapter when the idea of 'congruence' is discussed, but I hope that its comparative flexibility will prove an asset in the discussion of actual texts which is the main concern of this book. It may perhaps be noted in passing that such a view reveals the essential fallacy of the panallegorist interpretation of medieval literature, for it cannot be assumed that the relationship between a given word and its literary context will be constant. The Chaucer of Robertson is, in fact, a *Chaucer moralisé*, a mode which Chaucer would no doubt have regarded as perfectly legitimate but not the mode in which he originally wrote.

Such a simplistic approach may perhaps also enable us to

[1] Some discussion of the term 'image' with useful bibliography may be found in C. Brooke-Rose, *A Grammar of Metaphor* (London, 1958), pp.34–5. It will be observed that my use of the terms owes something to recent linguistic dichotomies such as *signifiant, signifié; expression, content; code, message.*

[2] Cp. M. Krieger, 'Bendetto Croce and the Recent Poetics of Organicism', *Comparative Literature,* vii (1955), 252–8.

[3] L. Hjelmslev, *Prolegomena to a Theory of Language,* translated by Francis J. Whitfield (Madison, 1961), p.60.

circumnavigate the 'problem of style'. Writers on linguistic stylistics commonly assume that the subject of investigation is of a binary nature in that style consists of deviation from a norm. This norm can be purely contrastive in the sense that, as language contains affective and descriptive elements, style consists in the exploitation of the affective elements of language.[1] In this sense, style deviates from a statistical norm. Other writers have seen in the concepts of transformational grammar or of discourse analysis the key to stylistic deviation,[2] while, for others, the concepts of levels and categories have seemed more significant.[3] Other scholars have held that the norm, from which style is a deviation, is contextual, and that the deviation is from the expectations aroused by the structure of the text itself.[4] These problems will not be my prime concern. Our task will be both broader and less rigorous. The structure of the literary image, like the structure of language itself, oper-

[1] Cp., for example, I. A. Richards, *Principles of Literary Criticism* (5th edn., London, 1934); C. K. Ogden and I. A. Richards, *The Meaning of Meaning* (4th edn., London, 1936); C. Bally, *Traité de stylistique française* (2nd edn., Heidelberg, 1921); *Linguistique générale et linguistique française* (2nd edn., Berne, 1944); *Le langage et la vie* (3rd edn., Geneva, 1952).

[2] Cp. A. H. Hill, 'An Analysis of *The Windhover*; An Experiment in Structural Method', *PMLA*, lxx (1955), 968–78; S. R. Levin, *Linguistic Structures in Poetry* (The Hague, 1962); 'Deviation – Statistical and Determinate – in Poetic Language', *Lingua*, xii (1963), 276–90; 'Poetry and Grammaticalness', in *Essays on the Language of Literature*, edited by S. Chatman and S. R. Levin (Boston, 1967), pp. 224–30; W. A. Koch, 'On the Principles of Stylistics', *Lingua*, xii (1963), 411–22; 'Recurrence and a Three-Modal Approach to Poetry', *De Proprietatibus Litterarum*, Series Minor 2 (The Hague, 1966); R. M. Ohmann, 'Generative Grammars and the Concept of Literary Style', *Word*, xx (1964), 423–39; J. P. Thorne, 'Stylistics and Generative Grammars', *Journal of Linguistics*, i (1965), 49–59; cp. R. Fowler, 'Linguistics, Stylistics; Criticism?', *Lingua*, xvi (1966), 155–6.

[3] Cp. R. Fowler (*Lingua*, 1966), 156–7; 'Linguistic Theory and the Study of Literature'; in *Essays on Style and Language*, edited by R. Fowler (London, 1966), pp.1–28; M. A. K. Halliday, 'The Linguistic Study of Literary Texts', in *Essays on the Language of Literature*, pp.217–23; N. E. Enkvist, J. Spencer and M. J. Gregory, *Linguistics and Style* (London, 1964).

[4] Cp. M. Riffaterre, 'Criteria for Style Analysis', *Word*, xv (1959), 154–74; 'Stylistic Context', *Word*, xvi (1960), 207–18; 'Vers la définition linguistique du style', *Word*, xvii (1961), 318–44; 'Problèmes d'analyse du style littéraire', *Romance Philology*, xiv (1961), 216–27.

ates at many levels; the phonological level, the grammatical and semantic levels and the level of connected discourse. Modes and genres are structural features just as much as metre or vocabulary, and they will therefore come within the scope of this book. And as language assumes meaning in its historical context, as well as by virtue of its syntagmatic relations, so art and literature too are in some degree contextual. An example from art may clarify this concept. A picture of a woman holding a child to her cheek may, in certain contexts, and, by virtue of a certain style (which in itself indicates a certain context), be interpreted as *Theotokos Glykophilousa*; a picture of a burning bush may equally be interpreted as the Virgin Mary. In this sense all works of art may be said metaphorically to belong to the area of 'speech' rather than 'language' and thus their structure depends upon organisation within a field. To understand the *meaning* we must therefore also consider the literary field of which the particular utterance is a part. But since we are concerned with an analysis of image and meaning we shall be concerned with the structure of the image at every level and not concerned only to distinguish stylistic features from non-stylistic features in the image.

Other concerns of this book may perhaps be most profitably indicated by a closer examination of some exemplary texts. I want to look first at the concepts of generality and particularity. Let us begin at the verbal level.[1] It might be said that there is a linguistic spectrum of generality and particularity. 'The beautiful girl' is more particular than 'the beauty of the girl' which involves an implication of the universal. That is to say,

---

[1] Though I have not adopted their terminology or their conclusions, I am indebted in my thinking on this topic to Christine Brooke-Rose and Viggo Brøndal, *Les parties du discours* (Copenhagen, 1948); cp. also W. K. Wimsatt, *The Verbal Icon* (Lexington, 1954), pp.133–51; R. Wells, 'Nominal and Verbal Style', in *Style in Language*, edited by T. A. Sebeok (New York, 1960), pp.213–20; Josephine Miles, *Eras and Modes in English Poetry* (2nd edn., Berkeley and Los Angeles, 1964). It should perhaps be noted that in the discussion that follows I am using the term 'range' in a general sense and not in the special sense which has been given it by Angus McIntosh. See 'Patterns and Ranges', *Language*, xxxvii (1961), 325–37.

the linguistic spectrum includes both the adjective 'beautiful' and the abstract noun 'beauty'. We could also say 'the girl who was beautiful moved me'; or 'the girl, who was beautiful, moved me'.[1] In each case we have a different emphasis. In the first, the emphasis is on the particularity and immediacy of the girl; in the second, on her beauty; in the third the defining clause serves to emphasise the girl's beauty and to define it more sharply; in the fourth, the girl's beauty is moved slightly into the background by the descriptive clause. In the last two examples the syntax serves as a focusing device. Some literary examples will make the differences more evident. The first example is a poem by Christine de Pisan:

> Vostre doulçour mon cuer attrait;
> Je ne vous vueil plus reffuser;
> Doulx ami, que vault le muser
> Quant par voz yeulx Amours me trait?
>
> Si vous vueil amer sans retrait
> A tousjours mais, car, sans ruser,
> Vostre doulçour mon cuer attrait.
>
> Or soyés tout mien, sans faulx trait;
> Ainsi pourrons noz jours user
> En grant doulçour, sans mal user;
> Car, pour vostre plaisant attrait,
> Vostre doulçour mon cuer attrait.[2]

> [*Your sweetness attracts my heart; I desire no more to refuse you. Sweet love, why waste time when through your eyes Love pierces me? I wish to love you unreservedly, for evermore, for, truly your sweetness attracts my heart. Now, be all mine, in true sincerity; thus could we pass our days in great sweetness, without ill doing. For, because of your delightful attractiveness, your sweetness attracts my heart.*]

---

[1] The places in the sentence in which variant modes of expression are possible have been termed 'free space', 'a position in the sentence in which word substitution over a fairly wide range can take place without alteration in what we might call the prose meaning of the sentence'. See A. L. Binns, ' "Linguistic" Reading: Two Suggestions of the Quality of Literature', in *Essays on Style and Language*, pp.118–34.

[2] Christine de Pisan, *Ballades, Rondeaux and Virelais*, edited by K. Varty (Leicester, 1965), No. 79.

The dominant ideas here are emphasised by the rhetorical play on words, 'attract', 'retract', 'attractiveness' and the rhymes also underline other elements in the poem. The pattern is effectively binary. The first theme is 'your sweetness draws my heart' and the second 'I will no longer refuse you, be mine for ever and we will use our time with great sweetness'.[1] The two parts are linked by the word 'sweetness'. Compare this with the following poem from the *Carmina Burana* on a comparable theme.

> Chume, chume, geselle min,
> ih enbite harte din!
> ih enbite harte din,
> chum, chum, geselle min!
>
> Süzer roservarwer munt,
> chum vnde mache mich gesunt!
> chum vnde mache mich gesunt,
> süzer roservarwer munt![2]

[*Come, come, my beloved, I wait for thy heart; Sweet, rose-red mouth, come and make me whole!*]

This poem also makes use of repetitions to outline its theme but the different effect is partly due to the way in which the poet modulates from the more general to the more particular. In the first stanza he speaks of waiting for his beloved's heart; in the second, the addition of the adjective *roservarwer* gives the impression, by its greater particularity, of drawing nearer to the lady. It may also be noticed that the poet is exploiting different semantic areas. In the first stanza he speaks of the heart which must, in such a context, be only a metaphor, although, by virtue of its associations, a highly charged metaphor. It thus belongs only mediately to the area of sense perception. It is not 'intuitive', but 'intellectual'.[3] On the other hand, as the poet

---

[1] Cp. R. Dragonetti, *La technique poétique des trouvères dans la chanson courtoise* (Brugge, 1960), pp.286–303.

[2] *Carmina Burana*, edited by A. Hilka and O. Schumann (Heidelberg, 1941), I, 2, No. 174a; 292.

[3] For these terms cp. W. M. Urban, *Language and Reality* (London, New York, 1939), pp.143–68; they are to be distinguished from the terms *affectif* and *intellectuel* and *emotive* and *referential* although they have certain features in common with these. Cp. P. Guiraud, 'Stylistiques', *Neophilologus*, xxxviii (1954), 8–9.

speaks of his beloved's lips, we move into the realms of the immediately sensible and 'intuitive'. This too gives a climactic effect to the poem and contributes to the sense of drawing nearer to the object of desire. The sense of close focus is further increased by the metonymy by which the poet speaks of his lady only by reference to her heart and her lips.

When we compare this with the poem by Christine de Pisan we find in the latter a style largely mediated by abstract words, particularly the key word *doulçour*. The adjectives *doulx*, *plaisant* also have less immediacy than the single adjective *roservarwer* with its complex associations of colour and fragrance. The poem by Christine de Pisan has a certain musical quality, both because the language is largely abstract, and because it is both less particular and less 'intuitive' than that of the poem from the *Carmina Burana*. This exploitation of the general and the particular, the typical and the individual, could be illustrated by another example from the *Carmina Burana*:

> Exiit diluculo
>   Rustica puella
> Cum grege, cum baculo,
>   Cum lana novella.
>
> Sunt in grege parvulo
>   Ovis et asella,
> Vitula cum vitulo,
>   Caper et capella.
>
> Conspexit in cespite
>   Scolarem sedere;
> 'Quid tu facis, domine?
>   Veni mecum ludere.'[1]

[*In the dawn, a rustic maiden went forth, with flock, with crook, with new wool. In the tiny little flock is a sheep and a little she-ass, female calf, with*

---

[1] See *Carmina Burana*, I, 2, No. 90; 86. Hilka and Schumann doubt the authenticity of the last stanza, which should perhaps be omitted. This would not affect the argument, but I have printed it for the sake of completeness. For the style, cp. the suggestive comments on the medieval Latin lyric by P. Damon, 'Modes of Analogy in Ancient and Medieval Verse', *University of California Publications in Classical Philology*, xv (1961), 299–313.

male-calf, goat and little she-kid. She saw a clerk sitting on the sward.
'What dost thou, master? Come and sport with me.']

Why has the poet of this charming pastoral chosen to cast it in a form so austerely typical? The *rustica puella* is never described, except in terms of the accompaniments of her avocation. The poem, until the last stanza, is almost entirely composed of common nouns, apart from conjunctions and prepositions. The adjectives *rustica, novella* and *parvulo* are general and commonplace. The diminutive category gives tone rather than precision to the whole. Even the particular animals are given a kind of generality by their congruence with the theme of the whole. Now this is necessary to achieve the 'cut away' technique by which the poet tells his story; in effect, simply by reference to a convention. Only because the story is in the tradition of the *pastourelle* are the implications of the last stanza clear. The *raison d'être* of the poem is the encounter between the shepherdess and the clerk. A description of, for example, the scene in which the encounter takes place would, by moving the tale from the general to the particular, create a disparity between the narrative kernel and its realisation in a naturalistic narrative. If we compare this poem with the poem in the Harley Lyrics, *De Clerico et Puella*, we note a significant difference. The Harley poem is in dialogue form and the clerk addresses the girl in the language of the courtly lover:

> My deþ y loue, my lyf ich hate, for a leuedy shene,
> heo is briht so daies liht, þat is on me wel sene;
> al y falewe so doþ þe lef in somer when hit is grene.
> ʒef mi þoht helpeþ me noht, to wham shal y me mene.[1]

This is evidently a move in the direction of the particularity of naturalism but it seems to me to detract from the poem's effectiveness. To name a clerk, as the Latin poem does, tells us all we need to know within the economy of the tale. That, like *hende* Nicholas and Absolon, he should use the language of the schools in his love-making, is an irrelevance, or, at best, a tautology.

[1] *The Harley Lyrics*, edited by G. L. Brook (Manchester, 1948), No. 24, ll.1–4.

But it might be argued that the second stanza of the Latin is just such another tautology. We are told that the heroine is a *rustica puella*. Do we need the enumeration of her flocks in the second stanza? How far, in fact, can a story be projected in its bare outline; or, in other words, where does narrative outline end and colouring begin? The story might be described as 'shepherdess meets clerk'! What then is the nature of the realisation? This is so delicately balanced that each part is proportionate to each other part, and none breaks out of the thematic narrative frame. In many medieval romances we find a strong visual realisation of the story but no psychological realisation; an imbalance between narrative theme and realisation. In this little story each part is seen from the same distance at the same focus. The dawn in which the *rustica puella* sets out, and the grassy sward on which the clerk sits, and the maiden's flocks are all at the same degree of generalisation. The result is a picture in flat washes, a primitive in which the beautifully balanced parts are all presented without detail or shading.

These then are two ways in which the general and the particular, the typical and the individual can be utilised in literature. On the one hand, we can have a use of the most general words, common nouns, abstracts even, which can be made more or less immediate by the use of the article or certain kinds of adjective.[1] The impact can also be made more or less intuitive or intellectual by these grammatical means. This, as we have tried to suggest, can be used to create a style which has, on the one hand, distant focus, on the other, a close focus. And we have tried to suggest that the same spectrum ranging from the general to the particular can be seen in relation to narrative. The more typical the figures and scenes in a narrative the more congruent it will probably be with the story kernel. The greater the pictorial realisation of the story kernel, the more the

[1] Cp. M. A. K. Halliday, 'The Linguistic Study of Literary Texts', in *Essays on the Language of Literature*, pp.217–23. Qualifiers, whether adjectives or definite articles, tend to shorten focus. We could construct a range of focus for the general to the particular as follows: *man, modern man, the man, the happy man, the black man*. This also illustrates the range from the less to the more intuitive.

narrative will move from the typical to the naturalistic and immediate. The typical in fact is one form of disengagement.

There are, however, other components in question. We have so far spoken of focus in relation to grammatical components of style. And we have spoken of close and distant focus to describe the amount of descriptive detail which a work may contain. But focus is not merely a matter of generality and particularity. It is also a matter of point of view, or aspect, the angle from which the author tells his story, the difference between 'telling' and 'showing'.[1] Aspect is of course different from focus but certain kinds of 'showing' give the effect of close focus. Thus authorial intervention often has the effect of bringing the story 'closer'. Grammatical manipulation, for example a sudden change of pronoun, can have the same effect. In the Latin *pastourelle* the change of aspect at the end to direct speech from the third person of the previous narration, is a focus effect of this kind. The verbal tenses essentially concerned with aspect can also have the effect of giving close or distant focus. A text can be written in a consuetudinal aspect or an indicative aspect. To some extent the former implies authorial intervention. It is the mode of the author who describes his heroine before telling us what she does. 'Emma Woodhouse handsome, clever and rich, with a comfortable home and happy disposition, seemed to unite some of the best blessings of existence; and had lived nearly twenty-one years in the world with very little to distress or vex her.' But 'On an evening in the latter part of May a middle-aged man was walking homeward from Shaston to the village of Marlott. . . . The pair of legs that carried him were rickety, and there was a bias in his gait which inclined him somewhat to the left of a straight line. . . .' It will be noted that the difference is not between the past and present tense, although the consuetudinal mode can be emphasised by the use of the present tense; nor is it a matter of direct or indirect speech. In both the example from *Emma*, and

[1] Cp. N. Friedman, 'Point of View in Fiction', *PMLA*, lxx (1955), 1160–84 and references; W. C. Booth, *The Rhetoric of Fiction* (Chicago, 1961), pp.3–20; 211–40.

the example from *Tess*, it is the author who is narrating. The distinction is rather that in *Tess* we are only told what an onlooker could have seen; in *Emma* the information has been gleaned over a period of time and refers to Emma's state and situation when the story opens. In one we are 'shown', in the other 'told'. This is a distinction which is particularly relevant to our discussion of the style of the romances, for they characteristically employ the consuetudinal aspect. It must also be noted that aspect differs from perspective, the composition of the literary picture.

But there is yet another way in which an author can exploit linguistic resources. This is by the exploitation of lexical sets. This I shall call the texture of a work.[1] The use of a number of words in the same semantic field, or of words which overlap in meaning, can create a close texture or lexical cohesion;[2] a number of words from different semantic fields, or with little semantic density, can create a loose texture. A simple example of close texture would be the second stanza of our pastoral where the names of the animals constitute a lexical set. From this it will be observed that it is possible for a poem to have distant focus but close texture. Let us look at some further examples:

> O myghty Mars, that wyth thy sterne lyght
> In armys hast the power and þe myȝt,
> And named art from est til occident
> The myghty lorde, the god armypotent,
> That, wyth schynyng of thy stremes rede,
> By influence dost the brydel lede

---

[1] I am not using 'texture' in precisely the sense in which it is often used by critics, namely as the product of the kind of overlap of determinate and indeterminate elements of sound and meaning which is assumed, for example, by J. C. Ransom and specially represented by the textual devices of ambiguity, paradox, irony (cp. 'Wanted: an Ontological Critic', in *Essays on the Language of Literature*, pp.269–82; cp. Brian Lee, 'The New Criticism and the Language of Poetry', in *Essays on Style and Language*, pp.29–52).

[2] See M. A. K. Halliday, 'The Linguistic Study of Literary Texts', in *Essays on the Language of Literature*, p.220, on 'lexical cohesion'. Cp. also J. R. Firth, 'Modes of Meaning', in *Papers in Linguistics, 1934–51* (London, 1957), pp.190–215; Enkvist, Spencer and Gregory, pp.73–5; G. Leach, '*This Bread I Break*', *A Review of English Literature*, vi (2) (1965), 66–75.

Of cheualry, as souereyn and patrown,
Full hoot and drye of complexioun,
Irows and wood and malencolyk,
And of nature brent and coleryk,
Of colour schewyng lyche the fyry glede,
Whos feerce lokes ben as ful of drede
As the levene that aly3teth lowe
Down by the skye from Iubiteris bowe![1]

Compare with this the following description of Mars from *The Knight's Tale*:

The statue of Mars upon a carte stood
Armed, and looked grym as he were wood;
And over his heed ther shynen two figures
Of sterres, that been cleped in scriptures,
That oon Puella, that oother Rubeus—
This god of armes was arrayed thus.
A wolf ther stood biforn hym at his feet
With eyen rede, and of a man he eet.[2]

These two passages bring out clearly the difference between close texture and close focus, not always an easy distinction to make. Close focus will generally involve the use of words which are particular rather than general and, more generally, of a number of such words in order to make a closely focused whole. When Chaucer speaks, for example, of the wolf with *red eyes*, he is shortening the focus because 'red eyes' is more precise than 'eyes'; the denotation is restricted by the addition of the adjective. But when Henryson, in his description of Mars in *The Testament of Cresseid*, speaks of Mars as clad

In hard Harnes, hewmound and Habirgeoun,
And on his hanche ane roustie fell Fachioun;[3]

the use of a number of words from a lexical set, *Harnes, hewmound, Habirgeoun, Fachioun*, gives close texture.

[1] Lydgate, *Troy Book*, edited by H. Bergen, EETS (ES) 97 (1906), I, ll.1–14.

[2] Geoffrey Chaucer, *The Canterbury Tales*, A, ll.2041–8; *The Complete Works*, edited by F. N. Robinson (2nd edn., London, 1957).

[3] Robert Henryson, *The Testament of Cresseid*, ll.186–7; *Poems and Fables*, edited by H. H. Wood (2nd edn., Edinburgh, 1958).

In the passage from Lydgate, we have close texture as a marked feature of the style. We notice, for example, the use of the synonyms or near synonyms *myghty, power, my3t, armypotent; schynyng, fyry, glede, rede; souereyn, patrown; irows, wood, malencolyk; brent, coleryk;* this is indeed semantic saturation. But it is also to be noted that in some of these examples we have a combination of close focus and close texture. Suppose we take for example, the words *schynyng, rede, fyry, glede.* On the one hand, as members of a lexical set they create close texture; on the other hand, by virtue of their particularity, they create close focus. Now it is to be noted that repetition of identical words does not necessarily create close texture. Consider the following well-known poem by Christine de Pisan:

> Seulete sui, et seulete vueil estre;
> Seulete m'a mon doulx ami laissée;
> Seulette sui, sanz compaignon ne maistre;
> Seulette sui, dolente et courroussiée;
> Seulette sui, en languour mesaisiée;
> Seulette sui, plus que nulle esgarée;
> Seulete sui sans ami demourée.[1]

[*Solitary am I and solitary wish to be; Solitary has my sweet love left me; Solitary am I without companion or lord; Solitary am I, grieving and distressed; Solitary am I, afflicted with languishment; Solitary am I, more destitute than any other woman, Solitary am I left without a love.*]

The anaphora in the poem does not create close texture, while the words which overlap in meaning do.[2]

Let us then try to summarise our stylistic observations so far. We have three factors in question. In the first place, we have general and particular modes. If we take the theme of 'a woman in love' we can present an image at close focus, the story of Dido of Carthage; or we can present it in a more distant focus in, for example, the form of a folk tale; 'there was a princess

---

[1] Christine de Pisan, *Ballades, Rondeaux and Virelais,* No. 5, ll.1–7.

[2] It should perhaps be pointed out that we distinguish between lexical sets and collocables. By a collocable we mean words such as 'red' and 'mouth' which are statistically likely to occur in conjunction with each other. As often been noted, poetry often exploits collocability by the use of variable collocations.

and she loved a prince' or something of the kind. In the second place, the image can be made more precise, for example, by the use of descriptive adjectives, defining words of various kinds, or narration in a deictic or indicative aspect rather than a consuetudinal aspect. These devices can also create close focus. In the third place, we can exploit lexical sets to create a close-textured style. This close-textured style is characteristic, both of Latinate styles, and of styles such as that of Old English poetry, which are rich in near synonyms.

We have also spoken in the course of our discussion of 'semantic shallowness'.[1] It is perhaps time to attempt some definition of this term. It is to be distinguished from the concepts of 'intuitive' and 'intellectual' expressions. Fenollosa observed that 'Poetry is finer than prose because it gives us more concrete truth in the same compass of words.'[2] The words which a poet uses *can* indeed be effective because they are words which evoke sense perceptions, the 'intuitive' words, but also because they are mediated by a symbolic process, the 'intellectual' mode of expression. But further, it is possible to write effectively by the exploitation of the impact of words, the intensity of their associations, the emotional resonance as one might say, to use a musical analogy. When Goethe writes

> Meine Ruh' ist hin,
> Mein Herz ist schwer;
> Ich finde sie nimmer
> Und nimmermehr,[3]

[*My peace is gone, my heart is heavy; never, nevermore shall I find it.*]

---

[1] But this must again be distinguished from the idea of semantic complexity and semantic simplicity; the actual complexity or simplicity of the concepts involved. We have yet so much to learn about the psychology of semantics that it is often difficult to classify terms accurately. But I think the distinction is valid. It might be said that *cold*, for example, was semantically less complex than *winter* or *heat* than *summer*; for general discussion and useful bibliography, cp. S. Ullmann, *The Principles of Semantics* (2nd edn., Oxford, 1957); *Semantics: An Introduction to the Science of Meaning* (Oxford, 1962).

[2] E. Fenollosa, *The Chinese Written Character as a Medium for Poetry* (London, 1936), p.27.

[3] Goethe, *Faust*, I, ll.3374–7.

he is, by general consent, writing poetry, although it might come under the condemnation, in imagist terms, of being abstract. The focus is not close, as we have defined this term, yet it cannot be denied that the verse has impact. The effectiveness of the lines depends both on the implicit associations of the word *ruh* and the contextual implications which, by contrast, emphasise and exemplify the nature of peace. Thus, within the context of the poem, as well as in the context of the reference, there is an intensification of the word's impact. It may also be noted that the echo of *mein* and *hin* also serves, by the forcible conjunction of the two words, to intensify the meaning of *mein*, to define possession in terms of its opposite. When we speak of semantic shallowness we mean the reverse of this. It will be evident that the term 'semantic shallowness' is relative. The full potential of semantic depth can be exploited or unexploited in a given context. In a more abstract field, the word *haste* has less semantic depth than the word *beauty*. And here we observe that the idea of semantic depth is relative in another sense also. It must be partly a matter of period what impact a word will have. That is to say, semantic depth can vary from period to period. The word *noble*, for example, a word of semantic depth for an Anglo-Saxon, is a shallow word for us. The semantic depth of a word is in fact a function of the emotive use of language.

In all these different cases we see the use of language as involving choice within a linguistic field. But we must now turn to a much more difficult topic, the area of discourse which by adaptation might be called *cosmos* in contrast with *logos*; or, in other terms, the *macro-context*;[1] that is to say, not the relationship of word to context, but the organisation of the literary image into a larger whole, the level of connected discourse. Ullmann has drawn attention to the problems raised by the *macro-context*. He cites J. R. Firth's reference to 'serial contextualization of our facts, context within context, each one being a function, an organ of the bigger context and all con-

[1] See E. Cassirer, *The Philosophy of Symbolic Forms*, III, translated by K. Manheim (New Haven, 1957); S. Ullmann, *Language and Style* (Oxford, 1964), p.127.

texts finding a place in what may be called the context of culture'. And he adds, 'Which of these ever widening circles will provide the best framework for style studies?'[1] The problem arises most acutely in regard to narrative works. These may be regarded as consisting of a number of episodes, each episode being bounded by a framework of time and space; that is to say, an episode is an action (to use the Aristotelian term) in which people are set within a limited and common context.[2] It is the organisation of these episodes that constitutes the structure of the work in question. It is to be noted that the smallest units, the episodes, must be in some degree an imitation of an action, in so far as they must involve the spatial and temporal contiguity of the persons involved. Thus when, for example, critics use the term 'episodic' as a term of disapprobation they refer, not to the existence of episodes, without which there could be no narrative structure, but to the way in which these episodes are put together. Clearly, a truly episodic structure, in this sense, would consist of episode A followed by episode B, followed by episode C, in which the first episode referred to John and Mary's activities in Never-never Land, episode B, to William and Henry's activities in Ruritania and so on. Yet even such disconnected episodes could be associated in a wider context if the episodes could be shown to be related to a common theme, taking the theme to be the prose or determinate meaning of the episode. On the other hand, if the episodes were not thematically related, we could have a structured whole if the first episode in Never-never Land, and the second episode in Ruritania, and the third episode in Illyria and the fourth in Cloud Cuckoo Land, and so on, were linked by the existence of a common central character. This is the structure of such picaresque novels as *Gil Blas* or *Peregrine Pickle*. Then again, the episodes could be linked by some common character or characters, a common chronology and a

[1] Ullmann, p.127; cp., also, Angus McIntosh, 'Some Thoughts on Style', in Angus McIntosh and M. A. K. Halliday, *Patterns of Language* (London, 1966), pp.93-4.

[2] I have preferred the more general term 'episode' to the term 'narreme'.

common location, a story in which the 'unities' were observed. And, finally, episodes can be linked by a common causation. The plots of Hardy's novels would afford an excellent example of this way of linking episodes. Not only have the stories common characters, locations and chronology, but each episode is *caused* by a previous one. Chaucer's *Knight's Tale* would be another example of this kind of structure. This is what is termed 'plot' and of this we shall have more to say in a later chapter.[1]

Now this is all obvious and well-known. What is not so clear is the way in which an author can effect the 'mutation of themes'; that is to say, whereas it is evident when an author is using episodes with common characters and settings, it is not so obvious how he effects thematic links, or when such thematic links are to be assumed. Suppose, for example, we take a scene from *Havelok the Dane*, the death of Havelok's father, and put beside it the death of Goldeboru's father. It is evident that the two scenes have a folk-tale parallelism of structure. They have a common subject matter but not, I think, a common theme. We have a figure but not a pattern. But such repetition of episodes can constitute a pattern where the parts form a common theme. The temptation scenes in *Sir Gawain and the Green Knight*, and the three hunting scenes, would afford a test case. If the three hunting scenes are purely rhetorical amplification, with no thematic implications, then we have purely a figure of repetition, in which three recognisably similar narrative outlines have been coloured differently and stood side by side. If, on the other hand, the episodes have thematic significance, then we have a pattern, and the three episodes imply a comment on a single theme, the temptation. The repetition of episodes in *Havelok*, on the other hand, though markedly symmetrical, bears no relation to a common theme. It is a figure and not a pattern. Of this we shall have more to say later. Here it is sufficient to note that the repeat bars, to use a musical term, can be of various kinds. In medieval literature we often

[1] Cp. R. Scholes and R. Kellogg, *The Nature of Narrative* (New York, 1966), pp.82–159.

have simple juxtaposition, or evident repetition of a narrative shape, to create a pattern; or the repeat bars may be a symbolic object such as a bell, or the harp in *Orfeo*;[1] a bar of music as in a Wagner opera, the *leitmotif*; a repeated symbol as in *Dombey and Son*; or it may be the symmetry of a narrative shape as in *Sir Gawain and the Green Knight*. Any or all of these can serve to convert a figure of repetition into a pattern by providing thematic links.

But how does a thematic narrative differ, on the one hand, from a folk-tale or myth; on the other from allegory? And how do these differ from mimetic narratives? The term *myth* is, to say the least, ambiguous in modern usage. It can be used in the Aristotelian sense of a plot; it can be used as in mythic criticism, to refer to an archetypal story pattern; or it can be used in the traditional sense of a Greek or pagan myth. I have used the term 'mythic narrative' in the sense of a thematic tale; that is, a tale which is not an allegory but has some discernible theme which the narrative exemplifies. This is not without difficulties. Suppose, for example, we take the story of the Widow of Ephesus, it may be said that the narrative exemplifies the fickle nature of women. The widow in the story is a type of all women and the story differs from a folk-tale only in making a judgement on the action. It is different, though only in degree, from a mimetic narrative; that is to say, one which contains, in a sense, both a narrative and a theme which, although related, are nevertheless discrete. This is akin to Panofsky's 'disguised symbolism'. It is a symbolism clothed in a naturalistic form. So the death of Paul Dombey is a narrative but the sea theme, which appears again later in the book, is a symbol of mutability. Yet it cannot be said that the episode of the child's death serves only to illustrate this theme in the sense in which the story of the Widow of Ephesus exists purely to illustrate the theme of woman's fickleness. The latter is purely an exemplary tale and is almost entirely without descriptive detail or characterisation. This distinction is, of course, evident at the poles but

[1] For the use of symbolic objects in medieval literature, cp. S. Bayrav, *Symbolisme médiévale* (Istanbul, 1957), pp.43–74.

often blurred in the actual instances. Suppose, for example, we take again the hunting and temptation scenes in *Sir Gawain and the Green Knight,* should we class them as mythic narrative or as mimetic narrative? I would suggest that they fall into the category of mimetic narrative, since, although their function may be partly as vectors of a theme, they also constitute a development of the description of the life at the Green Knight's castle. They are thus mimetic narrative in virtue of their naturalistic development of the story, which reduces the congruence of story-pattern and theme.

It will be noted that in the above section I have used the phrase 'mimetic narrative' and not the more usual 'symbolic narrative'. This leads us inevitably to some consideration of our use of the word *symbol.* This word has become so protean, and yet so popular, that it is essential to indicate how I intend to use the term. It is not part of my intention to discuss the philosophical implication of the term even were I competent to do so. Some uses I reject; not because I am concerned to discuss their validity but simply as a decision on a matter of terminology. In some cases, I have simply substituted other terms. For example, Coleridge in distinguishing between the two sentences 'Here comes a sail' [symbolism] and 'Behold our lion!' [allegory][1] is observing a distinction which I have termed simply 'metonymy' and 'metaphor'. The concept of the essentially autonomous nature of the symbol as against allegory, which seems to lie behind this distinction, I would also reject for reasons that I have partly stated already and which I shall indicate more fully later. Nor would I accept Ruskin's distinction between personification and symbolism: he writes

> It is to be noted that personification is, in some sort, the reverse of symbolism, and is far less noble. Symbolism is the setting forth of a great truth by an imperfect and inferior sign (as, for instance, of the hope of the resurrection by the form of the phoenix); and it is almost always employed by men in their most serious moods of faith, rarely in recreation. Men who use symbolism forcibly are

[1] Samuel Taylor Coleridge, *Miscellaneous Criticism,* ed. T. M. Raysor (London, 1936), p.99.

almost always true believers in what they symbolize. But personification is the bestowing of a human or living form upon an
abstract idea; it is, in most cases, a mere recreation of the fancy, and
is apt to disturb the belief in the reality of the thing personified.[1]

It seems to me that personification and symbolism cannot be
helpfully put in opposition.[2] Symbolism is essentially a polysemous form of expression. Personification in itself is not
polysemous as becomes evident in late medieval allegory.
Whether it is polysemous or not depends upon the context.
The device of capitalisation does not in itself create polysemy.
Symbolism is essentially a conjunction of two objects from
different classes but, whereas personification must be the conjunction of a concrete and an abstract in a symmetrical relationship, symbolism can be the conjunction of a concrete and
an abstract, or of two concrete objects as when, for example, the
writer of the *Ancrene Wisse* compares the cross of Christ to a
shield. Nor have I found Bergson's contrast between 'static'
and 'dynamic' symbolism useful,[3] nor that between 'ascending'
and 'descending' symbolism.[4] The quarrel about symbolism is,
of course, also a philosophical one, arising from a quarrel about
the nature of language itself. Hence, for example, springs the
debate about the definition of language, whether literal speech
should be regarded as a special form of sign or as symbolic.
Whatever the rights and wrongs of the philosophical debate,
there is, from our point of view, a case for making a distinction between the *sign* and the *symbol*. An example will show
the significance of this distinction.

The word rose is a verbal sign for a certain object, and this
object 'by any other name would smell as sweet'. But when I say
'gather ye rosebuds while ye may', rosebuds is no longer merely an
indicative sign; it becomes a symbol, in that there is not merely

---

[1] Ruskin, *The Stones of Venice*, II, 377.
[2] Cp. B. H. Bronson, 'Personification Reconsidered', *ELH*, xiv (1947),
163–77; C. Muscatine, 'The Emergence of Psychological Allegory in Old
French Romance', *PMLA*, lxviii (1953), 1160–82.
[3] Cp. E. Fiser, *Le symbole littéraire* (Paris, n.d.), pp.43–4.
[4] Cp. E. Kahler, 'The Nature of the Symbol', in *Symbolism in Religion and
Literature*, edited by R. May (New York, 1961), pp.65–70.

reference to the object, but a second reference depending upon the *meaning* of the sign to which we also now pay attention.[1]

This seems to me to lead into an important linguistic distinction which will underlie much of our discussion in the pages that follow. The primary function of a word in literary (or any other) discourse can be that of an 'intuitive' sign. For example, in descriptive passages, the aim of the writer is to evoke and recreate the physical context. This immediacy gives a particular colour to literary discourse. On the other hand, words can be used 'symbolically' in the sense in which Urban defines it, in allegory and in imagery. This is the 'intellectual' use of language in that it involves a particular kind of intellectual intermediary. It is to be noted, however, that we must distinguish clearly between 'symbol' and 'theme', and 'image' and 'meaning'. The 'theme' is the prose meaning of the 'symbol'. The rose is a symbol of transitoriness and in the 'gather ye rosebuds', rosebuds symbolise the theme of 'transitoriness'. But the 'meaning' can involve more than the 'theme'. Thus in the intellectual uses of language, as well as the connection with the stimulus, there is also a particular process of abstraction or reference by which some aspect of the object of sense assumes an additional significance. The degree of congruence between the symbol and the thing symbolised can vary considerably. I suspect that the distinction between the *extrinsic*, and the *intrinsic* and *insight* symbol is merely another aspect of this sliding scale of congruence.[2]

The concept of congruence is a fundamental one for our discussion. If we accept that a symbol involves a second reference or theme, it then follows that the congruence between the two parts is a matter of degree. When Broederlam introduces the lily or the prophets in a naturalistic setting, he increases the congruence of the image but reduces the congruence between symbol and theme. When the thirteenth-century illuminator pictures the Madonna with the sword in her bosom, he reduces the congruence of the image but maintains the congruence

[1] Urban, p.412.

[2] See H. Flanders Dunbar, *Symbolism in Medieval Thought* (New Haven, 1929).

between image and theme. The degree of congruence is a contextual matter.[1] Let us take as an example the following poem possibly by Alanus de Insulis:

Omnis mundi creatura
quasi liber et pictura
nobis est, et speculum;
nostrae vitae, nostrae mortis,
nostri status, nostrae sortis,
fidele signaculum.

Nostrum statum pingit rosa,
nostri status decens glosa,
nostrae vitae lectio;
quae dum primo mane floret,
defloratus flos effloret,
vespertino senio.

Ergo spirans flos expirat,
in pallorem dum delirat,
oriendo moriens.
simul vetus et novella,
simul senex et puella,
rosa marcet oriens.

Sic aetatis ver humanae,
iuventutis primo mane
reflorescit paululum.
mane tamen hoc excludit
vitae vesper, dum concludit
vitale crepusculum.

---

[1] *Congruence*, of course, raises the whole problem of metaphor. Cp. M. B. Hester *The Meaning of Poetic Metaphor* (The Hague, 1967) and references. I have again chosen a fairly general word to avoid for the moment considering the concept 'indeterminate meaning' in the structure of the literary image, or if, indeed, it is part of the structure at all. For a discussion of the whole question, cp. C. Day Lewis, *The Poetic Image* (London, 1947), pp.39–63. Another aspect of this concept is indicated by P. W. Damon, 'Style and Meaning in the Mediaeval Latin Nature Lyric', *Speculum*, xxviii (1953), 517–18. . . . 'the Carolingians were not interested in producing an intrinsically striking picture of nature. Their use of imagery was not based on its decorative appeal but on its symbolic or illustrative relation to the concepts informing their poetry.' He contrasts with Goliardic poetry's 'positive effort to include the maximum amount of natural detail and to introduce and juxtapose images in a casual, impressionistic manner'.

Cuius decor dum perorat
eius decus nox deflorat
aetas, in qua defluit.
fit flos fenum, gemma lutum,
homo cinis, dum tributum,
huic morti tribuit.[1]

[*The whole created world is for us, as it were, a book, a picture and a mirror; a faithful symbol of our life, our death, our condition, our lot. The rose pictures our condition, a fitting commentary on our condition, a moral tale about our life. The rose, blossoming in the early morning, in the evening blooms its last, a flower deflowered. Therefore, the flower breathing forth fragrance, breathes its last as it plays in its madness and grows pale and, springing up, it dies. At once old and young, an old man and a maiden, springing up, the rose withers. Thus the spring of human life, in the early morning of youth, blossoms for its own part a little. But the evening of life cuts off this morning when it brings to a close the twilight of life, whose beauty ended night deflowers, an age in which beauty flows away. The flower becomes hay, the gem mire, man dust, paying tribute to death.*]*

If we put this beside the use made of the rose image by Bonaventura in *The Mystical Vine*, we see the difference between two degrees of congruence:

Viso [ergo] de rosa [sanguinis], videndum est de [rosa] [caritatis] et [deinde passionis]. Ardorem rosae caritatis perpendimus, si diligentius videamus, *quis, quare, quales, quantum* amaverit amator misericors et mirabilis, amator noster ille, quo nihil maius, quo nihil ditius, nihil fortius, cui omnis spiritus confitetur, quoniam *Deus meus es tu.* In hoc verbo bene comprehenditur, *quis* amator sit: quia *Deus;* . . . Iam vero *quantum* amaverit, videamus. Quis vero hoc sufficienter dicat? Ecce, in expositione huius verbi necessarium habemus rosam passionis rosae caritatis coniungere, ut rosa caritatis in passione rubescat, et rosa passionis igne caritatis ardescat. Tantum enim dilexit nos noster dilector, ut, caritatis ardore cogente, ruborem passionis incideret *traderetque in mortem animam suam, mortem autem crucis* non breviter transeuntis, sed a principio ortus sui usque in finem mortis durissimae perdurantis. Omnia ergo, quae passus est bonus Iesus *in diebus carnis suae,* ad ruborem utique pertinent rosae passionis, quamvis

---

[1] Alanus de Insulis, *Omnis caro fenum; Oxford Book of Medieval Latin Verse,* edited by F. J. E. Raby (2nd rev. edn., London, 1959), No. 242, pp.369–70.

effusionibus crebris sacratissimi sanguinis ipsius specialiter fuerit rubricata.[1]

[*Having now therefore considered the rose of blood, let us now consider the rose of love and of the passion. We can measure the ardour of love's rose by considering more diligently who this merciful and admirable lover is, why, whom and how much he loved; he our lover than whom nothing is greater, richer, stronger, He to whom every spirit confesses, 'For Thou art my God'. This expression makes us understand clearly who the Lover is: God. . . . And now let us see how much he loved. But who can speak adequately of this? Behold, in the exposition of this word, 'quantum' we shall have to link together the rose of passion and the rose of love, that the rose of love may glow in the passion, and the rose of the passion burn with the fire of love. Our lover loved us so much that, the ardour of love compelling him, he turned scarlet in the passion and delivered himself to death, even the death of the cross; and not merely for a few passing hours but for the whole time between his birth and his most bitter death. For everything that Jesus, the good endured in the days of his flesh is implied in the redness of the rose of the passion, although the rose was coloured chiefly by his sacred blood, so bountifully shed.*]

Now, it is clear that, in the former text, the congruence between symbol and theme is considerable. The details of the symbol are fitted closely to the details of the theme. On the other hand, the symbol of the rose in the passage from *The Mystical Vine* is related to the theme mainly by virtue of the colour, the redness symbolising blood and suffering but also passion. It is, in the first instance, a development of the image of the vine:

Floret in vite nostra, benignissimo Iesu, rosa *rubens* et *ardens*, *rubens* sanguine passionis, *ardens* igne caritatis, *roscida* effusione lacrymarum dulcis Iesu.[2]

[*On our vine, Jesus most kind, there blossoms a red and ardent rose: red with the blood of the passion, ardent with the fire of love, roscid with the tears of Jesus most sweet.*]

---

[1] Bonaventura, *Opera Omnia*, *VIII* (Quaracchi, 1898), pp.182–3; *Vitis Mystica*, caps. XVI, XVII, translated by J. de Vinck, *The Works of Bonaventure* (Paterson, 1960), I, 190–1; my versions are a modification of this.

[2] Bonaventura, *Vitis Mystica*, cap. XV; *Opera*, VIII, 180; de Vinck, p.186.

Thus the love displayed in the Passion is symbolically linked by the common symbol, the red rose. The image of the rose is developed in the course of the enumeration of the sheddings of blood:

> Sicut enim rosa per frigus noctis clausa, solis ardore surgente, tota aperitur et foliis expansis in rubore demonstrat ardorem iucundum; ita flos caeli deliciosus, optimus Iesus, qui multo tempore a peccato primi hominis quasi in frigore noctis clausus fuit, peccatoribus nondum gratiae plenitudinem impendens, tandem plenitudine temporis accedente, radiis ardentis caritatis accensus, in omni corporis sui parte apertus est, et rosae caritatis ardor in rubore sanguinis effusi refulsit.[1]

> [*For as the rose throughout the chill of night is closed, but, when the heat of the sun rises, all unfolds and, opening up its petals, shows its flaming joy in its redness, so the delight-giving flower of heaven, the good Jesus – long closed, as in the cold of night, by Adam's sin, and still withholding from sinners the plenitude of grace – blazing at last in the fulness of time with the flames of a burning love, is opened up in every part of his body and the glow of the rose of love shone in the redness of his blood out-poured.*]

And, like Dante's many-petalled rose, the rose of the Passion also is many-petalled.

> Numera guttas sanguinis effusi de dulcissimo latere et corpore amantissimi Iesu, et habebis rosae passionis caritatisque folia enumerata. Singulae enim guttae sanguinis singula folia sunt.[2]

> [*Number the drops of blood that ran from the most sweet side and the body of the most loving Jesus, and you have counted the petals of the rose of suffering and love, for every single drop of blood is another petal.*]

In all these uses of the image the congruence is slight, that is to say, the resemblance upon which the comparison is based is minimal. But it must be noted that there is also a tonal congruence in that symbol and theme are emotionally in the same semantic area.[3] This, then, is our concept of congruence.

---

[1] Bonaventura, *Vitis Mystica*, cap. XXIII; *Opera* VIII, 186–7; de Vinck, p.200.

[2] Bonaventura, *Vitis Mystica*, cap. XXIII; *Opera*, VIII, 187; de Vinck, p.201.

[3] On semantic space see U. Weinreich, 'Travels through Semantic Space',

And, as we have said, the distinction between a mimetic and a mythic narrative is largely a matter of congruence. The mythic narrative is entirely congruent with its theme although, as the narrative develops in the direction of verisimilitude, it moves away from this complete congruence in the direction of the 'intuitive'. On the other hand, the narrative can move away from complete congruence in the direction of the symbolic. In this sense all imagery is symbolic.

I have tried in this introductory chapter to indicate some of the themes and topics which I hope to consider in the following chapters. There are clearly many aspects of the relationship of language to style in medieval literature which are omitted because our knowledge at present is simply inadequate for such a study. Such areas are those of syntax,[1] word order, and certain aspects of semantics. The studies that follow can be no more than an exploration of some parts of the field. It might be appropriate to conclude on a note of humility by quoting the words of Leo Spitzer: 'Once the architecture of the work of art has been laid bare, the scaffolding, which the critic had to erect provisionally for this purpose, can be scrapped. Stylistics, as I conceive it, is an exclusively auxiliary science. Just as, according to Pascal, for him who knows truth no style, no "art de persuader" is needed, so stylistics . . . must abdicate once the true nature of the work of art has been apperceived.'[2]

Word, xiv (1958), 346–66; 'A Rejoinder', *Word*, xv (1959), 200–1; C. E. Osgood, 'Semantic Space revisited', *Word*, xv (1959), 192–200.

[1] But cp. L. D. Benson, 'Chaucer's Historical Present', *English Studies*, xlii (1961), 65–77; S. B. Greenfield, 'Syntactic Analysis and Old English Poetry', *Neuphilologische Mitteilungen*, lxiv (1963), 373–8; F. T. Visser, 'The "Historical Present" in Middle English Verse Narratives', *English Studies presented to R. W. Zandvoort: English Studies*, xlv (1964), 135–42; P. C. Gage, 'Syntax and Poetry in Chaucer's *Prioress's Tale*', *Neophilogus*, l (1966), 252–61.

Some studies of the modern period may also be noted here; for example, Donald Davie, *Articulate Energy* (London, 1955) and M. A. K. Halliday, 'Descriptive Linguistics in Literary Studies', in *Patterns of Language*, pp.56–69; J. Mc. H. Sinclair, 'Taking a Poem to Pieces', in *Essays on Style and Language*, pp.68–81.

[2] L. Spitzer, *Linguistics and Literary History* (Princeton, 1948), p.218.

CHAPTER ONE

The Allegorical Picture

'The penalty for too earnestly probing and tapping at the surface of the image is that we fall through into the black waters beneath it, and the only consolation is that the poets have been there before us.'[1] Worse still befalls the critic who ventures on the surface of such topics as symbolism and allegory, a veritable 'Serbonian bog where armies whole have sunk'. Nevertheless, we must now attempt to look at allegory more closely, for allegory is a dominant mode of the Middle Ages. Let us then first consider a passage from John of Salisbury, incorporating an allegory which, not new when he wrote, was to have a long history:

'Si uerbis gentilium uti licet Christiano, qui solis electis diuinum et Deo placens per inhabitantem gratiam esse credit ingenium, etsi nec uerba nec sensus credam gentilium fugiendos, dummodo uitentur errores, hoc ipsum diuina prudentia in Eneide sua sub inuolucro fictitii commenti innuisse uisus est Maro, dum sex etatum gradus sex librorum distinctionibus prudenter expressit. Quibus conditionis humanae, dum Odisseam imitatur, ortum exprimere uisus est et processum, ipsumque, quem educit et prouehit, producit et deducit ad Manes. Nam Eneas, qui ibi fingitur animus, sic dictus eo quod est corporis habitator; *ennos* enim, ut Grecis placet, habitator est, *demas* corpus et ab his componitur Eneas ut significet animam quasi carnis tugurio habitantem. . . . Primus itaque liber Eneidos sub imagine naufragii manifestas infantiae, quae suis procellis agitatur, exponit tunsiones; et in fine suo habundantia cibi et potus adulta prosilit ad letitiam conuiualem.'[2]

---

[1] Day Lewis, p.135.

[2] John of Salisbury, *Policraticus*, VIII, xxiv, ed. C. C. I. Webb (Oxford, 1909), II, 415–16, translation based on Joseph B. Pike, *Frivolities of Courtiers*

[*If the words of the pagan may be employed by the Christian who believes that a nature divine and pleasing to God, because of the grace inherent in it, can belong to the elect alone (although I do not think that either the words or the thoughts of the pagans are to be shunned, provided their errors are avoided), Virgil seems by divine wisdom to have hinted at this very fact, when, under the cloak of poetic imagination, in his Aeneid, he subtly represents the six periods of life by the division of the work into six books. In these, in imitation of the Odyssey, he appears to have represented the origin and progress of man. The character he sets forth and develops he leads on and conducts down into the nether world. For Eneas, who therein represents the soul, is so named for the reason that it is a dweller in the body, for 'ennos', according to the Greeks, is 'dweller', and demas 'body'. The name Eneas is formed of these two elements to signify the soul dwelling, as it were, in a hut of flesh. . . . The first book of the Aeneid then, under the figure of a shipwreck, sets forth the manifest tribulations of childhood, which is shaken by its own tempests; and at the termination of the period the abundance of food and drink of manhood is in evidence at the gaiety of the banquet.*]

This is allegory, for *Allegoria rem totam per metaphoram obscurè tractat*.[1] That this is not the evident meaning of the *Aeneid* is beside the point, and would no doubt have been as freely admitted by John of Salisbury as by anyone else. That such an interpretation is both 'darke' and 'conceited' is consonant with its allegorical status. For it is important to distinguish between allegory and mythic narrative. There are also many exemplary tales in the *Policraticus*. For example, John of Salisbury uses the tale of the Widow of Ephesus, to which we have already referred, to illustrate the fickle nature of women. The story of Aeneas could also be used as mythic narrative. Dido then would stand for any woman in love and the myth would converge on the story of Anthony and Cleopatra. Nevertheless, Dido is

---

and Footprints of Philosophers; Being a Translation of the First, Second and Third Books and Selections from the Seventh and Eighth Books of the 'Policraticus' (Minneapolis, 1938), pp.402–3.

[1] Alexander Gil, *Logonomia Anglica*, edited by O. L. Jiriczek (Strassburg, 1903), p.104, quoted by J. McClennen, 'On the Meaning and Function of Allegory in the English Renaissance', *University of Michigan Contributions in Modern Philology*, i (6) (1947), 7; for a study of medieval allegory, cp. De Bruyne, II, 302–70.

still a real woman who performed the actions attributed to her in the narrative. Any inference as to the theme or implications of the story must accept this fact. In other words, narrative and theme are contiguous, they spring from the same context and partake of the nature of metonymy, not, as is the case with allegory, of the nature of metaphor. But when John of Salisbury interprets the *Aeneid* as telling of the ages of man, there is clearly a disjunction between narrative and theme and we have a relationship essentially of the nature of metaphor where the link between the two parts is one of similarity and not one of contiguity.[1]

Allegoria rem totam per metaphoram obscurè tractat. This sounds simple and comprehensive. But the endless debate since the time of Goethe[2] on the distinction between allegory and symbolism gives warning that the matter is not simple. It is now common to clear the ground by putting the whole of medieval allegory into cold storage in a refrigerator labelled 'personification allegory'.[3] But this is in fact highly misleading; partly because medieval allegory is not by any means entirely a matter of personification, as the example from John of Salisbury shows; partly because medieval allegory is itself highly complex; and partly because the distinction made by Proust between a *puissance de stricte signification* and a *puissance d'évocation*[4] is just as relevant to medieval allegory as it is significant for modern symbolism. Allegory and symbolism are not the products of different faculties such as fancy and imagination, but merely different ways of manipulating language.[5] I hope therefore in

[1] Cp. E. Stankiewicz, 'Linguistics and the Study of Poetic Language', in *Style in Language*, p.72.

[2] Goethe, *Maximen*, edited by G. Müller (Stuttgart, 1943), p.104.

[3] Cp. R. W. Frank, 'The Art of Reading Medieval Personification-Allegory', *ELH*, xx (1953), 237–50.

[4] Proust, *Chroniques*, p.141; cited in Fiser, p.53, fn. 85.

[5] For discussion of different types of medieval allegory see R. Tuve, *Allegorical Imagery* (Princeton, 1966); for the medieval theory of imagination see M. W. Bundy, 'The Theory of Imagination in Classical and Medieval Thought'; University of Illinois Studies in Language and Literature, xii (2 & 3) (1927), 177–256.

this chapter both to show that the term 'personification allegory' is misleading, and to consider both the different elements which make up medieval allegory and the use made of them by writers of allegory, especially Langland and Chaucer. To do this we must consider the three main streams which formed the watershed of medieval allegorical writing: biblical typology, the literary fiction and classical rhetoric.

The origin of biblical exegesis is no doubt to be sought in the Bible itself. The Pauline letters contain some well-known examples,[1] of which epistle to the Galatians is a classic instance:

> Scriptum est enim: Quoniam Abraham duos filios habuit: vnum de ancilla, et vnum de libera. Sed qui de ancilla, secundum carnem natus est; qui autem de libera, per repromissionem; quae sunt per allegoriam dicta. Haec enim sunt duo testamenta. Unum quidem in monte Sina, in servitutem generans; quae est Agar; Sina enim mons est in Arabia, qui coniunctus est ei quae nunc est Ierusalem, et servit cum filiis suis. Illa autem, quae sursum est Ierusalem, libera est, quae est mater nostra.[2]

> [*For it is written that Abraham had two sons, the one by a bondmaid, the other by a freewoman. But he who was born of the bondwoman was born after the flesh; but he of the freewoman was by promise. Which things are an allegory; for these are the two covenants; the one from the mount Sinai, which gendereth to bondage, which is Agar. For this Agar is mount Sinai in Arabia and answereth to Jerusalem which now is, and is in bondage with her children. But Jerusalem which is above is free, which is the mother of us all.*]

How far Hellenistic traditions of Homeric commentary, associated particularly with Alexandria, contributed to the Christian tradition is a matter of debate, but not significant for our purpose.[3] More significant is the early Christian debate as to the status of the literal sense. For some early biblical commentators such as Philo,[4] only the allegorical sense had

---

[1] See H. A. Wolfson, *The Philosophy of the Church Fathers* (Cambridge, Mass., 1956), pp.1–72; J. Pépin, *Mythe et Allégorie* (Paris, 1958), pp.247–52; H. de Lubac, *Exégèse Médiévale* (Paris, 1959 ff.); I, 2, 373–83.

[2] *Galatians*, iv, 22–6.

[3] See Pépin, pp.215–474.

[4] For Philo, see Pépin, pp.231–42.

true significance. For writers such as Origen, on the other hand, the Old Testament prophecies were as true as the New Testament events which they prophesied.[1] The point is put emphatically by Augustine.

Procul dubio figura est peregrinantis in hoc saeculo civitatis Dei, hoc est ecclesiae, quae fit salva per lignum, in quo pependit mediator Dei et hominum, homo Christus Iesus. Nam et mensurae ipsae longitudinis et altitudinis et latitudinis eius significant corpus humanum, in cuius veritate ad homines praenuntiatus est venturus et venit. Humani quippe corporis longitudo a vertice usque ad vestigia sexiens tantum habet quam latitudo, quae est ab uno latere ad alterum latus, et deciens tantum quam altitudo, cuius altitudinis mensura est in latere a dorso ad ventrem; velut si iacentem hominem metiaris supinum seu pronum, sexiens tantum longus est a capite ad pedes, quam latus a dextra in sinistram vel a sinistra in dextram, et deciens, quam altus a terra. Unde facta est arca trecentorum in longitudine cubitorum et quinquaginta in latitudine et triginta in altitudine. Et quod ostium in latere accepit, profecto illud est vulnus, quando latus crucifixi lancea perforatum est; hac quippe ad illum venientes ingrediuntur, quia inde sacramenta manarunt, quibus credentes initiantur. Et quod de lignis quadratis fieri iubetur, undique stabilem vitam sanctorum significat; quacumque enim verteris quadratum, stabit; et cetera, quae in eiusdem arcae constructione dicuntur, ecclesiasticarum signa sunt rerum. . . . (cap. xxvii) Non tamen quisquam putare debet aut frustra haec esse conscripta, aut tantummodo rerum gestarum veritatem sine ullis allegoricis significationibus hic esse quaerendam aut e contrario haec omnino gesta non esse, sed solas esse verborum figuras, aut quidquid illud est nequaquam ad prophetiam ecclesiae pertinere.[2]

[*Undoubtedly, the ark is a symbol of the City of God on its pilgrimage in history, a figure of the Church which was saved by the wood on which there hung the 'Mediator' between God and man, himself man, Christ Jesus.*

---

[1] See B. Smalley, *The Study of the Bible in the Middle Ages* (Oxford, 1952), pp.1–36; Wolfson, *passim*; E. Auerbach, *Scenes from the Drama of European Literature* (New York, 1959), pp.1–60; for Origen, see especially R. P. C. Hanson, *Allegory and Event* (London, 1959).

[2] *De Civitate Dei*, XV, 26, 27, edited by B. Dombart (3rd edn., Leipzig, 1909, 1905); II, 114–16; translation based on G. G. Walsh and Grace Monahan, *The Works of Augustine* (The Fathers of the Church, 14, Washington, 1952), pp.477–80.

Even the very measurements of the length, height and breadth of the ark are meant to point to the reality of the human body into which he came as it was foretold that he would come. It will be recalled that the length of a human body from head to foot is six times the length from one side to the other and ten times the thickness from back to front. Measure a man who is lying on the ground, either prone or supine. He is six times as long from head to foot as he is wide from right to left or left to right, and he is ten times as long as he is high from the ground up. That is why the ark was made 300 cubits in length and fifty in breadth, and thirty in height. As for the door in the side, that, surely symbolises the wound made by the lance in the side of the Crucified, the door by which those who come to him enter in, because it was from there that the sacraments flowed by which believers are initiated. It was ordered that the ark be made of squared timbers – a symbol of the four-square stability of a holy life, which, like a cube, stands firm however it is turned. So it is with every other detail of the ark's construction. They are all symbols of something in the Church . . . no one is free to think however that there is no deeper meaning in the written words or that all we should look for is the truth of the facts without regard to any allegorical purpose. On the other hand, no one should think that the whole story is merely a fabric of words and by no means facts, or, whether fact or fiction, that it has no prophetic relevance to the Church.]

Here the biblical story is treated as a sign in accordance with the definition of St. Augustine, *res praeter speciem, quam ingerit sensibus, aliud aliquid ex se faciens in cogitationem venire:* [a thing, which, beyond the impression that it conveys to the senses, makes something else known].[1] Such signs, when intentionally given by man to man or by God through man, says Augustine, can be called symbols,[2] and as Hugh of St. Victor points out, these are of numerous kinds;[3] for example, Jacob, his father's heir, is a symbol of Christ; Isaac, who gave a blessing to his son, is a symbol of God the Father; Egypt is a symbol of the world. Such symbols can be sought also in the New Testament as when the raising of Lazarus is seen as a symbol of the resurrection of the soul from sin, or Jesus's preaching in Solomon's porch in winter is seen as a symbol of the dullness and infidelity

[1] J. Chydenius, 'The Theory of Medieval Symbolism', *Acta Societatis Scientiarum Fennicae:* Commentationes Humanarum Litterarum, xxvii (2) (1961), 5.
[2] Chydenius, pp.6–7.   [3] Chydenius, pp.14–15.

of the Jews. Colour symbolism and number symbolism were also sometimes discussed under the general heading of interpretative signs. What is important to notice, however, is that a sign has, as it were, a double signification. Words, *signa propria*, have only the function of symbolising something else and their sense signification is purely aural, depending upon the *potestas* of the letters. But signs such as the burning bush of Moses or the stone of Jacob, *signa translata*, imply not only the actuality of the object but a secondary meaning also.[1] But this is not of course to deny the reality of the object or the events of which the objects are part. In bringing the Old and the New Testament into a prophetic relationship with each other, the truth of both is confirmed. Whether, however, the same is true in regard to vernacular literature is open to question. Chydenius points out that St. Thomas, in opposition to St. Augustine and Hugh of St. Victor, maintains that, in poetic expression, it is not the immediate sense but the metaphorical sense that matters. In other words, the image is of no importance, it is not *res et signum* but *signum tantum*, that is to say it is a descriptive symbol only and not a thing in its own right.[2] The same may be said of allegory, which is only a series of metaphors.

The medieval distinctions are not merely of historical interest. Let us take some examples. When the Old English poet, or the sculptor of Chartres, use Melchisedech as a type of Christ, they are essentially bringing together two images in order to express a theme. This device can be used with brilliant effect as when the writer of the Chester Isaac chooses to emphasise the typological relationship between the sacrifice of Isaac and the sacrifice of Christ on the cross. He not only makes a dogmatic point, but by the use of a tale with human protagonists, Abraham and Isaac, he implies the humanity of Christ as well as giving a special significance to the Old Testament story.[3] That

---

[1] Chydenius, pp.7–8; cp. A. Nemetz, 'Literalness and the *Sensus Litteralis Speculum*', xxxiv (1959), 76–89.

[2] Chydenius, pp.37–8.

[3] See R. Woolf, 'The Effect of Typology on the English Medieval Plays of Abraham and Isaac', *Speculum*, xxxii (1957), 805–25.

a knowledge of biblical typology penetrated vernacular writing cannot, I think, be denied. Not only does it appear in popularisations of the biblical narrative, such as the *Aurora* of Peter Riga[1], or in the vernacular sermon, or didactic narrative, such as the *Cursor Mundi*, but must, also, have been known from the liturgy, or from the art of the period, as Mâle and others have shown. But, I think it highly debatable how far the famous four senses are ever to be found in vernacular writings.[2] The literary significance of the typological method lies rather in its derivative, the *figura*.[3] Auerbach, in his well-known article on *figura* has written:

> Since in figural interpretation one thing stands for another, since one thing represents and signifies the other, figural interpretation is 'allegorical' in the widest sense but it differs from most of the allegorical forms known to us by the historicity both of the sign and what it signifies.[4]

He gives an illuminating example:

> Thus Virgil (in Dante) is not an allegory of an attribute, virtue, capacity, power, or historical institution. He is neither reason nor poetry nor the Empire. He is Virgil himself. Yet he is not himself in the same way as the historical characters whom later poets have set out to portray in all their historical involvement, as for example, Shakespeare's Caesar or Schiller's Wallenstein. These poets disclose their historical characters in the thick of their earthly existence; they bring an important epoch to life before our eyes, and look for the meaning of the epoch itself. For Dante, the meaning of every life has its place in the providential history of the

---

[1] Peter Riga, *Aurora*, edited by P. E. Beichner (Notre Dame, 1965).

[2] See H. Caplan, 'The Four Senses of Scriptural Interpretation and the Mediaeval Theory of Preaching', *Speculum*, iv (1929), 282–90; J. M. Campbell, 'Patristic Studies and the Literature of Mediaeval England', *Speculum*, viii (1933), 465–78; M. W. Bloomfield, 'Symbolism in Medieval Literature', *MP*, lvi (1958), 73–81; *Critical Approaches to Medieval Literature*, edited by Dorothy Bethurum (New York, 1960), pp.1–82; P. E. Beichner, 'The Allegorical Interpretation of Medieval Literature', *PMLA*, lxxxii (1967), 33–8; T. Silverstein, *ibid.*, 28–32.

[3] I use the term 'typology' of biblical typology. For the use of the terms 'allegory' and 'typology' in medieval exegesis see H. de Lubac, ' "Typologie" et "allégorisme" ', *Recherches de science religieuse*, xxxiv (1947), 180–226.

[4] Auerbach (1959), p.54.

world, the general lines of which are laid down in the Revelation which has been given to every Christian, and which is interpreted for him in the vision of the *Comedy*. Thus, Virgil in the *Divine Comedy* is the historical Virgil himself, but then again he is not; for the historical Virgil is only a *figura* of the fulfilled truth that the poem reveals, and this fulfillment is more real, more significant than the *figura*. With Dante, unlike modern poets, the more fully the figure is interpreted and the more closely it is integrated with the eternal plan of salvation, the more real it becomes.[1]

Again he writes of Cato in the *Purgatorio*:

> Beyond any doubt Cato is a *figura*; not an allegory like the characters from the *Roman de la Rose*, but a figure that has become the truth.[2]

It is important to notice here that figural writing is not limited to biblical figures. Any character, drawn from a known context, can be used as a *figura*. Thus Dante can use classical figures such as Virgil, Cato or a near contemporary figure such as St. Francis. To quote Auerbach again:

> If we think of the famous allegorical poems of late antiquity and of the Middle Ages, of Claudian's or Prudentius's works, of Alain de Lille or Jean de Meun, there is surely little in common between them and the biography of Francis in the *Comedy*. These works call up whole armies of allegorical figures, describe their persons, their clothes, their dwellings, make them discuss and fight with each other. Paupertas does indeed appear in some of these works, but as a vice or as the companion of a vice. Dante here introduces one single allegorical figure, Poverty, and connects her with a historical, that is to say, a concrete, real personality. This is something entirely different; he draws the allegory into actual life, he connects it closely with historical fact.[3]

This is the crux of the matter.

> Real historical figures are to be interpreted spiritually . . . but the interpretation points to a carnal, hence historical fulfilment.[4]

What is important about the figural way of writing is that the image exists in an actual context and therefore has a particular

[1] Auerbach (1959), pp.70–1. [2] Auerbach (1959), p.67.
[3] Auerbach (1959), p.83. [4] Auerbach (1959), p.34.

kind of associational richness, a *puissance d'évocation*, not evident in mythographic figures such as Hercules as used in early Christian art. There is surely all the difference in the world between the figure of Virgil in Dante and that figure whom

> Resoun men clepe . . . .
> Which from hir tour delyverly
> Com doun to me, withouten mor.
> But she was neither yong ne hoor,
> Ne high ne lowe, ne fat ne lene,
> But best, as it were in a mene.
> Hir eyen twoo were cleer and light
> As ony candell that brenneth bright;
> And on hir heed she hadde a crowne
> Hir semede wel an high persoune,[1]

or that 'freke' who

> Called Catoun his knaue . curteise of speche,
> And also Tomme Trewe-tonge – . telle-me-no-tales –
> Ne-lesyng-to-lawȝe-of – . for I loued hem neuere.[2]

A separate stream of allegorical writing is to be seen in the literary fiction. This is descended to some extent from traditional Hellenic commentaries on Homer and other classical writers.[3] There were, on the one hand, the rationalising commentaries, such as those of Euhemerus, purporting to show that the gods were but mortals,[4] a view known to Isidore of Seville who, in his *Etymologies*, states this view thus:

> Quos pagani deos asserunt, homines olim fuisse produntur, et pro uniuscujusque vita vel meritis, coli apud suos post mortem coeperunt.[5]

---

[1] Chaucer, *The Romaunt of the Rose*, ll.3193–202.

[2] William Langland, *The Vision of Piers the Plowman*, edited by W. W. Skeat (Oxford, 1886), B. iv, ll.16–18.

[3] Cp. Pépin, pp.85–214.

[4] For Euhemerus, see Pépin, pp.147–9; J. D. Cooke, 'Euhemerism: a Mediaeval Interpretation of Classical Paganism', *Speculum*, ii (1927), 396–410; J. Seznec, *The Survival of the Pagan Gods*, translated by Barbara F. Sessions (New York, 1953), pp.11–36.

[5] Isidore of Seville, *Etymologiae*, VIII, xi, 1; PL, lxxxii, col. 314; cp. Rabanus Maurus, *De Universo*, XV, vi; PL, cxi, col. 426.

[*Those whom the pagans assert to have been gods are said formerly to have been men and they began to be worshipped among their own people each one according to his life and merits.*]

A rationalising explanation of myth was also to be found in writers such as Macrobius.

Hoc animae sepulchrum, hoc Ditis concava, hoc inferos voca-verunt, et omnia, quae illic esse credidit fabulosa persuasio, in nobismet ipsis et in ipsis humanis corporibus adsignare conati sunt; oblivionis fluvium aliud non esse adserentes quam errorem animae obliviscentis maiestatem vitae prioris, qua antequam in corpus truderetur potita est, solamque esse in corpore vitam putantis. pari interpretatione Phlegethontem ardores irarum et cupiditatum putarunt, Acherontem quicquid fecisse dixisseve usque ad tristitiam humanae varietatis more nos paenitet, Cocytum quicquid homines in luctum lacrimasque compellit, Stygem quicquid inter se humanos animos in gurgitem mergit odiorum; ipsam quoque poenarum descriptionem de ipso usu conversationis humanae sumptam crediderunt, vulturem *iecur immortale tondentem* nihil aliud intellegi volentes quam tormenta conscientiae.[1]

[*They called this [the body] the tomb of the soul, the vaults of Pluto, the infernal regions; everything that fable taught us to believe was in the lower regions they tried to assign to us ourselves and to our mortal bodies. The river Lethe was to them nothing more than the error committed by the soul in forgetting its former high estate before it was thrust into a body, and in thinking that its sole existence was in a body. Similarly, they thought that Phlegethon was merely the fires of our wraths and passions, that Acheron was the chagrin we experienced over having said or done something, even to the point of becoming melancholy, as is the way with human beings, that Cocytus was anything that moved us to lamentation or tears, and that Styx was anything that plunged human minds into the abyss of mutual hatred. The description of the punishments, they believed, originated in human experience; and the vulture 'gnawing at the deathless liver', they would have us understand is nothing more than the pangs of conscience.*]

---

[1] Macrobius, *Commentarii in Somnium Scipionis*, I, x, edited by J. Willis (Leipzig, 1963), pp.43-4; translation by W. H. Stahl, *Macrobius, Commentary on the Dream of Scipio* (New York, 1952), p.128.

In some cases, myths were given physical interpretations. These are familiar from *The City of God*:

> Quodlibet igitur physicis rationibus et disputationibus adserant: modo sit Iuppiter corporei huius mundi animus, qui universam istam molem ex quattuor vel quot eis placet elementis constructam atque compactam implet et movet, modo inde suas partes sorori et fratribus cedat; modo sit aether, ut aerem Iunonem subterfusam desuper amplectatur, modo totum simul cum aere sit ipse caelum, terram vero tamque coniugem eandemque matrem (quia hoc in divinis turpe non est) fecundis imbribus et seminibus fetet; modo autem (ne sit necesse per cuncta discurrere) deus unus, de quo multi a poeta nobilissimo dictum putant:
> > deum namque ire per omnes
> Terrasque tractusque maris caelumque profundum.[1]

> [*On the basis of this argument drawn from physical phenomena and from their discussions, let the learned pagans maintain all they please about Jove: now let him be the soul of this material world, filling and moving the vast structure of the universe, formed and compounded of four elements, or of as many as they please. Now let Jupiter yield some parts of it to his sister and brothers. Again, let him be the ether embracing the underlying air, Juno. Now let him be the entire sky and air together, and let him with fertile rains and seeds fecundate the earth – his wife and mother at the same time, for this is no scandal among the gods. Finally, not to run through all their theories, let him be the unique god to whom, according to the thinking of many, the celebrated poet refers when he says, 'God pervades all lands and all depths of the sea, all heights of the heavens'.*]

Equally from the Stoic tradition of moral interpretation of myths came the so-called mythographic tradition, which may be said to have begun with the fifth-century writer Fulgentius. He, too, often explains the myths in physical terms as well as presenting them as *idola*, images or pictures. For example, Neptune represents the element water:

> Tridentem uero ob hac re ferre pingitur, quod aquarum natura triplici uirtute fungatur id est liquida, fecunda, potabilis. Huic et Neptuno Amphitritem in coniugium deputant – amphi enim

---

[1] Augustine, *De Civitate Dei*, IV, xi; I, 160, translation based on G. G. Walsh and D. B. Zema, *The Works of St. Augustine* (The Fathers of the Church, 8, Washington, 1950), p.206. Cp. also Pépin, pp.210–14.

Grece circumcirca dicimus – eo quod omnibus tribus elementis aqua conclusa sit, id est sit in caelo, sit in aere, id est in nubibus, et in terra, ut sunt fontes uel putei.[1]

[*He is depicted indeed for this reason as carrying a trident because the nature of the waters manifests a threefold capacity, namely liquid, life-bearing and drinkable. To this Neptune, also, they attribute a wife, Amphitrite for we interpret* amphi *in Greek as 'roundabout', for the reason that water is included in all three elements, that is, in the heavens and in the lower atmosphere, that is in the clouds, and on the earth, like springs and wells.*]

Such interpretations of classical myths were propagated in the Middle Ages partly through commentaries such as those of Remigius of Auxerre and John the Scot on Martianus Capella. The curious nature of these commentaries is perhaps worth illustrating as an example of the more eccentric species of medieval allegory. This is from John the Scot's ninth-century commentary on Martianus Capella:

AFRODITE id est spumea; Venus vocatur fabulose quidem quia de spumis castrati Saturni nata fingitur fuisse. Phisica vero consideratione, spumas ferventium seminum sive animalium sive aliarum rerum quibus nascuntur omnia quae in hoc mundo oriri videntur significat, ubi intelligendum quod praefata dona superiorum numinum bonas ac naturales humanae animae virtutes insinuant, que non aliunde nisi ex bonorum hominum causa et principio procedunt. Omne vero quod merito originalis peccati ex corruptibili et mortali creatura naturalibus animae virtutibus et miscetur et inseritur per illecebrosa Veneris donaria significat. Hinc est generalis et specialis libido, hinc avaricia, hinc insatiabilis connubendi pruritus ceteraque illici[t]a quae dinumerare longum est, florum pulchritudine, praetiosorumque unguentorum alatibus nec non supervacuis tinnitibus, infructuosa quoque quiet[e] corporibus veluti quadam somnolentia non inconvenienter significata.[2]

[*Aphrodite that is foamy; Venus is so-called indeed in fable because she is imagined to have been born of the spittle of castrated Saturn. Physically*

---

[1] Fulgentius, *Mitologiae*, I, iv; *Opera*, edited by R. Helm (Leipzig, 1898), p.19.

[2] Iohannes Scottus, *Annotationes in Marcianum*, edited by C. E. Lutz (Cambridge, Mass., 1939), p.13.

considered, she signifies the foam of the generating sperm of animals or other things, of which are born all things which are seen to spring up in this world; whence it is to be understood that the aforesaid gifts of superior beings indicate the good and natural virtues of the human soul which only proceed in the first instance from good men. Everything indeed that by virtue of original sin, arising from the corrupt and mortal creature, is mixed and added to in the natural virtues of the soul is signified by the enticing temples of Venus. Hence is general and particular lust, hence avarice, hence insatiable prurience and other illicit desires which it would take long to enumerate, through the beauty of flowers, and the allurements of precious unguents as well as by foolish janglings and, also, unfruitful repose of the body, as though in a kind of sleep, all these are not unfittingly signified.]

Such treatment of myths of all kinds was pervasive in the later Middle Ages. There are, for example, the descendants of Fulgentius represented by the so-called Third Mythographer of the twelfth century which became a standard text-book for the later Middle Ages.[1] Of later works in this tradition the most remarkable are *Fulgentius Metaforalis*[2] and Boccaccio's *De Genealogia Deorum*.[3] There were, however, other traditions. The *Ovid Moralisé* has a tradition of its own descending from twelfth-century writers such as Arnulfe of Orleans, John of Garland, through the *Ovide Moralisé* with the Copenhagen Commentary, Giovanni del Virgilio and the *Ovidius Moralizatus*, which formed part of the fifteenth book of Berchorius's *Reductorium Morale*.[4]

[1] See B. Smalley, *English Friars and Antiquity* (Oxford, 1960), p.111; Seznec, pp.84–121, 170–9.

[2] H. Liebeschütz, *Fulgentius Metaforalis* (Leipzig, 1926).

[3] Giovanni Boccaccio, *Genealogie Deorum Gentilium Libri*, edited by V. Romano (Bari, 1951).

[4] For Theodulph of Orleans on Ovid see Seznec, pp.89–91; Arnulfe of Orleans, *Allegoriae super Ovidii Metamorphosin*, edited by F. Ghisalberti, Memorie del Reale Istituto Lombardo di Scienze e Lettere (Classe di Lettere, Scienze Morali e Storiche), xxiv (1932), 157–234; John of Garland, *Integumenta Ovidii*, edited by F. Ghisalberti (Messina & Milan, 1933); *Ovide moralisé*, edited by C. de Boer, M. G. de Boer and J. T. M. van't Sant (Amsterdam, 1915–38); *Ovide moralisé en prose*, edited by C. de Boer (Amsterdam, 1954); *Le Commentaire de Copenhague de l'Ovide Moralisé*, edited by J. T. M. van't Sant (Amsterdam, 1929); F. Ghisalberti 'Giovanni del Virgilio espositore delle *Metamorfosi*', *Giornale Dantesco*, xxxiv (1933), 3–110; Petrus Berchorius, *Reductorium Morale*, Liber XV, caps. ii–xv, 'Ovidius Moralizatus', edited by J. Engels (Utrecht, 1962). Cp. also J. Engels,

There were also commentaries on Ovid's works in the Middle Ages, designed to provide scholars with bibliographical material, which may have contributed to the tradition of the moralised Ovid.[1] An example of the method of moralisation is Arnulfe of Orleans's explanation of the myth of Apollo and Marsyas, an example of some interest in view of the well-known references in Dante and in the painting of Raphael:

> Marsia cum Apolline disputans ab eodem victus vivus excoriatus in fluvium sui nominis fuit mutatus. *Allegoria:* Marsia *id est.* insipientia disputavit cum Apolline *id est.* cum sapientia, sed confutata per sapientiam, fuit excoriata. Insipiens enim a sapiente sibi non potest cavere quin totum quod dicit probetur nichil valere. In fluvium dicitur esse mutatus, vel ideo quia est fluvius eiusdem nominis, vel ideo quia quamvis a sapientia confutata diu est insipientia, tamen adhuc fluit.[2]

> [*Marsia disputing with Apollo, by him conquered and flayed alive, was changed into the river of his name. Allegory: Marsia, that is 'folly', disputed with Apollo, that is 'wisdom', but, refuted by wisdom, was flayed alive. For the fool cannot protect himself from the wise man but that all that he says proves to be of no value. He is said to have been changed into a river, either because there is a river of that same name, or because, although folly has, for long, been confuted by wisdom yet folly still flows.*]

We have mentioned some of the most influential traditions of moralisation in the Middle Ages but in effect anything could be moralised. We may recall the moralised tales about animals, the *Bestiary*, the moralised precious stone, the Lapidary[3], the

---

Études sur l'"Ovide moralisé' (Groningen, 1945); Smalley, pp.261–4. For the influence on Chaucer, cp. E. H. Wilkins, 'Descriptions of Pagan Divinities from Petrarch to Chaucer', *Speculum*, xxxii (1957), 511–22 and J. M. Steadman, 'Venus's *Citole* in Chaucer's *Knight's Tale* and Berchorius', *Speculum*, xxxiv (1959), 620–4; D. Bethurum Loomis, 'Saturn in Chaucer's "Knight's Tale" ', in *Chaucer und seine Zeit: Symposion für Walter F. Schirmer*, edited by A. Esch (Tuebingen, 1968), pp.149–61.

[1] F. Ghisalberti, 'Biographies of Ovid', *JWCI*, ix (1946), 10–59.

[2] Arnulfe of Orleans, *Allegoriae*, pp.217–18; for a discussion of the treatment of this theme in the Renaissance see E. Wind, *Pagan Mysteries in the Renaissance* (London, 1958), pp.142–6.

[3] For the Bestiary tradition see F. McCulloch, *Medieval Latin and French Bestiaries*; University of North Carolina Studies in Romance Languages and Literatures, XXXIII (1962); for the Lapidary see L. Pannier, *Les lapidaires*

Christian interpretation of the Zodiac in Philippe de Thaun's *Cumpoz*.[1]

In a passage to be echoed by many later writers on allegory, Boccaccio explains the significance of these fictions:

. . . . sciendum est his fictionibus non esse tantum unicum intellectum, quin imo dici potest potius polisenum, hoc est moltiplicium sensum. Nam sensus primus habetur per corticem, et hic licteralis vocatus est; alii per significata per corticem, et hi allegorici nuncupantur. Et ut quid velim facilius assummatur, ponemus exemplum. Perseus Iovis filius figmento poetico occidit Gorgonem, et victor evolavit in ethera. Hoc dum legitur per licteram hystorialis sensus prestatur. Si moralis ex hac lictera queritur intellectus, victoria ostenditur prudentis in vicium, et ad virtutem accessio. Allegorice autem si velimus assummere, pie mentis spretis mundanis deliciis ad celestia elevatio designatur. Preterea posset et anagogice dici per fabulam Christi ascensum ad patrem mundi principe superato figurari. Qui tamen sensus etsi variis nuncupentur nominibus, possunt tamen omnes allegorici appellari, quod ut plurimum fit. Nam allegoria dicitur ab allon, quod alienum latine significat, sive diversum, et ideo quot diversi ab hystoriali seu licterali sint sensu, allegorici possunt, ut dictum est, merito vocitari.[2]

[*It is to be understood in regard to these fictions that they are not to be thought of as having only one sense but may rather be said to be polysemous; that is multiple in sense. For the first sense is to be understood from the cortex or rind and this is called literal; other senses are to be understood through those things signified through the cortex and these are called allegorical. And that our intention be more readily grasped, we will give an example. Perseus, the son of Jupiter, by a poetic fiction, killed the Gorgon and, victorious, flew away into the air. If this is read literally, the historical sense appears; if its moral sense is sought, the victory of the prudent man against vice is demonstrated and his approach to virtue. If, however, we wish to adopt an allegorical sense, the elevation of the pious mind above those mundane delights which it despises, to celestial things, is designated. Further, anagogically it might be said to prefigure by a fable Christ's ascent*

français du moyen âge des xiie*, xiii*[e]*, et xiv*[e] *siècles* (Paris, 1882); P. Studer and J. Evans, *Anglo-Norman Lapidaries* (Paris, 1924); J. Evans and M. S. Serjeantson, *English Medieval Lapidaries*, E.E.T.S., 190 (1933); Seznec, pp.54–6.

[1] See Seznec, p.50, fn. 60. For *moralitates* in general see Smalley, *passim* and Tuve, pp.219–333.   [2] Boccaccio, *Genealogie*, I, iii; p.19.

*to the Father, having overcome the prince of this world; which senses, how-
ever, although they may be called by various names can equally all be
designated allegorical; which is often done. For 'allegoria' is derived from
'allon' which, in Latin, signifies 'other' or 'diverse'; and thus, whatever
deviates from the literal or historical sense may, as is said, properly be
called allegorical.*]

The concept of poetic fiction may also be illustrated from a
famous passage in Dante's *Convivio*:

L'altro si chiama *allegorico* e questo è quello che si nasconde sotto
il manto di queste favole, ed è una verità ascosa sotto bella
menzogna; siccome quando dice Ovidio che Orfeo facea colla
cetera mansuete le fiere, e gli arbori, e le pietre a sè muovere; che
vuol dire, che'l savio uomo collo strumento della sua voce faria
mansuescere e umiliare li crudeli cuori; e faria muovere alla sua
volontà coloro che non hanno vita di scienza e d'arte: e coloro
che non hanno vita ragionevole alcuna sono quasi come pietre.[1]

[*The other (sense) is called allegorical and this is the sense which is concealed
beneath the cloak of these fables, and it is a truth hidden beneath a fair lie;
as when Ovid says that Orpheus with his lyre made wild beasts tame and
drew the trees and the stones to himself; which implies that the wise man,
with the instrument of his voice, will soften and render humble cruel hearts;
and will draw to his will those who have not the life of science and art: and
those who have no rational life are, as it were, like stones.*]

Whereas the biblical exegesis revealed a truth beneath a veil
of truth, the poetic fiction *was* a fiction, whence the charge
that poets were liars, a charge from which Boccaccio was concerned to exonerate them by reference to the theory of poetic
fiction which I have just quoted. The distinction is neatly made
by Arnulfe of Orleans:

[1] *Le Opere di Dante Alighieri*, edited by E. Moore (4th edn. revised Paget
Toynbee; Oxford, 1924), p.252, ll.21–32; C. S. Singleton, 'Dante's
Allegory', *Speculum*, xxv (1950), 78–86, and R. H. Green, 'Dante's "Allegory
of Poets" and the Mediaeval Theory of Poetic Fiction', *Comparative Literature*,
ix (1957), 118–28; G. Paparelli, '*Fictio:* la definizione dantesca della
poesia', *Filologia Romanza*, vii (1960), fascicules 3–4, 1–83; C. Grayson,
'Dante e la prosa volgare', *Il Verri*, ix (1963), 6–26; J. Chydenius ('The
Typological Problem in Dante', *Acta Societatis Scientiarum Fennicae;* Commentationes Humanarum Litterarum, xxv (1), (1960), 45) suggests that
Dante's 'allegory of poets' is the old allegorial interpretation of myths
employed by the Stoics.

Re vera: Deus hominem de limo terre creavit, cuius rationem con-
tulit: *Fabulose:* Prometheus in Caucaso monte existens de limo
terre hominem faciens furatus est ignem de curru solis quem
homini suo ignem inspiravit et ita eum vivificavit. Unde pro tali
furto in Caucaso monte est extensus et iecur suum a vulturibus
corroditur. *Allegorice est talis:* Prometheus, re vera, fuit quidam
sapientissimus qui in Caucaso monte studens primus naturam
hominis duplam esse consideravit; secundum corpus terrenam,
unde fingitur hominem de limo terre fundasse; secundum animam
celestem, unde fingitur fasclulam currui solis apposuisse et
homini inspirasse. Quod vultures corrodebant iecur eius in
Caucaso nichil aliud est quam hoc quod cura cor eius in Caucaso
studentis corrodebat. Sicut adhuc corrodit corda quorumlibet
ubique studencium.[1]

[According to fact: *God created man from the slime of earth to whom He
gave reason:* According to fable: *Prometheus living in the Caucasian
mountain, while he was making man from the slime of earth, stole fire
from the chariot of the sun, which fire he breathed into his man and so
quickened him. Wherefore for this theft he was stretched out on the
Caucasian mountain and his liver consumed by vultures:* According to
allegory this: *Prometheus in fact was a certain very wise man who, studying in the Caucasian mountain, first understood the nature of man to be
twofold; in regard to his earthly body, wherefore it is fabled that he made
man from the slime of earth; in regard to a celestial spirit, wherefore he is
fabled to have thrust a piece of wood near the chariot of the sun and to have
breathed [fire] into man. The devouring of his liver by vultures, in the
Caucasus, is nothing else but that care devoured his heart in the Caucasus,
studying. Thus does care devour the hearts of all men everywhere who study.*]

Here the story of Prometheus is presented as a fable or *fictio*
adumbrating the fact of man's creation by God. This fiction
can in turn be moralised. The stealing of celestial fire is but an
involucrum[2] or fiction concealing the fact of man's divine nature
and the torments of Prometheus are but the labours by which
he is worn away. I have illustrated this point somewhat extensively because it seems to me important to note that medieval

[1] Arnulfe of Orleans, *Allegoriae*, p.201; cp. Ghisalberti, pp.43-4.
[2] Cp. M.D. Chenu, '*Involucrum:* Le mythe selon les théologiens médiévaux',
Archives d'histoire doctrinale et littéraire du moyen âge, xxii (1955), 75-9.

allegory has a whole world of allegorical material and practice to draw upon which has nothing whatever to do with biblical exegesis.

But the mythographic tradition is not important only as illuminating the concept of *fictio*, but because it introduced the concept of a particular kind of allegorical narrative which although it was, unlike biblical typology, fictitious was to some extent freed from the constraints of a narrative depending upon the manipulation of pure personifications. Above all, it was a tradition which became particularly associated with illustrations and which certainly enriched the pictorial content of allegory, not only by emblems, but by the use of classical figures as *idola* or concrete representations of abstract conceptions.[1] It is difficult to imagine Lydgate without Holcot and I would suspect that the static nature of late medieval allegory, in which we have, rather than a real action, a series of panels, was to some extent due to the popularity of moralised pictures, a popularity which manifested itself also in the late medieval passion for pageants. The pageant, the tournament, the plays, indeed, all testify to this late medieval urge towards visual representation, which is the logical outcome of the allegorical mode of thought; but in no small measure the mythographic tradition contributed to its satisfaction. And it must be noted that even the fiction itself is susceptible of a fourfold interpretation differing from the scriptural tradition. Thus, for example, the *De Formis Figurisque Deorum* uses the terms *litteraliter, naturaliter, historialiter, spiritualiter*. Thus Saturn is *naturaliter* 'time', *historialiter* 'a king of Crete', *spiritualiter*, or allegorically he can represent, for example, 'an evil prelate' or 'a tyrant'.[2]

Before passing to the third source of allegorical writing it may

---

[1] It is also connected with the physical tradition. See Seznec, pp.37–83; F. Saxl and H. Meier, *Catalogue of Astrological and Mythological Illuminated Manuscripts of the Latin Middle Ages*, III (London, 1953); IV, edited by McGurk (London, 1966).

[2] Berchorius, *De formis figurisque deorum; Reductorium Morale*, Liber, xv, cap. i, edited by J. Engels (Utrecht, 1960), pp.5–8. For medieval views of the fable, cp. also S. Manning, 'The Nun's Priest's Morality and the Medieval Attitude toward Fables', *JEGP*, lix (1960), 403–16.

be helpful to pause to consider the concept of 'moralisation' a little more closely. A characteristic piece of moralisation is the passage from the *Ancrene Wisse* about the shield of the Christ-knight. It runs as follows:

His scheld, þe wreah his Goddhead, wes his leoue licome þet wes ispread o rode, brad as scheld buuen in his istrahte earmes, nearow bineoðen, as þe an fot, efter monies wene, set up o þe oðer. Þet þis scheld naueð siden is for bitacnunge þet his deciples þe schulden stonden bi him & habben ibeon his siden, fluhen alle from him & leafden him as fremede, as þe godspel seið: *Relicto eo, omnes fugerunt.* Þis scheld is iȝeuen us aȝein alle temptatiuns, as Jeremie witneð: *Dabis scutum cordis laborem tuum.* Nawt ane þis scheld ne schilt us from alle uueles, ah deð ȝet mare, cruneð us in heouene *scuto bone uoluntatis.* Lauerd, he seið, Dauið, wið þe scheld of þi gode wil þu hauest us icrunet – scheld, he seið, of god wil, for willes he þolede al þet he þolede. . . . I scheld beoð þreo þinges, þe treo, & te leðer, & te litunge. Alswa wes i þis scheld – þe treo of þe rode, þet leðer of Godes licome, þe litunge of þe reade blod þet heowede hire se feire. Eft þe þridde reisun. Efter kene cnihtes deað, me hongeð hehe i chirche his scheld on his mungunge. Alswa is þis scheld, þet is, þe crucifix, i chirche iset i swuch stude þer me hit sonest seo forte þenchen þerbi o Iesu Cristes cnihtschipe þet he dude o rode. His leofmon bihalde þron hu he bohte hire luue, lette þurlin his scheld, openin his side to schawin hire his heorte, to schawin hire openliche hu inwardliche he luuede hire, & to ofdrahen hire heorte.[1]

Just as, in the *Bestiary*, the lion and the panther represent Christ, by a similar process the shield is here taken to represent Christ's passion. Various points may be noticed. In the first place, the image of the shield is an extension of an allegory of a different kind, the allegory of the Christ-knight to which we shall return later in connection with a passage from Langland. Secondly, the image of the shield shifts in the course of the passage. It represents the passion of Christ, but also, it is a shield against temptations and a crown for the victorious in heaven. These figures involve a double metaphor. The shield represents Christ's passion, but Christ's passion is a shield for

[1] *Ancrene Wisse*, pts. vi & vii, edited by G. Shepherd (London, 1959), pp.22–3.

the sinner. Then, the author has taken over, in virtue of a
verbal link, the curious metaphor from the Psalter, and the
shield becomes a crown. Further, the shield itself images two
slightly different things. In the first instance, the shield represents Christ's humanity, but also his body; its breadth his
outstretched arms, its narrow end his feet. Its lack of sides signifies those disciples who left his side when they should have remained with him. The sides, therefore, represent the side of
Christ but in a metaphorical sense. Secondly, the wood of the
shield represents the wood of the cross, its leather covering
Christ's body and the colouring Christ's blood. Moreover, by
another shift, the hanging of the knight's shield in the church
is like the placing of the crucifix in a church as a memorial of
Christ's chivalry. Now the shield is again Christ's body, which
was pierced for his beloved. It is indeed a kind of '*discordia
concors*'; a combination of dissimilar images, or discovery of
occult resemblances in things apparently unlike'. The term
'wit-writing' would not be ill-applied to it for the conjunction
of images depends upon intellectual rather than emotional
links.[1] These are sometimes verbal, as when the shield is
equated with a crown, or the sides of the shield with Christ's
side. But sometimes the image rests upon a resemblance of
shape. The shape of the cross recalls the shape of Christ's body
on the cross. But there is also a functional link. The shield
covers the knight's body; Christ's divinity was covered by his
human body. Then there is a configuration. As the leather of
the shield covers its wood so the body of Christ covered the cross
and as the colouring of the shield covered the leather so the
blood of Christ covered his body. Then, again, as the shield
hangs in the church as a memorial of past battles, so the crucifix
hangs in the church as a memorial of Christ's victory. In almost
every case, there seems to be a congruence of idea but an incongruence of feeling arising from the comparison of an
emotionally charged topic to an object which is emotionally
neutral. The same processes can be seen at work in moralisations

[1] For the synthesis of disparate materials in imagery see Philip Wheelwright, *The Burning Fountain* (Bloomington, 1968), pp.45–50.

of Virgil such as that of Bernard Silvestris,[1] or in the *Ovide Moralisé* when the story of Jason and Medea is made a type of the fall and redemption of man, the dragon's teeth the sowing of the Christian faith, the armed men who sprang up from the dragon's teeth those disciples of the Christian religion who fought against the enemies of the faith, and the golden fleece the human person of Christ, who by his death gave man immortality.[2]

The emblem is a particular example of this kind of allegorical picture. Whereas the elements in the description of a person, or object, in a non-allegorical narrative, are to some extent free, the emblem is essentially tied to its meaning. As Panofsky has said 'If the knife that enables us to identify a St. Bartholomew is not a knife but a cork-screw, the figure is not a St. Bartholomew.'[3] Such things speak primarily, not to the emotions, but to the intellect. They often imply an oblique reference to an object, story or some interpretation of a story. Such an emblem would be Pride falling from his horse at Chartres, for this is a curtailed reference to Pride's falling into the ditch of Fraud in Prudentius.[4] The emblems of Saints often refer to the stories of their passions. Such emblems are the knife of St. Bartholomew and the gridiron of St. Lawrence. Jewels and colours can assume emblematic qualities from association with moralisations of their qualities. Emblems are always visible, and a substitutional or emblematic mode of allegory may perhaps be distinguished from a verbal or narrative allegorical mode. When St. John speaks of God as *Alpha and Omega* he is using a metaphor. But when Boethius places the Greek letters on the border of Philosophy's robe these are emblems. The tradition of moralisation

---

[1] Bernard Silvestris, *Commentum super Eneidem*, edited by G. Riedel (Greifswald, 1924). Cp. also P. Courcelle, 'Les pères de l'église devant les enfers virgiliens', *Archives d'histoire doctrinale et littéraire du moyen âge*, xxii (1955), 5–74.

[2] *Ovide Moralisé*, VII, ll.709–806.

[3] E. Panofsky, *Studies in Iconology* (New York, 1939), p.7.

[4] Prudentius, *Psychomachia*, edited by M. P. Cunningham (Corpus Christianorum), Series Latina, cxxvi (Turnholt, 1966); ll.257–66, translation by H. J. Thomson, *Prudentius* (London & Cambridge, Mass., 1949), I, 297–9.

was richly productive of emblems in the Middle Ages. A particular and fascinating category of emblems are those pictures of which Miss Smalley has written. For example, Robert Holcot, in his Commentary on Wisdom, writes:

> Fingitur a quodam imaginem ebrietatis sic fuisse depictam, ut imago puerilis cornu habens in manu, et in capite coronam de uitro [viteo?]. Puer erat in signum quod facit hominem elinguem, insensatum more pueri; cornu habebat in manu in signum quod nullum celat secretum, sed clamando et clangendo reuelat. Coronam habet uitream [viteam?]: quia reputat se gloriosum et diuitem qui est ebrius, cum nicil habeat.[1]

> [*Someone feigns the image of Drunkenness to have been thus depicted, the image of a child, having in his hand a horn and on his head a crown of glass (vine). He was a boy in token that (drunkenness) makes a man speechless and senseless, in the manner of a child. He had a horn in his hand as a token that (the drunken man) conceals no secret but reveals (it) with clamour and clangour. He has a glass (vine) crown, because he considers himself glorious and wealthy, he who is drunk, whereas he has nothing.*]

Here as in the *Ancrene Riwle*, the link is accidental rather than substantial. The figure of a child holding a horn and wearing a crown is not an image of drunkenness which conveys any sense of the abstraction. We have merely a re-definition of the concept in terms of objects which share similar qualities. The sources of emblematic imagery are various, but it has been considered here since, not only was the mythographic tradition a fruitful source of emblems, but the same habit of mind can be seen in both.

So much for the implications of the mythographers and their kin. Their part in the genetic relationships of medieval allegory can best be considered in relation to our third category, the classical tradition. *Allegoria* is a rhetorical figure. Thus, for example, Quintilian:

> Allegoria, quam inversionem interpretantur, aut aliud verbis aliud sensu ostendit aut etiam interim contrarium. Prius fit genus plerumque continuatis translationibus, ut

---

[1] Robert Holcot, *In Librum Sapientiae* (1586), p.77. See Smalley, pp.133-202; for a slightly different text of this passage see p.171, fn. 5.

'O navis, referent in mare te novi
Fluctus; o quid agis? fortiter occupa
Portum,'

totusque ille Horatii locus, quo navem pro re publica, fluctus et
tempestates pro bellis civilibus, portum pro pace atque concordia
dicit. . . . Sine translatione vero in Bucolicis

'Certe equidem audieram, qua se subducere colles
Incipiunt mollique iugum demittere clivo
Usque ad aquam et veteris iam fracta cacumina fagi,
Omnia carminibus vestrum servasse Menalcan.'

Hoc enim loco praeter nomen cetera propriis decisa sunt verbis,
verum non pastor Menalcas, sed Vergilius est intelligendus.[1]

[Allegory, *which is translated in Latin by* inversio, *either presents one
thing in words and another in meaning, or else something absolutely
opposed to the meaning of the words. The first type is generally produced by
a series of metaphors. Take as an example:* 'O ship, new waves will bear
thee back to sea. What dost thou? Make a haven, come what may,' *and
the rest of the ode, in which Horace represents the state under the semblance
of a ship, the civil wars as tempests, and peace and good-will as the
haven . . . on the other hand, in the Bucolics Virgil introduces an allegory
without any metaphor:* 'Truth, I had heard Your loved Menalcas and his
songs had saved All those fair acres, where the hills begin To sink and
droop their ridge with easy slope Down to the water side and that old
beech With splintered crest.' *For in this passage, with the exception of
the proper name, the words bear no more than their literal meaning. But the
name does not simply denote the shepherd Menalcas, but is a pseudonym for
Virgil himself.*]

Two other figures combine to form a basic allegorical type of
narrative. By *prosopopoeia* was meant an imaginary monologue
which could, but need not be, attributed to inanimate objects.
Such personifications were part of the stock in trade of late
Latin poets, such as Statius. As C. S. Lewis has pointed out,[2]

[1] Quintilian, *Institutio Oratoria*, VIII, vi, 44–7, edited and translated by
H. E. Butler, *The Institutio Oratoria of Quintilian* (London & Cambridge,
Mass., 1921), III, 326–9.

[2] C. S. Lewis, *The Allegory of Love* (Oxford, 1936), pp.49–56; for the sub-
sequent development of this type of allegory see pp.56–111; for the 'School
of Chartres' see R. W. Southern, *Medieval Humanism and other Studies* (Oxford,
1970), pp.61–85.

these are often expanded in Statius to miniature allegories as in the following example:

> Iamdudum terris coetuque offensa deorum
> aversa caeli Pietas in parte sedebat,
> non habitu, quo nota prius, non ore sereno,
> sed vittis exuta comam, fraternaque bella,
> ceu soror infelix pugnantum aut anxia mater,
> deflebat, saevumque Iovem Parcasque nocentes
> vociferans, seseque polis et luce relicta
> descensuram Erebo et Stygios iam malle penates.[1]

[*Long time offended alike by earth and the company of the gods, had Piety been sitting in the remote region of the heavens, with unwonted dress and troubled countenance, and fillets stripped from off her hair; she bewailed the fraternal strife, as though a hapless sister or anxious mother of the fighters, and loudly chiding cruel Jove and the guilty Fates protested she would leave heaven and the light of day and descend to Erebus, for already she preferred the abodes of Styx.*]

Thirdly, the rhetorical device of *effictio* consists in depicting in words clear enough for recognition, the bodily form of some person. Thus to quote the *Rhetorica ad Herennium*:

> Effictio est, cum exprimitur atque effingitur verbis corporis cuiuspiam forma, quoad satis sit ad intellegendum, hoc modo: 'Hunc, iudices, dico, rubrum, brevem, incurvom, canum, subcrispum, caesium, cui sane magna est in mento cicatrix, si quo modo potest vobis in memoriam redire.'[2]

[*Portrayal consists in representing and depicting in words clearly enough for recognition the bodily form of some person as follows:* '*I mean him, men of the jury, the ruddy, short, bent man, with white and rather curly hair, bluegrey eyes, and a huge scar on his chin, if perhaps you can recall him to memory.*']

---

[1] Statius, *Thebaid*, XI, 457–64; edited and translated by J. H. Mozley, *Statius* (London & Cambridge, Mass., 1928), II, 422–5.

[2] *Cornifici Rhetorica ad C. Herennium*, edited by G. Calboli (Bologna, 1969), p.197; translation by H. Caplan, *Rhetorica ad Herennium* (London Cambridge Mass., 1954), p.387. For *effictio* see G. Misener, 'Iconistic Portraits', *Classical Philology*, xix (1924), 97–123; E. C. Evans, 'Roman Descriptions of Personal Appearance in History and Biography', *Harvard Studies in Classical Philology*, xlvi (1935), 43–84.

These traditions could give rise to two sorts of allegorical narrative. On the one hand, there developed 'the morality' in which the actor was an abstraction but his actions were not allegorical, the non-metaphorical allegory of Quintilian. Thus in the passage from Statius, Piety is personified but her actions are dramatic rather than allegorical. A true sister to Piety in Statius is Jean de Meung's Reason who displays her encyclopaedic knowledge to the Dreamer in a quite unallegorical manner. Examples can also be found in late medieval allegories such as *The Assembly of Ladies* in which the lady falls asleep in an arbour and dreams that she is addressed by a series of abstractions such as Perseverance, Lady Loyalty, and Temperance and Diligence. On the other hand, one could create a fully-developed allegorical narrative in which, as in Quintilian's first example, the whole narrative consists of two parts, the picture and the theme, the metaphorical allegory of Quintilian. It would perhaps be true to say that allegories of action or conversation, as in parts of the morality play, tend towards the first type and allegories of description towards the second. The reason for this is not far to seek. 'Fame tells a tale and Victory hovers over a general, or perches on a standard; but Fame and Victory can do no more,' as Johnson observed. An abstraction is not in itself allegorical. When Jean de Meung speaks of Reason he means reason and not something else; when Langland speaks of Reason and Conscience, Faith, Dame Study, Scripture and so on, he is not referring to some other entity but to these abstractions. We tend to find, therefore, that personification allegory usually includes long descriptive passages which serve, I think, not only to give concreteness to the abstractions, but some allegorical machinery. For the writer of personification allegory is up against the problem which Coleridge shrewdly noted in relation to the *Psychomachia*, that 'if the allegoric personage be strongly individualised so as to interest us, we cease to think of it as allegory; and if it does not interest us, it had better be away'.[1]

---

[1] Coleridge, *Miscellaneous Criticism*, p.31.

But let us now look at some specific examples of this kind of allegory. The *Psychomachia* itself, probably written towards the end of the fourth century, is based upon Tertullian's elaboration of the Pauline image of the Christian life as warfare:

> Vis et pugillatus et luctatus? praesto sunt, non parva sed multa. Aspice impudicitiam deiectam a castitate, perfidiam caesam a fide, saevitiam a misericordia contusam, petulantiam a modestia adumbratam; et tales sunt apud nos agones, in quibus ipsi coronamur.[1]

> [*Would you have fightings, and wrestlings? Here they are, things of no small account and plenty of them . . . see Impurity overthrown by Chastity, Perfidy slain by Faith, Cruelty crushed by Pity, Impudence thrown into the shade by Modesty; and such are the contests amongst us and in them are we crowned.*]

So he exhorts his fellow-Christians to shun the games and spectacles of his day and to battle against the vices of the soul. The *Psychomachia* of Prudentius is an extension of this metaphor. If we take a passage we can see how each detail, at one and the same time, projects the picture and illustrates the theme.[2]

> Ecce modesta graui stabat Patientia uultu
> per medias inmota acies uariosque tumultus
> uulneraque et rigidis uitalia peruia pilis
> spectabat defixa oculos et lenta manebat.
> Hanc procul Ira tumens, spumanti feruida rictu,
> sanguinea intorquens suffuso lumina felle,
> ut belli exsortem teloque et uoce lacessit
> inpatiensque morae conto petit, increpat ore
> hirsutas quatiens galeato in uertice cristas.
> 'En tibi, Martis' ait 'spectatrix libera nostri,
> excipe mortiferum securo pectore ferrum;
> nec doleas quia turpe tibi gemuisse dolorem.'

---

[1] Tertullian, *De Spectaculis*, XXIX, edited by E. Castorina (Florence, 1961), pp.379–82; translation by T. R. Glover, *Tertullian* (London, 1931), p.297.

[2] Cp. H. R. Jauss, 'Form und Auffassung der Allegorie in der Tradition der *Psychomachia*', *Medium Aevum Vivum: Festschrift für Walther Bulst* (Heidelberg, 1960), edited by H. R. Jauss and D. Schaller, pp.179–206.

Sic ait, et stridens sequitur conuicia pinus
per teneros crispata notos et certa sub ipsum
defertur stomachum rectoque inliditur ictu;
sed resilit duro loricae excussa repulsu.
Prouida nam uirtus conserto adamante trilicem
induerat thoraca umeris squamosaque ferri
texta per intortos commiserat undique neruos.[1]

[*Lo, mild Long-suffering was standing with staid countenance, unmoved amid the battle and its confused uproar, with fixed gaze watching the wounds inflicted as the stiff javelins pierced the vital parts while she waited inactive. On her from a distance swelling Wrath, showing her teeth with rage and foaming at the mouth, darts her eyes all shot with blood and gall and challenges her with weapons and with speech for taking no part in the fight; irked by her hanging back, she hurls a pike at her and assails her with abuse, tossing the shaggy crests on her helmeted head. 'Here's for thee,' she cries, 'that lookest on at our warfare and takest no side. Receive the death-stroke in thy calm breast, and betray no pain, since it is dishonour in thine eyes to utter a cry of pain.' So speaks she and the quivering pineshaft launched through the yielding air goes hissing after her angry words. Sure-aimed it hits the stomach and smites hard with full force but is struck off by the resistance of a hard cuirass and rebounds; for the virtue had prudently put on her shoulders a three-ply corslet of mail impenetrable, the fabric of iron scales joined every way with leathers interlacee.*]

The visual effectiveness of the narrative is demonstrated by the series of illustrations to the *Psychomachia*.[2] But let us consider it more closely. In the first place it will be noted that the passage consists of a developed similitude or metaphor. The character of Wrath and of Patience is indicated by two warriors, one aggressive, the other clad in the impenetrable mail of patience. Wrath is further characterised by a literal translation of Wrath into a wrathful person, baring his teeth, foaming at the mouth, his eyes bloodshot. This is not a metaphor but a simple shift of key from the abstract to the concrete, from similarity to contiguity. The description is an *effictio* not strictly an *allegoria*.

---

[1] Prudentius, *Psychomachia*, ll.109–27; based on Thomson, I, 287–9.
[2] R. Stettiner, *Die Illustrierten Prudentiushandschriften* (Berlin, 1905); Raimond van Marle, *Iconographie de l'art profane: allégories et symboles* (The Hague, 1932), pp.1–110; A. Katzenellenbogen, *Allegories of the Virtues and Vices in Medieval Art* (London, 1939), pp.1–13.

Nevertheless, the work as a whole is an allegory, for it images man's psyche as a battlefield. There is a congruence between picture and theme, although the relationship between them is not always the same. Further, the picture is not only congruent but the narrative has a surface consistency; it is a naturalistic and coherent narrative. Substitute the names of people for the abstractions and it might be a description of a battle from Statius.[1] We find therefore that we have three variables: firstly, the nature of the relationship between the picture and the theme; secondly, the degree of congruence of picture and theme, thirdly, the self-consistency of the picture. All these factors, as I hope to show, are important when analysing and evaluating allegory. A consideration of two other passages at this point is revealing and will serve to develop our analysis. The first is from Langland:

> Thanne cam Coueityse. and caste how he myghte
> Ouercome Conscience. and cardynal vertues,
> And armed hym in auaryce. and hungriliche lyued.
> His wepne was al wiles. to wynnen and to hyden;
> With glosynges and with gabbynges. he gyled the peple.
> Symonye hym sente. to assaille Conscience,
> And preched to the peple. and prelates thei hem maden,
> To holden with Antecryste. her temperaltes to saue;[2]

At first sight we have the same picture. The passage is part of the Psychomachia at the end of *Piers Plowman* and here we have a conflict between Covetousness, and Conscience with the virtues. But differences immediately emerge when we look at it more closely. In the first place, if we try to separate the picture and the theme we run into difficulties. The theme is presumably the attack of Covetousness on Conscience and the virtues, but the picture is rarely metaphorical. When we are told, for example, that Covetousness's weapon is guile and his armour is avarice we have a reversal of theme and picture. Instead of describing the armour and weapons of Covetousness,

---

[1] For the influence of Roman battle scenes on the pictorial tradition see Katzenellenbogen, p. 5.

[2] Langland, *Piers Plowman*, B. xx, ll.120–7.

these accoutrements are themselves abstractions, avarice and guile. Indeed, what we really have is a dramatic picture strictly comparable, not to the allegory of Prudentius, but to a morality play such as *Everyman*. The metaphorical content is external. The difference is indeed that between metaphorical allegory and non-metaphorical allegory in the terminology of Quintilian; between a true allegory and a narrative couched in the most abstract terms. There is an essential difference between saying that the armour of Avarice was of such and such a kind and saying that Covetousness wore avarice like armour and used guile as his weapon. It is indeed to move away from allegory towards symbolism. The shift of key which we noted in Prudentius is here reversed. Our second variable thus becomes irrelevant in regard to this passage. Yet it is significant that, notwithstanding the shift away from metaphorical allegory to non-metaphorical allegory, the picture is not self-consistent. This is because Langland treats his character mythically rather than allegorically. What the passage is saying is that Covetousness was rapacious and deceitfully gained money and concealed it. He deceived people with confidence talk and, corrupted by Simony, persuaded the church to think more of its temporal goods than of its office. The passage shifts, in fact, from an allegorical to a literal action. Thus, while the whole passage starts from the metaphor of the battle for man's soul, a metaphor which we still can trace in the armour of avarice and the weapons of wiles and in the command to attack Conscience, this metaphor is blended with action on a literal, exemplary level, earning money, preaching and so on.[1] An interesting case is the phrase 'live hungrily' which, it seems, could mean either that he was hungry for money, a metaphor, or that he was physically hungry and therefore always seeking food. In this exploitation of the literal level we surely have much of the secret of Langland's effectiveness as a writer. From this springs his dramatic liveliness of speech and action, for we

[1] Cp. Tuve, *passim*; and R. Woolf, 'The Tearing of the Pardon', in *Piers Plowman: Critical Approaches*, edited by S. S. Hussey (London, 1969), p.73.

are always being catapulted into the real world of fourteenth-century England. In short, Langland's abstractions are so lively just because they are so often treated dramatically rather than allegorically.

The second passage is from *The Assembly of Gods*:

> Forthe then went Cerberus with hys fyry cheyne
> And brought thedyr Vyce, as he commaundyd was,
> Ageyn noble Vertew that batayll to dereygne.
> On a glydyng serpent rydyng a gret pas,
> Formyd lyke a dragon, scalyd harde as glas,
> Whos mouth flamyd feere without fayll.
> Wyngys had hit serpentyne and a long tayll.
>
> Armyd was Vyce all in cure boyle,
> Hard as any horn, blakker fer then soot
> An vngoodly soort folowyd hym parde,
> Of vnhappy capteyns. Of myschyef croppe and roote
> Pryde was the furst þat next hym roode, God woote
> On a roryng lyon; next whom came Enuy,
> Syttyng on a wolfe – he had a scornfull ey.
>
> Wrethe bestrode a wylde bore, and next hem gan ryde.
> In hys hand he bare a blody nakyd swerde.
> Next whom came Couetyse, that goth so fer and wyde,
> Rydyng on a olyfaunt, as he had ben aferde.
> Aftyr whom rood Glotony, with hys fat berde,
> Syttyng on a bere, with hys gret bely.
> And next hym on a goot folowyd Lechery.[1]

This passage is superficially like the passage from Prudentius and unlike the passage from Langland. The relationship between picture and theme is one of similarity or metaphor, the metaphor of the spiritual battle between the vices and virtues. The abstractions, however, are not on the whole delineated with human characteristics, but by emblematic animals and objects. This necessarily affects the surface impression which the passage gives. It has a picturesque quality absent in the other two. The abstractions are never given the depth and immediacy of the people in the *Psychomachia*, which,

[1] Lydgate (?), *The Assembly of Gods*, edited by O. L. Triggs, E.E.T.S. (ES) 69 (1896), ll.610-30.

if not complex characters, have at least something of the immediacy of a human being whose emotions are familiar to us. The world of the *Psychomachia* may be only part of a world, but it is part of a human world. The animal emblems in Lydgate, on the other hand, convey a picture to the eye but no quality to the mind. They are essentially tautologies since to say that Envy is sitting on a wolf is to say that the wolf symbolises Envy.[1] The scene in Lydgate is thus picturesque but semantically thin. How different are his beasts from the sinister animals which Dante meets in the humanly significant context of the *selva oscura*!

This leads us straight into the heart of the matter, the allegorical picture. When we say *allegoria rem totam per metaphoram obscurè tractat* we emphasise an essential point, the similarity between imagery and allegory. When Auden in his *Paysage Moralisé* or in *The Ascent of F6* uses the mountain as an image of futile endeavour, he is operating in essentially the same way as Dante when he uses a mountain as an image of moral endeavour. The fundamental difference is merely between a narrative and a non-narrative kind. C. Day Lewis has said that word-pictures 'only become images in relation to a general truth'.[2] This makes an essential distinction between description in the mythic mode, such as the descriptions of Blanche in the *Book of the Duchess* or Gawain in *Sir Gawain and the Green Knight* or the portraits of Troilus, Criseyde and Diomede in *Troilus and Criseyde* and imagery, which is essentially a linking device between picture and theme. The exact nature of the link varies from author to author and from period to period according to the congruence of picture and theme, and the exploitation of meaning and associations of words. But the essential nature of the allegorical picture remains and it differs, as C. Day Lewis observes, from the word picture in that the word picture is intuitive only. Of course a word-picture can have relevance to the theme of a story. When we are told that the Green Knight has a holly bob and an axe, these details are significant and not

[1] For the wolf as a symbol of Covetousness see Katzenellenbogen, p.61.
[2] Day Lewis, p.139.

random. But their significance is secondary in the sense that their implications for the story is routed through the person of the Green Knight and his actions. On the other hand, when Langland describes Wrath, the description is directly relevant to the theme. This difference constitutes the nature of the allegorical picture. Thus the essential dichotomy in linguistic terms is not between personification and allegory or even between symbolism and allegory, but between an allegorical and a mythic mode of writing. The mythic mode of writing we have already tried to define briefly both in this chapter and in our introductory chapter. We have suggested that, while both forms are binary, the relationship between the parts is different; in one a relationship of similarity, in the other a relationship of contiguity.

We have tried to show that under the umbrella of allegory shelter a number of different modes of writing, both linguistically and genetically distinct. On the one hand, we have the kind of relationship which Auerbach has called figural. He is no doubt right in supposing that the origin of this is to be seen in the tradition of biblical typology but, as a mode of writing, it extends beyond the scriptural tradition as can be seen from Auerbach's treatment of the figures of Virgil, Beatrice, Cato and Francis in *The Divine Comedy*. If Francis can be used as an exemplum of poverty, it is because he exemplified this quality and the figure is an example of *pars pro toto*. This, of all allegorical modes, is the nearest to the mythic mode of writing and differs from it only in that the figure is tied in a particular way to the allegorical narrative and it is an abstraction only in the sense that a particular character is abstracted and viewed in a context other than its actual historical context. That is to say that, while the *figura* of Francis brings with it certain emotional overtones deriving from a known historical context, in *The Divine Comedy* he appears in an allegorical narrative which is quite different from his actual historical context. Again, when Cato is presented in the context of *The Divine Comedy* he is a *figura*; when he appears in Valerius Maximus, he is purely exemplary. It is also possible for a type, such as a ploughman, to be treated as a *figura*, as we shall see in a later discussion of *Piers Plowman*, although such a figure will tend to be seen within the historical context of his time and the figural mode is re-enforced in Langland by the conjoining of the figure of a ploughman with the implications of the proper name 'Peter'. He is thus, if one may so put it, 'more figural' than his prototype the ploughman, who appears as a type of zeal in the illustrations of the *Somme le Roy*. It is also to be noted that the degree of congruence between theme and picture in figural allegory can vary. For example, Virgil, in Dante, is a much freer figure than the figure of Abraham in Langland.

A very different type of allegorical machinery is the emblem or fiction. When the writer of the *Ancrene Wisse* takes the shield as a type of the cross, or the writer of the *Ovide Moralisé* takes the golden fleece as a type of Christ's humanity, or we take the Phoenix as a type of the Resurrection, then we are bringing together two different universes of discourse; the shield is made of wood, the cross is made of wood, so one may stand for the other; the phoenix rises from its ashes, Christ rose from the dead, so one may stand for the other. Or, when Boccaccio tells us that Perseus rising into the air to fight the Gorgon represents the prudent man avoiding vice or, in an abstract mode, the pious mind rising above the wretchedness of life, the pivot of the allegory is the idea of rising into the air. As Perseus rises literally, so a man can rise metaphorically above vice, for example, or above the sorrows of life. It may be noted in passing that the moral sense is that which applies to the type, the moral man, the exemplary level, while the allegorical sense, in Boccaccio's usage, is the abstract sense, the pious mind. But in each case we have a transference from a literal to a metaphorical sense of the verb 'rising' and the consequential conjunction of two different universes of discourse. In this case, we notice also a large area of incongruence between the image and the theme which gives a distinctive and often slightly ludicrous tone to the whole.

But the complexity of the allegorical mode of writing does not depend only upon the different relationships between the picture and the theme but also upon the relationship of the whole picture to the whole theme. For example, Quintilian's non-metaphorical allegory is non-metaphorical because it contains a single component only which is not to be understood literally; namely, the substitution of the name Menalcas for the name Virgil. But the rest of the poem is to be understood literally. We have suggested that, in essence, the use of personification is of this nature. There is clearly a difference between saying Beauty speaks and Helen of Troy speaks. To say that Beauty speaks is an allegory, in the sense that it cannot be literally true. But it is not truly polysemous because Beauty is the subject of the discourse. There are not, as it were, two subjects of discourse, as is the case when we regard Perseus as man rising above vice. And, as we have seen, it is possible to have an 'allegory' in which the allegorical mode is not consistently maintained. This is the comprehensible result of the complex relationships of allegory, the relationships of picture to theme, of picture to picture, an elaborate pattern of linguistic concords and discords. This complexity is not the inevitable result of its binary nature, but of the particular nature of the relationships between picture and theme, a relationship essentially metaphorical.

Let us now turn to a more detailed consideration of two authors, Langland and Chaucer. I want to consider Langland under two headings; firstly, a comparative treatment of the theme of avarice and a consideration of the allegorical portrait, and, secondly, a closer study of a single scene of allegorical narrative from Langland. The first account of avarice is from Holcot's *Commentary on the Prophets*:

Notandum quod amphora dicitur esse avaritia et avarus etiam describitur secundum Chrysostomum super Mat., omelia 28, esse homo ab oculis ignem emittens, niger, ab alterutris humeris dracones habens (loco) manus dependentes. Fit autem ei os pro dentibus gladios acutos habens infixos, pro lingua autem veneni et pestiferi formati fortem (fontem) emanantem, habens etiam ventrem caminum; pedes sunt subalati; facies ipsa a lupo et cane constructa, et loquitur nichil humanum sed sonitum habet non delectabilem, sed terribilem, et in manibus flammam habet. Terribilia esse videntur que dicta sunt, sed nondum secundum quod est avaritie formavimus. Hec ille. Ex istis dictis posset dici quod avarus pingitur esse homo denigratus in cute, gladio trans-verberatus, cum fonte venenato et oculis igneis cum flamma in manibus, ex humeris draconibus dependentibus, cum vultu lupino, habens os pro dentibus cum subalatis pedibus et sonis terribilibus.[1]

[*It is to be noted that the amphora (in reference to the text Zach. v, 7 Ecce* mulier sedens in medio amphorae) *is said to be avarice and the avaricious man is also described by Chrysostom in his gloss on Matthew, in Homily 28, as being a man sending forth fire from his eyes, black, and having, in place of hands, dragons hanging from both shoulders. He gives him also a mouth with sharp, inset swords for teeth, and for a tongue a fountain spewing forth, of poisonous and pestilent form, his belly is like a furnace; his feet are feathered; the face built up from a wolf and a dog; his speech is not in any way human but has a sound not pleasant to hear, but terrible and he has a flame in his hands. The things we have described are evidently terrible; yet have we not described what avarice truly is. Thus Chrysostom describes him. From these words it could be said that the avaricious man is depicted as being blackened in skin, transfixed with a sword, with a fountain of poison, and eyes of fire, with a flame in his hands, having dragons hanging from his shoulders, with the face of a wolf, having a tusk for teeth, with winged feet and making terrible sounds.*]

Let us put beside this the following passage from Langland:

> And thanne cam Coueytise. can I hym nouʒte descryue
> So hungriliche and holwe. sire Heruy hym loked.
> He was bitelbrowed. and baberlipped also,
> With two blered eyghen. as a blynde hagge;
> And as a letheren purs. lolled his chekes,
> Wel sydder than his chyn. thei chiueled for elde;
> And as a bondman of his bacoun. his berde was bidraueled.
> With an hode on his hed. a lousi hatte aboue,
> And in a tauny tabarde. of twelue wynter age,
> Al totorne and baudy. and ful of lys crepynge;
> But if that a lous couthe. haue lopen the bettre,
> She sholde nouʒte haue walked on that welche. so was it
>   thredebare.
> 'I haue ben coueytouse,' quod this caityue. 'I biknowe it here;

---

[1] Quoted by Smalley, p.177.

> For some tyme I serued. Symme atte stile,
> And was his prentis ypli3te. his profit to wayte.
> First I lerned to lye, a leef other tweyne,
> Wikkedlich to weye. was my furst lessoun.
> To Wy and to Wynchestre. I went to the faire,
> With many manere marchandise. as my maistre me hi3te;
> Ne had the grace of gyle. ygo amonge my ware,
> It had be vnsolde this seuene 3ere. so me god helpe!'[1]

If we consider other literary representations of the theme of avarice, for example in *Martin Chuzzlewit, Le Père Goriot, The Threepenny Novel*, it is obvious that the passages from Holcot and Langland, different though they are from each other, have certain features in common which differentiate them from the treatment in the novels. Whereas a novelist such as Dickens or Balzac puts us in an actual context of avarice in action, an allegorical writer, as we have already pointed out, presents the reader with an extended metaphor. Nevertheless, the differences between the two passages are significant. In Holcot we have a monster, in Langland a human being. Holcot's monster has the face of a wolf and a dog, he is painted with tusks, winged feet and with a flame in his hand. Like Virgil's picture of Fame, the portrait has little regard for human verisimilitude. The image is an emblem, that is to say, it must be understood by grasping an intellectual *distinctio* or reference. The wolf is a symbol of avarice, his winged feet no doubt represent the prevalence of avarice in the world and the flame in his hand the destructive nature of avarice both in the macrocosm and microcosm. We might compare it with the *femina balba* of the *Purgatorio*,[2] whose stuttering tongue probably represents the equivocal speech of avarice, the stuttering of the drunkard and the flattering words of the luxurious man; whose squinting eyes have been thought to represent the blind lust for possessions of cupidity, the bleariness of gluttony and the distortion of values of luxury, whose crooked gait may represent the distorted judgement of avarice, the staggering gait of gluttony and debilitation of luxury; the

[1] Langland, *Piers Plowman*, B. v, ll.188–208; cp. C. vii, ll.196–214.

[2] Dante, *Purgatorio*, xix, ll.7–18; *La Divina Commedia*, edited by T. Casini and S. A. Barbi (Firenze, 1923).

hands, as in Prudentius, are a symbol of giving, and thus she has maimed hands, both unwilling to give and, enfeebled by luxury and gluttony, incapable of doing so. It is perhaps worth noticing, however, that the picture of the *femina balba* stands to some extent half way between Holcot and Langland. For while avarice in Dante's portrait is defined as an intellectual sin, in intellectual terms, though represented by physical equivalents, the sins of the flesh are defined in physical terms. Thus avarice is defined as equivocal of speech, lustful for possessions, distorted in judgement, unwilling to give; gluttony, on the other hand, is defined as stuttering, bleary-eyed, staggering, too feeble to give. Thus the *femina balba* is both a literal picture of the gluttonous man and a metaphorical picture of an avaricious one. And the total effect is further modified by Dante's addition to this picture of the emblem of the siren, followed by the historical incarnation of avarice in Pope Adrian V. When we turn to Langland, we find that, like Guillaume de Lorris, he has described Avarice as an old man who, like Elde in *The Parlement of the Three Ages*, is *babirlippede* and blind. Like Elde, he is presumably toothless, for his beard (Elde is bearded too) is all beslobbered. His clothes, as befits a miser, are old and dirty. His life has been one of petty pilfering and sharp practice among the tradesmen of London. There he has learnt to cheat at the fair, to draw out the selvedge of cloth with the drapers, and stretch it out; and with his wife, Rose the retailer he employed false measures, and adulterated the ale. The picture has not quite the consistency of a portrait. We might compare Sir Harvey with Chaucer's Doctor:

> And yet he was but esy of dispence;
> He kepte that he wan in pestilence.
> For gold in phisik is a cordial,
> Therefore he lovede gold in special.[1]

Although both authors draw upon contemporary detail, the use of this is different in each. Chaucer is drawing a portrait of a doctor and the details of the image are drawn from his experience of this class of men. It is, as it were, a composite, a type

---

[1] Chaucer, *The Canterbury Tales*, A. ll.441–4.

of a class of men whom Chaucer has met in life or literature. The image and the theme are contiguous. In Langland, on the other hand, the portrait is not of a type, but of an abstraction, Avarice. Consequently, the Doctor, although only a type, has the potential of real life; that is to say, he is not a tied image but a free one. His conduct is unpredictable in theory and therefore what he actually does is interesting. With Langland, on the other hand, although his portrait is vividly realised in terms of real life, the figure is tied and the less congruent the image is with the theme the more unreal it becomes. Langland, in fact, poses in an acute form the problem of the allegorist. In so far as he must present us with an incarnation of an abstraction, with an image or metaphor, he must use words which evoke a picture. But to produce this immediacy of impression he can either use images which are in themselves vivid, as with the emblem, but where the relationship with the theme is intellectual and oblique which means that the emotional impact, the *puissance d'évocation* is at a minimum, or he can draw, as Langland often does, upon images which are both intellectually appropriate and emotionally evocative in relationship to the theme. Such an image is the portrait of the dirty, miserly old man in his portrait of avarice. But this in itself leads to difficulties. As our expectation of an actual situation is evoked, we are correspondingly disappointed by the limitations imposed by the nature of the allegorical image. Avarice, as portrayed by Langland, can do many things in life but he must always do them avariciously, even though he can be avaricious in an indefinite number of contexts, or be represented by a number of different types, just as Chaucer attributes avarice to his Doctor, his Pardoner and his Friar. I would therefore sum up my observations on the allegorical portrait as follows: there are as many ways of drawing allegorical portraits as there are allegorical methods. On the one hand, the allegorical figure may be like the pictures of Holcot or the hag Avarice, in *Le Pèlerinage de la Vie Humaine*, a collection of emblems. This lady, for example, has six hands because Deguileville wishes to have her holding certain emblematic objects, or to exhibit emblematic qualities. Thus, she has the palms of a griffin, in the third hand she holds a file to file bridles, in the fourth she holds a pair of scales to weigh the zodiac and the sun and to cast them away, and a large dish. In the fifth hand she holds a crook and her sixth hand she laid on her haunch wherefore she limped like a cripple. The moralisation of this is later explained. Her hands, like the paws of a griffin are made to take and not to give. Her first hand is Ravine, and her second 'Cutpurse'. Her third hand is Usury, for with it she 'wasteth bothe gret and smal'. Her balance indicates that she wants the light of the world for herself. With her dish Truanty she begs. The crook in her sixth hand symbolises Simon Magus, for, like the initial S of his name, it is crooked. Thus is simony an inevitable result of avarice. Moreover, simoniac priests cripple the grace of God. The haunch on which she lays her hand is Lying and with her sixth hand she cheats simple folk. Like Langland's Avarice, when she is a draper, she hangs out 'courteyns in the lyght, for to blynde folkes syght'.[1] Each of these relationships depends upon a *distinctio* rather than a natural fitness of image for theme. In spite of the topical illustrations of the theme, there is not even the concern for the consistency of the surface image which we see in Prudentius when he describes his figure of Greed:

> fertur Auaritia gremio praecincta capaci,
> quidquid Luxus edax pretiosum liquerat unca
> corripuisse manu, pulchra in ludibria uasto
> ore inhians aurique legens fragmenta caduci
> inter harenarum cumulos. Nec sufficit amplos
> inpleuisse sinus; iuuat infercire cruminis
> turpe lucrum et grauidos furtis distendere fiscos,
> quos laeua celante tegit laterisque sinistri
> uelat opermento. Velox nam dextra rapinas
> abradit spoliisque ungues exercet aënos.[2]

[*Tis said that greed, her robe arranged to make a capacious fold in front, crooked her hand and seized on everything of price that gluttonous Indulgence left behind, gaping with mouth wide open at the pretty baubles as she*

---

[1] Lydgate, *The Pilgrimage of the Life of Man*, edited by F. J. Furnivall, E.E.T.S. (ES) 83 (1901), ll.17148–18194.

[2] Prudentius, *Psychomachia*, ll.454–63; Thomson, I, 311.

> *picked up the broken bits of gold that had fallen amid the heaps of sand.*
> *Nor is she content to fill her roomy pockets but delights to stuff her base gain*
> *in money bags and cram swollen purses to bursting with her pelf, keeping*
> *them in hiding behind her left hand under cover of her robe on the left side,*
> *for her quick right hand is busy scraping up the plunder and plies nails*
> *hard as brass in gathering the booty.*]

Whereas Prudentius paints a picture of a human figure in action (note that, just as the nails of Spenser's Mammon *'like* clawes appeared', so Prudentius uses *aënus*, for which both literal and metaphorical uses are recorded). Deguileville constructs a static, picturesque grotesque. The activities of Prudentius's Avarice can be interpreted; those of Deguileville have to be explained. On the other hand, as we have suggested, allegorical portraits can be constructed on a different pattern. Instead of a loose parataxis of emblems which are convincingly coherent only in relation to their theme, we find Langland in his portrait of Avarice attempting a picture of some surface coherence. Since this results in a figure with an actual context in experience, its actions, although limited by the theme, can be dramatic like those of figures in a morality play. On the other hand, they differ from the *figura*, such as the figure of Adrian V in Dante because, since their picture is conditioned by the theme, by the metaphorical relationship to the picture, they lack the complexity and the apparent unpredictability of life. The difference, of course, is not absolute in the sense that, even in allegory, picture and theme need not be absolutely congruent as we have already said. But where the picture is not self-consistent, then the areas of incongruence do not create a life-like impression as they may do where the picture is self-consistent. For example, Langland equates men with apples and describes how he asks for an apple from the tree;

> thanne comsed it to crye,
> And wagged Wydwehode. and it wepte after.
> And whan it meued Matrimoigne. it made a foule noyse,
> That I had reuth whan Piers rogged. it gradde so reufulliche.[1]

---

[1] Langland, *Piers Plowman*, B. xvi, ll.75–8; cp. C. xix, ll.108–10; for unity of authorship see G. Kane, *Piers Plowman: The Evidence for Authorship* (London, 1965).

These apples are the kin of Adam. As the C text says 'Adam was as tre. and we aren as hus apples.'[1] But mankind lives in one of three states, Virginity, Widowhood or Matrimony bringing forth fruit, a hundred-fold, sixty-fold and thirty-fold. As men fall from the tree and die, they are gathered up by the devil. Now, if the apples on the tree represent mankind, and mankind is made up of three classes of people, then these classes of people must grow on the tree; and so they do, but at the expense of a grotesque image though one which is perhaps justified within the dream framework of Langland's poem.

Let us now turn to an example of an allegorical narrative from Langland. The passage is from the B text, Langland's account of the Crucifixion:

> One semblable to the Samaritan. and some-del to Piers the Plowman,
> Barfote on an asse bakke. botelees cam prykye,
> Wyth-oute spores other spere. spakliche he loked,
> As is the kynde of a knyʒte. that cometh to be dubbed,
> To geten hem gylte spores. or galoches ycouped.
> Thanne was Faith in a fenestre. and cryde, '*a! fili Dauid!*'
> As doth an heraude of armes. whan auntrous cometh to iustes.
> Olde Iuwes of Ierusalem. for Ioye thei songen,
>   *Benedictus qui venit in nomine domini.*
> Thanne I frayned at Faith. what al that fare be-mente,
> And who sholde Iouste in Iherusalem. 'Iesus,' he seyde,
> 'And fecche that the fende claymeth. Piers fruit the Plowman.'
> 'Is Piers in this place,' quod I. and he preynte on me
> 'This Iesus of his gentrice. wole Iuste in Piers armes,
> In his helme and in his haberioun. *humana natura;*
> That Cryst be nouʒt biknowe here. for *consummatus deus,*
> In Piers paltok the Plowman. this priker shal ryde;
> For no dynte shal hym dere. as *in deitate patris.*'
> 'Who shal Iuste with Iesus?' quod I. 'Iuwes or scribes?'
> 'Nay,' quod he, 'the foule fende. and Falsdome and Deth.
> Deth seith he shal fordo. and adown brynge
> Al that lyueth or loketh. in londe or in watere.

---

[1] Langland, *Piers Plowman* C. xix, ll.68.

Lyf seyth that he likth. and leyth his lif to wedde,
That for al that Deth can do. with-in thre dayes,
To walke and fecche fro the fende. Piers fruite the Plowman,
And legge it there hym lyketh. and Lucifer bynde,
And forbete and adown brynge. bale and deth for euere:
O mors, ero mors tua!'[1]

What are we to make of this jumble? The following elements
may be distinguished. Firstly, Christ at his Triumphal Entry
into Jerusalem is compared to the Good Samaritan and to Piers
the Plowman and to a knight going to be dubbed. But when the
Dreamer asks Faith who is to joust in Jerusalem we hear that
he is to joust for the fruit of Piers the Plowman whom he resembles. Then we are told that Jesus is to joust in Piers's
armour, *humana natura* and in the jacket of Piers the Plowman.
We are then told that he is to joust against the devil, falsehood
and death. Thus we have a mixture of a personification and of
the analogies with Piers Plowman and the Good Samaritan
and a knight going to joust, so that, at first sight, the passage
appears as jumbled as the macaronic language itself. But as
the Latin quotations are, by virtue of their Latinity, designed
to indicate the doctrinal substructure, so the allegorical machinery is designed to evoke certain ideas. At the mimetic level
the whole passage has a dream-like quality as suggestive as the
fantasies of Bosch. But, like the fantasies of Bosch, the components have both a level of intellectual symbolism and a
puissance d'évocation and it is the combination of these two which,
in my opinion, constitutes the peculiar genius of Langland as
a writer of allegory. This passage well illustrates the point. The
intellectual level is plain. The Good Samaritan is a type of
Christ in his redeeming love, a typological metaphor. The image
of the Christ-knight is again commonplace and we have already met it in the *Ancrene Wisse*.[2] It is a pure metaphor. The
figure of Piers is, in my view, a *figura*. To this I shall return in a

[1] Langland, *Piers Plowman*, B. xviii, ll.10–35b; cp. C. xxi, ll.8–35.
[2] W. Gaffney, 'The Allegory of the Christ-Knight in *Piers Plowman*',
PMLA, xlvi (1931), 155–68. R. Woolf, 'The Theme of Christ the Lover-
Knight in Medieval English Literature', *RES*, xiii (1962), 1–16.

later chapter. For the moment let it suffice to say that we know from contemporary illustrations, such as those to the *Somme le Roi*, and from the sermons of the period, that the ploughman was a type of Zeal, or, negatively, of Sloth.[1] Just as St. Francis could be extracted from his historical setting by Dante and stand as a type of poverty, so, from the class of labourers, Piers the Plowman is taken as a type of his class. When he pursues his avocation of ploughing, he is a type of Zeal; when he falls asleep beside his plough, he is a type of Sloth as he is pictured in the illustrations to the *Somme*. Of course, other metaphors are caught up in the figure of Piers. He is not just a ploughman, but Piers the Plowman, Peter, the apostle who sowed the seed of the Gospel; in the Life of Dobet, in the triumph of Piers Plowman, he is in a sense Christ's humanity since the Plowman is perfected humanity. All this is well known, but does not explain why Langland chose just these images to describe the Triumphal Entry into Jerusalem. Now, it is just this juxtaposition which gives the poetic effectiveness to Langland's allegory. The first point to notice is the figure of Faith. Why does Langland choose a personification here rather than a *figura* as he later uses the *figura* of Abraham for the same idea? I think the answer is that Langland wants to speak of the interpretation which faith demands of the historical events which the Dreamer witnesses. The Dreamer sees these events in his dream and since *this*, rather than faith, is the theme, he chooses to represent Faith by an image which has comparatively little metaphorical depth. On the other hand, to the subject of Faith's discourse, the Triumphal Entry, he gives all the range and subtlety of association, all the depth of feeling, which derives from the *figura* of Piers, from the Good Samaritan and from the Christ-knight. Nevertheless, it might be objected that it would have been better to present us with a sustained picture depending upon one of the three figures. I think not. The Good Samaritan could clearly have provided an allegorical narrative but not one which would not have been entirely congruent with

---

[1] See pages 90–2 for details and further discussion.

the Triumphal Entry. Piers could have had a narrative in-
vented for him, but this would not have had the richness of
association of a story already known. On the other hand, the
Christ-knight provided just the kind of allegorical narrative
needed, with the advantage that as a person and not a personification, his actuality conveys a sense of actuality and of
excitement to the scene, as well as giving both actuality and
definition to Faith watching from the window rather as Criseyde
watches Troilus ride back from battle. But why, then, is Christ
both like Piers and also about to fight for his progeny? The poet
could, of course, have said merely that Christ was about to fight
in *humana natura*, but by using the figure of Piers the poet has
introduced something of the complexity of imagery at this point
in the poem. Man is the fruit of Piers, in so far as Piers represents
human nature perfectible by grace. The figure of Piers thus
highlights an aspect of human nature which is particularly
relevant to the theme of redemption. But as Christ fights for
the redemption of man, man himself engages too in spiritual
warfare in his human nature. And then in the B text the image
shifts again. Piers is no longer in his 'helme' and his 'haberioun'
but in the 'paltok' of a labourer, the symbol of his humanity.
Thus, by means of a central figure, Piers, Langland has emphasised certain aspects of his central concept, human nature.
Piers here represents Christ's human nature but also man's
nature as perfectible by grace. Piers in his armour represents
man in his spiritual battle, and Piers the Plowman in his paltok
represents man, the son of Adam, who earns his bread by the
sweat of his brow. Thus by the use of the figure of Piers the
Plowman, rather than of a personification, the poet has introduced a prismatic image which refracts the situation into all its
implications. And the key-note of the whole passage is set by the
first line: 'One semblable to the Samaritan and somedel to
Piers the Plowman.' The Good Samaritan is a *figura* of Christ
in his aspect of redeemer. A *figura* takes colour from its context
and the use of such a figure not only indicates the particular
aspect of Christ with which the poet is here concerned, but
brings with it emotional overtones deriving from its own con-

text. Moreover, the action of theme and image are adequately congruent: 'A certain man went down from Jerusalem to Jericho' the parable of the Good Samaritan begins and so the figure naturally merges with that of Christ entering Jerusalem on Palm Sunday. Thus it seems to me that we have in this passage an excellent example of the way in which a good poet can use the various resources of medieval allegorical writing to give depth and subtlety, variety of texture and a perspective to his allegorical writing, features which have been noted by more than one critic.[1] Let us now turn to our final example, *The Parlement of Foules*.

It will be remembered that the poem falls into three main sections: the vision of Scipio Africanus, the Garden of Venus and the Parlement of Birds. It is with the first two that I am mainly concerned. The first part is essentially based upon Cicero's *Dream of Scipio* in which Scipio the Younger dreams of his grandfather, Scipio Africanus the Elder. But, in fact, the version of the story in Petrarch's *Africa* seems to me more relevant to Chaucer's poem. For Petrarch has made a significant change in Cicero's tale. He shifts the situation found in Cicero's text 'so that it is Scipio Africanus the Elder who dreams of his father rather than Scipio the Younger who dreams of the Elder'. This no doubt is, as A. S. Bernardo has suggested, consistent with Petrarch's attempt to keep the Elder Scipio as the central figure of his poem.[2] The *Africa* has broadly two main themes. On the one hand, it portrays Scipio the Elder as the patriot, the great soldier and saviour of his country. But, more significantly for Chaucer's poem, in Book V we find the Elder Scipio playing

[1] Cp. for example, E. Vasta, *The Spiritual Basis of 'Piers Plowman'* (The Hague, 1965), p.27; R. Woolf, 'The Tearing of the Pardon', in *Piers Plowman: Critical Approaches*, p.73; R. Tuve (1966), *passim*. Further references to discussion of the meaning and function of Piers in the poem will be found on pp.98–113. E. Salter, *Piers Plowman* (Oxford, 1962), p.76, speaks of 'fluctuations of allegorical depth' as a feature of the whole poem. But particularly see Frank, (1953), pp.237–50 and *passim* in *'Piers Plowman' and the Scheme of Salvation* (Yale Studies in English, 136, New Haven, 1957). Why I do not entirely agree with Frank's analysis will emerge in the next chapter.

[2] See A. S. Bernardo, *Petrarch, Scipio and the 'Africa'* (Baltimore, 1962), p.22 and fn. 2.

a new role, the mediator between passion and virtue. The core of the book deals with Massinissa's overwhelming passion for Sophonisba, the queen of Lybia. To quote Bernardo

> 'As the drama unfurls, however, it is the figure of Scipio that looms larger and larger in Massinissa's mind and slowly saves him from the clutches of a lust that could have not only ruined him but the entire campaign and consequently Rome and Italy as well. . . . It is clear therefore that notwithstanding the lyrical and literary effectiveness of the Massinissa-Sophonisba episode, recalling, as it does, not only Petrarch's personal drama with Laura but highly Virgilian tones, its true value in the artistic strategy of the epic lies in the new dimension it gives Scipio: not only is he a leader of men and nations, but a savior of souls.'[1]

Here I think we have the significance of Scipio in Chaucer. Like Petrarch's Scipio he is a *figura*. Bernardo points out that in 'the last five books that were apparently intended to anchor the epic in historical reality, we see Petrarch focusing attention on a drama which exemplifies, in microcosmic form, the ultimate accomplishment of Roman civilisation; the rule of reason and law, and the defeat of cupidity'.[2] Thus in the first section of *The Parlement of Foules*, we have the *figura* of Scipio the Elder brought before us as offering one attitude towards love; that of the ascetic who rejects passion in favour of virtue and regards love as concupiscence which the virtuous man will reject for the common good, as Massinissa did at the behest of Scipio.[3]

When we turn to the temple of Venus we find an allegory of quite another kind. The passage follows quite closely the Seventh Book of the *Teseida*. Moreover, Boccaccio's *chiose* for his text are a useful commentary on the text of Chaucer. Details apparently naturalistic in the *Teseida* are given an allegorical interpretation by Boccaccio.[4] For example, his temple is set

---

[1] Bernardo, p.25, 30.

[2] Bernardo, p.151.

[3] My attention was first directed to this aspect of Scipio by a reading of the *Trionfi*. But this view was reinforced by the exposition of a similar view by Bernardo, who discusses Chaucer's use of Scipio on pages 183–5.

[4] Giovanni Boccaccio, *Teseida: Delle Nozze d'Emilia*, edited by A. Roncaglia (Bari, 1941), pp.417–30.

fra altissimi pini, chosen because their fruits are aphrodisiac; the animals which appear there, rabbits, sparrows and doves are types of libidinous animals.[1] The beautiful flowers and the myrtle are there because their scent incites to love.[2] The songs and instruments are there because they drive away melancholy, the enemy of love. The place is shady and full of fountains because these give the ease and shade which the pursuit of love requires. These details are, as Boccaccio himself explains, those things which in general can naturally incite to love. They are merely figures of love, which differ from the emblem in that, whereas the association between an emblem and its theme is at the thematic level, that of a figure and its theme functions at both levels. Thus if a child is an emblem of drunkenness this is only because both are incapable of speaking. There is no general resemblance between a boy and a drunkard. On the other hand, when a pine tree stands for love because the fruits if eaten are aphrodisiac, then there is a causal connection at the literal level of the picture as well as at the thematic level. There is also a level of personification in Boccaccio's interpretation. Thus Charm is found at the entrance of Venus's dwelling because this all lovers desire to possess. And similar incentives to love are Beauty, Youth, Nobility, Affability and the like. Mythological figures are also used. There is Cupid whose arrows represent either the suddenness of his attack or the anguish of desire. Cupid is said to manufacture these arrows with the help of Pleasure, Idleness, Memory. Pleasure is the daughter of Cupid and Psyche, for by Psyche is represented Hope and the hope of lovers is the mother of pleasure:

> e questa cotale dilettazione è quella che tempera le saette d'Amore, cioè che le fa forti a potere bene passionare il cuore; e temperale nella fonte della nostra falsa estimazione, quando per questa dillettazione, nata d'amore e di speranza, giudichiamo che la cosa piacuta sia da preporre ad ogni altra cosa o temporale o divina. Ma perchiò che queste cose dette non si possono senza ricorda-

---

[1] Cp. Guy de Tervarent, *Attributs et symboles dans l'art profane 1450-1600* (Geneva, 1958–64), sub. *lièvre, colombe, passereau*.

[2] Cp. de Tervarent, sub. *myrte*.

mento della cagione d'esse e senza spazio di tempo fermare, perciò agiugne Memoria e Ozio a ferrare queste saette, fabricate dal fervore d'amore e temperate dalla dilettazione intrinseca, nata dalla speranza.[1]

[*and this same delight is that which tempers the arrows of Love, that is which makes them strong to inflame the heart well with passion; and they are tempered in the fountain of false estimation, when through this delight, born of love and of hope, we judge that the object of pleasure is to be preferred to every thing temporal or divine. But because these aforesaid things cannot be established without recollection of the reason of their being and without space of time, therefore, Memory and Idleness join in tipping these arrows with iron, arrows made from the fervour of love and tempered by the inward delight born of hope.*]

How far Chaucer would have subscribed to these interpretations it is difficult to say. Certainly he substitutes for the plants of Boccaccio a conventional list of trees, and his rabbits, like the fishes with their red fins and silver scales, seem more in place in the borders of a manuscript than in Boccaccio's ponderous allegory. But there is one detail which is perhaps more significant.

The copper of which the temple is made is elaborately allegorised in Boccaccio. The temple is of copper because copper and brass are found on the planet Venus; because they, like love, strengthen, unite and alloy every metal; then again brass, being polished, shines like gold; also it has, when struck, a most pleasing sound. So these three things represent the effects of Venus because under her influence all things are linked and procreate. Then again, just as it can be burnished to look like gold, love appears like gold but in the end is full of bitterness. Then again by its pleasant sound it represents the sweetness of love talk.[2] Certainly, Chaucer's temple of brass must imply at least part of this explanation, and here Chaucer is using a purely emblematic technique. He employs too the technique of pictures. Dame Peace sitting at the door 'with a curtyn in hire hond' reminds us that the desires obtained by force are not

---

[1] Boccaccio, *Teseida*, p.420.
[2] Boccaccio, *Teseida*, pp.421–2.

consonant with true love, as has been observed by courtly men from Andreas Capellanus to Gawain. Presumably Dame Peace holds the curtain to show the way into the temple; that is, to the consummation of love. Dame Patience, too, is a picturesque figure whose hill of sand perhaps represents the frustration of desire.[1] What we have then in the first two parts of the *Parlement of Foules* is, I think, a contrast between the *figura* of Scipio, the ascetic view of love and the Temple and Garden of Venus representing the cult of love.[2] The choice of a *figura* for the first part was partly no doubt to provide a guide for the Dreamer. But this guide could have been a personified abstraction and I suspect that the technical contrast between the human figure of Scipio, and the emblematic and abstract nature of much of the allegorical machinery, in the second part of the poem, was intended to give a difference of tone, a sombre figure representing a sombre theme, whereas the machinery of the second part gives an artificial tone, a certain brassiness, if I may so put it, suitable also for its theme.[3] So I would suggest that Chaucer is simply saying in the poem that by marriage we can reconcile love with duty to the state, a theme very fitting for a poem written to celebrate a state marriage, if the poem was indeed so intended. A similar contrast is noted by Boccaccio in a traditional gloss on Venus:

> La quale Venere è doppia, perciò che l'una si può e dee intendere per ciascuno onesto et licito disiderio, si come è disiderare d'avere moglie per avere figliuoli . . . La seconda Venere è quella per la quale ogni lascivia è disiderata, e che volgarmente è chiamata dea d'amore; e di questa disegna qui l'autore il tempio e l'altre cose circustanti ad esso, come nel testo appare.[4]

> [*Which Venus is twofold, because the one can and must refer to every honest and licit desire such as the desire to have a wife for the procreation of*

---

[1] Cp. H. R. Patch, 'Chaucer's Desert', *MLN*, xxxiv (1919), 321–8.

[2] For the poem as a *contentio*, cp. D. Everett, 'Chaucer's Love Visions, with particular reference to the *Parlement of Foules*', in *Essays on Middle English Literature* (Oxford, 1955), pp.97–114.

[3] One might compare C. S. Lewis's remarks on the Bower of Bliss; Lewis, p.325.

[4] Boccaccio, *Teseida*, p.417.

children . . . the second Venus is the goddess through whom all con-
cupiscence is desired and who is commonly called the goddess of love; it is the
temple of this Venus which the author here describes and other things con-
nected with it, as appears in the text.]

The effectiveness of this *contentio* in Chaucer lies very largely in
the variety of allegorical techniques which are employed, and
the degrees of semantic depth and subtlety which such variety
implies.

In conclusion, I should like to say something further about
the surface consistency of allegory since this is the point which
most alienates the modern reader of allegory. We have seen
how certain kinds of allegory, such as the emblematic way of
writing, tend away from surface consistency; while others, such
as the *figura* and the morality, tend towards it. I should make it
clear that surface consistency is not necessarily a virtue in
allegory; for allegory can please by virtue of its very obscurity.
Mutatis mutandis one might apply the words of Mallarmé: 'To
name an object is to do away with the three-quarters of the enjoyment of the poem which is derived from the satisfaction of
guessing little by little: to suggest it, to evoke it – that is what
charms the imagination.'[1] Reverse the roles of theme and image
and we have a picture of the emblem; the object is named indeed but the imagination is teased by its relationship to the
theme, just as it is in the emblems of the baroque period. One
might indeed apply to medieval allegory Maritain's observation that 'If it pleases a futurist to paint a lady with only one
eye, or a quarter of an eye, nobody denies him such a right:
all one is entitled to require – and here is the whole problem
– is that the quarter eye is all the lady needs *in the given case.*'[2]
But the allegorical writer is not concerned, on the other hand,
solely to present the reader with an intellectual challenge. He
will also seek to recommend his theme by an appeal to the
emotions through the language and the images he chooses. And
long before the Renaissance, with its concern for 'tactile values',
the Middle Ages was not untouched by the 'despotism of the

[1] Quoted by Edmund Wilson, *Axel's Castle* (New York, 1931), p.20.
[2] J. Maritain, *Art and Scholasticism* (London, 1930), pp.27–8.

eye', a despotism encouraged by 'the long rhetorical tradition
that a speaker is most emotionally effective when he visualises
and evokes the scene he describes'.[1] A memorable and moving
picture will have its effect in allegory as in any other kind of
writing. But it is perhaps true to say that this is not the only
way in which allegory can affect us. The metaphor of 'organic
unity' is particularly misleading in relation to allegorical writing. More appropriate would be the metaphor of a 'field' since
the unity is not necessarily that of a living being, as it presents
itself to the eye of an observer, but one that depends for its
effectiveness upon a network of relationships between words and
their associational fields. To the modern reader, presented with
a temple of brass as a symbol of love, the allegorical method
seems arid. How much better, we think, would it have been to
present us with a portrait of a person in love, a person in some
familiar and coherent context. With such a person we can
sympathise and by such a response our sympathies are enlarged
and our understanding enriched. But the temple of brass is not
entirely a pictorial gimmick. We are presented with a temple
because a temple is a place of worship, and love is an act of
worship. The image thus does in fact predicate something of
love. When Mâle writes 'Art was at once a script, a calculus
and a symbolic code'.[2] he is making a profound comment on
the nature of allegory. The images of allegorical writing are
signs comparable with words but different from words in that
they have, as Augustine observed, a double sense; they are both
res and *signa*. As we have tried to show in relation to Langland's
descriptions of the dreamer's vision of the Triumphal Entry,
the unity of impression in allegory, as well as its emotional impact, may well depend upon such a network of associations in a
linguistic field rather in the manner of a symbolist poem.

   This topic can well be concluded by discussion of a device
which did much to increase the effectiveness of medieval
allegory, a device which gave allegory an impetus in the
direction of naturalism. I mean the dream vision. Glunz has

[1] M. H. Abrams, *The Mirror and the Lamp* (New York, 1953), p.160.
[2] E. Mâle, *The Gothic Image* (London, 1961), p.22.

emphasised the essential egotism of Dante and the significance of the egotism, as he sees it, as a move away from the medieval mode of thought.[1] But, in fact, it is to Guillaume de Lorris that the credit must go for seeing the potentialities of this device. For, in *The Romance of the Rose*, the dreamer and the dream both serve to give a naturalistic colour to the allegory; this and the prevalent use of the morality, serve as dramatic devices from which the allegory derives much of its liveliness. Moreover, this device makes it possible to introduce a human response to the events of the allegory which increases its emotional impact. This is superbly exploited by Dante. Was ever, for example, allegorical shade given a farewell as moving as Virgil:

> Ma Virgilio n'avea lasciati scemi
>   di sé, Virgilio dolcissimo patre,
>   Virgilio a cui per mia salute die'mi;
> né quantunque perdeo l'antica matre,
>   valse a le guance nette di rugiada,
>   che, lacrimando, non tornasser atre.[2]

> [*But Virgil had left us bereft of himself, Virgil most beloved father, Virgil to whom, for my salvation, I gave myself; nor did all that our ancient mother lost prevent my cheeks wet with dew from turning dark with weeping.*]

Did ever the deadly sins, so beloved of medieval writers, inhabit a world as solid as those of Dante? Not only 'the structure of emotions, for which the allegory is the necessary scaffold',[3] but also the physical details of the allegory are concretised for us by Dante's response to them. Of English allegorists it is Langland who is most like Dante in this technique as in other matters.[4] The textual problem necessarily makes anything like a final statement impossible and there are passages in which the

---

[1] H. H. Glunz, *Die Literarästhetik des europäischen Mittelalters* (Bochum-Langendreer, 1937), pp.450–7.

[2] Dante, *Purgatorio*, xxx, ll.49–54.

[3] T. S. Eliot, *The Sacred Wood* (7th ed., London, 1950), p.169.

[4] For the unifying function of the Dreamer cp. Vasta, p.26; R. Woolf, 'Some Non-Medieval Qualities of *Piers Plowman*', *Essays in Criticism*, xii (1962), 111–25; for the psychology of the Dream Vision, cp. C. B. Hieatt, 'The Realism of Dream Visions', *De Proprietatibus Litterarum*, Series Practica, 2 (The Hague, 1967).

Dreamer comes to life which are peculiar to one or other of the texts. Such would be the dubious ending of A xii in which the Dreamer steps outside the poem and narrates the death of the poet. As he journeys with *omnia probate* he falls in with Hunger and Fever and

> Deþ delt him a dent and drof him to þe erþe.[1]

Thus the end is incongruent with the beginning:

> In a somer sesoun whanne softe was the sonne
> I shop me into a shroud as I a shep were:[2]

but at the end the conclusion is again in the third person

> Wille þurgh inwit (wiste) wel þe soþe,
> Þat þis speche was spedelich, and sped him wel faste,
> And wrouȝthe þat here is wryten and oþer werkes boþe
> Of peres þe plowman and mechel puple also.[3]

The C text likewise provides us with a long passage about the Dreamer which is lacking in the other texts:

> Thus ich a-waked, god wot. whanne ich wonede on Corne-
> hulle,
> Kytte and ich in a cote. clothed as a lollere,
> And lytel y-lete by. leyue me for sothe,
> Among lollares of London, and lewede hermytes;
> For ich made of tho men. as reson me tauhte;
> For as ich cam by Conscience with Reson ich mette
> In an hote heruest. whanne ich hadde myn hele,
> And lymes to labore with. and louede wel fare,
> And no dede to do. bote drynke and to slepe.[4]

The Dreamer then has a conversation with Reason in which we learn much of his life. Reason asks him what useful work he can do and he replies:

> 'Whanne ich ȝong was,' quath ich. 'meny ȝer hennes,
> My fader and my frendes. founden me to scole,

---

[1] Langland, *Piers Plowman*, A. xii, l.104.
[2] Langland, *Piers Plowman*, A. Prologue, ll.1–2.
[3] Langland, *Piers Plowman*, A. xii, ll.99–102.
[4] Langland, *Piers Plowman*, C. vi, ll.1–9.

> Tyl ich wiste wyterliche. what holy wryt menede,
> And what is best for the body. as the bok telleth,
> And sykerest for the soule. by so ich wolle continue.'[1]

But there are sufficient passages of this kind common to more than one text to give some assurance that we may reasonably regard this as part of the technique of the poems. The Dreamer often ponders, after he has woken up, on the meaning of the vision which he has just seen. Thus, after the tearing of the pardon, he awakens out of his dream 'meteles and moneyles on maluerne hilles'[2] and he wanders about pondering on the significance of his dream. And he concludes:

> Dowel at þe day of dome is digneliche vndirfongen
> He passiþ al þe pardoun of seint petris chirche.[3]

And, as he roams about 'robed in russett' he falls in with two friars minor with whom he debates the biblical text *septies in die cadit iustus*. And it is only after this encounter that he walks into a wood and lying down in a clearing, lulled by the bird song, he falls asleep and dreams of Thought, Wit, Study, Clergy and Scripture. In the same way, after the vision of Imaginatyf we see the dreamer roaming about, dressed like a mendicant, and pondering on the dream from which he has just awakened. He thinks how Fortune has failed him and Age come upon him. He ponders too on the corruption of the clergy and how Imaginatyf showed him a vision of nature but warned him that *vix justus saluabitur*, or, in the words of the C text

> That *iustus* by-fore Iesu. *in die iudicii*
> *Non saluabitur*. bote *uix* helpe;[4]

The author of the B text makes effective use of the 'waking-up' technique. After Patience's sermon, Haukyn 'wepte and weyled'[5] and, in so doing, woke up the dreamer. And he is

---

[1] Langland, *Piers Plowman*, C. vi, ll.35–9.
[2] Langland, *Piers Plowman*, A. viii, l.129.
[3] Langland, *Piers Plowman*, A. viii, ll.155–6.
[4] Langland, *Piers Plowman*, C. xvi, ll.22–3.
[5] Langland, *Piers Plowman*, B. xiv, l.332.

indignant at the sufferings of the poor and many thought him mad, he tells us, for he was loth to reverence lords and ladies:

> Lordes or ladyes. or any lyf elles,
> As persones in pellure. with pendauntes of syluer;
> To seriauntz ne to suche. seyde nouȝte ones,
> 'God loke ȝow, lordes!'. ne louted faire;[1]

And after the triumph of Piers the Plowman he is awakened by the ringing of bells on Easter Day and we see him with 'Kitte my wyf and Kalote my douȝter' going to church.[2] Finally, not the least interesting of these 'extra-somnary' meetings with allegorical figures, is the meeting with Need which precedes the Vision of Antichrist.[3] The Dreamer is hungry and he knows not where to eat. Need tells him that need

> at grete nede. may nymen as for his owne,
> Wyth-oute conseille of Conscience. or cardynale vertues
> So that he suwe and saue. *spiritus temperancie*.[4]

The encounter, in fact, seems to be a comment on the vision that the Dreamer has just seen, in terms of the actual situation of the Dreamer. In this way, the person of the Dreamer is used to give actuality to the dream and, in a sense, himself becomes part of the reader's own experience. This actuality is reinforced by small touches of detail. The Dreamer goes to sleep in Lent after walking about 'as a reccheles renke', 'wolleward (C. wo-werie) and wete-shoed'.[5] Sometimes, when he wakes, we have a vivid phrase indicating his response to the preceding dream; so, after the stern words of Scripture, the Dreamer weeps and when he wakes he grieves that he has not dreamt more and he says to himself: 'Now wote I what Dowel is,' quod I. 'by dere god, as me thinketh!'[6] When he wakes from the vision of the

[1] Langland, *Piers Plowman*, B. xv, ll.6–9.
[2] Langland, *Piers Plowman*, B. xviii, ll.425–xix, 5; C. xxi, ll.472–xxii, 5.
[3] Langland, *Piers Plowman*, B. xx, ll.1–49; C. xxiii, ll.1–50; see also R. M. Frank, 'The Conclusion of *Piers Plowman*', *JEGP*, xlix (1950), 310–11 for discussion of this episode.
[4] Langland, *Piers Plowman*, B. xx, ll.20–2; C. xxiii, ll.20–2.
[5] Langland, *Piers Plowman*, B. xviii, ll.1–2; C. xxi, ll.1–2.
[6] Langland, *Piers Plowman*, B. xi, l.399; C. xiv, ll.218–19.

D

Soul and the Tree of Charity, he looks 'estwarde and west-warde' for Piers the Plowman, or, in the C text, for *Liberum Arbitrium*.[1] And sometimes the Dreamer breaks out of the dream itself as when he swoons for pure joy at the revelation of Piers in the vision of the Tree of Charity. This gives us a vivid sense of one of those mysterious and significant experiences of the dream world where the emotion seems inexplicable in terms of the imagery of the dream.

But perhaps even more remarkable than these autobio-graphical passages are those details which Langland often gives of his allegorical figures, details which are an extension of the image horizontally without apparent regard to the vertical dimension, such as his use of proper names,[2] what Kaske has called 'the *Piers* poet's capacity for representing the intangible in familiar and colorful forms'.[3] Thus, for example, we see Spes 'rapelich renne forth'[4] and Abraham 'as hore as an hawethorne'[5] and even where the details have an evident allegorical significance the particular choice of allegorical image coincides with the visual image. Such a picture is the Bible:[6]

> Thanne was there a wiȝte. with two brode eyen,
> Boke hiȝte that beupere. a bolde man of speche,[7]

where presumably the 'two brode eyen' represent the Old and New Testament. More subtly, we often get the sense of the Dreamer watching the dream by virtue of this descriptive over-plus.[8] So when Piers prepares himself for his role as pilgrim

[1] Langland, *Piers Plowman*, B. xvi, ll.168–9; C. xix, ll.181–2.

[2] Many writers have commented on Langland's eye for vivid detail. For example, see J. Lawlor, *Piers Plowman* (London, 1962), 209 ff., 262 ff.

[3] R. E. Kaske, 'The Use of Simple Figures of Speech in *Piers Plowman* B: A Study in the Figurative Expression of Ideas and Opinions', *SP*, xlviii (1951), 596.

[4] Langland, *Piers Plowman*, B. xvi, l.273.

[5] Langland, *Piers Plowman*, B. xvi, l.173.

[6] For 'Boke' see R. E. Kaske, 'The Speech of "Book" in *Piers Plowman*', *Anglia*, lxxvii (1959), 117–44; R. L. Hoffman, 'The Burning of "Boke" in *Piers Plowman*', *MLQ*, xxv (1964), 57–65.

[7] Langland, *Piers Plowman*, B. xviii, ll.228–9; C. xxi, ll.240–1.

[8] Cp. R. E. Kaske, 'Langland's Walnut Simile', *JEGP*, lviii (1959), 650–4.

He caste on his cloþis, ycloutid and hole,
Hise cokeris and his cuffis for cold of his nailes,
And heng his hoper at his hals in stede of a scrippe.[1]

It has been observed that there is little sense of place in Langland.[2] But if *Piers Plowman* has not the topographic exactitude
of Dante it is because, as has often been remarked, the technique is so strongly dramatic even though it is a drama without
a setting. It is people and not places that one remembers in
Langland. But he is like Dante in the ability to fuse the sensuous and immediate with the symbolic. It is true, as Elizabeth
Suddaby observed, that he has a 'constant awareness of and
power to communicate physical reality',[3] but he has more than
this. An admirable example of this further capacity occurs in
the account of the crucifixion:

'*Consummatum est,*' quod Cryst. and comsed forto swowe
Pitousliche and pale. as a prisoun that deyeth;
The lorde of lyf and of liȝte. tho leyed his eyen togideres.
The daye for drede with-drowe. and derke bicam the sonne,
The wal wagged and clef. and al the worlde quaued.[4]

On the one hand, we have the physical picture of the dying
Christ compared to the dying prisoner while, on the other, we
have the choice of detail which will indicate the underlying
theme, the paradox of the 'lorde of lyf and liȝte' closing his
eyes in death and shutting out the light, and the indication
of the sympathetic darkness of nature. Thus, the third line, at
first sight, merely a picture of the dying figure on the cross,
is also the catalyst of symbolic implications of the scene. Kaske
has well spoken of the 'metaphysical firmness which underlies
some of Langland's most picturesque imagery'.[5] And this
quality is nowhere more evident than in the interplay between

---

[1] Langland, *Piers Plowman*, A. vii, ll.54–6.
[2] See, for example, Woolf, (1962), pp.115–17.
[3] E. Suddaby, 'The Poem *Piers Plowman*', *JEGP*, liv (1955), 95.
[4] Langland, *Piers Plowman*, B. xviii, ll.57–61; C. xxi, ll.58–62.
[5] Kaske (1959), p.653. Cp. G. Kane's remark on 'the close connexion
between the poet's imaginative and symbolic perception' in *Middle English
Literature* (London, 1951), p.240.

the allegorical and the visual made possible by the response of dreamer to dream in the poem. Goethe wrote that 'Allegory transforms phenomenon into concept, the concept into an image.'[1] But in Langland we have more than an image of a concept. We have a human response to the image.

But before we leave the topic of allegory, we should perhaps step back and look at the picture as a whole. We have tried to analyse the components of medieval allegory and to suggest ways in which these can be exploited by writers of allegory. Yet it is, I think, doubtful whether it is consonant with medieval ways of thinking to divide what we should call allegory from other didactic modes of writing. The allegory and the exemplum in fact overlap in medieval practice in a way which calls in question our rigid distinctions between allegorical and non-allegorical writing.[2] A good example of this would be the illustrations of the vices and virtues in the manuscripts of the *Somme le Roi*. We might take, for example, the series from the MS. BN. f. fr. 1895.[3] The illustrations of the vices and virtues in this manuscript are in the form of pictures enclosed in squares symmetrically divided into four. The pictures are accompanied by instructions which serve also to explain them. Thus, for example, the four cardinal virtues are pictured as follows: at the top, right-hand corner sits a lady, Prudence, holding an open book, her pupils sitting at her feet. Alongside her to the left is Temperance, represented by two ladies seated at a table laden with food. On his knees before them is a poor man, drinking from a cup. Fortitude is pictured below in the form a of a lady holding a lion in a medallion and on her left is Justice holding in one hand a sword and, in the other, a

[1] See page 34, note 2.

[2] Cp. W. F. Bolton, 'Parable, Allegory and Romance in the Legend of Barlaam and Josaphat', *Traditio*, xiv (1958), 359–66; G. Hough, 'The Allegorical Circle', *Critical Quarterly*, iii (1961), 199–209.

[3] For illustrated manuscripts of the *Somme* see E. G. Millar, *An Illuminated MS. of 'La Somme le Roy' attributed to the Parisian miniaturist Honoré* (Roxburghe Club, Oxford, 1953), pp.12–20; to Millar's list should be added our manuscript and BM. MS. Royal 19 C. ii. Millar prints instructions to the miniaturist from MSS. BN. f. fr. 958 and 14939, on pp.49–51.

balance. A similar combination of the emblematic and the exemplary can be seen in the pictures of humility and pride in which Humility is represented in one square by the figure of a lady holding a lamb in a medallion,[1] in another square by a sinner kneeling before another man; and that of Pride is represented, in one square, by a man shooting arrows from a tower and, in the other square, by a picture of a hypocrite kneeling before an altar. He is not looking at the altar, the text tells us, but at another figure behind him. The other figure points at him. In the same way, Amity is represented by a lady holding a dove, Peace by a lady holding an Agnus Dei. Mercy is pictured by a lady giving a coat to a poor man and the contrast between Idleness and Labour is pictured by a man asleep beside his plough, on the one hand, and by a man sowing corn on the other. The conventional and traditional nature of these representations is beyond question. They can be paralleled, for example, by the series of vices and virtues, referred to by Katzenellenbogen[2] in the windows of Lyons and Auxerre cathedrals, both of the first half of the thirteenth century. At Lyons, Largitas, not unlike the figure of Mercy in the *Somme*, is giving away valuables, and at Auxerre she is clothing the poor exactly like her sister in the *Somme*. Likewise Avarice at Lyons and Auxerre is, as in the *Somme*, collecting, or holding, treasure. At Auxerre Sapientia is holding a book like Prudence in the *Somme*. But more significant than these correspondences of detail, the windows show exactly the same blend of the emblematic and the exemplary. Superbia at Lyons is a falling monarch, at Auxerre a knight falling off a horse, while Humilitas at Auxerre has a medallion with a dove, and so on.

Biblical stories are also used in the *Somme* illustrations. Thus, Noah's ark is used as symbol of peace and Equity is represented by Moses horned, standing between two figures, and restraining them from killing each other with clubs. David and Jonathan represent Amity, Saul and David the antitype. David and

[1] Cp. Katzenellenbogen, pp.27–56.
[2] Katzenellenbogen, p.83; for the use of exemplary human figures see plates 54 and 55.

Goliath represent Fortitude,[1] Hester, Chastity and the story of Joseph and Potiphar's wife, Luxury. Thus the emblematic figure, the exemplary action, and the *figura* are used indifferently as alternative modes of expressing the same idea. The aim of this chapter has been to show the complexity of the relationship of theme and picture in medieval allegorical writings. The distinction between a dynamic and a static symbol, the latter a symbol with a fixed meaning and the former a symbol reflecting the author's consciousness, is sometimes invoked to the detriment of medieval allegory. This I have tried to show is a gross oversimplification of the nature of medieval allegory. On the contrary, here too it is possible to find that a 'symbolisation de la vie profonde est faite par le jeu des images'.[2] It is precisely this 'jeu des images' a play depending upon the constantly shifting relationship between image and theme, which is the strength of the allegorical manner of writing.

[1] Katzenellenbogen, pp.9, 24.
[2] Fiser, p.41.

CHAPTER TWO

Literary Structures

'Basically the invention is faulty; it is not Dante's at all, but is taken from Virgil, and Dante borrows it "storpiandola e confondendola e riempiendola d'episodii alieni e indecenti a materia heroica, e d'interessi priuati e abbietti".' So judged Castravilla in 1572. He judged indeed, not merely that Dante's plot was faulty, but that *The Divine Comedy* had no single plot.[1] This judgement may indicate, as Weinberg says,[2] that Castravilla merely reflects the confusions of his contemporaries with respect to 'the nature of imitation, the nature of plot and the nature of episodes'; the judgement is not uninteresting, however, in relation to medieval literary structures. The famous quarrel over the structure of Ariosto, and attempts to bring Ariosto into line with the precepts of Aristotle, likewise bring into prominence the changed concept of structure which developed in the sixteenth century and which has in a greater or lesser degree influenced thinking on this topic ever since.[3] Despite the much-advertised precepts of the rhetoricians, medieval authors were not unaware of the need for a well-proportioned tale or of the dangers of a straggling plot. No less an authority than Augustine defines physical beauty as 'partium congruentia cum quadam suauitate coloris',[4] and Brunetto Latini, in his much used *Livres dou Tresor*, warns the narrator: 'mais se li trespas n'est

---

[1] B. Weinberg, *A History of Literary Criticism in the Italian Renaissance* (Chicago, 1961), p.833 and note 23; Anselmo (?) Castravilla, *Discorso di (Ridolfo) Castravilla, nel quale si mostra l'imperfettione della 'Commedia' di Dante*, edited by Mario Rossi (Città di Castello, 1897), p.25.

[2] Weinberg, p.832.   [3] Weinberg, pp.954–1073.

[4] Augustine, *De Civitate Dei*, XXII, 19; cited in H. Brinkmann, *Zu Wesen und Form mittelalterlicher Dichtung* (Halle, 1928), p.3; cp. Maritain, pp.23–30.

bien dou tout acordans a la matire, certes il sera mauvais et desprisables'.[1] Rather, the judgement of Castravilla on what is now generally accepted as the great masterpiece of medieval literature must suggest that a radical change of view had taken place; indeed the argument as to whether Dante's poem consisted of three voyages or of one single voyage divided into three parts[2] is not unreminiscent of the great quarrel over 'Malory one or eight' which has troubled us in our day. In discussing this matter we may usefully distinguish between 'a plot' and 'a pattern'. By 'a plot' I mean the presentation of the action in such a way that each event is related to every other event within the 'frame', by explicit or implicit motivation, and by space and time relationships, so that the action appears 'necessary' and comprehensible. This kind of 'necessity' is rightly linked with the concept of 'imitation'. For it is an aspect of verisimilitude that the actions played out before us should be credible and that the actors should inhabit a world which has the dimensions of the world of our senses; or if the action be incredible, that the writer should make it credible by the use of sense data of a familiar kind. By 'a pattern' I mean, as I have already indicated, the presentation of an action in such a way that the events within the frame bear a thematic relationship to each other and not a space-time relationship. The kind of distinction I am trying to make can be well illustrated by reference to Dürer's Melencolia (I). Here is a woman of melancholy and saturnine countenance, her posture indicating 'grief, fatigue and meditation', surrounded by a clutter of symbolic objects. From her belt hangs a key, signifying power, and a purse, signifying riches, for 'among the medieval descriptions of the melancholic there was none in which he did not appear as avaricious and miserly and hence, implicitly, as rich'.[3] The

---

[1] Brunetto Latini, *Li Livres dou Tresor*, edited by F. J. Carmody, University of California Publications in Modern Philology, xxii (1948), 331.

[2] Cp. Weinberg, p.835; Giacopo Mazzoni, *Discorso in difesa della 'Commedia' del divino poeta Dante*, edited by Mario Rossi (Città di Castello, 1898), pp.77–83.

[3] R. Klibansky, Erwin Panofsky and Fritz Saxl, *Saturn and Melancholy* (London, 1964), pp.284, 287.

clenched fist and the black face also indicate the melancholic humour.[1] She has compasses in her hand, as well as other geometric symbols, a sphere, writing materials, signifying pure geometry. In the background, is a building under construction, and near it a moulding plane, a set-square and a hammer, symbols of the builder's trade and, beside these, a polyhedron symbolising descriptive geometry. This series of geometrical objects is in the picture because it was held that Saturn, the type of the melancholic man, governed the art of geometry.[2] At the feet of Melancholy lies a dog, the typical beast of Saturn, of melancholics and, in particular, of scholars and prophets.[3]

Klibansky, Panofsky and Saxl show convincingly that these objects, and others, appear in the picture because they have a thematic relationship to the subject of the picture. In this sense the unity of the picture depends upon the idea of melancholy and not upon the creation of a human scene presenting melancholy, as we might say, dramatically. This is our first impression. But we might carry our distinction a little further. Klibansky, Panofsky and Saxl comment:

> The idea behind Dürer's engraving, defined in terms of the history of types, might be that of Geometria surrendering to melancholy, or of Melancholy with a taste for geometry. But this pictorial union of two figures, one embodying the allegorised ideal of a creative mental faculty, the other a terrifying image of a destructive state of mind, means far more than a mere fusion of two types; in fact, it establishes a completely new meaning . . . the new meaning . . . communicates itself to eye and mind with the same directness as that with which the outward appearance of a man approaching us reveals his character and mood.[4]

Here we have the essential distinction. The picture might, by a metaphor, be said to have evolved from 'a pattern' to 'a plot', from a composition in which the details are linked as part of an 'allegorised ideal' to one in which the details are formed into a spatial whole which communicates itself directly to mind and

[1] Klibansky, Panofsky and Saxl, pp.289–90.
[2] Klibansky, Panofsky and Saxl, pp.328; 331–8.
[3] Klibansky, Panofsky and Saxl, pp.322–3.
[4] Klibansky, Panofsky and Saxl, pp.317, 321.

eye as our sense impressions in real life communicate, and are classified and interpreted. Our response to the scene is a response to a dramatic whole not an interpretation of separate parts by reference to an underlying meaning. The latter is a 'pattern' because it implies, not only that the parts are related by virtue of an underlying meaning, but that the juxtaposition of the parts is itself part of the meaning. It is indeed a kind of parataxis whereas the concept of 'plot', to continue the grammatical metaphor, is a kind of syntaxis.

Now, I do not intend to suggest that the chronological distribution of 'plot' and 'pattern' is exclusive. One has only to think of Chaucer's fabliaux to find an admirable example of 'plot' in medieval literature. The fabliau is a realistic genre, with little or no intellectual content and we should, therefore, expect it to be constructed in this way. If I concentrate almost exclusively upon structures of another kind, it is because it is here that the medieval works are in need of interpretation and may benefit from being measured by a new yardstick. I should like therefore to turn to the consideration of the class of structure which I have called 'patterns'. These may conveniently be divided into two sub-classes. On the one hand, we have purely symbolic structures; on the other, what might be called thematic structures.

By a symbolic structure I mean those structures which, like a Gothic cathedral (or indeed a renaissance church)[1] are built upon a symbolic framework. Of such structures the most typical is number symbolism, where the structure itself and not merely what is structured, is symbolic. The sanction was, perhaps, as Curtius has suggested, the words from the book of *Wisdom*: *omnia in mensura et numero er pondere disposuisti*.[2] It was a way in which the work of art could imitate nature or, as in the case of Dante, reveal divine truth. For, as Curtius points out,

---

[1] Cp. R. Wittkower, *Architectural Principles in the Age of Humanism* (2nd edn., London, 1952), especially pp.89–124; Otto von Simson, *The Gothic Cathedral* (London, 1956).

[2] E. R. Curtius, *European Literature and the Latin Middle Ages*, translated by W. R. Trask (London, 1953), p.504; *Wisdom*, xi, 21.

from the three times three symbolism of the *Vita Nuova*, Dante proceeded to the elaborate numerical structure of the Comedy with its interweaving of triads and decads. Here, in the words of Curtius, 'number is no longer an outer framework, but a symbol of the cosmic *ordo*'.[1] Similar structures have been seen in French and German literature of the Middle Ages and also for Spenser.[2] In Middle English a numerical structure has been found in *Pearl*,[3] in itself not improbably in view of the author's liking for elaborate and artificial word patterns. On this view the poem would be based on a pattern of 3, 4, 12 reflecting the construction of the heavenly Jerusalem described in *Revelations* 21. The heavenly city has

> twelve gates, and at the gates twelve angels, and names written
> thereon, which are the names of the twelve tribes of the children
> of Israel; on the east three gates; on the north three gates; on the
> south three gates; and on the west three gates. And the wall of the
> city had twelve foundations and in them the names of the twelve
> apostles of the Lamb.... And the city lieth four-square...
> And (the angel) measured the city with the reed, twelve thousand
> furlongs... And he measured the wall thereof, an hundred and
> forty and four cubits, according to the measure of a man, that is,
> of the angel.

---

[1] Curtius, p.509.

[2] M. Ittenbach, *Deutsche Dichtungen der salischen Kaiserzeit* (Würzburg, 1937); V. H. Hopper, *Medieval Number Symbolism* (New York, 1938); W. S. Woods, 'The Symbolic Structure of *La Chanson de Roland*', *PMLA*, lxv (1950), 1247–62; H. Eggers, *Symmetrie und Proportion epischen Erzählens* (Stuttgart, 1956); F. Tschirch, 'Zum symbolbestimmten Umfang mittel-alterlicher Dichtungen', in *Stil u. Formprobleme in der Literatur*, edited by P. Böckmann (Heidelberg, 1959), pp.148–56; E. W. Bulatkin, 'The Arithmetic Structure of the Old-French *Vie de Saint Alexis*', *PMLA*, lxxiv (1959), 495–502; C. A. Robson, 'The Technique of Symmetrical Composition in Medieval Narrative Poetry', in *Studies in Medieval French presented to Alfred Ewert* (Oxford, 1961), 26–75; M. S. Batts, 'Numbers and Number Symbolism in Medieval German Poetry', *MLQ*, xxiv (1963), 342–9; A. Fowler, *Spenser and the Numbers of Time* (London, 1964); *Silent Poetry: Essays in Numerological Analysis* (London, 1970); R. A. Peck, 'Number Symbolism in the Prologue to Chaucer's *Parson's Tale*', *English Studies*, xlviii (1967), 205–15.

[3] C. O. Chapman, 'Numerical Symbolism in Dante and the *Pearl*', *MLN*, liv (1939), 256–9; M.-S. Røstvig, 'Numerical Composition in *Pearl*: a Theory', *English Studies*, xlviii (1967), 326–32.

Thus each stanza has twelve lines and three rhymes. Each line has four stresses and often three or four alliterating words. Of the hundred and one stanzas, ninety-nine are divided, like *The Divine Comedy*, into three groups of approximately equal length + two as an epilogue. The 101 is made up of 33 in part 1, +32 in part 2, +34 in part 3, =99 + 2 = 101 (or perhaps, as P. M. Kean has suggested, 1212 lines).[1] Transitions occur in stanzas 33 and 65 in each of which the dreamer asks the Pearl maiden questions regarding the life she leads. Note especially 389–92 and 771–4 and the verbal echoes of 392/774. In Chapman's opinion, the reality of the tripartite division is shown by an examination of the mood and subject of each of the main divisions: the vision, the dialogue, the vision. While it seems impossible to prove this thesis, it is quite in keeping with the known schemes of numerical symbolism. Certainly, however curious and fantastic, however improbable or preposterous these schemes may seem to the modern reader, there appear to be sufficient authentic cases to warrant calling attention to them as exemplifying a distinctive kind of structure; namely one in which a symbolic concept, in this case number, is used as a unifying principle.

Before proceeding to discuss thematic structure proper, something should be said of the structure of allegory. Already in our chapter on allegorical imagery, we have drawn attention to the varying degrees of surface consistency we find in allegories and of devices by means of which the image can be given a dramatic immediacy. It is indeed true that, as in Dürer's Melancholia, the allegorical image tends towards the dramatic, as we have shown it to do in the work of the greatest of medieval allegorists, Dante and Langland. But allegory cannot properly have a plot, since plot is essentially a web of cause and effect in a human setting, exemplifying, or imitating, a human situation. And this plot situation is a paradigm of experience. But in allegory the meaning is not primarily in the surface

---

[1] P. M. Kean, 'Numerical Composition in *Pearl*', *NQ*, ccx (Feb. 1965), 49–51.

picture as a whole, but in its parts, as they are related to some other thing, by a relationship, not of cause and effect, or of place and time, but in the intellectual relationship of *signum* and *significatum*. On the other hand, allegory can have pattern. So, for example, *Piers Plowman* has been seen as having a pattern of repeated symbols and themes, such as the seven deadly sins, or the figure of Piers, these figures and themes being modified at each appearance by their context. Thus H. W. Wells argued that the definitions of Dowel describe the active life and that this section of the poem is a presentation of this way of life. In the presentation of Dobet, he sees the contemplative life and, in Dobest, he sees the active life as exemplified by the episcopal office, each section contextually modifying the dominant symbol.[1] This view was further developed by N. K. Coghill, who supposed Dowel to be the life of faith and work, the layman and manual worker; Dobet the life of contemplation and the clerk; and Dobest the life of the bishop. Later he supposed that these could be fitted into a pattern of four-fold interpretation. More important for our purpose, Piers, in Coghill's view, was an allegorical symbol for these three ways of life and his entries into the poem indicated a change from one theme to another just as his nature changed at each appearance. In other words, the structure of the poem depended upon a central symbol which shifted contextually at each appearance.[2] Piers is the unifying symbol of the poem. A similar view was put forward by Troyer who assumed that Piers was a multiple symbol conditioned by its context.[3] The concept of the three states as a clue to the poem was adopted also by R. W. Chambers, and

[1] H. W. Wells, 'The Construction of *Piers Plowman*', *PMLA*, xliv (1929), 123-40.

[2] N. K. Coghill, 'The Character of Piers Plowman considered from the B text', *Medium Aevum*, ii (1933), 108-35; 'The Pardon of *Piers Plowman*', *PBA*, xxx (1944), 303-57; a more recent view assumes that the poem deals with the different stages of the Dreamer's life, Piers being a variable ideal 'the arbiter between man and the proper understanding of Grace'. See J. F. Adams, '*Piers Plowman* and the Three Ages of Man', *JEGP*, lxi (1962), 23-41.

[3] H. W. Troyer, 'Who is Piers Plowman?', *PMLA*, xlvii (1932), 368-84.

further elaborated by Wells, and it may be said that this was generally the fundamental assumption behind much early discussion of the structure of the poem.[1] This view has recently been under fire from a number of critics but a tendency to regard Piers as an evolving symbol is still evident. Thus, for example, Father Dunning considers him to be identified, amongst other things, with Christ in the *Vita*, with St. Peter, the Church itself, and with 'the vital spirit of religion in the Church', but also, in the A text, as 'the conventional ideal of the just man, living in simplicity and truth'.[2] A complex role for Piers has been assumed by some scholars ever since Skeat conjectured that he represented the type of Honesty, or the ideal honest man, in the *Visio*, but later Christ and St. Peter.[3] So Burdach thought him to represent Everyman, the type of uncorrupted nature, but also Christ and St. Peter,[4] and Glunz has suggested that he represents a developing symbol, the godly king, but also aspects of Christ.[5] Mrs. Salter has seen a developing symbol of another kind. In her view, the poem shows us the spiritual progress of Piers from a humble worker to 'the truth of God reposed in man'.[6] Other critics have regarded Piers as an increasingly complex symbol; Lawlor assumes that '*Piers Plowman* in the conclusion is, like the Plowman of the *Visio*, individual man not given over to corruption. But also, with all the cumulative

---

[1] H. W. Wells, 'The Philosophy of Piers Plowman', *PMLA*, liii (1938), 339–49; R. W. Chambers, *Man's Unconquerable Mind* (London, 1939), pp. 88–171; 'Poets and their Critics: Langland and Milton', *PBA*, xxvii (1941), 120–3; cp. also, T. P. Dunning, 'The Structure of the B-Text of *Piers Plowman*', *RES*, vii (1956), 225–37; S. S. Hussey, 'Langland, Hilton and the Three Lives', *ibid.*, 132–50.

[2] T. P. Dunning, *Piers Plowman: An Interpretation of the A-Text* (Dublin, 1937), pp.116–17, 119–20.

[3] W. W. Skeat, *Piers Plowman*, II, xxv–xxvii, 102.

[4] K. Burdach, *Der Dichter des Ackermann aus Böhmen und seine Zeit vom Mittelalter zur Reformation*, III, 2 (Berlin, 1926–32), pp.165, cp. also 297–353.

[5] Glunz, pp.534–5

[6] Salter (1962), p.83; cp. E. Zeeman, 'Piers Plowman and the Pilgrimage to Truth', *Essays and Studies*, 1958, 1–16. Mrs. Salter has called attention to the 'figural' aspect of Piers in 'Medieval Poetry and the Figural View of Reality', *PBA*, liv (1968), 73–92.

force the poem has developed, he might be the Church's head, a true Pope who would destroy Pride and set the Friars in order.'[1] Piers has also been regarded as the semi-divine quality in man.[2] How consistently this symbol has been used throughout the poem is also a matter of debate.

There is much truth in many, if not most, of these views. I propose, not so much to combat them, as to look at the problem from a different point of view. I shall first consider Piers as a *figura* and then consider how far this analysis can enable us to understand, not every detail of the poem, for this can hardly be possible until we have an established text, but something of the principles upon which the text is constructed. Let us then first consider Piers as a *figura*. To do this we must analyse the appearance of Piers in the poem, and we will begin with the *Visio*.

When Chaucer wished to represent one of those members of society who laboured honestly with their hands for the good of the community, he chose a ploughman to represent this class.

> A trewe swynkere and a good was he,
> Lyvynge in pees and parfit charitee.
> God loved he best with al his hoole herte
> At alle tymes, thogh him gamed or smerte,
> And thanne his neighebor right as hymselve.
> He wolde thresshe, and therto dyke and delve,
> For Cristes sake, for every povre wight,
> Withouten hire, if it lay in his myght.[3]

This is Piers the Plowman. Its very generality and lack of visual detail link it with Piers, who, like *Peres the Pardoner* or *Sir Piers*

---

[1] Lawlor, p.185.

[2] Cp. E. T. Donaldson, *Piers Plowman: The C Text and its Poet* (Yale Studies in English, 113, New Haven, 1949), p.186; Frank (1957), pp.23, 117; E. Vasta, 'Truth, the Best Treasure in *Piers Plowman*', *PQ*, xliv (1965), 17–29; B. Raw, 'Piers and the Image of God in Man', in *Piers Plowman: Critical Approaches*, pp.143–79.

[3] Chaucer, *The Canterbury Tales*, A. 531–8. Cp. J. Horrell, 'Chaucer's Symbolic Plowman', *Speculum*, xiv (1939), 82–92; but cp. Gardiner Stillwell, 'Chaucer's Plowman and the Contemporary English Peasant', *ELH*, vi (1939), 285–90.

of Prydie in Langland, is plain 'John Smith', as Dunning has pointed out.[1] The ploughman in Chaucer and in Langland is a type of virtuous living; but he is a ploughman and not a symbol. His function as a typical figure is suggested, too, by the illustrations of the *Somme Le Roi* where ploughing, he represents Zeal or Prouesse, and, sleeping beside his plough, he represents Idleness. There were biblical texts which suggested this view of the ploughman as the man who, having put his hand to the plough, did not turn back or who, as in the second epistle to Timothy, was the labourer in the field of the spirit. But this does not mean that he is an allegorical figure in the sense of being polysemous. He is merely an abstraction from the concrete, not an analogy. Such a type is, of course, peculiarly appropriate in the *Visio* with its concern for man in society, with its 'field of folk', classified into the traditional three, those who labour with their hands, those who labour by praying, and those who labour by fighting. The poet summarises this traditional classification in the Prologue:

> Thanne come there a kyng . knyȝthod hym ladde,
> Miȝt of the comunes . made hym to regne,
> And thanne cam kynde wytte . and clerkes he made,
> For to conseille the kyng . and the comune saue.
> The kyng and knyȝthode . and clergye bothe
> Casten that the comune . shulde hemself fynde.
> The comune contreued . of kynde witte craftes,
> And for profit of alle the poeple . plowmen ordeygned,
> To tilie and trauaile . as trewe lyf asketh:[2]

This pattern is constantly repeated at each stage of the poem. We see the classes of society confessing their sins, we see them labouring in the half-acre and we learn the terms on which they may receive the pardon from Truth. This social imagery is, indeed, the most pervasive in the *Visio* and is, I believe, a significant pointer to the function of Piers. The *Visio* is certainly concerned with the search for Truth; but the answer of the

---

[1] Dunning, p.120.
[2] Langland, *Piers Plowman*, B. Prologue, ll.112–20; C. i, ll.139–46.

Visio is that man must labour at his avocation in a spirit of charity. In the words of the B text:

> The kynge and the comune . and kynde witte the thridde
> Shope lawe and lewte . eche man to knowe his owne.[1]

or, as a later generation might have put it, 'each member of society should do his duty in that station of life to which it has pleased God to call him'. If the ploughing of the half-acre in Passus VI appears to be an interruption of the pilgrimage to Truth, as many critics have thought, when we regard the nature of the pilgrimage itself, this interruption is more apparent than real. For the court which they seek on the pilgrimage to Truth is man himself, for the walls are of 'witte to holden wille out'. This must be an allegory of man's soul. But it is the soul of the virtuous man, for it is protected by the crenellations of Christendom and buttressed by Faith and, unlike the coat of Haukyn, its Christendom seems to be in good repair. It is protected from the elements by Love and Humility. Prayer, Penance and Almsdeeds are the bridge, the pillars and the hinges of the gate. The janitor is Grace and his servant Amends and the sacrament of penance gives entrance. This might suggest that the court cannot be the heart of man, since a man can scarcely enter his own heart. Yet he does precisely this:

> And if Grace graunte the . to go in in this wise,
> Thow shalt see in thi-selue. Treuthe sitte in thine herte,
> In a cheyne of charyte . as thow a childe were,
> To suffre hym and segge nouȝte . aȝein thi sires wille.[2]

The ploughing of the half-acre must precede the pilgrimage because honest labour is the prerequisite of man's salvation. The figure of Hunger makes it difficult to suppose that the half-acre is, as Robertson and Huppé suggest, 'the preparation of the human heart through good works for the building of the

---

[1] Langland, *Piers Plowman*, Prologue, ll.121–2; Cp. P. M. Kean, 'Love, Law and *Lewte* in *Piers Plowman*', *RES*, xv (1964), 241–61.

[2] Langland, *Piers Plowman*, B. v, ll.614–7; C. viii, ll.254–60. Cp. A. vi, ll.92–4. For the castle of Truth in the heart of man, cp. D. W. Robertson and B. F. Huppé, *Piers Plowman and Scriptural Tradition* (Princeton, 1951), pp.77–8.

tabernacle'.[1] The work of the half-acre is rather to be defined as giving 'the image of the man of good works' and as indicating that 'Truth is attainable only by the fruitful laborer'.[2] The allegory here is figurative only.[3] The ploughing is a figure of all honest labour truly performed. The ladies sowing their fine seams, no less than the knights and ploughmen, are 'ploughing' and poverty comes upon society when the social orders neglect their avocations. Poverty, that great medieval topic from the days of St. Francis onwards, the problem of *temporalia* in all its secular and spiritual complexities, is a constant theme in the poem.[4] The three necessities of life common to all men, clothing, meat and drink, of which Holy Church speaks at the beginning of the poem,[5] are the subject of Need's discourse at the end of the poem.[6] There is no difficulty here.

The problems arise in the scene of the tearing of the pardon. Yet the difficulties have perhaps been exaggerated. The pardon is granted to all those classes of society who fulfil their social obligations in a spirit of charity rather than cupidity. The attempt to plough the half-acre has failed. Hunger reigns. Piers is destitute because society has failed him:

> 'I haue no peny,' quaþ piers, 'pulettis to biggen,
> Noþer gees ne gris, but two grene chesis,
> And a fewe cruddis and crem, and an hauer cake,
> A lof of benis and bren ybake for my children;'[7]

Now Truth, hearing of the plight of Piers under the domination of hunger, sends him a pardon. Truth tells him to plough his fields and stay at home. And this pardon is granted to all who labour justly, to all who help Piers to plough or to sow, kings and knights who protect Holy Church, bishops who teach and tend their flock, merchants who spend their gain for the good

---

[1] Cp. Robertson and Huppé, p.79.

[2] Frank (1957), p.23.

[3] Cp. Frank (1957), p. 23, 'but the scene is to be read literally'.

[4] For the theme of *bona temporalia* in the A text see T. P. Dunning, *passim.*

[5] Langland, *Piers Plowman*, A. i, ll.20–6; B. i, ll.20–6; C. ii, ll.20–4.

[6] Langland, *Piers Plowman*, B. xx, ll.1–49; C. xxiii, ll.1–50.

[7] Langland, *Piers Plowman*, A. vii, ll.264–7; B. vi, ll.282–5; C. ix, ll.304–7.

of the community, lawyers who plead without fees for the poor. All those members of society, in short, who rectify the cupidity which the Dreamer observed in the Field of Folk. These are the people who receive the pardon from Truth. Here then is the problem. The pardon comes from Truth. It must be good, for it demands virtuous living. It indeed indicates, in the words that the Dreamer himself later uses, that

> Dowel at þe day of dome is digneliche vndirfongen;
> He passiþ al þe pardoun of seint petris chirche.[1]

This is evidently not a pardon in the sense of remission of punishment, as the priest rightly says, but it would seem to be the pardon of Truth and it wins the approval of the Dreamer. Why then does Piers tear it? Is it a sign of disapproval or annulment, of regret or even rejection, as critics have thought,[2] or a sign that Piers repents?[3] The confusion has, I believe, arisen from a misunderstanding of the nature of Piers and of the *Visio*, as well as a misunderstanding of the problem that is under discussion.

For Piers, in the *Visio* at least (and we shall proceed to his function in the *Vita* later), is a *figura*, not an abstraction. It is accordingly fruitless to try to equate him with a single idea or concept. For a *figura*, while typifying some general idea, at the same time acts as a person and not as a personified abstraction. Thus, for example, when we learn that Piers has neither pig nor goose, we are not to suppose that these details are allegorical nor, on the other hand, that they are irrelevancies. As Piers is a *figura*, it is proper that he should operate at a literal level. We have already said that he represents all honest workers who live

---

[1] Langland, *Piers Plowman*, A. viii, ll.155–6; B. vii, ll.171–2; C. x, ll.323–4.

[2] Cp. Dunning, p.148; Robertson and Huppé, pp.93–4; Frank (1957), pp.28, 33; Woolf, 'The Tearing of the Pardon', in *Piers Plowman: Critical Approaches*, pp.50–75; according to H. Meroney ('The Life and Death of Longe Wille', *ELH*, xvii (1950), 18) the tearing represents the breaking of the tables of the law; M. C. Schroeder, '*Piers Plowman:* The Tearing of the Pardon', *PQ*, xlix (1970), 8–18.

[3] Cp. Lawlor, p.79; for the treatment of the scene in the C text, see Donaldson (1949), pp.161–8.

in humility and charity. But what of his encounter with the
priest in the pardon episode? Here it is important to notice how
the scene closes. So much attention has been focused upon the
dramatic moment of the tearing of the pardon that the episode
has been viewed out of focus. When the Dreamer awakes, he
leaves Piers and the priest arguing about the pardon. And his
reflections upon the dream seem to run somewhat as follows:
he considers

> how þe prest inpugnid it al be pure resoun,
> And demide þat dowel indulgence passiþ,
> Bienalis and trienalis and bisshopis lettres.[1]

Now, this is grammatically ambiguous, but I would translate
it: 'The priest reasonably impugned the pardon and deemed
that indulgence, *biennalis* and *triennalis* and bishops' letters
surpassed Dowel'. This reading seems to be supported by the
B and C texts. The sentiment that, at the Day of Judgement,
Dowel is worthily received is, I believe, the beginning of the
Dreamer's final musings, not an observation of the priest as,
indeed, the reading of the A text would suggest. The Dreamer
is a good son of the church, he accepts 'þat pardoun, and
penaunce, and preyours do salue'.[2] Nevertheless

> to triste on þis trionalis, trewely, me þinkeþ,
> It is not so sikir for þe soule, certis, as is do wel.[3]

Why then does Piers tear the pardon? Seemingly, it represents
the virtues of Dowel as against man-made pardons. Here the
understanding of Piers as a *figura* is of assistance. An allegorical
figure presupposes a moral stance. This is a necessary prerequisite to choice of an allegorical image. This is not equally
true of a *figura*, which has areas of ambiguity. Piers in the pardon
scene is representative, in my opinion, of a point of view, a
factor in a problem, even a person in an equivocal situation.

---

[1] Langland, *Piers Plowman*, A. viii, ll.152–4; B. vii, ll.168–70; C. x,
ll.318–20.

[2] Langland, *Piers Plowman*, A. viii, l.161; B. vii, l.177; C. x, l.328.

[3] Langland, *Piers Plowman*, A. viii, ll.163–4; B. vii, ll.179–80; C. x,
ll.330–1.

When he faces the priest, he is the virtuous layman facing the Church in the form of the priest. I suspect that, behind the confrontation, lies the Wycliffite concept of the saved layman, one of the elect who was, in Wycliffe's view, a priest in his own right, and who, as such, could function as a priest in giving absolution or hearing confession. For Wycliffe, the Church consisted of the elect and essentially its function was to imitate the life of Christ and the apostles in a life pledged to poverty, humility and charity.[1] I am not suggesting that Langland was a Lollard, but merely that the question of the relationship between Church and laity, the nature of the Church and function of the priesthood, which had been raised by Wycliffe in an acute form in the fourteenth century, and which reverberated widely throughout the fourteenth and fifteenth centuries, was a current issue, greatly discussed, and an issue with which Langland here concerns himself. This appears to me to be the core of the discussion. But, we might ask, if Piers, the virtuous layman, living a life of poverty and toil, in humility and charity, is on the side of Dowel, why does he appear to reject it by tearing the pardon? Primarily, I think, because he is a person and not a personification. To the Dreamer he appears to be in the right, but he himself is not sure. The tearing of the pardon is a dramatic crystallisation of the problem, a dilemma later stated explicitly by the Dreamer in his musings on the scene. 'I do believe,' Piers might have said, 'that pardon, penance and prayers *do* save, yet surely Dowel *must* avail too. What then is the nature of Dowel? And, if we believe that a man in virtue of honest toil and loving service of the community, and by a life of patient poverty (whether spiritual or physical), must be saved, what then is the function of the church and of the priesthood?' Such I believe to be the problem of the *Visio* and it is focused by the picture of the ploughman. Will he find Truth is the question of the *Visio* and leads us to the *Vita*. But, the sceptic might object, it is, after all, the Dreamer and not Piers

[1] See G. Leff, *Heresy in the Later Middle Ages* (Manchester, 1967), II, 525-7.

who sets off in search of Dowel. This is surely because Piers is, in effect, the *alter ego* of the Dreamer, the ideal to which he hopes to attain. In this sense, it is true that Piers is man's better nature, his ideal self.

But such a theory must clearly be tested against the *Vita* before we can proceed to consideration of some characteristics of the poem's structure. I believe it can be shown that our interpretation of Piers does not conflict essentially with his later appearances in the poem. For example, in the C text, at the dinner party of Conscience, Clergy and Patience, we are told that

> Pacience as a poure thyng cam . and preide mete for charite,
> Ylike to Peers Plouhman.[1]

Here Piers is introduced as an example of patient poverty. A more difficult passage occurs later in the same scene. Conscience asks Clergy to explain the nature of Dowel. In the B text Clergy replies that

> For one Pieres the Ploughman . hath inpugned vs alle,
> And sette alle sciences at a soppe . saue loue one.[2]

The C text, as usual, is more explicit, but makes essentially the same point:

> For Peers loue the Plouhman . that enpugnede ones
> Alle kyne konnynges . and alle kyne craftes,
> Saue loue and leaute . and louhnesse of herte.[3]

Both texts cite the text *Dilige deum* (*et proximum*) and the fifteenth psalm 'Lord who shall dwell in thy tabernacle', already extensively used in the Meed Episode to delineate the righteous man. Poverty is further defined in C, where we are told that Piers Plowman affirms that *pacientes vincunt*. It has been thought that Piers here represents Christ but, certainly in the B text, and possibly in the C text, he may equally well represent the

[1] Langland, *Piers Plowman*, C. xvi, ll.33–4.

[2] Langland, *Piers Plowman*, B. xiii, ll.123–4.

[3] Langland, *Piers Plowman*, C. xvi, ll.131–3; cp. Donaldson (1949), pp.169–80.

Ploughman himself, the type of honest toil, the unlettered man who reaches heaven by virtue of his love for his neighbour. That such a man is Christ-like does not mean that he represents Christ in an allegorical sense but, like St. Francis, he may stand for loving poverty. Piers figures also in the picture of Haukyn, the Active man, as we should expect.

> I haue none gode gyftes. of thise grete lordes,
> For no bred that I brynge forth . saue a beneson on the Sonday,
> Whan the prest preyeth the peple . her *pater noster* to bidde
> For Peres the Plowman . and that hym profite wayten.
> And that am I, Actyf . that ydelnesse hatye,
> For alle trewe trauaillours . and tilieres of the erthe;[1]

Surely this must mean, 'I have no good gifts from these great lords for any bread that I bring forth, except a blessing on Sunday, when the priest begs the people to pray their *pater noster* for Piers the Ploughman and those that desire his well-being. And I am Active, who hate idleness, for I provide with wafers all true toilers and tillers of the earth.'[2] Now it would seem that Haukyn is, as it were, the antitype of Piers, the Hyde, as it were to Piers's Jekyll. In the C text, indeed, Haukyn appears as the apprentice of Piers the Plowman. In both texts, the figure of Piers can be considered the virtuous layman, the body of the Church.[3]

Perhaps the most controversial of all Piers's appearances is in the Vision of *anima* and the Tree of Charity. His first appearance, in this section of the poem, is in the *Distinctio Caritatis*, as

---

[1] Langland, *Piers Plowman*, B. xiii, ll.234–9; C. xvi, ll.209–16; for some discussion of the symbolism of this passage, cp. A. C. Spearing, 'The Development of a Theme in *Piers Plowman*', *RES*, xi (1960), 241–53.

[2] For different views of Haukyn see S. Maguire, 'The Significance of Haukyn, *Activa Vita*, in *Piers Plowman*', *RES*, xxv (1949), 97–109; for the husbandman as deserving the protection of society as the man upon whom the whole of society depends, see John of Salisbury, *Policraticus*, V, ii; I, 283. The passage in Langland, of course, refers to the petition 'Give us this day our daily bread'.

[3] Skeat, in fact, was not far out in considering Piers to represent the Church Militant here; Skeat, *Piers Plowman*, II, 201.

it is headed in the C text. The passage begins with an approximate paraphrase of I *Corinthians* xiii. We are shown the humble and contrite heart washing away pride. 'I wish I knew Love,' says the Dreamer; and he is told that he cannot see him without the help of Piers Plowman. 'Do clerks know him who keep Holy Church?' the Dreamer asks. 'Clerks only know by words and deeds,' he is told, 'but Piers sees more deeply, for God knows their thoughts'. 'Many are the hypocrites', we are told, 'and only by the will can charity exist and only Piers Plowman knows the heart, *Petrus id est Christus*.[1] It is well-known that the C text omits these last words. Yet even the C text has the words

> 'Peers the Plouman' quath he. 'most parfitliche hym knoweth;
> *Et uidit deus cogitationes eorum.*'[2]

These passages seem to suggest that Piers here is equated with God. Yet I believe that this is the only passage in the poem where Piers could be equated with Christ and this alone must give us pause. It is possible to get some idea of what the poet's intentions were if we look at the second passage in this section, the episode of the Tree of Charity. In the B text, when the Dreamer hears that the human heart, in which grows the Tree of Charity, is farmed by Liberum Arbitrium, under Piers the Plowman, he swoons for joy. Why? Many critics would again suppose because Piers is Christ. But I believe this is not so. It is helpful at this point to remember the place of Piers in the passion scene. Here Piers is *not* Christ. Christ is 'somewhat like Piers the Plowman';[3] mankind is the fruit of Piers the Plowman;[4] Faith tells the Dreamer that Jesus jousts in Piers's armour, *humana natura*[5] and lastly that Christ shall ride 'In Piers paltok the Plowman' or in Piers's armour.[6] Here it is undeniable that Piers is human nature, however precisely

---

[1] See Langland, *Piers Plowman*, B. xv, ll.145–206.
[2] Langland, *Piers Plowman*, C. xvii, ll.337–7b.
[3] Langland, *Piers Plowman*, B. xviii, l.10; C. xxi, l.8.
[4] Langland, *Piers Plowman*, B. xviii, ll.20, 33; C. xxi, ll.18, 32.
[5] Langland, *Piers Plowman*, B. xviii, ll.22–3; C. xxi, ll.21–2.
[6] Langland, *Piers Plowman*, B. xviii, l.25; C. xxi, l.24.

defined, not Christ himself. He is the son of Adam, who eats his bread in the sweat of his brow, as his children have done ever since. In the episode of the Tree of Charity, it looks as though Piers may also represent mankind, or Everyman. Donaldson has pointed out that to equate Piers with Christ in the B text is difficult and he views Piers in this scene as mankind, or rather that elevated portion of mankind which includes the patriarchs and prophets.[1] According to Frank the passage is confused because the poet has tried to say two things at the same time; on the one hand, that man has free-will and, on the other that man is assisted in the fight against sin by the Holy Ghost. With the help of the Trinity man can do good deeds. But man's good deeds alone will not win salvation.[2] This can be clarified if we summarise what the poet of the B text seems to be saying. The Tree of Charity grows in the heart of man and it is cared for by Free Will and Piers the Plowman.[3] The tree is attacked by the world, the flesh and the devil and Piers strikes at them with the power of the Father and the wisdom of the Father, but Free Will wields the third stake. The fruit of the tree, as we pointed out in Chapter I, is mankind living in three acceptable states, and, as the fruit falls, devils pick up patriarchs and prophets and carry them off to Hell. Yet if Piers is Christ, why does he shake the tree so that the patriarchs and prophets go to hell? And why does the Dreamer faint with joy at the mention of Piers? It is, I think, because the Dreamer realises that, as man has free-will, he is capable of attaining to Charity. Piers is the Dreamer's *alter ego*, an idealised projection of himself. The Dreamer therefore swoons with joy at the realisation of his own perfectibility. Yet the initial vision is clouded by what follows. When Piers shakes the tree (a symbol

[1] Donaldson (1949), pp.183-7.

[2] Frank (1957), p.87.

[3] For the tree see M. Day, 'Duns Scotus and *Piers Plowman*', *RES*, iii (1927), 333-4; Robertson and Huppé, pp.191-6 and M. W. Bloomfield, review of Robertson and Huppé, in *Speculum*, xxvii (1952), 246-7; '*Piers Plowman* and the Three Grades of Chastity', *Anglia*, lxxvi (1958), 227-53; *Piers Plowman as a Fourteenth Century Apocalypse* (New Brunswick, 1961), pp.74-5, 117, 122-3.

perhaps of man's fall), only grief and sorrow follow and the
Dreamer learns that free-will must be aided by grace, the
grace which follows when Piers (here both man's ideal self
and the means of Christ's incarnation) strikes at the devil
with the prop of the Son; that is to say, only the incarnation
makes man capable of attaining charity. Man's free-will alone
is insufficient. And what more fitting symbol of the limitation
of man's unaided will could be chosen than the tree, at once
the symbol of Charity, of Adam's fall, and a figure of the cross,
the instrument of his redemption.[1] The Tree of Charity, like
the cross in *The Dream of the Rood*, is a shifting symbol; it represents, not only charity growing in the heart of man, but mankind himself, as he progressed from the fall to the redemption,
from the tree of the Garden of Eden to the tree of Golgotha. It
may be noticed that, if this view is accepted, the omission of
the figure of Piers in the C text does not very materially change
the argument.[2]

And, finally, in the last section, Piers is a pope but this too
does not conflict with our interpretation. This is the ploughman's spiritual function as the ideal ruler of the church. It is
plain that Langland, like Dante, was deeply concerned with
the government of the world and, like Dante, he saw the world
under the rule of the just king and the just pope. And when
Conscience sets out, as a pilgrim, to find Piers Plowman to
destroy Pride, he is surely not seeking only a good pope, but
the righteous man, living in humility and charity, the ploughman who, unlike the friars, does not need to flatter for his
necessity. And Conscience calls upon Nature to avenge her,
and to send fortune and health, until she has Piers the Plowman,
the type of self-reliance and natural toil, and a humble poverty
unlike that of the friars. In view of all this, it seems to be impossible to accept that, when the poet of the B Text says *Petrus
id est Christus*, he can be taken literally. If Piers does not represent Christ at the crucifixion, it seems unlikely that he can

[1] Cp. K. J. Höltgen, 'Arbor, Scala und Fons Vitae', in *Symposion für
Schirmer*, pp.355–91.

[2] Cp. Donaldson (1949), pp.187–92 for discussion of the C. text.

do so here. In the absence of an authoritative text, we may
hazard the guess that the poet is trying to say that only those
who live a good life, in humility and charity of heart, and not
merely a life of apparent good works, can be equated with Piers
as, indeed, from this point of view, Christ also can be equated
with Piers. It is perhaps a phrase parallel to Holy Church's
remark that

> For whoso is trewe of his tunge, telliþ non oþer,
> Doþ þe werkis þerwiþ and wilneþ no man ille,
> He is a god be þe gospel on ground and on lofte,
> And ek lyk to oure lord be seint lukis wordis.[1]

This surely means that the good man is Christ-like, like Christ
in his human ministry? Such too would I suspect to be the
meaning of *Petrus id est Christus*.

The structure of *Piers Plowman* is a structure characteristic
of the dream allegory and essentially different from that of an
allegory such as *The Faery Queene*. The structure is built round
the person of the Dreamer. But in *Piers Plowman* we have, also
the person of the ploughman, a real person, even though used
figurally, who is, as I have suggested, to some extent a reflection
of the Dreamer himself. He is both the dominant theme of the
poem and the centre of the Dreamer's attention as he appears
elusively at crucial moments in the poem. It is this figural
nature of Piers, I believe, which explains why, in spite of his
comparatively rare appearances, he takes the title role in the
poem. The apparently literal element in the poem, moreover,
becomes relevant once we realise the true nature of Piers. The
structure is a function of the dramatic interplay between the
Dreamer and Piers, vitalised by Piers's figural nature.

Let us now turn from allegory to some non-allegorical works
whose structure has puzzled modern critics. Isidore of Seville
has the following entry under the heading *Sententia*:

Sententia est dictum impersonale, ut: Obsequium amicos, veritas
odium parit. Huic, si persona fuerit adjecta, *chria* erit, ita:

---

[1] Langland, *Piers Plowman*, A. i, ll.86–9; B. i, ll.88–91; C. ii, ll.84–7.

Offendit Achilles Agamemnonem vera dicendo, Metrophanes promeruit gratiam Mithridatis obsequendo.[1]

[*A* sententia *is an impersonal statement as: Flattery brings friends, truth hatred. To which, if a person be added, it will be* chria, *thus: by telling the truth Achilles offended Agamemnon; Metrophanes attracted the favour of Mithridatis by flattery.*]

This summarises neatly one dimension of our problem. The structure of a work is, of course, related to the nature of the people in the work in question. We have at the one extreme, the most general concepts, abstractions such as faith, hope, charity, solitude, purity, impurity, whose proper realm is allegory. But as we move across the spectrum in the direction of *chria*, or, the particular, from the abstract noun, in the direction of the proper name, we can observe two other bands not specified by Isidore. Firstly, we have the *type* figure, the ploughman, the exile, the *peregrinus*, the last survivor and so on. Secondly, we have the *figurae*, Virgil, Cato, Belshazzar, Scipio, Peter. This class differs from the preceding in containing individuals who existed within a precise historical context. They are, in grammatical terms, proper names. Now it might reasonably be asked how these differ from characters, also individuals, real or imagined, in, say, a nineteenth-century novel. I think the answer lies in the nature of the structure within which they are placed and within which they function. In allegory, development takes place at the conceptual level. Thus, in Chaucer's *Parlement of Foules*, the argument runs somewhat as follows: there can be three attitudes to human love: that of asceticism, that of lust, and that of nature; the way of marriage reconciles the claims both of morality and of desire. This argument is projected by means of a *figura*, Scipio, an *idolum*, Venus, and a personification, Nature, each in an appropriate setting. Apart from the dream context, there is no connection at the mimetic level between the three scenes of the poem. Further, in the case where an historical figure is used, Scipio, he is not presented as a rounded

[1] Isidore, *Etymologiae*, II, xi; cited by G. Paré, A. Brunet, P. Tremblay, *La renaissance du xiie siècle: les écoles et l'enseignement* (Paris & Ottawa, 1933), p.268-9.

human being, but as representative of a point of view. He is the link, as it were, between *sententia* and *chria*. In the same way, Dante uses St. Peter, St. James and St. John as *figurae* of faith, hope and charity, Langland uses Abraham and the Good Samaritan as *figurae* of faith and charity. Development at the conceptual level is essential to allegory. Works, such as *The Wanderer*, *The Seafarer* in Old English, and *Purity* and *Patience* in Middle English, which use type figures to exemplify a single theme, mutability, renunciation, purity, patience, are not strictly allegorical. On the one hand, the characters in these poems are clearly different from both the *figura*, which is a proper name, and from the individual character in a modern novel, which is also a proper name, but which, unlike the *figura*, motivates and is revealed by plot; on the other hand, their structure is not strictly allegorical nor yet, though narrative, can they be said to have a plot. Let us now look, in the light of these observations, at the structure of some of these texts.

We might begin with the Old English companion pieces, *The Wanderer* and *The Seafarer*. In my view, the two poems are built round three type figures, an exile, a sage and a seafarer.[1] The latest editors of the former poem, T. P. Dunning and A. J. Bliss, compare *The Wanderer* to a musical piece in binary form, and refer to the two parts as 'movements'. That is to say, the structure of the poem is thematic, and consists of the juxta-position of thematic elements,[2] in this case the monologue of an exile, and the reflections of a sage, both parts dealing with the transitoriness of human life. Confusion as to the poem's

---

[1] For the abundant literature on these texts see *The Seafarer*, edited by I. L. Gordon (London, 1960), and *The Wanderer*, edited by T. P. Dunning and A. J. Bliss (London, 1969); all quotations are taken from these editions. For *The Seafarer* as a *peregrinus* poem see D. Whitelock, 'The Interpretation of *The Seafarer*', *The Early Cultures of North-west Europe* (H. M. Chadwick Memorial Studies), edited by C. Fox and B. Dickins (Cambridge, 1950), pp.261–72.

[2] We might perhaps compare the technique of the ideogram which juxtaposes signs for various ideas and concepts, in order to form a new concept, a technique of juxtaposition common in modern poetry. Cp. Brooke-Rose, pp.91–3.

meaning has arisen because critics assumed that in a poem which appeared to be a narrative, there must be a plot; but this is not the case. The exile's narrative is merely exemplary. The second part of the poem is not so easy to define and critics have differed as to where the division should come. In my view, the second part begins at line 73 with the introduction of the sage. But it differs from the first part in being reflective rather than narrative, and the dominant image, the ruined building, has no narrative context. Nevertheless, the two sections are structurally parallel. Each part has a section introducing the type figure and the dominant image; the exile awaits God's mercy as he rows across the sea, the sage looking upon the ruined building reflects upon the end of the world. In these two parts we have mutations of a common theme; the exile and the sea as symbols of loneliness, and the building, a symbol of security, as so often in Anglo-Saxon poetry, when ruined becomes a symbol of desolation. The organisation of the material in the two parts is slightly different. In the first part, the image of the exile is presented in the form of a narrative monologue; in the second part, we have first the image of the building and then, in lines 88–91, we hear that, like the exile, the sage thinks of past conflicts:

> Se þonne þisne wealsteal wise geþohte,
> ond þis deorce lif deope geondþenceð,
> frod in ferðe, feor oft gemon
> wælsleahta worn, ond þas word acwið:

[*So he who wisely pondered upon the site of this wall and who is accustomed to consider deeply this dark life, wise in heart, often calls to mind many battles and he speaks thus.*]

Then, in each part, we have a moralising conclusion. But the two movements, although not exactly parallel, are sufficiently parallel to indicate that they belong together. But if one applies a musical analogy the terms 'theme' and 'development of theme' would perhaps be closer to the structural facts than the term 'movement'. For the theme of mutability as presented by the exile is more particular than that of the sage. The exile's conclusions are personal. The sage takes up the theme where the exile lays it down and his thoughts are impersonal, his conclusions supernatural.

When we turn to *The Seafarer* we find a similar use of paratactic structure to express the theme. The apparent shifts of tone and theme in the poem led early commentators to think that the poem was a dialogue.[1] In fact, it seems probable that the speaker, like the speaker in the poem *Resignation*, is turning away from earthly sorrow and, *longunge fus*, turns his thoughts to a voyage across the sea.[2] He describes vividly his hardship on the sea. His kinsmen cannot comfort him, for those who dwell on land know not the hardships endured by those who voyage on the sea.[3] Yet he longs to return to it, even though he knows not what God will decree for him on that tempestuous element. He is, I believe, the type of those who suffer in this world. It is not unnatural, therefore, that in the second part of the poem his thoughts should turn from this mortal life, transitory on earth, to heaven and the joys of the Lord. The word *lond* in line 66 is indeed crucial, for it involves a change of meaning; the first part of the poem is speaking of the seafarer's feelings about the sea and his attitude to those who live on land, and the life they lead, the life of happiness and security. But in the second part of the poem *lond* means 'earth' as opposed to 'heaven', not 'land' as opposed to 'sea'. Thereafter, the themes of *lof* and *dream* are transposed into a religious context and, like Guthlac, on the night before his conversion, the speaker thinks of:

antiquorum regum stirpis suae per transacta retro saecula miserabiles exitus flagitioso vitae termino . . . necnon et caducas

---

[1] M. Rieger, 'Der Seefahrer als Dialog hergestellt', *ZfDP*, i (1869), 334–9; E. Hönncher, 'Zur Dialogeinteilung im *Seefahrer*', *Anglia*, ix (1886), 435–46.

[2] *Resignation*, ll.89–104; *The Exeter Book*, edited by G. P. Krapp and E. van Kirk Dobbie; the Anglo-Saxon Poetic Records, III (New York, 1936); cp. E. G. Stanley, 'Old English Poetic Diction and the Interpretation of *The Wanderer*, *The Seafarer* and *The Penitent's Prayer*', *Anglia*, lxxiii (1956), 413–66.

[3] I assume that lines 25–6 mean, not that the seafarer has no kinsmen, but that they are unable to comfort him. The meaning 'because' for *forþon* is well-evidenced in Old English. It often translated Latin *quia*.

mundi divitias contemtibilemque temporalis vitae gloriam . . . et finem inevitabilem brevis vitae.[1]

[*the wretched deaths and the shameful ends of the ancient kings of his race in the course of the past ages . . . also the fleeting riches of this world and the contemptible glory of this temporal life . . . and the inevitable finish of this brief life.*]

The two parts of the poem are not simply juxtaposed but juxtaposed in a meaningful way. The themes of the first part, the secure life on land which the seafarer rejects and the sea voyage itself become, in the second part of the poem, symbols of the mutability of earthly things, and of the life to come. The use of the figure of seafaring as a type of hardship may be paralleled by the words of Adam in *Genesis A*, uttered in remorse after the fall:

Gif ic waldendes willan cuðe,
hwæt ic his to hearmsceare habban sceolde,
ne gesawe þu no sniomor, þeah me on sæ wadan
hete heofones god heonone nu þa,
on flod faran, nære he firnum þæs deop,
merestream þæs micel, þæt his o min mod getweode,
ac ic to þam grunde genge, gif ic godes meahte
willan gewyrcean.[2]

[*If I knew the Lord's pleasure, what punishment I must have of him, thou hadst never the more speedily seen me in my mind ever doubt him, though He, the God of heaven had now commanded that I should traverse the sea, journey on the ocean, however mightily deep it be, however great the ocean stream, but I would go to the bottom of it, could I do God's pleasure.*]

I would therefore assume that, just as *The Wanderer* is built up round two type figures, the exile and the sage, so *The Seafarer* is built up round the figure of the seafarer, a type of distressed humanity, one of those who 'go down to the sea in ships' and that 'do business in great waters'; and like the seafarer of the Psalmist, he cries unto the Lord in his trouble and is brought out of his distress. The joys of life on land are not for him, for

[1] Felix, *Life of Guthlac*, pp.82–3.
[2] *Genesis* A, ll.828–35; *The Junius Manuscript*, edited by G. P. Krapp; The Anglo-Saxon Poetic Records, I (New York, 1931).

he knows that he must ever set out again to sea. He sets his mind, therefore, on the joys of heaven. The poem thus falls naturally and effectively into two contrasting parts: the first, in which the theme of the 'hall joys' represents that earthly happiness which the seafarer can never fully enjoy; then those 'hall joys' of heaven which will be his reward when earthly joys have crumbled away. The poem, therefore, like *The Wanderer*, is a poem in which a type figure is built into a thematic structure.

We have a structure of essentially the same kind in the Middle English poems *Purity* and *Patience*. Since *Purity* is perhaps the more interesting as well as the least understood, I should like to look at it in some detail.

A brief summary of the poem may be helpful. The poem falls into the following sections, each section being indicated in the manuscript by a special capital. First, there is an introduction in which the poet praises 'Cleanness', and this is followed by the parable of the wedding supper (an account combining the accounts of Matthew and Luke) which is then interpreted:

> Thus comparisunez Kryst þe kyndom of heven
> To þis frelych feste þat fele arn to called;
> For alle arn laþed luflyly, þe luþer and þe better,
> Þat ever wern fulȝed in font þat fest to have;
> Bot war þe wel, if þou wylt, þy wedez ben clene,
> And honest for þe halyday, lest þou harme lache,
> For aproch þou to þat Prynce of parage noble –
> He hates helle no more þen hem þat ar sowle.
> Wich arn þenne þy wedez þou wrappez þe inne,
> Þat schal schewe hem so schene schrowde of þe best?
> Hit arn þy werkez, wyterly, þat þou wroȝt havez,
> And lyved wyth þe lykyng þat lyȝe in þyn hert,
> Þat þo be frely and fresch fonde in þy lyve,
> And fetyse of a fayr forme, to fote and to honde,
> And syþen alle þyn oþer lymez lapped ful clene;
> Þenne may þou se þy Savior and his sete ryche.[1]

---

[1] *Purity*, edited by R. J. Menner (Yale Studies in English, 61, New Haven, 1920), ll.161–76.

This is followed by the story of Adam and of Lucifer, and, in section four, by the story of Noah and the flood. These narrative sections are followed by a homiletic conclusion, appropriately headed by Menner *A Warning of God's wrath against Sinners*.[1] Another narrative section follows, which tells the stories of the visit of the three angels to Abraham, and the fall of Sodom and Gomorrah. This narrative section is again concluded by a homiletic section, containing an exhortation to purity. The last section tells the story of the fall of Jerusalem, the capture of the holy vessels from the temple at Jerusalem, and their defilement at the hands of Belshazzar and the overthrow of his kingdom by the Medes and Persians. This is again concluded with a brief homiletic section:

> Þus upon þrynne wyses I haf yow þro schewed,
> Þat unclannes tocleves in corage dere
> Of þat wynnelych Lorde þat wonyes in heven,
> Entyses hym to be tene, teldes up his wrake;
> Ande clannes is his comfort, and coyntyse he lovyes,
> And þose þat seme arn and swete schyn se his face.
> Þat we gon gay in oure gere þat grace he uus sende,
> Þat we may serve in his syʒt þer solace never blynnez.[2]

The poem has often been criticised as a mere pretext for telling our stories connected, more or less loosely, with the theme of purity. Yet, though the structure is less elegant and sophisticated than that of *Gawain* and *Pearl*, it nonetheless repays consideration. It must be noted, in the first place, that the word 'cleanness' does not only mean purity of sexual morals.[3] It can also mean 'integrity', 'wholeness', 'soundness' and is often used to translate Latin *sinceritas*. We may, therefore, suppose that the interpretation of the parable refers generally to 'purity of heart', 'innocence', in which a man must be clothed to enter the kingdom of heaven. The poet, indeed, tells us that the garments which a man must wear to enter the kingdom of heaven, the feast of the mighty lord, are his works; these must

---

[1] *Purity*, p.23. [2] *Purity*, ll.1805–12.
[3] For an analysis of the different senses, cp. David J. Williams, *A Literary Study of the Middle English Poems 'Purity' and 'Patience'* (B.Litt. thesis, Oxford, 1965).

be noble and unsullied. Moreover, the poet has combined with the version of Matthew that of Luke, which adds the excuses of the wedding guests, and this links the poem more firmly with what Menner calls the sub-theme, that of *trawþe*, 'loyalty'. This sub-theme is illustrated in the tale of Adam, the tale of Lucifer and the tale of Lot's wife. Both Adam and Lucifer rejected the authority of God, just as the wedding guests rejected the invitation of the heavenly lord. Lucifer is represented as a *feloun*,[1] who, though given the highest position, like a churl, gives an unnatural return for these favours. Adam too is said to have 'fayled in trawþe'.[2] Lot's wife, also, is disobedient, putting salt in the food against the command of the angel and, contrary to God's command, turning round to look at the burning cities of the plain. So she is turned into a pillar of salt 'for two fautes þat þe fol watz founde in mistrauþe'.[3] The theme is picked up again in the last section where we are told that Jerusalem fell because 'þat folke in her fayth watz founden untrwe'.[4] We thus have a kind of musical canon. 'Virtue' the poet says, 'is necessary for the man who wishes to enter the kingdom of heaven and of all virtues purity is the best'; and he illustrates the sin of impurity by narrating the stories of the Flood and of Sodom and Gomorrah. At the same time, he picks up another theme, implicit in the parable, rejection of God's command, pride and lack of faith. This theme he develops alongside the major theme, purity. But the story of Belshazzar does not seem to illustrate either the theme of purity or the theme of loyalty. Rather it is, as Menner pointed out, the theme of defilement. The link is a purely verbal one, not unlike the concatenation of *Pearl*. After the two episodes illustrating the theme of fleshly impurity, the poet, having exhorted the reader to purity, passes to the theme of shrift. As the pearl can be purified, so may man be purified by shrift. Yet after shrift let a man sin no more for:

> War þe þenne for þe wrake; his wrath is achaufed
> For þat þat ones watz his schulde efte be unclene,

---

[1] *Purity*, l.217.
[3] *Purity*, l.996.
[2] *Purity*, l.236. Cp. p.xlvii.
[4] *Purity*, l.1161.

> Þaȝ hit be bot a bassyn, a bolle, oþer a scole,
> A dysche, oþer a dobler, þat Dryȝtyn onez served,
> To defowle hit ever upon folde fast he forbedes,
> So is he scoymus of scaþe þat scylful is ever.[1]

And as vengeance fell upon Nebuchadnezzar who stole the vessels from the temple, and upon Belshazzar who defiled them at the banquet, so shall a man suffer who defiles the vessel of his soul.

The conclusion, however, to which we have already referred, would suggest that yet another theme may be woven into the fabric of the poem:

> Thus in three ways have I quickly shown you that uncleanness rends the precious heart of the gracious lord who lives in heaven, leads him to anger and rouses his wrath; and purity of heart is his comfort, and elegance (or wisdom) he loves, and those who are seemly and fair shall see his face. May he give us grace to be joyously clad (i.e. to wear the wedding garment), that we may serve before him where joy never ceases.

The theme of wisdom (punningly referred to in this passage together with the clothes imagery of the parable of the 'wedding-garment') can be traced in the story of Nebuchadnezzar. When he recovers from his degradation as a beast of the field, we are told that he came to himself when

> he wyst ful wel who wroȝt alle myȝtes,
> And cowþe uche kyndam tokerve and kever when hym lyked.
> Þenne he wayned hym his wyt, þat hade wo soffered,
> Þat he com to knawlach and kenned hymselven;
> Þenne he loved þat Lorde and leved in trawþe
> Hit watz non oþer þen he þat hade al in honde.[2]

The structure of the poem thus consists of a number of juxta-posed exemplary narratives which develop a number of themes implicit in the initial parable. On the one hand, we have an exploration of the implications of the parable which leads the

---

[1] *Purity*, ll.1143–8. [2] *Purity*, ll.1699–704.

poet in two directions; the direction of 'purity' and the direction of 'loyalty'. In the second place, the poem is an exploration of the implications of the concept of 'purity'. The poem might thus be summarised as follows. The parable of the wedding feast presents us with the need for integrity and loyalty in those who seek the banquet of the kingdom of heaven. The poet then presents his major and minor themes, fleshly purity and loyalty and illustrates these by *exempla* against lechery and pride. We then pass to the theme of confession as a means of purification (a theme linking with the reference to impure priests in the beginning and linked to what follows by the 'vessel' image) and from there to the story of the sack of Jerusalem and Belshazzar's feast, illustrating the themes of defilement and perhaps again loyalty to God. The function of the paratactic structure of homiletic exhortation and exemplary narrative is thus a means by which the poet explores the implications of both the meaning of the parable and the implications of the word 'cleanness'. As Williams has observed, the effect is cumulative.[1] At the same time, it should be noted that the word 'cleanness' itself is throughout the poem semantically enriched, so that when we come to the poet's conclusion, with its repetition of the garment metaphor, the words *coyntyse, clannes,* are ambiguous. On the one hand, they can mean 'skill', 'wisdom' and 'purity', on the other, 'elegance' and 'cleanliness'. The context is carefully organised so that the introductory words raise an expectation of the first group of meaning but the abrupt return to the clothing image in *gay in oure gere,* 'fittingly clothed in our virtues', suggests the other set of meaning also. The whole is thus linked together by a pattern of imagery. The comment of A. C. Spearing on *Patience* could well be applied also to *Purity*: 'One of the poet's great gifts is for the symmetrical ordering of his material, in such a way that one detail always answers another, and a single story grows an extraordinary richness of meaning.'[2]

[1] Cp. Williams, p.216.
[2] A. C. Spearing, '*Patience* and the *Gawain*-Poet', *Anglia,* lxxxiv (1966), 308.

In our discussion of the poems *The Wanderer*, *The Seafarer* and *Purity* we have tried to demonstrate the structure of poems which, while they are not allegorical, are not narrative poems in the usual sense of the word, although they do, in varying degrees, contain a narrative element. Still less has any of them a plot in the sense in which we have been using the word. Their structure, as I have tried to show, is paratactic. The two Old English poems, however, differ from the Middle English poem in that the central figures are types, whereas those in *Purity* are individuals. The surface is, therefore, more richly ornamented, although less suggestive, than that of the Old English poems. One has only to compare the description of the ruin in *The Wanderer* with the description of the destruction of Sodom and Gomorrah to perceive the difference of key between the two poems. Nor would the figure of the exile be readily treated with the particularity of the figure of Nebuchadnezzar in *Purity*.

There are medieval works, however, which, while appearing to be continuous narratives and to deal with individuals not types, have a structure, nevertheless, which has been little understood. The charge against all of them would be that of being episodic in their plot structure. We may best approach these through a famous passage by Chrétien de Troyes. The passage is from his romance *Erec et Enide*:

> Li vilains dit an son respit
> que tel chose a l'an an despit
> qui molt valt mialz que l'an ne cuide;
> . . . .
> Por ce dist Crestïens de Troies
> que reisons est que totevoies
> doit chascuns panser et antandre
> a bien dire et a bien aprandre;
> et tret d'un conte d'avanture
> une molt belle conjointure
> par qu'an puet prover et savoir
> que cil ne fet mie savoir
> qui s'escïence n'abandone
> tant con Dex la grasce l'an done:

d'Erec, le fil Lac, est li contes,
que devant rois et devant contes,
depecier et corronpre suelent
cil qui de conter vivre vuelent.[1]

[*The peasant in his proverb says that many a thing is despised that is worth
much more than is supposed. . . . So Chrétien de Troyes says that it is right
that one should always try and intend to speak and learn well; and he draws
from a story of adventure a very good 'argument' by which it may be proved and
shown that he is not wise who does not make liberal use of his knowledge so
long as God may give him grace. The tale is of Erec, son of Lac which those
who earn their livings by telling stories are accustomed to mutilate and
spoil before kings and counts.*]

This much-debated passage is clearly important as putting
forward Chrétien's view of the difference between his own work
and the tale as told by popular story-tellers. Clearly both he and
the minstrel have in common a tale, a *conte*. The difference must
lie in the treatment of the tale, in the *conjointure*. It seems probable that the term *conjointure* is drawn from Horace's *Ars Poetica*:

In verbis etiam tenuis cautusque serendis
dixeris egregie, notum si callida verbum
reddiderit iunctura novum.[2]

[*Moreover, with a nice taste and care in weaving words together, you will
express yourself most happily, if a skilful setting makes a familiar word
new.*]

And later Horace speaks of *series iuncturaque*, 'order and setting'.[3]
In the first passage the phrase *callida iunctura* seems to imply
that a word or phrase, not in itself new, can be made effective
in a new context. In the second passage, it seems to have the
sense of 'relevance'. It seems likely therefore that Chrétien

---

[1] Chrétien de Troyes, *Erec et Enide*, edited by Mario Roques (Paris, 1955),
ll.1–22; for the related concepts of *sen* and *matière* see *Le Chevalier de la
Charrete*, edited by Mario Roques (Paris, 1958), ll.26–9.
[2] Horace, *Ars Poetica*, ll.46–8; edited by E. C. Wickham (Oxford, 1903);
translation by H. R. Fairclough (London, 1926). It may be noted that
Peter of Blois (*De Amicitia Christiana et de Charitate Dei et proximi*, PL, ccvii,
cols. 871–95) quotes this text in his Prologue to justify the adaptation of old
material to a new use. On Peter of Blois see Southern, pp.105–32.
[3] Horace, *Ars Poetica*, l.242.

intends to use an old tale in a new way by giving it a particular
contextual significance and by setting it within the framework
of a particular theme and so using it as a rhetorical 'argumentum'. The relevance of the parts is to be found in the theme.

Auerbach has an illuminating observation to make on structure of this kind in his book *Mimesis*. He is speaking of the
Old French *Alexis* and he writes

> This figural tradition played no small part in discrediting the
> horizontal, historical connections between events and in en-
> couraging rigidification of all categories. Thus the prayers cited
> above exhibit the figures of redemption completely rigidified. The
> parceling of the events of the Old Testament, which are inter-
> preted figurally in isolation from their historic context, has become
> a formula. The figures – as on the sarcophagi of late antiquity –
> are placed side by side paratactically. They no longer have any
> reality, they have only signification. With respect to the events of
> this world, a similar tendency prevails: to remove them from their
> horizontal context, to isolate the individual fragments, to force
> them into a fixed frame, and, within it, to make them impressive
> gesturally, so that they appear as exemplary, as models, as
> significant, and to leave all 'the rest' in abeyance.[1]

We are in the realm of exemplary action, a realm where action
is not character-revealing but theme-revealing. As Bezzola has
suggested[2] this kind of symbolic action is common in Chrétien.
He demonstrates his thesis for *Erec and Enide* but it could equally
apply to *Yvain*, where we seem to have a working out of the
concept of the proper relationship between prowess, love and
man's duty to society. In these terms the episodes become
meaningful, for the story is not to be seen in terms of individual
character but of exemplary action. With each adventure Yvain

---

[1] E. Auerbach, *Mimesis: The Representation of Reality in Western Literature*,
translated by Willard Trask (Princeton, 1953), p.116. The references have
been checked against the German second edition of 1959. Cp. R. M. Jordan,
Chaucer and the Shape of Creation: the Aesthetic Possibilities of Inorganic Structure
(Cambridge, Mass., 1967) and E. Salter, 'Medieval Poetry and the Visual
Arts', *Essays & Studies*, 1969, 29–31.

[2] R. R. Bezzola, *Le sens de l'aventure et de l'amour* (Paris, 1948), *passim*;
J. Finlayson, '*Ywain and Gawain* and the Meaning of Adventure', *Anglia*,
lxxxvii (1969), 312–37.

learns something of the true nature of the relationship of man to woman and man to man, within the context of chivalric society, and it is the 'demonstrative' nature of the episodes, to use a rhetorical term, and not any revelation of Yvain's character, which is significant. The poem is not an allegory but rather an example of a thematic structure in which the actors are exemplary but neither types nor abstractions. Nor are they *figural* as I have defined the term, because they do not merely represent a point of view as part of an abstract discussion. The *figura* does not so much represent a class of people as one person or member of a class in relation to a particular concept.

Ong has suggested that associated with the development of printing is the development of a particular visual and spatial sense in rhetoric and with the development of Copernican space 'so much more truly spatial than Aristotle's less abstract, directional space', the 'development of the painters' feeling for a similar, abstract space climaxed in the work of Jan van Eyck'.[1] This spatial model is in some degree a structural model also. It is reasonable to distinguish between a modern novel in which a strongly thematic element is projected by a mannered plot and strongly individualised characters, in short, in a naturalistic manner as a temporal and spatial continuum, and a medieval work such as Chrétien's *Yvain*, in which the theme is projected by exemplary characters and whose structure is one of contrasting episodes rather than a plot. The distinction could further be illustrated from *Beowulf*. The structure of the poem has been a battle-ground for critics for so long that it would seem that little remains to be said. Yet the poem is so apposite that it must be considered. Tolkien justified the two parts by assuming a binary structure 'rising and setting'[2] and this view contains much truth. But, while essentially true, it seems to be an oversimplification. It does not explain why the poet chose to make the 'rising' consist of two separate, but similar, episodes, the

[1] W. J. Ong, *Ramus: Method, and the Decay of Dialogue* (Cambridge, Mass., 1958), p.314.

[2] J. R. R. Tolkien, 'Beowulf: the Monsters and the Critics', *PBA*, xxii (1936), 271.

slaying of Grendel and the slaying of Grendel's mother, nor why the poet prefaced the 'setting' by the elaborate section of retrospect generally termed 'Beowulf's return'. For a poet who so ingeniously introduced a whole world of historical references (even though he misguidedly placed them on the perimeter of his tale), this is perhaps surprising. For it seems to me clear that the structure of the poem, if puzzling, is not naïve. And, indeed, if we look at the poem as a pattern of exemplary action, much becomes comprehensible. The fundamental pattern of the poem can be seen in the Scyld prologue. It is one of those elegiac themes which, as we have already pointed out, occupied the mind of Guthlac at the point of conversion: 'antiquorum regum stirpis suae per transacta retro saecula miserabiles exitus flagitioso vitae termino'. The *dramatis persona* is an heroic king. There are brought together into a pattern of exemplary action, the arrival, the rise to fame, and the death of the hero. All the rest of the poem is a development of, and a comment on, this schema. But the development and the comment essentially (in spite of a loose narrative frame) take the form of a paratactic arrangement of similar episodes. It has been rightly observed that 'the narrative method involves juxtaposition of events whose logical connection, at first sight, seems vague'.[1] The first act after the prologue shows the arrival of the hero, his slaying of Grendel and his triumph. But here the pattern of the prologue alters. The theme of the hero's success is further developed and a new theme, that of 'sorrow after joy' introduced. Just so, the different aspects of kingship are explored in the figure of Hrothgar, in the theme of precarious peace in the Fin episode, and in the theme of succession in the Wealhtheow episode. In short, the second adventure, the slaying of Grendel's mother, is necessary, not in order to tell us any more about the hero, who simply goes on being heroic, but to introduce a new theme, the theme of the reversal of fortune. Moreover, it is significant that the elaborate account of the rejoicing after the

---

[1] J. Leyerle, 'Beowulf the hero and the king', *Medium Aevum*, xxxiv (1965), 89; 'The Interlace Structure of *Beowulf*', *University of Toronto Quarterly*, xxxvii (1967), 1–17.

death of Grendel is not repeated after the death of Grendel's mother even though there might seem to be more cause for rejoicing here. Grendel's head is borne back to the Danes and the whole of the fiendish race is destroyed. Yet, instead of a long ritual of panegyric and banquet, we have instead a remarkable example of rhetorical abbreviation:

> Geat wæs glædmod, geong sona to,
> setles neosan, swa se snottra heht.
> Þa wæs eft swa ær ellenrofum,
> fletsittendum fægere gereorded
> niowan stefne. Nihthelm geswearc
> deorc ofer dryhtgumum. Duguð eal aras;
> wolde blondenfeax beddes neosan,
> gamela Scylding.[1]

[*The Geat was glad at heart, he went straight to his seat, as the wise one commanded. Then, yet again, as before, was a feast elegantly prepared for the brave men, the hall-dwellers, on a fresh occasion. The shade of night became more intense, dark over the noble company. The veteran band all arose. The grey-haired warrior wished to seek his bed, the aged Scylding.*]

In the scene of which this passage is the conclusion, the contrast is not as formerly, between the sorrow of King Hrothgar, his triumph after the death of Grendel, and renewed sorrow at the death of Aeschere, but a contrast between Beowulf's triumph and the old king's sorrow at Beowulf's departure. The scene is indeed symbolic. The old king, looking at the sword from the cave, with its reminder of the punishment which falls upon the enemies of God, is moved to warn the triumphant warrior of the dangers of greatness and of its inevitable end. It must be emphasised that the scene is a human scene, its dynamic is human emotion. This is not allegory. Nevertheless, the interest is centred, not in the actors as individuals, but as representative types. It might be entitled 'any king, in his old age, bids farewell to the warrior who has been as a son to him and warns him of the deceitfulness of power and of life's mutability'. We see, as

---

[1] *Beowulf and the Fight at Finnsburg*, edited by F. Klaeber (3rd edn., London, 1950), ll.1785-92.

it were, Hrothgar in three significant postures; the grief-stricken king, the generous rewarder of heroism, and the old man, warning his beloved son of future sorrow. The initial scheme, as set forth in the prologue, arrival, fame, death, is here set forth again but, to use a musical analogy, in a developed form. In the last section, the pattern is repeated for the third and last time. Beowulf arrives home, becomes king and slays, and is slain by, the dragon. The pace is slower, the picture dilated,[1] the king's action projected against a wide historical canvas of feud and death. We have now three pictures of the life of a hero, firstly Scyld, the triumphant hero-king whose departure is more splendid than his arrival. Even in death he seems to triumph as he departs into the mysterious unknown. Then King Hrothgar and Beowulf are seen in success and reversal of fortune; and finally we have the picture of Beowulf himself, whose rise and fall straddles and links the last two parts of the poem, and whose life presents us with a mirror image of the life of Scyld. For Scyld's death presaged the rise to glory of his people, whereas that of Beowulf presaged the downfall of his nation. If this sounds fanciful and over-sophisticated, it must be remembered that both themes and actions are conventional. No Anglo-Saxon poet would have to sit down to work out their significance to combine them into a meaningful pattern. They would surely come to him as naturally as the leaves on the tree. All the poet has told is three traditional types of story three times over, varying them at each stage of the telling.[2] This is the technique of fairy tales the world over.[3]

[1] Cp. G. J. Engelhardt, '*Beowulf:* a study in Dilatation', *PMLA*, lxx (1955), 825–52.

[2] It is impossible to summarise all the literature on the topic of the poem's structure, but some recent discussion may be noted such as A. Bonjour, The Digressions in '*Beowulf*' (Oxford, 1950); A. G. Brodeur, 'The Structure and the Unity of *Beowulf*', *PMLA*, lxviii (1953), 1183–95; *The Art of Beowulf* (Berkeley & Los Angeles, 1959), pp.132–81; H. L. Rogers, 'Beowulf's Three Great Fights', *RES*, vi (1955), 339–55; K. Sisam, *The Structure of Beowulf* (Oxford, 1965). For the rest the reader may refer to Klaeber's bibliography.

[3] For the structure of primitive literatures see especially Axel Olrik, 'Epische Gesetze der Volksdichtung', *ZfDA*, xxxix (1909), 1–12; H. & A. Thornton and A. A. Lind, *Time and Style* (London, 1962).

I have said nothing of the 'episodes and digressions'.[1] They introduce new themes and elaborate old ones but I have not discussed them in detail because the technique they imply is essentially the same as that which I have suggested for the main plot. They too come within the field of exemplary action. This is all I have to add to the immense and ingenious discussion; any interpretation of the structure of *Beowulf* must be in terms of the typical, the general, the conventional. The poem is not an allegory nor is it a novel, but it belongs to that large class of exemplary tales which is so characteristic of the Middle Ages and whose nature is only now coming to be understood. The exemplary character has a natural corollary in the exemplary action, and the exemplary action has a natural corollary in the thematic structure. All three I believe to be present in *Beowulf*.

It is instructive to compare the structure of *Beowulf* with some medieval symmetrical structures such as *Sir Gawain and the Green Knight*, or Chaucer's *Knight's Tale*. The view I have put forward, that *Beowulf* is a neat threefold structure, with the last two episodes linked by a kind of thematic bracket, might suggest that I am trying to claim that its structure is as mannered as that of the two late medieval poems. This is clearly not the case. The apparent difference in the poems is perfectly real. It is true that *Gawain*, like *Beowulf*, has a repetitive structure. Just as similar episodes continually recur in *Beowulf*, two ship burials, three monster slayings, two dragon slayings, three hall defences, and so on, so the *Gawain* poet repeats themes and episodes. Thus the poem is placed in a frame of Arthurian legend. The scene at Arthur's court at the beginning is balanced by a scene at Arthur's court at the end. The challenge is made on New Year's Day; the requital is given on New Year's Day. Life at the Green Knight's court is equally symmetrical. We have three evening parties, three temptation scenes, there hunting scenes. Moreover, each hunting scene is used as a kind of frame for the equivalent temptation scene. Thus we find the episode of the first kiss inserted into the first hunt, dividing it

[1] Cp. A. Bonjour, 'The Technique of Parallel Descriptions in *Beowulf*', *RES.* ii (1951), 1–10.

into two parts and so with the other two. The rendering of the kiss in each case is accompanied by festivities.[1] We have parallel journeys through a winter landscape, parallel arming scenes and so on. Why then is the structure of *Beowulf* obscure to a modern reader, while that of *Gawain* is lucidly clear? I think there are two reasons. In the first place, and most obviously, the Gawain poet has created suspense by a kind of encapsulating technique. The two beheadings not only match each other but the second was predicted at the same time as the first. The careful interweaving of the temptation and the hunting scenes is necessitated by the exchange of winnings just as the second beheading is causally connected with the first, while the *Beowulf* poet's plot elements are complete narratives in themselves, and the pattern is in a sense self-sufficient at each stage, with its own rise and fall. There are thus no necessary narrative links between the parts. Whereas the death of Scyld does not cause the ravages of Grendel and all that follow therefrom, nor the slaying of Grendel and Grendel's mother necessitate Beowulf's return and his death, the *Gawain* poet has given us a plot in which the events are necessitated by the actions of the characters within the story. In *Beowulf*, all we appear to have is a loose chronological sequence and the connections are all thematic. In *Gawain* on the other hand, the events all spring from the initial challenge; and, if the visit to Hautdesert appears at first sight yet another chivalric adventure of the kind familiar to readers of medieval romances, this is only part of the poet's practical joke upon the reader. The identity of Bertilak and the Green Knight locks the episode firmly into the structure of the whole. It is as though Beowulf's dragon should turn out to be Grendel in disguise, and Hrothgar a reincarnation of Scyld.

---

[1] S. Barnet, 'A Note on the Structure of *Sir Gawain and the Green Knight*', *MLN*, lxxi (1956), 319; D. B. J. Randall, 'A Note on Structure in *Sir Gawain and the Green Knight*', *MLN*, lxxii (1957), 161–3; D. R. Howard, 'Structure and Symmetry in *Sir Gawain*', *Speculum*, xxxix (1964), 425–33; for the balancing of sound effects cp. A. Renoir, 'An Echo to the Sense; The Patterns of Sound in *Sir Gawain and the Green Knight*', *English Miscellany*, xiii (1962), 9–23; V. F. Petronella, '*St. Erkenwald*: style as the Vehicle for Meaning', *JEGP*, lxvi (1967), 538–9.

The fact that these are only parallel types and not identical persons (if I may be allowed to term the dragon a person) makes it difficult for the modern reader to identify them. The first difference between the structure of *Beowulf* and *Sir Gawain and the Green Knight* is thus in the way the episodes are arranged, those of the *Beowulf* poet being, as it were, stood in a row, and those of the *Gawain* poet being interlaced. The structure of *Beowulf* is that of a folk-tale, of *Gawain* that of a *virelai* or *ballade*. It thus appears that the links which, in *Beowulf*, are purely thematic, are, in Gawain, part of a space-time continuum, and the episodes are linked by a pattern of causation as well as by a simple symmetry of arrangement. Something of the difference between the two poems can be seen in miniature, if we compare the *hund missera* that Grendel ravaged Heorot, with the year within which the action of *Sir Gawain and the Green Knight* takes place. In the Old English poem we are looking into the 'dark backward and abysm of time', in the other at a brightly lit peep-show.

The second difference is perhaps more interesting. In *Beowulf* we compare a number of different people from different eras of Danish and Geatish history. To equate Beowulf with Scyld, we have to perform a process of abstraction. Only then can we understand the thematic relationship of the different parts of the poem. In Gawain it is different. We have the parts linked together in a plot-like structure. Yet the marked symmetry of structure has a function which is comparable to the technique of juxtaposition in *Beowulf*. If we consider the two scenes in which Gawain encounters the Green Knight, the function of this symmetry of structure becomes apparent. In the first, the brusque challenger, whose rudeness is apparent even in his speech,[1] although, as John Burrow has pointed out,[2] his station is evident in his dress and figure, is contrasted with the brave and courtly Gawain who is the

---

[1] See C. Clark, '*Sir Gawain and the Green Knight:* Characterisation by Syntax', *Essays in Criticism*, xvi (1966), 361–74.

[2] See J. A. Burrow, *A Reading of 'Sir Gawain and the Green Knight'* (London, 1965), pp.14–17.

epitome of knighthood even down to his courteous request to leave the table. But when he encounters the Green Knight again the roles are reversed; or not quite reversed. The fabric of the tale does indeed reverse them neatly. The challenger returns the blow. This is necessary to emphasise the structural parallel. But the roles of the two men have not been precisely reversed but rather we have moved on a kind of upward spiral. Gawain has moved into the sphere of self-knowledge and sees the nature of his fault – or so he thinks. But his remorse is perhaps excessive. When the Green Knight tells him that he took the green girdle because he loved his life, 'I blame you the less', we may think that the author himself speaks, for we remember *Patience* 'For be monnes lode neuer so luþer, þe lyf is ay swete.'[1] Clearly, Gawain's conduct has been at fault but nevertheless we have moved into an area of moral casuistry. At the beginning of the tale the moral dimensions are clear-cut. Gawain exemplifies them, his shield symbolises them. Now we return to a parallel encounter with the Green Knight in which absolutes have been replaced by priorities. We see Gawain in truly human proportions, angry with the Green Knight, angry with himself and angry with all womankind. And another reversal is to come. When Gawain returns to the court they laugh and comfort him and tell him that he has done well and, by their very praise, they cut him down to size. In the first scene, at King Arthur's court, they laugh at the Green Knight as he rides out of the hall. Now it is at Gawain that they laugh and again the earlier scene is a mirror image of the other. And the Green Knight too has assumed human proportions; he is no longer the stern supernatural challenger but the moral mentor and humane judge who politely asks Gawain to return and visit him. Thus the structural parallel serves to underline the changed perspective and the ironic reversal of the second part of the poem.

Gawain's two journeys to the Green Chapel would serve as another example. In the first, we have Gawain as the typical knight errant. Like Alexander in the romances bearing his

---

[1] *Patience*, edited by J. J. Anderson (Manchester, 1969), l.156.

name, he fights against supernatural and mythical creatures;
bulls, bears and satyrs. The poet praises him in hyperbolical
terms:

> Mony klyf he ouerclambe in contrayez straunge,
> Fer floten fro his frendez fremedly he rydez.
> At vche warþe oþer water þer þe wyȝe passed
> He fonde a foo hym byfore, bot ferly hit were,
> And þat so foule and so felle þat feȝt hym byhode.
> So mony meruayl bi mount þer þe mon fyndez,
> Hit were to tore for to telle of þe tenþe dole.
> Sumwhyle wyth wormez he werrez, and with wolues als,
> Sumwhyle wyth wodwos, þat woned in þe knarrez,
> Boþe wyth bullez and berez, and borez oþerquyle,
> And etaynez, þat hym anelede of þe heȝe felle;
> Nade he ben duȝty and dryȝe, and Dryȝtyn had serued,
> Douteles he hade ben ded and dreped ful ofte.[1]

In the second journey, to the Green Chapel, we have again moved
on an upward spiral. For one thing, we see events closer at hand.
Instead of a catalogue of dangers surmounted, we have a
genuine moral temptation in the person of the guide; on the other
hand, there is again a certain area of moral ambiguity because
Gawain is wearing the green girdle. There is also an increasing
duality of vision. As Gawain approaches the Green Chapel,
we are presented with two contrary movements of mood. On
the one hand, a mood of deflation.

> Þenne he boȝez to þe berȝe, aboute hit he walkez,
> Debatande with hymself quat hit be myȝt.
> Hit hade a hole on þe ende and on ayþer syde,
> And ouergrowen with gresse in glodes aywhere,
> And al watz holȝ inwith, nobot an olde caue,
> Or a creuisse of an olde cragge, he couþe hit noȝt deme
> with spelle.
> > 'We! Lorde,' quoþ þe gentyle knyȝt,
> > 'Wheþer þis be þe grene chapelle?
> > Here myȝt aboute mydnyȝt
> > Þe dele his matynnes telle!'[2]

---

[1] *Sir Gawain and the Green Knight*, edited by J. R. R. Tolkien and E. V.
Gordon; revised by N. Davis (Oxford, 1968), ll.713–25.
[2] *Sir Gawain and the Green Knight*, ll.2178–88.

But Gawain's response is not one of relief but of panic:

> 'Now iwysse,' quoþ Wowayn, 'wysty is here;
> Þis oritore, is vgly, with erbez ouergrowen;
> Wel bisemez þe wyȝe wruxled in grene
> Dele here his deuocioun on þe deuelez wyse.
> Now I fele hit is þe fende, in my fyue wyttez,
> Þat hatz stoken me þis steuen to strye me here.
> Þis is a chapel of meschaunce, þat chekke hit bytyde!'[1]

Here too the poet has differentiated the two journeys. In the first we see merely externals. Here we see both the actuality and Gawain's response to it. Gawain is becoming more and more detached from his background. Yet he is still moving in the world of the supernatural; he does not yet realise the true nature of his trial. And here too we see the function of the symmetrical structure. Not only does the story constantly increase in complexity but the scale alters as between one 'shot' and another. If, for example, we compare Gawain's arrival at the Green Knight's castle with his arrival at the chapel we see a neat reversal of situation; in the first instance, he thinks the castle is natural, although the reader suspects that it is supernatural. In the last scene, the dreaded Green Chapel, the enchanted destination of his journey, turns out to be 'nobot an olde caue'.

Moreover, if we compare the two beheading scenes it is like passing from the land of the Lilliputians to the land of the Brobdingnagians. In the second, every detail of Gawain's reactions is described. Let us put the two passages side by side.

> The grene knyȝt vpon grounde grayþely hym dresses,
> A littel lut with þe hede, þe lere he discouerez,
> His longe louelych lokkez he layd ouer his croun,
> Let the naked nec to þe note schewe.
> Gauan gripped to his ax, and gederes hit on hyȝt,
> Þe kay fot on þe folde he before sette,
> Let hit doun lyȝtly lyȝt on þe naked,
> Þat þe scharp of þe schalk schyndered þe bones

---

[1] *Sir Gawain and the Green Knight*, ll.2189–95.

And schrank þurȝ þe schyire grece, and schade hit in twynne,
Þat þe bit of þe broun stel bot on þe grounde.
Þe fayre hede fro þe halce hit to þe erþe.
Þat fele hit foyned wyth her fete, þere hit forth roled;[1]

If we compare this with the final decapitation scene, several
points emerge. In the first place, whereas the description in the
first scene is largely visual there is, in the second, not only visual
detail, such as the axe with the long lace, the Green Knight's
puckering 'lip and brow' as he prepared to strike, the blood
shining on the ground as a sign that Gawain had fulfilled his
bargain and can now return the Green Knight's hostility; far
more than these we notice the careful recording of Gawain's
reactions. He greets Bertilak's stupendous whetting with the
rueful remark

> þat gere, as I trowe,
> Is ryched at þe reuerence me, renk, to mete
> bi rote.
> Let God worche! 'We loo' –
> Hit helppez me not a mote.
> My life þaȝ I forgoo,
> Drede dotz me no lote.[2]

When the Green Knight reproves him for flinching, he replies

> I schunt onez,
> And so wyl I no more;
> Bot þaȝ my hede falle on þe stonez,
> I con not hit restore.[3]

We see the Green Knight feinting:

> He myntez at hym maȝtyly, bot not þe mon rynez,
> Withhelde heterly his honde, er hit hurt myȝt.
> Gawayn grayþely hit bydez, and glent with no membre,
> Bot stode stylle as þe ston, oþer a stubbe auþer
> Þat raþeled is in roché grounde with rotez a hundreth.[4]

---

[1] Sir Gawain and the Green Knight, ll.417–28.
[2] Sir Gawain and the Green Knight, ll.2205–11.
[3] Sir Gawain and the Green Knight, ll.2280–3.
[4] Sir Gawain and the Green Knight, ll.2290–4.

But Gawain, screwed up to the limit, standing as still as a stone, or a tree stump in rocky ground, does not realise what he is doing. He is angry, his nerves taut and he protests:

> Wy, þresch on, þou þro mon, þou þretez to longe;
> I hope þat þi hert arȝe wyth þyn awen seluen.[1]

Then the Green Knight takes up his position to strike:

> No meruayle þaȝ hym myslyke
> Þat hoped of no rescowe.[2]

But we have not only a marvellously realistic picture of Gawain's emotions in the situation, but an interplay of emotion. We are told that when Gawain springs up to attack Bercilak, 'in hert hit him lykez'[3] and he speaks to Gawain in much the same terms as those in which God speaks to Jonah:

> Bolde burne, on þis bent be not so gryndel.
> No mon here vnmanerly þe mysboden habbez,
> Ne kyd bot as couenaunde at kyngez cort schaped.[4]

Thus, as we are referred back to the original covenant, we realise that we have seen the counterpart in one sense of the first scene, so like in visual details, the sharpness of the axe, the bowing of the head, the falling of the axe so that it cut into the flesh. But the story line has been enriched by the addition of harmonies. I have looked at only two passages in detail but there are other instances in which the circular structure serves to emphasise the psychological evolution of the characters or to add another dimension to the story. The parallel hunting and temptation scenes are an obvious case. It might be objected that one can find a similar use of the technique in works outside the Middle Ages. Some of the novels of Dickens, for example, would afford illustration of the use of a sub-plot as a comment upon the main action, or the plays of Shakespeare. But the *Gawain* poet is distinctive in using what is basically a decorative and

---

[1] *Sir Gawain and the Green Knight*, ll.2300–1.
[2] *Sir Gawain and the Green Knight*, ll.2307–8.
[3] *Sir Gawain and the Green Knight*, l.2335.
[4] *Sir Gawain and the Green Knight*, ll.2338–40.

rhetorical device for this purpose. It is perhaps, in the last re-
sort, a matter of proportion. The intention to contrast large
blocks of narrative seems to be demonstrated by the treatment
of the hunting and temptation scenes where the three hunts
and the three temptations are described at equal length, like
contrasting and complementary triptychs. This is not the interweaving of a plot and sub-plot but a deliberate juxtaposition
of amplifications. Like the *Beowulf* poet, he brings the camera
nearer as the poem draws to its conclusion, but he is not contrasting complex narrative sequences, as the *Beowulf* poet does,
but rather single shots, carefully laid side by side, in what is a
single carefully constructed plot. One might summarise by
quoting the observations of Ferdinand Lot on the topic of
entrelacement: '. . . Le *Lancelot* n'est pas une mosaïque d'òu l'on
pourrait avec adresse enlever des cubes pour les remplacer par
d'autres, c'est une sparterie ou une tapisserie; si l'on tente d'y
pratiquer une coupure, tout part en morceaux.'[1]

This leads us to our last topic, the technique of *entrelacement*.
Vinaver has written:

> A character, according to the modern critical convention, does
> certain things because of what he is; or, to be more precise, be-
> cause what we know of the laws of human behaviour makes it
> necessary for him to act as he does. There is, however, another
> form of motivation – more closely related to the narrative medium
> and divorced from all logical or psychological reference: a form
> which depends for its effect upon a perceptible structural relation-
> ship between two or more incidents.

He gives an example from the Vulgate Lancelot. To clear
Guinevere of a false accusation and rescue her from punishment, Lancelot has to fight single-handed three knights.

> But as the combat is about to begin Gawain steps forward, ties
> with his own hands the leather straps of Lancelot's helmet, and
> girds his own sword, Excalibur, about Lancelot, praying him to
> carry it for his, Gawain's sake. And Lancelot says that he would
> do so willingly.

---

[1] F. Lot, *Étude sur le Lancelot en Prose* (Paris, 1918), p.28.

This appears a pointless episode, since Lancelot's own sword is also invincible. But it is intended, in Vinaver's opinion, as a foil to the episode later in the story where Lancelot and Gawain become bitter enemies:

> in the ensuing struggle between the two best knights of Arthur's kingdom Excalibur appears again; it is with Excalibur that Gawain strikes Lancelot in a fierce combat in which he himself receives a fatal wound. What was once a symbol of his love for Lancelot now becomes a reminder of the broken bond between the two truest friends united by ties stronger than those of blood.

And he concludes

> An awe-inspiring sense of continuity, of a constantly unfolding panorama stretching as far into the past as into the future – such are the rewards to be reaped by a reader whose memory can meet the challenge of interwoven 'branches' and themes and who can detect beneath and behind them an uninterrupted chain of events.[1]

Interesting examples of this technique can be found in the works of Malory. Vinaver has argued that Malory largely destroyed the *entrelacement* of his rendering of the French texts.[2] I believe this to be a matter of degree rather than of kind, and propose, in this connection, to consider the story of Balin and *The Book of Sir Launcelot and Queen Guinevere*. Let us begin with the story of Balin. The story has one main linked theme and two main independent themes. The linked theme is the tale of destruction of the eleven kings, already predicted in *The Tale of Merlin*:

> For thes eleven kyngis shall dye all in one day by the grete myght and prouesse of armys of two valyaunte knyghtes – as hit tellith

---

[1] E. Vinaver, *Form and Meaning in Medieval Romance*, The Presidential Address of the Modern Humanities Research Association, 1966, pp.18–20; cp. 'King Arthur's Sword', *Bulletin of the John Rylands Library*, xl (1958), 513–26; *The Rise of Romance* (London, 1971).

[2] *The Works of Sir Thomas Malory*, edited by E. Vinaver (2nd edn, Oxford, 1967), pp.lxiv–lxxiii.

aftir. Hir namys ben Balyne le Saveage and Balan, hys brothir, that were marveylous knyghtes as ony was tho lyvynge.[1]

The linked theme is thus part of a larger theme, King Arthur's Northern Wars, and it is structurally significant in that Pellinore's slaying of King Lot, there related, is the cause of Gawain's slaying of Pellinore and Lamorak, his son, and this slaying, in turn, is the reason why Sir Pynell tried to poison Sir Gawain – the disastrous episode which ends in the indictment of Guinevere and her rescue by Lancelot. This first theme, then, the theme of the Northern Wars, is part of a pattern of vendetta which forms, as it were, the skeleton of the whole work. As Moorman has pointed out, Malory has made certain alterations to his source to underline the pattern of feud running through it. Most notably, Sir Pynell is made a relative of Lamorak and thus the poisoning of Sir Patryse, attributed to Guinevere, exacerbates the feud with Lancelot. Lancelot is thus drawn into a double feud, that with Arthur, and that with the sons of Lot.[2] Thus the intricate pattern of relationships cuts across the artificial structure of the tales and forms a tragic framework enclosing the whole work. *The Tale of Balin* thus has not only internal contrasts but links with a larger whole of which it forms a part, and is a good example of the technique of *entrelacement*.

The first independent theme is Balin's acquiring of the sword from the Lady Lyle of Avilion, the cursed sword with which he kills his brother Balan. The second is the story of the death of Lanceor at the hands of the ill-fated knight, Balin and the consequential death of the Lady Columbe. This Balin fails to prevent. Later, the quest for the felon knight Garlon ensues. This in turn results in the striking of the Dolorous Stroke in the hall

---

[1] Malory, *Morte Darthur*, p.40; cp. Vinaver's note (*Works*, III, 1297) on p.41, 3–10; for the structure of *Balin* see pp.1276–8.

[2] Cp. C. Moorman, 'Lot and Pellinore: The Failure of Loyalty in Malory's *Morte Darthur*', *Mediaeval Studies*, xxv (1963), 83–92, and C. Moorman, *The Book of Kyng Arthur* (Lexington, 1965), pp.49–63. For emphasis on the essential unity of the work, cp. also D. S. Brewer, 'Form in the "Morte Darthur" ', *Medium Aevum*, xxi (1952), 14–24.

of King Pellam. These two stories are episodically narrated in the course of the book. With these we shall deal in detail. There are also two episodes which appear to be unrelated to the book as a whole. One is the story of the Maiden's Blood, which is, however, later connected with the Grail theme of which it forms a part. The other is the story of Garnyssh of the Mounte, the knight who kills himself because Balin shows him the unfaithfulness of his lady. This has a function in the portrayal of Balin, although it is told as a self-contained episode and is therefore irrelevant to our discussion of the use of *entrelacement* in *The Tale of Balin*.

If we compare Malory's story of Balin with a modern rendering, such as Tennyson's treatment in the *Idylls of the King*, our first reaction is that it has too many episodes. Yet, a closer inspection shows that Malory has produced a perfectly balanced tale. For the technique of *entrelacement* provides exactly that tension which the *sententia* of the tale requires. If Tennyson's Balin is an exemplum of wrath, Malory's Balin is the doomed man whose every action brings disaster and who defies his fate until it at last overcomes him. Mrs. Loomis has written: 'It is [Malory] alone who releases the tragic primary episodes of the story from trivial and unrelated things, who has focussed all the interest on the figure of Balin, and who has enhanced . . . the sense of mystery and of "swift oncoming doom".'[1] Malory indeed has shown excellent judgement, not only in what he omits, but in what he keeps, the shape of the story. For what we have is a separation of the two parts, prophecy and fulfilment, by examples of Balin's fated actions. The first act is the drawing of the magic and fated sword (later used by Lancelot to slay Gawain) and the slaying of the Lady of the Lake. This is followed by a series of interwoven episodes. The actions of Balin are welded into the fabric of the whole work by his departure to fight King Rions, a figure already familiar from earlier

---

[1] L. H. Hibbard, 'Malory's Book of Balin', in *Medieval Studies in Memory of Gertrude Schoepperle Loomis*, edited by R. S. Loomis (Paris & New York, 1927), p.179.

books.[1] But he does not yet begin his war against the northern kings. For an Irish knight, Lanceor, rides after Balin to slay him but, before the battle takes place, we have an explanation from Merlin of the earlier episode of the Lady of the Lake. Thus even before the fight with Lanceor begins we have, as it were, a shadow thrown by the figure of Merlin and his explanation of the earlier episode. Indeed his only function is to be prophetic and fateful. And appropriately, for the fight with Lanceor, for all its random appearance, leads to the Dolorous Stroke. Malory then continues the story of the fight and Lanceor is slain. His lady, Columbe, commits suicide, a death which is to cost Balin dear; for, as Merlin explains, this death shall result in the striking of the Dolorous Stroke. Then the story changes course. Balan and Balin set off in search of King Rions and the battle against the northern kings takes place. Here again Malory introduces a seemingly irrelevant episode. A knight, Berbeus, arrives at court and is slain by an invisible knight, Garlon. This appears to be a trivial marvel. Yet it is this supernatural knight who leads Balin to his doom; ironically, because Balin hopes to avenge the victims of Garlon, Berbeus, Peryne de Mounte Belyarde and the knight whose son has been wounded by Garlon. Balin indeed achieves his vengeance but, in the course of achieving it, he takes up the Grail spear and strikes the Dolorous Stroke for which vengeance falls upon him. Thus Balin brings disaster to those whom he seeks to help; as he does yet again in the encounter with Garnyssh of the Mounte whose death he causes by showing to him his lady's unfaithfulness. Then we move to the final scene. Balin arrives at the castle where his death is to take place.

> And soo he herd an horne blowe as it had ben the dethe of a best; 'That blast,' said Balyn, 'is blowen for me, for I am the pryse, and yet am I not dede.'[2]

---

[1] Other links may be noted, such as the inscription of the tomb of Lanceor and Columbe with the names of Lancelot and Tristram. Cp. also, T. C. Rumble, 'Malory's *Balin* and the Question of Unity in the *Morte Darthur*', *Speculum*, xli (1966), 68–85.

[2] Malory, *Morte Darthur*, p.88.

They explain to him the custom of the castle and he agrees to joust.

> 'Wel,' sayd Balyn, 'syn I shalle, therto I am redy; but traveillynge men are ofte wery and their horses to, but though my hors be wery my hert is not wery. I wold be fayne ther my deth shold be.'[1]

They take away his shield, and give him a better one. Thus he is unknown to Balan when he meets him in the tournament. He fights his brother and they slay each other.

> Ryght so cam the lady of the toure with four knyghtes and six ladyes and six yomen unto them, and there she herd how they made her mone eyther to other and sayd 'We came bothe oute of one wombe, that is to say one moders bely, and so shalle we lye bothe in one pytte.' So Balan prayd the lady of her gentylnesse for his true servyse that she wold burye them bothe in that same place there the bataille was done, and she graunted hem with wepynge it shold be done rychely in the best maner.[2]

And so ends the story of Balin about whose head

> the wind of fate,
> Blew storm and cloud from death's wide gate.

Saintsbury speaks of 'a wonderful symphonic arrangement, as in the close of the story of Balin';[3] a 'symphonic arrangement' indeed but, if by this is meant a complex interrelation of contrasting themes and tones,[4] it is equally true of the story of Balin as a whole.

At first sight it may seem to the modern reader that the same theme is better managed in *Sohrab and Rustum* or the *Hildebrandslied*. In these the one combat between father and son is concentrated in a single episode of impressive intensity. The chance that brought together father and son *was* a chance, as in the story of Balin, but chance ironically and purposefully directed to a single tragic climax. The episodes in the Balin story do not spring from character; yet neither do they appear

---

[1] Malory, *Morte Darthur*, p.88.

[2] Malory, *Morte Darthur*, p.90.

[3] G. Saintsbury, *A History of English Prose Rhythm* (London, 1912), p.91.

[4] For contrasting tones cp. E. Vinaver, *Le Roman de Balain*, edited by M. D. Legge (Manchester, 1942), pp.xxiii–xxv.

essential for the tragic climax. They are simply further exemplifications of the ill-fated actions of Balin. They repeat with paratactic insistence the theme of Balin's mortal touch. Their function is not to explore or exemplify the character of Balin but rather to form a relentless concatenation of events which can destroy a man. It is the actions themselves that matter and not any light that they might cast upon Balin as an individual. And as the web is woven, we become aware of the schematic nature of the episodes, a schematic quality necessary to make the thematic pattern plain. If, for example, we take the story of Garnyssh of the Mounte this quality is plainly exemplified. Balin searches for the lady

> fro chamber to chambir and fond her bedde, but she was not there. Thenne Balen loked into a fayr litil gardyn, and under a laurel tre he sawe her lye upon a quylt of grene samyte, and a knyght in her armes fast halsynge eyther other, and under their hedes grasse and herbes.[1]

This brief pastoral, pared away from a longer and more circumstantial account in the French, gives the essence of the scene. And when Garnyssh sees her

> for pure sorou his mouth and nose brast oute on bledynge.[2]

And the conversation that passes between them, after Garnyssh has slain the lovers, says with the greatest brevity all that the scene implies.

> O Balyn! Moche sorow hast thow brought unto me, for haddest thow not shewed me that syght I shold have passed my sorow.[3]

Balin replies, 'God knoweth I dyd none other but as I wold ye dyd to me.'[4] Yet the outcome is the suicide of Garnyssh. Here we have, in one brief episode, the essence of *The Tale of Balin*; the sense of swift, unpredictable reversal of fortune, the ironic relationship between a man's intentions and his fate; all

---

[1] Malory, *Morte Darthur*, p.87.
[2] Malory, *Morte Darthur*, p.87.
[3] Malory, *Morte Darthur*, p.87.
[4] Malory, *Morte Darthur*, p.87.

narrated with a brevity which brings into prominence the structure of the whole tale. And thus by the interweaving of the episodes, each one apparently new, yet each contributing to the sense of doom, a doom as inexplicable as the appearance of Merlin or of the invisible knight himself, as relentless and inconsequential as a dream, Malory has achieved the richly orchestrated tale of the Knight with the Two Swords.

Our second episode is the story of the Maid of Astolat. The story is well known from Tennyson's telling of it in the *Idylls of the King*. At first sight, Tennyson's retelling of it as an independent episode has much to commend it. Yet when we look more closely at the tale as told by Malory, and the French *Mort Artu*, we observe some of the characteristic merits of the medieval method of story-telling. The story itself is simple and well known. The Fair Maid of Astolat dies for love of Lancelot and her body is laid, at her request, on a barge and floats down to Camelot. Since this is a case where Malory has altered his material, it will be useful to look at both versions. The French *Mort Artu*[1] has the following story: after the return from the quest of the Grail, Agravain, the brother of Gawain denounces Lancelot to the king. The king does not heed him but departs for a tournament at Winchester. Lancelot, also intending to go to the tournament, but *incognito*, takes his leave of the queen. He lodges with a rich vavasour and borrows his son's shield in order to avoid recognition at the tournament. The vavasour's daughter, the Maid of Astolat, falls in love with Lancelot and makes him promise to wear her sleeve at the tournament. In the tournament, Lancelot is wounded by Bors and departs. Gawain and Gaheriet go in search of him but return unsuccessful. In the meantime, another tournament has been proclaimed at Tanebourc. Gawain and Gaheriet have left Winchester and lodge at Escalot and Gawain is put to sleep in the room in which is Lancelot's shield. He hears the whole story from the vavasour's daughter. Gawain then returns to Camelot and the king tells him of the suspicions of Agravain. Gawain, thinking,

[1] *La Mort le Roi Artu*, edited by Jean Frappier (Geneva & Lille, 1954); for the structure cp. *Étude sur 'Le Mort le Roi Artu'* (Geneva, 1968), pp.347–71.

as a result of his visit to Escalot, that Lancelot is in love with the vavasour's daughter, bids him take no heed of Agravain's suspicions. But the queen also hears the story and is deeply distressed. Renewed search is made for Lancelot, who, because of his wound, cannot come to the tournament at Tanebourc. The queen, however, does not believe that his absence is due to the wound. The story then tells how Arthur spends a night at the castle of Morgan le Fay. There a series of murals reveals to him Lancelot's love for Guinevere. He swears that he will avenge his shame. In the meantime, Lancelot is cured and hopes to attend the tournament. The Maid of Astolat is dying for love of him and the queen is still angry. There follows the episode of the poisoned apple and the burial of Gaheriz. In the meantime Lancelot has been wounded again in a hunting accident. Then Mador de la Porte learns of the death of his brother by the poisoned apple. At this point, the death-boat of the Maid of Astolat arrives at Camelot and Gawain realises that he has misjudged Lancelot and so does the queen. Lancelot sets out to defend the queen against the charge of giving Gaheriz the poisoned apple and is victorious. Then we pass to the story of how Agravain entrapped Lancelot with the queen.

Now when we consider this narrative certain points of interest emerge. In an obvious sense, the episodes are interlaced. The author, for example, breaks up the story of the Maid of Astolat and intersperses the tournaments and the story of the king's suspicions of Lancelot. The theme of Lancelot's incapacity and disappearance is used more than once. Thus in an obvious way the story could be described as episodic. In fact, the French writer frequently proclaims that this is his intention. 'Now the story leaves so and so,' he says, 'and turns to so and so.' Equally obvious is it that Malory has detached the story of the Maid of Astolat from the story of the poisoned apple. But I believe there is rather more than a simple change from a medieval structure in the French tale to a modern type of narrative in Malory. It must firstly be observed that the French tale, although apparently flouting the principle of 'one action', in fact moves within a psychological continuum. Analysed not

as a series of episodes, but in relation to the psychological movement of the whole, three psychological forces are seen to be at
work in a unified field; the mounting suspicions of the king, the
jealousy of the queen, the devotion of Lancelot. All these inter-
act to bring about the downfall of the Round Table. Now, the
action, apparently so fragmented, is carefully related to this
psychological field, and forms, one might say, a contrapuntal
system of motivation and action. The story might be analysed
as follows: we have, on the one hand, the tournaments of
Winchester and Tanebourc, two focal points of the action. On
the other hand, the psychological motivation has four focal
points; the denunciation of Agravain at the beginning; the king's
visit to Arthur's castle; the conversation of the brothers of
Gawain about the love of Lancelot and Guinevere; the trap
of Agravain. These four scenes, all concerned with the theme
of the king's jealousy, are carefully interwoven with the theme
of Guinevere's jealousy. Thus the story of the Maid of Astolat
has a two-fold function in the plot; namely, to increase the
jealousy of Guinevere and to lull the suspicions of Gawain,
since he thinks that Lancelot is in love with the Maid of Astolat.
His suspicions, however, revive upon the death of the Maid.
Thus the death of the Maid is significantly placed so that it has
a double function in the psychological development of the
story. It firstly proves to Guinevere that her suspicions of
Lancelot are unfounded, and this just at the moment when
she is accused of the death of Gaheriz. It thus increases her
anguish. In the second place, it increases the suspicions of
Gawain and others of the queen's guilt just at the moment
when she most needs a champion to defend her. In the same
way, the search for Lancelot, on the face of it a senseless romance
convention, brings Gawain into contact with the Maid of
Astolat and thus has a function in the psychological development of the tale. Malory seems indeed to have made this closely
woven tale, truly a tapestry, with the threads running throughout the fabric, into a mosaic, in which each piece can be removed without substantial damage to the whole. But has he,
in fact, moved, as Vinaver claims, from the world of medieval

narrative to the modern world? The most strikingly obvious point is that he has rearranged the tale, as it were, in larger blocks. Thus, for example, although he keeps the interwoven narrative of the tournament at Winchester and the Maid of Astolat, he detaches the story from that of the poisoned apple and altogether omits the episode of Arthur's visit to Morgan's castle; partly, no doubt, because it refers back to an episode in the Vulgate Lancelot which he had omitted. Yet he has not rejected completely the technique of *entrelacement*, although he has certainly modified it. In making the stories less fragmented, he has also broken the relentless psychological movement of the French. Thus, after the episode of the poisoned apple happily resolved, we have the story of the Maid of Astolat, preserving certainly the contrast between the Maid and the queen, but cut away from its function of fostering the growing suspicions of the king and Gawain's part in these. It is also noteworthy that Malory adds three episodes absent in the French, the Great Tournament, the Knight of the Cart, and the Healing of Sir Urry, all intended to exalt Lancelot before his downfall. Inevitably Malory has lost some of the psychological subtlety and impetus of the French. But what has he put in its place? His story is still episodic but the episodes, like the episodes in a saint's life, are exemplary. They are primarily linked by a common reference to the characters whose virtues they exemplify. Their spatial and chronological reference is irrelevant, whereas in the French the chronological relationship is important for its essential part in the motivation of the action. That Malory's tales can exploit the technique of *entrelacement* seems evident from *The Tale of Balin*. But *The Book of Sir Launcelot and Queen Guinevere*, while not devoid of interwoven episodes, seems to show a thematic narrative of a different kind. Yet, as I have tried to suggest, it is less a modern narrative technique, than a different one, the technique of the exemplary tale.[1]

[1] For an interesting analysis of the exemplary narrative cp. O. Kratins, 'The Middle English *Amis and Amiloun*', *PMLA*, lxxxi (1966), 347–54; Hanspeter Schelp, 'Exemplarische Romanzen im Mittelenglischen', *Palaestra*, 246 (Göttingen, 1967), especially pp.242–8.

How, then, should we summarise the main points which we have been trying to make about medieval literary structures? We have tried to suggest that there is a distinction between plot and pattern; further, that characteristic of the Middle Ages are thematic structures in which the actors are often exemplary types rather than individuals. Works having such thematic structures use narrative in varying ways and degrees; little, as in the Old English elegies, narrative interspersed with homiletic material as in *Purity* and *Patience*; almost entirely as in *Beowulf* or the romances of Chrétien. In yet other medieval works, such as *Sir Gawain and the Green Knight*, a plot is combined with the technique of thematic contrast. Finally, we have considered a special kind of thematic contrast, the technique of *entrelacement*. In reply to a critic who objects that such disposition of material can equally be found, for example, in the works of Dickens, it may be said that, in a sense, the characteristic feature of these medieval narratives is a negative one; not merely that the material is arranged in a certain order but that the episodes often appear discrete; for they need not be placed in a space-time continuum and the actions narrated in them are often apparently unmotivated. The typical character is thus as important in the structure as the episodes themselves and as much of the apparently loose structure of medieval narrative springs from the use of typical characters as from the use of thematic narrative structure.

If verisimilitude is the aim, then the disposition of material must give the illusion of actuality in scene and character; it must exhibit an apparently orderly and comprehensible system of time and space even though on investigation this may turn out to be a *trompe d'œil* – but one which serves to enroll our sympathy and engage our belief. But medieval narrative appears to spring from a principle of multiplicity rather than unity. It might be compared, as Vinaver points out, with a foliated initial. He writes:

> The expansion is not, as in classical ornament, a movement to-wards or away from a real or imaginary centre – since there is no

centre – but towards potential infinity. And yet the artist, like the author of a fully interlaced cyclic composition, has the entire design in mind, knows where the point of departure is for each ramification – or digression. . . . There is no limit to what a cycle might eventually receive within its orbit, just as there is no limit to what the pictorial or sculptural ornament might absorb in its conquest of space; everything we see or read about is part of a wider canvas, of a work still unwritten, of a design still unfilled.[1]

Yet, illuminating though the analogy from art may be, it would perhaps be better to call it a musical principle of statement and development or even better perhaps an 'isometric' principle, the principle of the *Ars Nova* of the thirteenth century, a principle which was to be carried over into the poetry of the later Middle Ages. It is also a method of abstraction in which the unifying principle is the pattern to which the narrative is conformed rather than the use of a narrative as a template of life. Thus again we find those abstract and general principles of which Pächt speaks; a paratactic idiom which requires a field of reference to complete its sense, and a dualism which requires us to project one order of meaning into another. But above all a richness and multiplicity of form, a musical technique which has nothing to do with organic unity.

[1] Vinaver (1966), pp.14–15.

F

CHAPTER THREE

Daughters of Earth

> Footfalls echo in the memory,
> Down the passage which we did not take. . . .

Language also has its echoes and because language is the raw
material of literature, linguistic echoes are part of our experience of literature. When Chaucer writes

> A nyghtyngale, upon a cedir grene,
> Under the chambre wal ther as she ley,
> Ful loude song ayein the moone shene,
> Peraunter, in his briddes wise, a lay
> Of love, that made hire herte fressh and gay[1]

the bird is a conventional symbol of love realised in a particular
context. It is semantically two dimensional; on the one hand,
it has a contextual dimension; on the other hand, like Eliot's
nightingales in the bloody wood, it has a chronological dimension as part of a literary tradition. Literature at all periods
affords examples of this kind of echo. The mock heroic depends
upon the reader's knowledge of the epic for its full effect to be
apparent; or literary echoes can be purely verbal rather than
formal. Such are the quotations used by Eliot in *The Waste
Land*, the Horation echoes in the eighteenth-century verse
epistle, or the classical echoes in Milton. Yet the literary echo
is peculiarly interesting in relation to medieval literature as
medieval literature was peculiarly conventional. The rhetorical
commonplace provided a schema which was immediately
recognisable. The advantages of this in the sculpture of the
Middle Ages is evident; its advantages in literature are perhaps

[1] Chaucer, *Troilus and Criseyde*, II, ll.918–22.

not so apparent, especially to an age which prizes originality in art. Yet many a reader of medieval literature must have shared the Proustian experience of hearing 'la rumeur des distances traversées', though it has not been a material object which aroused this pleasurable sensation, part intellectual, part intuitive, but a remembered phrase or pattern in some conventional mode. Some of the ways in which conventional modes in medieval literature can be so exploited is the theme of this chapter.

The most obvious point of departure is the formulaic style of the Old English alliterative poetry. It has long been understood in a general way that the Old English poetic style was an oral style based on the use of formulae. But it is only in the last twenty years, since Magoun instituted a systematic application of the findings of the American scholar, Milman Parry, to Old English poetry, that the technique of alliterative poetry has been intensively studied.[1] The work of Milman Parry was centred in the Homeric poems but, as he studied the formulaic expressions which abound in these poems, he came to realise that this manner of writing was associated with oral composition. He turned therefore to the study of oral poetry as still practised in Yugoslavia early in the twentieth century.[2] Briefly defined, oral poetry is narrative poetry composed in a manner evolved over many centuries by minstrels who were illiterate. Its main characteristic is the building of metrical units, by means of formulae and formulaic expressions, and the building of songs by the use of traditional motifs. A formula may be defined as 'a group of words which is regularly employed under the same metrical conditions to express a given essential idea'.[3]

[1] F. P. Magoun, 'Oral Formulaic Character of Anglo-Saxon Narrative Poetry', *Speculum*, xxviii (1953), 446–67. No attempt is made here to give a complete bibliography of works on this topic.

[2] Milman Parry died before his work was systematised in a definitive form. But much of his material was incorporated in the book of his pupil, A. B. Lord, *The Singer of Tales* (Cambridge, Mass., 1960).

[3] The definition of the formula has been much debated. Cp. R. E. Diamond, 'The Diction of the Signed Poems of Cynewulf', *PQ*, xxxviii (1959), 228–41; R. D. Stevick, 'The Oral Formulaic Analyses of Old

An oral poem thus has no fixed form but merely a narrative nucleus which will be differently presented each time the poem is performed. The nature of the Old English poetic style may be conveniently illustrated by the poem *Caedmon's Hymn*.

> Nu sculon herigean heofonrices Weard,
> Meotodes meahte ond his modgeþanc,
> weorc Wuldorfæder, swa he wundra gehwæs,
> ece Drihten, or onstealde;
> He ærest sceop eorðan bearnum
> heofon to hrofe, halig Scyppend.
> Þa middangeard, monncynnes Weard,
> ece Drihten, æfter teode
> firum foldan, Frea ælmihtig.[1]

[*Now must we praise the Guardian of the heavenly Kingdom, the might of the Creator and the thought of his mind, the work of the father of Glory; as he, eternal God, established the beginning of every marvel. He first created, for the children of men, heaven as a roof, the holy creator; then the earth, the Guardian of mankind, the eternal Lord, the almighty Ruler afterwards established for men of earth.*]

If we examine this in relation to the Old English corpus we find that it contains stereotyped phrases appearing in a number of other poems such as *heofonrices Weard* and *ece Drihten*. In the manner characteristic of formulae, these appear also in variant forms in other poems. Thus the metrically complete phrase *eorðan bearnum* may appear in another poem as *dryhta bearnum*, *hæleþa bearnum*, *leoda bearnum*, *manna bearnum*, and so on. We also find stereotyped grammatical formulae. Thus a pattern such

---

English Verse', *Speculum*, xxxvii (1962), 382–9; H. L. Rogers, 'The Crypto-Psychological Character of the Oral Formula', *English Studies*, xlvii (1966), 89–102; D. K. Fry, 'Old English Formulas and Systems', *English Studies*, xlviii (1967), 193–204. My use of the term will be conservative; that is to say, we shall distinguish between a formula and a conventional epithet. The verbs *cleopode*, *maþelode*, though frequently used in Old English poetry do not, in my view, constitute formulae any more than the poetic words *beorn*, *freca*, *þeoden*, or words such as *cyning* which happen to be used frequently in poetry although they are ordinary prose words. I shall limit the term formula to those phrases which form metrical half-lines.

[1] See *Bede's Account of the Poet Cædmon*, in Sweet's *Anglo-Saxon Reader*, revised by D. Whitelock (Oxford, 1967), No. X, pp.46–7.

as *Nu sculon herigean* may appear as *Nu me mæg hreowan* or *nu þu meaht gecnawan*; *nu þu meaht gehieran*; *nu ge moton gangan*.[1] In each of these we have a verbal phrase which is preceded by 'nu'. In this regard, therefore, the poem may be shown to be 'formulaic'.[2] It is not, however, merely the formulaic nature of Old English poetry which gives it what Northrop Frye has called the 'curiously inwrought' quality of Old English poetry.[3] Equally important are the parallelism,[4] the synonym and the kenning. The difference between the last two may be illustrated by the series *cyning, þeoden, beaga brytta*. The first two are synonyms, the last a *kenning* or metaphor. The antiquity of these periphrases or 'gripped epithets'[5] as Gavin Bone called them,

[1] Cp. F. P. Magoun, 'Bede's Story of Cædman: The Case History of an Anglo-Saxon Oral Singer', *Speculum*, xxx (1955), 49–63.

[2] Whether this implies that it was orally composed is another question. Recently, scholars have been more willing than formerly to admit that a formulaic style does not necessarily imply oral composition. Of special interest in this connection are those OE poems which are translated from a Latin original. Cp. R. E. Diamond, 'The Diction of the Anglo-Saxon Metrical Psalms', *Janua Linguarum*, Series Practica 10 (The Hague, 1963); L. D. Benson, 'The Literary Character of Anglo-Saxon formulaic Poetry', *PMLA*, lxxxi (1966), 334–41; cp. also A. Bonjour, '*Beowulf* and the Beasts of Battle', *PMLA*, lxxii (1957), 563–73; 'A Postscript on *Beowulf* and the Singer Theory', in *Twelve Beowulf Papers, 1940–60* (Neuchatel & Geneva, 1962), pp.147–9; R. P. Creed, 'The Singer Looks at His Sources', *Comparative Literature*, xiv (1962), 44–52; Alison Jones, '*Daniel* and *Azarias* as Evidence for the Oral-formulaic Character of Old English Poetry', *Medium Aevum*, xxxv (1966), 95–102; A. Gyger, 'The Old English *Soul and Body* as an Example of Oral Transmission', *Medium Aevum*, xxxviii (1969), 239–44; R. F. Lawrence, 'The Formulaic Theory and its Application to English Alliterative Poetry', in *Essays on Style and Language*, pp.166–83; A. G. Brodeur, 'Three Anglo-Saxon Narrative Poems', in *Nordica et Anglica: Studies in Honor of Stefán Einarsson* (The Hague, 1968), 97–114; A. Jabbour, 'Memorial Transmission in Old English Poetry', *Chaucer Review*, iii (1969), 174–90.

[3] Northrop Frye, *The Anatomy of Criticism* (Princeton, 1957), p.280.

[4] For the possible origins of the *bogenstil* see A. Campbell, 'The Old English Epic Style', *English and Medieval Studies presented to J. R. R. Tolkien*, edited by N. Davis and C. L. Wrenn (London, 1962), pp.13–26.

[5] Cp. Gavin Bone, *Anglo-Saxon Poetry* (Oxford, 1943), p.17. The propriety of the term *kenning* in relation to Old English has been questioned, but I have retained the term since it is sanctioned by usage and can hardly give rise to any confusion.

seems to be vouched for, not only by their appearance in other Germanic literatures, but also because they usually form a metrical unit and can be the basis of formulaic variation. If we look again at *Cædmon's Hymn* we notice at once the use of synonyms, *meotod, ece Drihten, halig Scyppend, Frea ælmihtig*, and the kennings *heofonrices Weard, Wuldorfæder, moncynnes Weard*. We notice that the poet has chosen epithets which emphasise certain aspects of God, his kingship and his creative power. The Hymn also illustrates conveniently what is meant by parallelism. The sentence structure of Old English poetry is essentially paratactic, and built up of a series of parallel words and phrases. In some ways it is not unlike the Miltonic verse paragraph, for the articulation of the verse is from caesura to caesura, even though the extent of the line is contained by the alliteration, except in those cases where the alliteration runs on from line to line to form a kind of enjambement. Thus in the Hymn we find three kinds of parallelism. Firstly, we have balanced phrases, noun balancing noun, adjective adjective and so on. Thus *ece Drihten, halig Scyppend, Frea ælmihtig*, or *Meotodes meahte, weorc Wuldorfæder*. Secondly, we have apposition. This differs from balance in that two balanced phrases must have the same grammatical form whereas in apposition the referent of the one element is defined by the other. A common type is that in which one component is a pronoun as in *He ærest sceop, heofon to hrofe, halig Scyppend*. The third type is enumeration, as for example, *Nu sculon herigean heofonrices Weard, Meotodes meahte, and his modgeþanc, weorc Wuldorfæder*. Here the objects of praise are four related but distinct entities: God's protection, his power, his providence and his creation.[1] Logically, this is the outcome of the paratactic style and should not perhaps be called parallelism but it has been included here because it is often spoken of as such.[2]

The manipulation of parallels is a great part of the skill of the

---

[1] Cp. R. F. Leslie, 'Analysis of Stylistic Devices and Effects in Anglo-Saxon Literature', in *Stil-und Formprobleme in der Literatur*, pp.129–36. For paratactic structure, cp. also Thornton and Lind, *passim*.

[2] For a useful discussion of these topics cp. Brodeur, pp.39–70, 247–83.

Anglo-Saxon poet and some poets show a preference for certain patterns. As Laborde noted,[1] balanced phrases may be single, complex or compound, a single type consisting of two members only, the compound of more than two and a complex set of several parallels which, like the themes of contrapuntal music, pursue each other through the verse. Some Old English poems favour the complex type of parallelism and a peculiarly elaborate example can be quoted from the opening lines of *Exodus*:

> Hwæt, we *feor and neah* gefrigen habbað
> *ofer middangeard Moyses domas*
> (*wræclico wordriht wera cneorissum*
> *in uprodor eadigra gehwam*
> æfter bealusiðe *bote lifes,*
> *lifigendra gehwam langsumne ræd*)
> *hæleðum* secgan.[2]

[*Lo, we have heard, far and near, throughout the world, proclaimed to men, the judgements of Moses, his wonderful decrees, to the generations of men — for each of the blessed ones, in the world above, after the grievous journey, the recompense of life, for each of the living ones, enduring counsel.*]

Schematically, this can be represented as having the pattern *xa, ab, 'bc, ac, xb, cb, cx* where *a–c* represent parallels and *x* a half line or part of a line without parallels. The *a* series is represented by *feor and neah, ofer middangeard, in uprodor,* the *b* series by *Moyses domas, wræclico wordriht, bote lifes, langsumne ræd* and the *c* series by *wera cneorissum, eadigra gehwam, lifigendra gehwam* and *hæleðum.* It will be noted that these combine balance with enumeration so that we get a kind of step pattern in which the meaning moves forwards and upwards. In general, however, compound or complex grammatical sentences tend to have less parallelism than simple sentences. In *Elene* for example, the

[1] E. D. Laborde, 'The Style of *The Battle of Maldon*', *MLR*, xix (1924), 401–17.

[2] *Exodus*, edited by E. B. Irving (Yale Studies in English, 122, New Haven, 1953), ll. 1–7.

conventional expansions of the source, such as the battle scene, have more parallelism than those parts of the text which are closely dependent upon a Latin source. When complex parallelism does occur in a compound or complex sentence, it is usually confined to one clause only, although one parallel may be interclausal. Thus as syntaxis increases, parallelism decreases. Then we find, instead of true parallelism, of which the matrix is the half-line, parallel themes, occupying whole lines, as in the following:

> Him seo æðele cwen aʒeaf andsware,
> 'Wiðsæcest ðu to swiðe soðe ond rihte,
> ymb þæt lifes treow ond nu lytle ær,
> sæʒdest soðlice be þam siʒebeame
> leodum þinum ond nu on liʒe cyrrest'.[1]

[*To him the noble queen gave answer, 'Too vehemently dost thou deny what is true and right concerning the tree of life; yet now, but a little while previously, thou didst speak the truth to thy people about the tree of victory and now thou turnest to a lie.*]

The organisation of parallels is also a matter of some complexity. In narrative poetry they are often consecutive and in such cases the parallels usually run over the line as in

> *heofonengla þreat,*
> *weorud wlitescyne, wuldres aras,*
> cwomun on corðre.[2]

[*The band of heavenly angels, the radiant host, glorious messengers, came in a troop.*]

On the other hand, the parallels can be intercalated, an order which is common with complex parallels. Thus

> Ic up ahof *eaforan ʒinʒne*
> ond *bearn cende* þam ic *blæd* forʒeaf,
> *haliʒe hiʒefrofre.*[3]

[*I reared a young child and gave birth to a son to whom I granted prosperity, blessed consolation.*]

---

[1] *Elene*, edited by P. O. E. Gradon (London, 1958), ll.662–6.
[2] *Christ*, ll.492–4.
[3] *Elene*, ll.353–5.

ond þa þy þriddan dæʒ
ealles leohtes leoht lifʒende áras,
ðeoden enʒla, ond his þeʒnum
soð siʒora frea, seolfne geywde
beorht on blæde[1]

[*And then, on the third day, the light of lights rose living, the prince of angels and showed himself to his thegns, the true lord of victories, radiant in joy.*]

In some cases the parallelism can be inclusive, as in the following example from the *Fates of the Apostles*:

Sume on Romebyrig
frame, fyrdhwate, feorh ofgefon,
þurg Nerones nearwe searwe,
Petrus ond Paulus.[2]

[*Some gave up their lives in Rome, brave and bold in battle, through the cruel cunning of Nero, namely Peter and Paul.*]

This technique of parallelism is characteristically Old English. It virtually disappears in the alliterative poetry of the Middle English period.[3] Its function is distinctive and is capable of particular literary effects. This can be illustrated very clearly from the following passage from *Beowulf*:

Gewat þa ofer wægholm winde gefysed
flota famiheals fugle gelicost,
oð þæt ymb antid oþres dogores
wundenstefna gewaden hæfde,
þæt ða liðende *land* gesawon,
brimclifu blican, *beorgas steape*,
side sænæssas.[4]

[*Then, impelled by the wind, the foamy-necked ship, most like to a bird, journeyed over the sea until, after a due period of time, on the next day(?),*]

---

[1] *Elene*, ll.485–9.

[2] *Andreas and The Fates of the Apostles*, edited by K. R. Brooks (Oxford, 1961), ll.11–14.

[3] But cp. R. A. Waldron, 'Oral Formulaic Technique and Middle English Alliterative Poetry', *Speculum*, xxxii (1957), 792–804; J. Finlayson, 'Formulaic Technique in *Morte Arthure*', *Anglia*, lxxxi (1963), 372–93.

[4] *Beowulf*, ll.217–24.

the ship with its curved prow, had so voyaged that the sailors saw land, the sea-cliffs shining, the lofty headlands, the broad sea promontories.]

In the first place we have a kind of echo technique.[1] In more technical language, both the paradigmatic and the syntagmatic recurrence are borne mainly by the parallels which we have underlined. We notice, for example, the formal pattern of the last three lines with noun followed by verb and then a chiastic pattern of noun and adjective. On the other hand, the semantic aspect of the parallels acts as a kind of prism which refracts the image which the description conveys. But most important, we have at one and the same time a principle of recurrence and a principle of variation. The poet is saying that the cliffs are 'white', 'high' and 'broad' but by the use of parallel epithets, *brimclifu, beorgas, sænæssas,* he has imposed upon the verse a formal pattern not unlike the development of a theme in music.

But it is not only the technique of parallelism which gives Old English poetry its elaborate musical pattern, its echoing style. The use of formulae also contributes to this effect. Poetry written in the oral tradition is a continuum and its very conventionality contributes to its suggestiveness. As Creed has said 'the audience, singer included, *hears* each new performance of a theme *counterpointed* against all the old performances it has heard'.[2] He has suggested that in *Beowulf*, lines 1769–81, the conclusion of Hrothgar's Sermon, the choice of epithets is intended to echo the opening lines of the poem. And there are many similar parallels to which he calls attention. It seems to me, however, that there is a more subtle way in which the

---

[1] The repetitive nature of the style is seen also in the narrative technique. Misunderstandings of this are not uncommon, cp. for example, D. R. Evans, 'The Sequence of Events in *Beowulf*, lines 207–16', *Medium Aevum*, xxxii (1963), 214–16; for recent discussion of the verbal structure cp. R. Quirk, 'Poetic Language and Old English Metre', in *Early English and Norse Studies presented to Hugh Smith*, edited by A. Brown and P. Foote (London, 1963), 150–71; J. L. Rosier, 'The Literal-Figurative Identity of *The Wanderer*', *PMLA*, lxxix (1964), 366–9.

[2] R. P. Creed, 'On the Possibility of Criticizing Old English Poetry', *Texas Studies in Literature and Language*, iii (1) (1961), 101. Cp. T. C. Rumble, 'The *hyran-gefrignan* formula in *Beowulf*', *Annuale Mediaevale*, v (1964), 13–20.

conventional diction can be made to serve the purpose of semantic enrichment. The compound *cearseld* in *The Seafarer*,[1] serves as an admirable example. The Seafarer says that, in his hard life on the sea, he has experienced many a *cearseld* 'dwelling of sorrow'. This is surely meant to evoke the conventional *meoduseld*, 'mead-hall' with all its Anglo-Saxon associations of happiness and security. Thus the compound *cearseld*, by its very conventionality, implies an ironic contrast with *meodoseld*. When the last survivor in *Beowulf* has committed his treasure to the earth the poet tells us that

> unbliðe hwearf
> dæges ond nihtes, oð ðæt deaðes wylm
> hran æt heortan[2]

[*He went in sorrow, day and night, until the surge of death reached his heart.*]

This variation on the conventional *wintrys wylm* used, for example, in the episode of the swimming match with Breca, implies not only a metaphor, in the conjunction of the two parts, by which death overwhelms the man like a wave or surge of water, but also the coldness of death.

But the manipulation of formulae, effective though it can be, is perhaps less important in Old English poetry than the exploitation of conventional themes. These themes are well-known and have been widely discussed.[3] Every reader of

---

[1] *The Seafarer*, l.5.   [2] *Beowulf*, ll.2268-70.

[3] Cp. S. B. Greenfield, 'The Formulaic Expression of the Theme of "Exile" in Anglo-Saxon Poetry', *Speculum*, xxx (1955), 200-6; F. P. Magoun, 'The Theme of the Beasts of Battle in Anglo-Saxon Poetry', *Neuphilologische Mitteilungen*, lvi (1955), 81-90; also Bonjour, pp.563-73; D. K. Crowne, 'The Hero on the Beach: an Example of Composition by Theme in Anglo-Saxon Poetry', *Neuphilologische Mitteilungen*, lxi (1960), 362-72; R. E. Diamond, 'Theme as Ornament in Anglo-Saxon Poetry', *PMLA*, lxxvi (1961), 461-8; J. E. Cross, 'The Old English Poetic Theme of "The Gifts of Men"', *Neophilologus*, xlvi (1962), 66-70; G. Clark, 'The Traveler recognizes his Goal: A Theme in Anglo-Saxon Poetry', *JEGP*, lxiv (1965), 645-59; D. K. Fry, 'The hero on the beach in *Finnsburh*', *Neuphilologische Mitteilungen*, lxvii (1966), 27-31; 'The hero on the beach in *Judith*', *Neuphilologische Mitteilungen*, lxviii (1967), 168-84; 'Old English Formulaic Themes and Type-scenes', *Neophilologus*, lxii (1968), 48-54.

Anglo-Saxon poetry is familiar with the sea-scenes, the battle scenes, with the gathering of the birds and beasts of prey; there are the feasts and, above all, the understood and pervasive relationship of lord and man, with the related elegiac imagery of the deserted hall and the slain or exiled warrior. It is as commonplace as the ideology of Brecht but gains strength from its very familiarity. Two examples may be taken of the use of these conventional configurations. The first is from the poem *The Wanderer*. It is now generally understood that the poem is built round two conventional themes: the theme of exile and the theme of the empty and ruined building. These themes are primarily derived from contemporary and earlier social structures. The Old English poets write about thegns and overlords because to them these were appropriate figures of some of the most basic human emotions. Originally, no doubt, to be taken literally, they were transmuted into a kind of figurative language, generally understood and profoundly suggestive. If Old English poetry lacks imagery, it is because the figures on which it relies have themselves the suggestiveness of metaphorical language. This is evident in *The Wanderer*. The theme, as we have already said, is 'mutability'. The theme is presented first in the figure of an exile:

> Donne sorg ond slæp somod ætgædre
> earmne anhogan oft gebindað,
> þinceð him on mode þæt he his mondryhten
> clyppe ond cysse, ond on cneo lecge
> honda ond heafod, swa he hwilum ær
> in geardagum giefstolas breac.[1]

[*Then sorrow and sleep together often bind the heart of the wretched solitary man, he imagines that he embraces and kisses his lord, and lays head and hands on his knee, as in days gone by he previously, from time to time, enjoyed the gift-throne.*]

The conclusion is plain enough:

> Swa þes middangeard
> ealra dogra gehwam dreoseð ond fealleþ.[2]

[*Thus, every day, this world decays and declines.*]

---

[1] *The Wanderer*, ll.39–44.　　　　[2] *The Wanderer*, ll.62–3.

The second image is that of the ruined building. A wise man, the poet tells us, will understand the desolation which will come to the world in its last days. The creator of man is also He who lays waste the cities of men:

> Swa nu missenlice geond þisne middangeard,
> winde bewaune, weallas stondaþ,
> hrime behrorene, hryðge þa ederas.
> Woniað þa winsalo, waldend licgað
> dreame bedrorene; duguþ eal gecrong
> wlonc bi wealle. . . .
> yþde swa þisne eardgeard ælda Scyppend,
> oþþæt burgwara breahtma lease,
> eald enta geweorc idlu stodon.[1]

[*As now in various places throughout this earth, stand walls wind-swept, covered with frost, the buildings snow-covered (?). The wine-halls crumble, the warriors lie dead, deprived of joy; the veteran band has all fallen, proud by the wall. . . . Thus has the creator of men laid waste this earth, until the ancient works of giants stood empty, deprived of the clamour of citizens.*]

Whoever wisely ponders on these ancient ruins, will inevitably lament the mutability of earthly things. But the poet's lament is not that of a Villon, for example; he does not invoke the universally understood image of the melting snow. Nor, indeed, does he use the style of some of the earlier examples of this theme. The point emerges plainly if we compare the imagery of *The Wanderer* with the treatment of the same theme by Isidore of Seville in his *Synonyma*:

> Brevis est hujus mundi felicitas, modica est hujus saeculi gloria, caduca est et fragilis temporalis potentia. Dic ubi sunt reges? ubi principes? ubi imperatores? ubi locupletes rerum? ubi potentes saeculi? ubi divites mundi? quasi umbra transierunt, velut somnium evanuerunt. Quaeruntur, et non sunt.[2]

[*Brief is the joy of this world, trifling the glory of this generation, temporal power is fleeting and fragile. Say, where are the kings? where are the princes, where are the emperors, where the rich in possessions? where are the*

---

[1] *The Wanderer*, ll.75–87.
[2] Isidore of Seville, *Synonyma*, II, 91, PL, lxxxiii, col. 865.

powerful of this world? where the rich of the earth? they have passed as a
shadow, vanished as a dream. Men seek them and they are not.]

The theme is itself conventional. In origin, both the *ubi sunt*
theme and its corollary, the ruined building theme, may well
have been biblical[1] and it was, no doubt, already rich with
associations when Isidore of Seville used it. But the Old English
poet has added another dimension by the imagery in which he
chooses to incorporate it. The images in Isidore are quite
general. Not so in the Old English poem. A traditional theme is
yet further enriched by the use of heroic imagery and, as in
Isaiah, is given a local habitation:

> Hwær cwom mearg? hwær cwom mago? hwær cwom
> maþþumgyfa?
> Hwær cwom symbla gesetu? Hwær sindon seledreamas?
> Eala beorht bune! Eala byrnwiga!
> Eala þeodnes þrym! Hu seo þrag gewat,
> genap under nihthelm, swa heo no wære!
> Stondeð nu on laste leofre duguþe,
> weal wundrum heah wyrmlicum fah –
> eorlas fornoman asca þryþe,
> wæpen wælgifru, wyrd seo mære.[2]

[*Where has gone the horse, where the rider, where the giver of treasure?*
Where have gone the places of feasting, where are the joys of the hall? Alas,
the bright cup! Alas, the mail-clad warrior! Alas the prince's glory! How
has the time departed, grown dark beneath the shroud of night, as though it
has never been! There stands now, in place of the beloved veterans, a wall
wondrously high, adorned with serpentine patterns (?), the multitudes of
spears have destroyed men, weapons greedy for slaughter, glorious fate!]

It might be thought that the Old English example merely
seems more particular because it is less familiar. The modern
reader is struck by the 'treasure giver' in a way he is not struck
by Isidore's *reges* simply because, to the modern reader, the less
familiar term has more impact. Yet the Old English poet

---

[1] Cp. I *Corinthians*, i, 20; *Isaiah*, xxxiii, 18; *Baruch*, iii, 16–19; J. E. Cross
' "Ubi sunt" passages in Old English – Sources and Relationships', *Veten-*
skaps-Societeten i Lund, Årsbok, 1956, pp.25–44; for the ruined building cp.
Isaiah, xxxiv, 10–15.

[2] *The Wanderer*, ll.92–100.

evokes a context in a way that Isidore does not. Isidore's examples are all *potentes saeculi*, kings, princes, emperors, potentates, those of the Old English poet are not in themselves symbols of power. We have, instead, a submerged image of a ruined hall to which the details are subordinate. And this hall is thought of as having an existence in time and space in a way that the princes and rulers of Isidore have not. They are a continuous succession of the great ones of the earth. But the Old English poet, like his Hebrew counterpart, has chosen to mirror the passing of time in a figure, the figure of a ruined hall. Time does not merely pass but has passed already, the 'iniquity of oblivion' has scattered her poppy and all we see of the once prosperous life in the hall is a 'wall wondrously high'.

Yet the Old English does not differ from the Latin merely in its greater particularity. Compare the Old English with the following later passage on the same theme:

> Hwer is paris and heleyne,
>> Þat weren so bryht and feyre on bleo,
> Amadas and dideyne,
>> tristram, yseude and alle þeo,
> Ector, wiþ his scharpe meyne,
>> And cesar, riche of wordes feo.
> Heo beoþ i-glyden vt of þe reyne
>> so þe schef is of þe cleo.[1]

The use of concrete universals in this passage gives it a particularity lacking in Isidore. The examples are figures famous in legend and history and have therefore their own echoes in the corridors of time. The image at the end, like Villon's image of the melting snow, is one which suggests the cyclic nature of time rather than its obliterating power. The fields are full of corn another year and when the snows melted

> oþer com
> gear in geardas – swa nu gyt deð[2]

[Another year came into men's dwellings, as it still does]

---

[1] Thomas de Hales, *Love Ron*; *English Lyrics of the XIIIth Century*, edited by Carleton Brown (Oxford, 1932), No. 43, ll.65–72.

[2] *Beowulf*, ll.1133–4.

But whereas the particulars of Thomas de Hales's *Love Ron* are merely examples of great men and women who have died and stand for other great ones who have passed away, the details of the Old English, while less particular, are more concrete in that they are part of a single image. And it is possible to re-assemble this image in the mind because it corresponds to an image already familiar from tradition.

This use of a traditional diction to create a kind of submerged imagery can be illustrated from other Old English poetry. Thus, for example, when the *Beowulf* poet speaks of Grendel as a 'hall thegn', he is drawing upon a conventional theme to say something about the monster and when he goes on to say that he cannot receive treasure he implies that Grendel is an evil thane.[1] In a different way, the poet of *Christ I* uses conventional imagery in his rendering of the first advent antiphon: *O rex gentium et desideratus earum, lapisque angularis qui facis utraque unum: veni, et salva hominem quem de limo formasti.* To this corresponds in part the following Old English:

> Ðu eart se weallstan þe ða wyrhtan iu
> wiðwurpon to weorce. Wel þe geriseð
> þæt þu heafod sie healle mærre
> ond gesomnige side weallas
> fæste gefoge, flint unbræcne,
> þæt geond eorðbyrg eall eagna gesihþe
> wundrien to worlde wuldres ealdor.
> Gesweotula nu þurh searocræft þin sylfes weorc,
> soðfæst, sigorbeorht, ond sona forlæt,
> weall wið wealle. Nu is þam weorce þearf
> þæt se cræftga cume ond se cyning sylfa,
> ond þonne gebete – nu gebrosnad is –
> hus under hrofe. He þæt hra gescop,
> leomo læmena. Nu sceal liffrêa
> þone wergan heap wraþum ahreddan,
> earme from egsan, swa he oft dyde.[2]

---

[1] This assumes that lines 168-9 mean: 'Grendel could not approach the gift-throne (i.e. receive treasure as a good thane), treasure on account of the Creator nor did He take heed of him'.

[2] *The Advent Lyrics of the Exeter Book*, edited by J. J. Campbell (Princeton, 1959), ll.2–17.

[*Thou art the building stone which the workmen formerly rejected from the work. Well it befits thee that thou be the headstone of the glorious hall and join the wide walls with a firm joint, inviolable flint, so that throughout the cities of the earth, all things with the gift of sight (?) may marvel eternally, O lord of glory! Reveal now skilfully thine own work, true, victorious, and forthwith leave standing wall against wall. Now is need for the work, that the mighty one, the king himself come and then repair – what is now decayed – the house under its roof. He created the body, limbs of clay. Now must the Lord of Life save the accursed multitude from the wrathful ones, wretched men from terror, as He has often done.*]

To bring out clearly the poet's technique let us look at another passage which uses the building image, King Alfred's Preface to his translation of the Soliloquies of St. Augustine.

Gaderode me þonne kigclas, and stuþansceaftas, and lohsceaftas, and hylfa to ælcum þara tola þe ic mid wircan cuðe, and bohtimbru and bolttimbru, and, to ælcum þara weorca þe ic wyrcan cuðe, þa wlitegostan treowo be þam dele ðe ic aberan meihte. Ne com ic naþer mid anre byrðene ham þe me ne lyste ealne þane wude ham brengan, gif ic hyne ealne aberan meihte; on ælcum treowo ic geseah hwæthwugu þæs þe ic æt ham beþorfte. Forþam ic lære ælcne ðara þe maga si and manigne wæn hæbbe, þæt he menige to þam ilcan wuda þar ic ðas stuðansceaftas cearf, fetige hym þar ma, and gefeðrige hys wænas mid fegrum gerdum, þat he mage windan manigne smicerne wah and manig ænlic hus settan, and fegerne tun timbrian and þær murge and softe mid mæge oneardian ægðer ge wintras ge sumeras, swa swa ic nu ne gyt ne dyde.[1]

[*Then I gathered for myself staves and props and bars, and handles for all the tools I knew how to use, and crossbars and beams for all the structures which I knew how to build, the fairest pieces of timber, as many as I could carry. I neither came home with a single load, nor did it suit me to bring home all the wood, even if I could have carried it. In each tree I saw something that I required at home. For I advise each of those who is strong and has many waggons, to plan to go to the same wood where I cut these props, and fetch for himself more there, and load his wagons with fair rods, so that he can plait many a fine wall, and put up many a peerless building,*]

---

[1] King Alfred's Version of St. Augustine's *Soliloquies*, edited by T. A. Carnicelli (Cambridge, Mass., 1969), p.47; *English Historical Documents*, I, edited by Dorothy Whitelock (London, 1955), 844.

*and build a fair enclosure with them; and may dwell therein pleasantly,
and at his ease, winter and summer, as I have not yet done.*]

King Alfred then goes on to express the desire that he may rest
in the house of learning until he obtains a more permanent
dwelling:

Nis it nan wundor þeah man swilc ontimber gewirce, and eac on
þare lade and eac on þære bytlinge; ac ælcne man lyst, siððan he
ænig cotlyf on his hlafordes læne myd his fultume getimbred
hæfð, þæt he hine mote hwilum þar-on gerestan, and huntigan,
and fuglian, and fiscian, and his on gehwilce wisan to þere lænan
tilian, ægþær ge on se ge on lande, oð þone fyrst þe he bocland and
æce yrfe þurh his hlafordes miltse geearnige.[1]

[*It is not to be marvelled at that one expends labour on such material both in
the carriage and in the building; but every man, when he has built a village
on land leased to him by his lord, with his help, likes to stay in it sometimes,
and to go hunting and fowling and fishing, and to support himself in every
way on that leased land, both on sea and land, until the time when through
his lord's mercy he may acquire bookland and a perpetual inheritance.*]

Now, in both these instances, we have a building image; the
poet of *Christ* is extending the Latin image of Christ as the
corner-stone, Alfred is using the image of a house of learning,
which he has built, and now wishes to enjoy until he is called
by death to the eternal mansions. But there is an essential difference in the way the two images are used, not explicable
purely in terms of different subject matter. For Alfred's image
is explicit and precise; the poet's implicit and evocative.
Alfred's image is an adornment of the subject, a rhetorical
amplification, precise in its domestic details of tools and leases.
The distinction between a house on lease and a house held by
charter is a happy comparison neatly twisting the conventional
reference to 'heavenly mansions'. But the poet of *Christ* is
drawing on poetic convention for his image and it is correspondingly evocative and generalised. The image woven into
the biblical image of the rejected corner stone is that of the
ruined hall which Christ, at his coming, will repair. This is

---

[1] Alfred, *Soliloquies*, p.48; *English Historical Documents*, p.844.

made clear by the words *nu gebrosnad is / hus under hrofe*. Thus a particular twist is given to the thought of the antiphon.[1] Christ is the headstone of the corner. His coming will be to save men. To this the Old English poet adds elegiac overtones by his use of the conventional image of the deserted building and, also, by implication, Christ is the king whose coming will restore the ruined hall to life. Thus, the poet, using traditional imagery, writes figurally; King Alfred, using an illustration, not from literary tradition, but from everyday life, does not. Thus it might be said that Old English poetry has its own iconography which can be used subtly as a kind of submerged imagery. This is, indeed, the most significant and interesting achievement of the Old English Christian poets, the true miracle of Caedmon, the transition from a literal, heroic manner of writing to a figurative one.[2]

The point could again be illustrated by reference to *The Wife's Lament* contrasted with the Norse *Hamðismál*. When Guðrun laments her fate she gives the reader a series of single, sharp images:

> Einstœð, em ek orðin
> sem ǫsp í holti,
> fallin at froendum
> sem fura at kvisti,
> vaðin at vilia
> sem viðr at laufi,
> þá er in kvistskœða
> kømr um dag varman.[3]

[*I am left standing alone like the aspen in the woodland, shorn of kins-men as pine-tree of branch, stripped of joy, as wood of leaf when the girl, branch-robbing, comes on a hot day.*]

---

[1] Cp. R. B. Burlin, 'The Old English *Advent*' (Yale Studies in English, 168, New Haven, 1968), pp.58–66.

[2] C. L. Wrenn, 'The Poetry of Cædmon', *PBA*, xxxii (1946), 277–95; J. J. Campbell, 'Learned Rhetoric in Old English Poetry', *MP*, lxiii (1966), 189–201; B. K. Martin, 'Aspects of Winter in Latin and Old English Poetry', *JEGP*, lxviii (1969), 375–90.

[3] *Hamðismál*, stanza 5; text and translation from *The Poetic Edda*, I, edited by Ursula Dronke (Oxford, 1969), 161–2.

The woman in *The Wife's Lament* uses language so generalised and conventional that we do not know what is actual and what is image.

> Sindon dena dimme, duna uphea,
> bitre burgtunas, brerum beweaxne,
> wic wynna leas . . .[1]

[*The valleys are dim, the hills lofty, the dwellings of men are bitter, overgrown with briars, joyless dwellings.*]

Her exile and solitary dwelling, if actual (and the oak tree may suggest that they are), merge with the conventions of elegiac imagery. Just as we do not know whether the exile in *The Wanderer* has actually rowed across a wintry sea, so we do not know how actual are the details of the lot of the Wife's lover:[2]

> min freond siteð
> under stanhliþe, storme behrimed,
> wine werigmod wætre beflowen,
> on dreorsele, dreogeð se min wine
> micle modceare.[3]

[*. . . my friend sits beneath a rocky slope, frost-covered by storm, a sorrowful man, encompassed by water, in a desolate hall, this companion of mine endures much grief of heart.*]

Thus, as so often in Old English poetry, the scene is primarily not actual but emblematic, fact and setting blending with imagery; yet the imagery, being figurative, derives its strength in another sense from its actuality. There is no sudden recognition of similarity between dissimilars as in the image from the *Hamðismál*. On the contrary, we are in a world in which, by virtue of the exploitation of conventional motifs, the actual is

---

[1] *The Wife's Lament*, edited by R. F. Leslie in *Three Old English Elegies* (Manchester, 1961), ll.30-2.

[2] For discussion see the bibliography in *Three Old English Elegies* and R. C. Bambas, 'Another View of the Old English *Wife's Lament*', *JEGP*, lxii (1963), 303-9; M. J. Swanton, '*The Wife's Lament* and *The Husband's Message*: A Reconsideration', *Anglia*, lxxxii (1964), 269-90.

[3] *The Wife's Lament*, ll.47-51. Cp. R. W. V. Elliott, 'Form and Image in the Old English Lyrics', *Essays in Criticism*, xi (1961), 1-9.

constantly irradiated by the use of imagery carrying with it associations which are archetypal (in the correct sense of this abused word). And, because the images are conventional, they can be evoked without explicit reference. They are like the opening bar of a familiar piece of music.

How greatly failure to appreciate this fact can vitiate the understanding of Old English poetry can be further illustrated from the critical battle over the location of Grendel's mere.[1] The passage is well-known:

> Hie dygel lond
> warigeað wulfhleoþu, windige næssas,
> frecne fengelad, ðær fyrgenstream
> under næssa genipu niþer gewiteð,
> flod under foldan. Nis þæt feor heonon
> milgemearces, þæt se mere standeð;
> ofer þæm hongiað hrinde bearwas,
> wudu wyrtum fæst wæter oferhelmað.
> Þær mæg nihta gehwæm niðwundor seon,
> fyr on flode. No þæs frod leofað
> gumena bearna, þæt þone grund wite.
> Ðeah þe hæðstapa hundum geswenced,
> heorot hornum trum holtwudu sece,
> feorran geflymed, ær he feorh seleð,
> aldor on ofre, ær he in wille,
> hafelan beorgan; nis þæt heoru stow![2]

[*They inhabit a secret land, the wolf-slopes, windswept headlands, the perilous fenpath, where the mountain stream falls down under the shadows of the cliffs, the flood under the earth; it is not far hence, in measure of miles, that the mere stands, over which hang frost-covered groves, a wood, fast-rooted, overshadows the water. There every night can a sinister marvel be seen, fire on the water. There is none of the children of men so wise that he may know the depth. Though the stag, harassed by hounds, the hart*

---

[1] Cp. R. W. Chambers, *Beowulf: An Introduction* (3rd edn., with a supplement by C. L. Wrenn, Cambridge, 1959), and bibliography, and K. Malone, 'Grendel and his Abode', *Studia Philologica et Litteraria in Honorem L. Spitzer*, edited by A. G. Hatcher and K. L. Selig (Bern, 1958), pp.297–308; D. A. H. Evans, 'The Lake of the Monsters in *Beowulf*', *Studia Neophilologica*, xl (1968), 148–54.

[2] *Beowulf*, ll.1357–72.

strong with lofty antlers, driven from afar, seek the forest, rather he gives up his life, his being on the shore, than enter to seek protection; that is not a pleasant place!]

Whether or not the author of *Beowulf* knew the *Visio Pauli*, and whatever the relation of this passage to the *Blickling Homilies*, it is clear that the orientation of the passage is to be explained by reference to Germanic conventional motifs. It is not necessary to assume that the description must form a geographically comprehensible whole. The monsters live in a waste land, a no-man's land. Grendel is a *mære mearcstapa*, a renowned wanderer in those waste borderlands which constituted territorial boundaries in primitive times. His home is in all desolate places *moras, fen ond fæsten*, uplands, marsh and impenetrable places. But these places are, by implication, blended with the biblical wilderness, for Grendel is a descendant of Cain and the poet mentions the exile of Cain. And the poet of *Genesis A* like the *Beowulf* poet, uses the language of Germanic exile to image the tragedy of Cain:

> Him þa Cain gewat,
> gongan geomormod gode of gesyhðe,
> wineleas wrecca, and him þa wic geceas
> eastlandum on, eðelstowe
> fædergeardum feor.[1]

[*Cain then departed, sorrowful left the sight of God, a joyless exile, and then chose for himself a dwelling in the eastern lands, a homeland far from his paternal dwellings.*]

There is no need to visualise the setting of Grendel's mere. Each detail exists, not as part of a coherent whole, but for its evocative value. The wolfslopes suggest the outlaw who, like the wolf, is solitary and savage. As the *Gnomic Poem* says:

> wulf sceal on bearowe,
> earm anhaga.[2]

[*The wolf lives in a barrow, the wretched solitary one.*]

---

[1] *Genesis A*, ll.1049–53.
[2] *Maxims*, ll.18–19; *The Anglo-Saxon Minor Poems*, edited by E. Van Kirk Dobbie; The Anglo-Saxon Poetic Records, VI (New York, 1942).

The perilous fen-path indicates the loneliness of the place; the *Gnomic Poem* again makes the relevant point:

> þyrs sceal on fenne gewunian
> ana innan lande.[1]

[*The giant dwells in a fen, alone in the land.*]

The mountain-stream, falling down into the shadowy water, evokes the image of darkness, used elsewhere in the poem to mark the forces of evil.

> Com on wanre niht,
> scriðan sceadugenga. Sceotend swæfon,
> þa þæt hornreced healdan scoldon,
> ealle buton anum. Þæt wæs yldum cuþ,
> þæt hie ne moste, þa Metod nolde,
> se scynscaþa under sceadu bregdan; –
> ac he wæccende wraþum on andan
> bad bolgenmod beadwa geþinges.[2]

[*The walker in the shadows came gliding in the dark night. The warriors slept who should have guarded the antler-adorned hall, all but one. It was known to men that the spectral ravager might not, since the Creator willed it not, draw them beneath the shadows – but he watching, with hostile intent towards his foes, waited, angry, the outcome of the conflicts.*]

Again, the rimy trees are purely evocative of those winter scenes which the Old English poets used to suggest desolation and sorrow. It is illuminating to put this account beside one of the winter scenes in *Gawain*:

> For werre wrathed hym not so much þat wynter nas wors,
> When þe colde cler water fro þe cloudez schadde,
> And fres er hit falle myȝt to þe fale erþe;
> Ner slayn wyth þe slete he sleped in his yrnes
> Mo nyȝtez þen innoghe in naked rokkez,
> Þer as claterande fro þe crest þe colde borne rennez,
> And henged heȝe ouer his hede in hard iisse-ikkles.[3]

---

[1] *Maxims*, ll.42–3.
[2] *Beowulf*, ll.702–9.
[3] *Sir Gawain and the Green Knight*, ll.726–32.

The stream clattering down from the mountain tops and the spray freezing in the cold air is pictured with a clear, hard, physical precision. The only suggestive word (as distinct from a descriptive word) is the somewhat uncommon *fale* 'pale', 'faded' which suggests both the paleness of the frost- or snow-covered earth, and the paleness of sorrow and suffering. But, in the *Beowulf* poet's account of the waterfall falling from the headlands, the phrases lack this clarity. Not only is the picture not composed as a visual unity, but the individual items are evocative rather than precise. Thus his choice of epithets is conditioned by their metaphorical as well as their literal sense. As we have already pointed out these metaphors are conventional ones used elsewhere in the poem, darkness and cold. Even the hunted stag, perhaps taken from a learned source, is described in terms of exile, *feorran geflymed*, and his fate in refusing the sinister refuge is made, by a kind of double metaphor, yet more poignant.

I have tried to illustrate how the conventional nature of Old English poetic diction is capable of exploitation, by a competent poet, to enrich his poetry by the evocation of stock responses. The world of Anglo-Saxon poetry is a world of fundamental contrasts, designed, like gnomic poetry, to illustrate the substance rather than the accidents of things. Many of these contrasts have often been remarked; the hall and its life of security contrasted with exile or the cold and storm of nature; the hero and the coward; heroic pride and disaster; these stock characters and situations appear constantly. But they also underlie many poems, as a kind of imagery, so familiar that the briefest reference serves to recall the dialectic of sorrow and joy, courage and fear, security and desolation. This has perhaps been sufficiently illustrated, but we might take one concluding example, of a slightly different kind, to illustrate the force of this conventional and generalised diction. It is the messenger's account of the death of Beowulf:

> Wiglaf siteð,
> ofer Biowulfe, byre Wihstanes,
> eorl ofer oðrum unlifigendum,

healdeð higemæðum heafodwearde,
leofes ond laðes.[1]

[*Wiglaf sits, the son of Wihstan, over Beowulf, one man over another life-less; he keeps watch, sad at heart (?), over friend and foe.*]

The generality of the words *eorl ofer oðrum unlifigendum,* cuts away, as it were, the background so that it becomes not the description of a particular grief, but a model of the retainer mourning over his dead lord, a situation familiar but none-theless moving. The description of the first line and a half is pared away to the barest of symbolic postures. Its visual content is at vanishing point; its significance immense because it de-picts one of the primary emotions. 'With grief of heart he keeps a watch over friend and foe alike' says the poet. The irony of Wiglaf's enforced watch over the dragon, as well as over Beo-wulf, is indicated by the barest and most conventional of formulae, *leofes ond laðes.* But because it is a formula, with all its contextual associations, it suggests in the most general manner, not only the irony of Wiglaf's particular situation, but, behind this, the inevitable dialectic of life, the warring factions of enemy and friend. Thus, in these few lines, the poet has called upon a rich texture of association made possible for him by the conventional nature of his poetic medium.

Our second example of the exploitation of conventional language is taken, not from a literature that draws upon an oral and formulaic poetic diction, but from a literature which uses conventional imagery of a learned origin. I propose to use the patristic imagery familiar from the medieval lyric. A well-known category of this is the biblical imagery taken to repre-sent or foreshadow the Virgin Mary.[2] So the burning bush in

---

[1] *Beowulf,* ll.2906–10; for *higemæðum* cp. Klaeber's note.

[2] Cp. F. J. E. Raby, *Christian-Latin Poetry* (2nd edn., Oxford, 1953), pp.363–75; H. Barré, *Prières anciennes de l'occident a la mère du sauveur* (Paris, 1963), pp.330–41; R. T. Davies, *Medieval English Lyrics* (London, 1963), pp.371–8; A. Salzer, *Die Sinnbilder u. Beiworte Mariens in der deutschen Literatur u. lateinischen Hymnenpoesie des Mittelalters* (Darmstadt, 1967). Useful medieval collections are to be found in Albertus Magnus, *Biblia Mariana* and the *De Laudibus Beatae Mariae Virginis* in *Opera Omnia,* XXXVII, 365–443, XXXVI, edited by A. Borgnet (Paris, 1898).

which God appeared to Moses (*Exodus*, iii, 2) symbolised her unconsumed virginity.[1] She can be compared to the unicorn because, as a unicorn will lay its head on the lap of a virgin, and can then be caught

> Sic et Dominus Jesus Christus spiritualis unicornis descendens in uterum virginis.[2]

> [*Likewise the Lord Jesus Christ, the spiritual unicorn, descending into the womb of the Virgin.*]

Then, again, she was compared to Gideon's Fleece. In *Judges* we read:

> Dixitque Gedeon ad Deum: Si salvum facis per manum meam Israel, sicut locutus es, ponam hoc vellus lanae in area: si ros in solo vellere fuerit, et in omni terra siccitas, sciam quod per manum meam, sicut locutus es, liberabis Israel. Factumque est ita. Et de nocte consurgens expresso vellere, concham rore implevit.[3]

> [*And Gideon said unto God: 'If thou wilt save Israel by mine hand, as thou hast said, behold I will put this fleece of wool on the floor; and if the dew be on the fleece only, and it be dry upon all the earth beside, then shall I know that thou wilt save Israel by mine hand, as thou hast said.' And so it was; for he rose up early on the morrow, and thrust the fleece together, and wringed the dew out of the fleece, a bowl full of water.*]

In the words of Adam of St. Victor:

> Super vellus ros descendens,
> et in rubo flamma splendens,
>   (neutrum tamen laeditur),
> fuit Christus carnem sumens,
> in te tamen non consumens
>   pudorem, dum gignitur.[4]

> [*The dew descending on the fleece and the flame glowing in the bush (yet was neither damaged), was Christ taking flesh yet not consuming thy virginity when he was born.*]

---

[1] Cp. Salzer, pp.12–14.

[2] Pseudo-Hugh of St. Victor, *De bestiis* (PL, clxxvii, col. 59), cited in Davies, p.372; Salzer, pp.44–50.

[3] *Judges*, vi, 36; cp. Salzer, pp.40–2.

[4] See Raby, p.372.

The perpetual virginity of the Blessed Virgin was thought to be prefigured by the vision of Ezechiel (*Ezechiel*, xliv, 2). A large number of images were drawn from the *Song of Songs*. The sealed fountain and the garden enclosed depend upon *Canticles*:

> Hortus conclusus, soror mea, sponsa, hortus conclusus, fons signatus. Emissiones tuae paradisus malorum punicorum cum pomorum fructibus, cypri cum nardo; nardus et crocus, fistula et cinnamomum, cum universis lignis Libani; myrrha et aloe, cum omnibus primis unguentis; fons hortorum, puteus aquarum viventium, quae fluunt impetu de Libano.[1]

> [*A garden enclosed is my sister, my spouse, a garden enclosed, a fountain sealed. Thy plants are an orchard of pomegranates, with fruits of apple trees; of henna with spikenard; spikenard and saffron, calamus and cinnamon with all trees of Lebanon; myrrh and aloe with all chief spices; a fountain of gardens, a well of living waters which flow rushing down from Lebanon.*]

To these might be added the mountain of Daniel (*Daniel*, ii, 34–5); Jesse's rod (*Isaiah*, xi, 1); a rose of Jericho (*Ecclesiasticus*, xxiv, 18); the lily among thorns (*Canticles*, ii, 2); the rod of Aaron (*Numbers*, xvii, 8); Solomon's temple (I *Kings*, vi–vii) and so on. These types became entirely commonplace and had a long life before them in baroque art and finally in the 'sadistic profanation' of Swinburne.[2]

There was a long tradition of commentaries on *Canticles* in the early and medieval church. There were two main traditions of interpretation: on the one hand, the Bride was interpreted as the Church, on the other, as the soul of man. Both these traditions were blended in the influential commentary of Origen. Origen composed his commentary about the middle of the third century, but his work was known to the later Middle Ages through the Latin translation of Rufinus. Many other commentaries existed but the most influential for the later Middle Ages were those of St. Bernard and of his contemporary Wm.

---

[1] *Canticles*, iv, 12–15.
[2] Mario Praz, *The Romantic Agony* (2nd edn., Oxford, 1951), p.231.

of St. Thierry.[1] How familiar this exegetical tradition was to the Middle Ages, partly no doubt through the medium of the liturgy, is suggested by the speech in *The Merchant's Tale* in which January invites May into the garden in a speech full of echoes of the *Song of Songs*:

> Rys up, my wyf, my love, my lady free!
> The turtles voys is herd, my dowve sweete;
> The wynter is goon with alle his reynes weete.
> Com forth now, with thyne eyen columbyn!
> How fairer, been thy brestes than is wyn!
> The gardyn is enclosed al aboute;
> Com forth, my white spouse! out of doute
> Thou hast me wounded in myn herte, O wyf![2]

This is based on *Canticles*:

> En dilectus meus loquitur mihi, surge, propera, amica mea, columba mea, formosa mea, et veni; iam enim hiems transiit; imber abiit, et recessit; . . . vox turturis audita est in terra nostra.
>
> [*My beloved spake and said unto me, 'Rise up, hasten my love, my dove, my fair one, and come away; for lo, the winter is passed, the rain is over and gone; . . . the voice of the turtle-dove is heard in our land'.*]

and

> Ecce tu pulchra es, amica mea, ecce tu pulchra es! Oculi tui columbarum.
>
> [*Behold, thou art fair, my love; behold thou art fair; thou hast doves' eyes.*]

and again in

> Quam pulchrae sunt mammae tuae, soror mea sponsa! Pulchriora sunt ubera tua vino.[3]
>
> [*How fair are thy breasts, my sister, my spouse; thy breasts are fairer than wine.*]

The 'garden enclosed' is a symbol of the Virgin and it is to be presumed that Chaucer's readers would be able to appreciate

---

[1] Cp. P. C. Spicq, *Esquisse d'une histoire de l'exégèse latine au moyen âge*, (Paris, 1944), p.397; De Bruyne, III, 30–71.

[2] Chaucer, *The Canterbury Tales*, E. 2138–45.

[3] *Canticles*, ii, 10–12; i, 14; iv, 10.

the ironic undertones of the references. Indeed, in the whole range of literature, from the lyric *Blow, northerne wynd* of the Harley collection,[1] to Henry Vaughan's lines

> Gods silent searching flight:
> When my Lords head is fill'd with dew, and all
> His locks are wet with the clear drops of night[2]

there is perhaps no text which has been so fruitful a source of literary reference.

Let us consider now some of the ways in which this exegetical tradition is utilised and the critical problems which such utilisation poses. There are a number of poems which consist effectively of a list of the types of the Virgin. Latin poems, such as the famous sequence of Adam of St. Victor, may have been the model, or simply the incantatory pattern of the liturgy; and, indeed, we shall be considering an example in which the liturgy provides the inspiration. Well known are the poems in this class by William of Shoreham, by Lydgate and by Dunbar. But it is not with these that I am here concerned. I want rather to consider some of the more oblique uses of material of exegetical and liturgical origin. I should like to look first at the poem *Quia amore langueo*.[3] The refrain of the poem is taken from *Canticles* v, 8 and ii, 5. What the implications of these passages were for the medieval reader, may be seen from the following passage from St. Bernard's *De Diligendo Deo*.[4]

> .... plane fideles norunt, quam omnino necessarium habeant Iesum, et hunc crucifixum: dum admirantes et amplexantes supereminentem scientiae caritatem in ipso, id vel tantillum quod sunt, in tantae dilectionis et dignationis vicem non repen-

---

[1] *The Harley Lyrics*, No. 14; cp. *Canticles*, iv, 16; v, 1; for a different view see L. Spitzer, '*Explication de Texte* Applied to Three Great Middle English Poems', *Archivum Linguisticum*, iii (1951), 1–22, 164–5.

[2] Henry Vaughan, *The Night*, ll.31–3; *Works*, edited by L. C. Martin (2nd edn., Oxford, 1957); cp. *Canticles*, v, 2.

[3] I am using the Douce text. See Carleton Brown, *Religious Lyrics of the XIVth Century* (2nd edn., Oxford, 1952), No. 132.

[4] Bernard, *De Diligendo Deo*, III, 7; *Opera Omnia*, edited by J. Leclercq and H. M. Rochais (Rome, 1963), III, 124.

dere confunduntur. . . . Iudaeus sane, sive paganus nequaquam talibus aculeis incitatur amoris, quales Ecclesia experitur, quae ait: *Vulnerata caritate ego sum* et rursum: *fulcite me floribus, stipate me malis, quia amore langueo*. Cernit regem Salomonem in diade-mate, quo coronavit eum mater sua; cernit Unicum Patris, crucem sibi baiulantem; cernit caesum et consputum Dominum maiestatis; cernit auctorem vitae et gloriae confixum clavis, percussum lancea, opprobriis saturatum, tandem illam dilectam animam suam ponere pro amicis suis. Cernit haec, et suam magis ipsius animam gladius amoris transverberat, et dicit: *Fulcite me floribus, stipate me malis, quia amore langueo.*

[*Christians well know how entirely they should depend upon Jesus and Christ crucified; admiring and loving in him this love rising above knowledge, they would be ashamed not to repay what little they are in return for such love and honour . . . the Jew and the pagan certainly, do not feel their love stimulated by such goads as that which the Church feels that says* 'I am wounded with love' (Canticles, *iv, 9*). *And yet again* 'Sustain me with flowers, compass me with apples, for I languish with love' (Canticles, *ii, 5*). *She sees King Solomon beneath the crown with which his mother crowned him; she sees the only son of the Father carrying his cross; she sees the Lord of majesty smitten and spat upon; she sees the Author of life and of glory pierced with nails, struck with the lance, heaped with contumely. She sees him finally yield up his beloved spirit for those whom he loves. She sees these things and the sword of love pierces, rather, her own soul and she says:* Sustain me with flowers, encompass me with apples, for I languish with love.]

The poem takes the form of an address from the Virgin to man, in which she expresses her love and sorrow for him and here it is she and not, as in Bernard, the Church, that feels the languor of love. But as well as the refrain, the poet has built into the poem a pattern of relationships. The speaker, the Virgin, refers to herself as the mother of Christ, but also as the mother of mankind and, because all men are the children of God, and Christ is the Son of God, she is, also, the sister of man. Yet further she invokes another kind of love and speaks as though mankind were to be her husband. The relationship of Christ and Mary is, as it were, dissolved, and placed in relation to mankind: 'thy syster ys a quene, þy broþer ys a kynge . . . take me for þy wyfe'; yet again, man is the son of

Mary and Christ for the heavenly heritage is entailed on him;
he is the rightful heir. This imagery too is entirely conventional.
It is used again, for example, in a poem by the Franciscan poet,
William Herebert:

> Þou wommon boute uere,
> Þyn oune uader bere:
>   Gret wonder þys was
> Þat on wommon was moder
> To uader and hyre broþer –
>   So neuer oþer nas.
>
> Þou my suster and moder, –
> And þy sone my broþer –
>   Who shulde þoenne drede?
> Who-so hauet þe kyng to broder
> And ek þe quene to moder
>   Wel auhte uor to spede.
>
> Dame, suster and moder,
> Say þy sone my broþer,
>   Þat ys domes-mon,
> Þat uor þe þat hym bere
> To me boe debonere –
>   My robe he haueth opon.[1]

This is not in fact, as might appear at first sight, merely a play
of fancy on the poet's part. The image can be traced back at
least to St. Anselm:

> Sed et tu, Iesu, bone domine, nonne et tu mater? An non est mater,
> qui tamquam gallina congregat sub alas pullos suos? . . . Paule
> mater, et te ipse genuit. Pone ergo mortuum filium tuum ante
> pedes Christi, matris tuae; quia filius eius est. . . . Ora pro filio
> tuo, quia mater es, ut vivificet filium suum, quia mater est. Fac,
> mater animae meae, quod faceret mater carnis meae.[2]
>
> [*But thou too Jesus, dear Lord, art thou not also a mother, for is not he
> a mother who as a chicken gathers his chicks under his wings? Paul too is
> a mother who gave birth to thee. Place then thy dead son, Anselm, before*

---

[1] *Religious Lyrics*, No. 16, ll.1–18.

[2] Anselm, *Opera Omnia*, edited by F. S. Schmitt (Edinburgh, 1946), III,
40–1. Cp. D. A. Castel, *Méditations et prières de S. Anselme* (Collection Pax,
Paris etc., 1923). Cp. Bernard, *Liber de Passione Christi et Doloribus et Planctibus
Matris Ejus*, PL, clxxxii, col. 1136.

the feet of Christ, thy mother, for he is his son. . . . . *Pray thou, Paul, for thy son, Anselm, for thou art a mother, that Christ may give him life; for Christ too is a mother. Mother of my soul, do what the mother of my flesh would do.*]

In the centuries which followed St. Anselm, we find developing a pious devotion to 'Christ our mother', a devotion reflected in the *Revelations* of Juliana of Norwich:

Our hey fader, God almyty, which is beyng, he knew us & lovid us fro aforn any tyme; of which knoweing in his mervelous depe charite & the forseing endless Counsel of all ye blissid Trinite, he wold that ye second person shuld becom our Moder, our brother, & our savior: wherof it folowith that, as verily as God is our fader, as verily God is our Moder; Our Fader (willeth) our Moder werkyth, our Good Lord the Holy Gost confirmith; & therfore it longyth to us to loven our God in whom we have our being, him reverently thankyng & prayeyng of our makyng, mytily prayeing to our Moder of mercy & pite, & to our Lord ye holy Gost of helpe & grace.[1]

It is thus evident that the poetic image which we find in our poem has, in fact, a liturgical background and is entirely conventional.[2]

What are the critical implications of this? We have demonstrated that the refrain and the imagery of relationships in *Quia Amore Langueo* have a referential background in liturgy and exegesis. But is it to be assumed that the quotation will be recognised as such and is this a part of the poetic texture? And does the referential background act as a control on the apparently erotic implications of the text? Let us turn for a moment to a quite different example. It is taken from George Herbert's poem *The Sacrifice*:

> *O all ye who passe by, behold and see;*
> Man stole the fruit, but I must climbe the tree;
> The tree of life to all, but onely me:
> >   Was ever grief like mine?

---

[1] *The Revelations of Juliana of Norwich*, MS. Sloane, 2499, f. 43; modernised by Dom Roger Hudleston (2nd edn., London, 1952), p.122.

[2] Cp. P. Molinari, *Julian of Norwich* (London, 1958), pp.169–76 and references.

Rosamund Tuve has commented on this passage as follows:

> I think it can be shown that this at first surprising and contra-
> dictory antithesis-identification of the two trees is thematically
> related to Herbert's idea of the Atonement, and had been felt to
> be so related by innumerable writers of poems or meditations or
> other treatments of the Passion for centuries. . . . Empson speaks
> of Christ climbing the tree 'as if he was putting the apple back';
> although the tradition in a sense carries this meaning, it would be
> too loose and careless an image to suit earlier minds, too incapable
> of conceptual reverberations.[1]

More simply, the reference is to the commonplace identification
of the cross with the tree of life. The compressed reference is
possible because the identification of the two trees is commonplace. Because of the conceptual reverberations, due to the
intellectual nature of the reference, the witty juxtaposition of
the ideas of life and death becomes possible. But let us look
more closely at the passage from Empson:

> He climbs the tree to repay what was stolen, as if he was putting
> the apple back; but the phrase in itself implies rather that he is
> doing the stealing, that so far from sinless he is Prometheus and
> the criminal. Either he stole on behalf of man (it is he who appeared
> to be sinful, and was caught up the tree) or he is climbing upwards,
> like Jack on the Beanstalk, and taking his people with him back to
> Heaven. The phrase has an odd humility which makes us see him
> as the son of the house; possibly Herbert is drawing on the medieval
> tradition that the Cross was made of the wood of the forbidden
> trees. Jesus seems a child in this metaphor, because he is the Son
> of God, because he can take the apples without actually stealing
> (though there is some doubt about this), because of the practical
> and domestic associations of such a necessity, and because he is
> evidently smaller than Man, or at any rate than Eve, who could
> pluck the fruit without climbing. This gives a pathetic humour and
> innocence; . . . on the other hand, the son stealing from his
> father's orchard is a symbol of incest; in the person of the Christ
> the supreme act of sin is combined with the supreme act of virtue.
> Thus in two ways, one behind the other, the Christ becomes

---

[1] Tuve, *A Reading of George Herbert* (Chicago, 1952), pp.85–6. On the
topic of ambiguity, cp. also W. Nowottny, *The Language Poets Use* (London,
1962), pp.146–73; G. N. Leech, *A Linguistic Guide to English Poetry* (London,
1969), pp.205–24.

guilty; and we reach the final contradiction:

> Lo, here I hang, charged with a world of sin
> The greater world of the two. . . .

as the complete Christ; scapegoat and tragic hero; loved because hated; hated because godlike; freeing from torture because
tortured; torturing his torturers because all-merciful; source of all
strength to men because by accepting he exaggerates their weakness; and, because outcast, creating the possibility of society.[1]

Now, this has a subtlety which might well have pleased a
medieval commentator. It is not my concern to discuss the
interpretation of Herbert's poem but the example is a useful
model. It is, of course, possible to look at the language of
imagery in at least two ways. If one believes the language of
poetry to be necessarily 'untrue' as not susceptible of verifica-
tion, then the only ascertainable fact about poetic language is
our response to it. On such a premise, a post-Freudian reading
of Herbert must be different from a pre-Freudian reading.
And, on such a view, it will be possible to see similar Freudian
implications in the middle English lyric *Quia Amore Langueo*; for
each critic creates his own poem. On the other hand, on the
historicist's view the only relevant implications are those which
were available to the author when he wrote. The battleground
between these two points of view is familiar, but the dividing
line between the two points of view is not always evident. If
the historicist may invoke the liturgy and the exegetical tradition to explain a poem, may not Empson invoke the Prometheus myth, Jack and the Beanstalk, the story of the Fall,
Freud's interpretation of dreams, and the Old Testament
scapegoat, not to mention several rather oblique references to
the biblical narrative of the Passion? With the exception of
Freud, all of these sources could have been known to Herbert.
On the other hand, it is not necessary to prove that Herbert
did know of the tradition of the first and second Adam to infer
that it is used in the poem. Indeed, we should feel that the poem
was evidence that he did. It is clearly not merely a matter of

---

[1] W. Empson, *Seven Types of Ambiguity* (3rd edn., London, 1953), pp.232–
233; cp. Empson's note to the third edition, p.xvi.

historical availability of certain sources that is the essential criterion in judging how far we may proceed outside the poem. Let us take another case. It is the little poem entitled by Carleton Brown *Sunset on Calvary*.[1] It runs as follows:

> Nou goth sonne vnder wod, –
> me reweth, marie, þi faire Rode.
> Nou goþ sonne vnder tre, –
> me reweþ, marie, þi sone and þe.

It has been pointed out that this English quatrain is introduced into the text of Edmund Rich's *Speculum Ecclesiae*. In the *Speculum*, the lines occur in connection with the meditation on the Annunciation and the Passion. The English quatrain is preceded by a rhythmical passage in French:

> Ci doit tu penser de la duce Marie de quel angusse ele estoit replenié quant estut a son destre e receust le disciple pur le mestre; cum ele avoit grant dolur quant le serf receust pur le seignur – le fiz au peschur pur le fiz al emperor – Iohan, le fiz Zebedeu, pur Ihesu, le fiz deu. E pur ceo poeit ele dire de soi ceo ke dist Neomi, 'Ne me apelez bele, taunt ne quant, mes amere me apelez des or ne avant; kar de amerete e dolur grant m'ad replenie le tot*pussant'. Meimes cele tenuire dit ele en le chançon de amur, 'Ne vus amerveillez mie que io su brunecte e haslée, car le solail me ad descolurée.'[2]

> [*And thus must thou think of the sweet Mary, with what anguish she was filled when she stood on his right and took the disciple for the master; what great sorrow she had when she received the vassal for the lord, the son of a sinner for the son of an emperor, John, son of Zebedee for Jesus, Son of God. And therefore could she say of herself that which Naomi said, 'Call me not fair but henceforth bitter; for the almighty has filled me with great bitterness and sorrow'. The same she says likewise in the song of love: 'Marvel not that I am dark and burnt, for the sun has discoloured me'.*]

This may be elucidated by St. Bernard's Commentary on *Canticles*. Commenting on the *Canticles* text *Nigra sum sed formosa*, he writes:

---

[1] *English Lyrics*, No. 1; and cp. J. L. Cutler, '*Nou goth Sonne under Wod*', *The Explicator*, iv (1945), 1, 7; S. Manning, '*Nou goth Sonne vnder wod*', *MLN*, lxxiv (1959), 578–81.

[2] H. W. Robbins, *Le Merure de Seinte Eglise by Saint Edmund of Pontigny* (Lewisburg, 1925), p.63; cited in *English Lyrics*, p.165–6.

Est et persecutionis, quae etiam pro summo ornamento habetur, si quidem suscipio pro iustitia et veritate . . . unde et addit sponsa: *Nolite me considerare quod fusca sim, quia decoloravit me sol:* hoc est: Nolite me notare quasi deformem, quia cernitis pro ingruente persecutione minus florentem, minus secundum gloriam saeculi coloratam. Quid exprobratis nigredinem, quam fervor persecutionis, non conversationis pudor invexit? . . . vel sic: Sol iustitiae decoloravit me Christus, cuius amore langueo. Languor iste coloris quaedam exterminatio est, et defectus in desiderio animae.[1]

[*There is also (the blackness) of persecution, which is even counted, if only I endure it, as an exalted ornament, when it is endured for the sake of righteousness and truth . . . on this account the Bride adds:* Scrutinise me not because I am black, because the sun hath discoloured me (*1, 6*); *that is, 'Do not consider me repulsive, because it is the violence of persecution which renders me less attractive and less blooming according to the glory of the world. Why do you impute as a blemish to me the blackness which the heat of persecution and not any fault in my behaviour caused?' or the text may be interpreted thus: the Sun of Righteousness, Christ, has discoloured me, for whose love I languish. This languor is a certain extermination of colour and weakness in the desire of the spirit.*]

If we assume that the poet intends to suggest this identification with the Bride of *Canticles*, then we have not only a metaphor, not unlike the Old English exploitation of conventional metaphor, but a distinctive shape given to the poem. For we have a parallel between the first and the third, and the second and the fourth lines; the sun sets, both the natural sun and the Sun of Righteousness, the son of Mary; but it is the sun of sorrow which darkens Mary's face, before the setting of the sun brings darkness, both actual and spiritual, to the world. To those for whom it is axiomatic that appeal to anything outside the text under consideration is an offence against the autonymous nature of poetry, such an interpretation will be offensive. But it seems to me that this axiom is based upon an illusion. It is true that literary criticism must be an analysis of the words on the page. In this sense it is true also that the clue to the poem must be in the poem; it is not true, however, that aesthetic

---

[1] Bernard, *Sermones super Cantica Canticorum*, 28; *Opera* I (1957), 201.

judgements are independent of the lexical meaning of the words on the page and lexical meaning can involve literary reference. This granted, other conclusions follow. As we have already pointed out, Empson invokes, in the interests of understanding Herbert, a considerable number of outside sources from Jack and the Beanstalk to the Prometheus myth. He would, no doubt, regard these as part of a legitimate structure of reference. A similar structure of reference has been revealed by our study of exegetical and liturgical reference. The study of sources and analogues is no more than a preliminary to understanding, not a substitute for it. But to be involved in assessing the associations of the words on the page is necessarily to be involved in looking outside them. We should, in fact, not look merely at the words but through them. Yet the relevance, or irrelevance, of the semantic fringe must depend upon the structure of the poem as a whole. The implication of incest in Herbert's poem is irrelevant in terms of the poem's total structure, and conversely, in *Sunset on Calvary*, the assumption of an underlying reference to the *Song of Songs* (although, of course, one cannot *prove* that the poet knew the text though this is likely) is consonant with the total structure of the poem as I have tried to show. It is an 'imposed' meaning but one which fits the fundamental structure of the text as we have it.

Let us now return to the poem *Quia Amore Langueo*. How far are we justified in reading into the poem the background of the imagery of *Canticles* and of the cult of God our mother? Does it help our understanding of the poem to know that this background exists? The implication of the use of erotic terminology in religious contexts is difficult to assess. But it seems reasonable to assume that the mystics chose such language to express the inexpressible because they were concerned with a relationship which, while different from carnal love, was *love*. When a Richard of St. Victor speaks of the carnal love it is to illuminate the nature of divine love.[1] When Mechthild of Magdeburg pictures Christ as a noble youth whom she meets

---

[1] Richard of Saint Victor, *De Quatuor Gradibus Violentae Caritatis*, edited by G. Dumeige (Textes philosophiques du moyen âge, III, Paris, 1955).

in a wood full of singing nightingales and when the noble youth invites her

> Come at midday
> To the shade by the brook
> To the resting-place of love.
> There thou mayest cool thyself,[1]

or when a medieval writer uses the image of the Christ-knight, in all these and many more, the image is surely used to portray an emotion which is different from, but has characteristics in common with, human love. I think, therefore, it is a reasonable assumption that the refrain of the *Quia Amore Langueo* carries with it, not only, by virtue of being a quotation, the implications of its context, but, also, by virtue of its use of the word *amor*, the idea of earthly love.[2] We should, perhaps, make a distinction here. If we take a word like English 'chest' it is reasonable to assume that, in most cases, the context will determine which of the two senses is in question. That is to say, the semantic overlap is of such a kind that it will rarely be relevant to the context. In 'he had a weak chest', and 'he packed his luggage in a chest' there is no possibility of ambiguity. The semantic overlap, the idea of 'a container', which is the basis of the divergent development, is such that it is no longer part of the meaning of 'chest' in the sense of the 'container in which a human being keeps his lungs'. Whether this is true in a language where we have free compounding like Old English, it is difficult to say. It may be that the Old English compounds with 'loca' have a greater degree of semantic overlap. But with later English this is not so. It must not be assumed that homonymity necessarily implies polysemy.

[1] *The Revelations of Mechthild of Magdeburg or The Flowing Light of the Godhead*, translated by Lucy Menzies (London, 1953), p.22. For the treatment of the four daughters of God in a romantic setting, cp. R. A. Klinefelter, 'The Four Daughters of God: A New Version', *JEGP*, lii (1953), 90–5 and references.

[2] It is to be presumed that the word *amor* being more sharply contrasted with *caritas* than English *love* with *charity*, tends to underline the ambiguity. Thus Bonaventura's *rosa caritatis* has different overtones from the English *rose of love*. Cp. pp.29–30.

But when we come to a word like *love* the case is different. Here the semantic overlap between the different uses is much greater, partly because the boundaries between the different senses are more difficult to define. Whereas, in the case of 'chest' an ambiguity is unlikely, unless the writer conditions his context with an ambiguity in mind, in the latter, ambiguity is probable. Furthermore, in this particular case, the context of the quotation favours this semantic ambiguity, for, as we have said, the use of erotic terminology in religious writing must be supposed to keep some of its emotional flavour. In the same way, the evocation of the cult of Christ our mother not merely explains the reference but indicates the emotional tone of the poem. It indicates that God's love for us is, like the love of a mother for a child, tender, forbearing and sacrificial.

But the sceptical reader might yet object that this last point could have been made by a simple metaphor, without the evocation of the underlying liturgical cult. Here I think we must understand that there is a difference between an emotional ambivalence and an intellectual paradox. Just as *O felix culpa* does not express the ambivalence of human attitudes to sin, but a paradox that sin could result in good fortune, in the same way, in regard to Herbert's poem, there is a difference between an interpretation assuming that, on the one hand, when Christ speaks of himself climbing the tree from which the apple was stolen, this evokes emotional ambivalence on the part of the reader by virtue of the contextual juxtaposition of 'fruit' and 'tree' and an interpretation assuming, on the other hand, that it involves the paradox that the sinless man has been treated as a robber. And it is surely the tone of the reference which makes this difference and the implied context which conditions that tone. And this is particularly significant where the words used are in themselves polysemous or tend to polysemy.

I should therefore assume that in the poem *Quia Amore Langueo* the structure of the poem is conditioned by the quotation from the *Song of Songs* which forms its refrain and by the literary context which this implies. What we have in the poem is a conventional address of the Virgin to mankind, reproving him for sin and offering him her mediating love and grace. This is a commonplace theme. What makes the poem effective is the paradoxical and polysemous use of imagery, its structure in fact. This is created by the pattern of relationships, ever shifting, even contradictory, a kind of word play on the theme of love. If the love appears on the surface to be erotic or even incestuous it is important to understand that the poem assumes emphatically that this is only a *jeu d'esprit*. When one has guessed the riddle the idea is emphatically negatived. And the shape of the poem is a shape of paradox.

And finally, this technique of literary reference contributes to semantic fullness. Dante, in *Purgatorio* xxx, describes the longing of the waiting church by a reference to the *Song of Songs*:

> un di loro, quasi da ciel messo,
> '*Veni, sponsa, de Libano*' cantando
> gridò tre volte. . . .[1]

> [*One of them, as though sent from heaven, cried out three times, chanting, 'Come spouse from Lebanon'.*]

This is not just a puzzle, although the process of identification is part of our aesthetic pleasure. The bringing together of two discrete contexts belongs to what Philip Wheelwright has called *compositive imagining*:

> Fresh associations can generate fresh meanings, and the semantic function of poetry consists largely in this: that poetry quickens and guides the associative faculty, keeps it in athletic trim, and thus actually generates new meanings – meanings that would lose their identity outside the individual poetic context, but which are authentically real within it.[2]

But further than this, the quotation from *Canticles*, by virtue of all its rich associations in medieval writing and liturgy, achieves a remarkable semantic enrichment to the context in which it occurs. For the same reason it seems to me entirely legitimate

[1] Dante, *Purgatorio*, xxx, ll.10–12; for different interpretations of the *Sponsa de Libano* see E. Auerbach, 'Figurative Texts Illustrating Certain Passages of Dante's *Commedia*', *Speculum*, xxi (1946), 477–82; Charles Singleton, *Dante Studies* I (Cambridge, Mass., 1954), pp.45–60.

[2] Wheelwright, p.50.

to assume that the poet of 'I sing of a maiden' had in mind the conventional image of the Virgin as Gideon's Fleece on which fell the dew of heaven, as the dew of divine grace fell upon the Virgin Mary. But here we have an enrichment of a somewhat different kind since the image can be taken literally as well as typologically. Yet if we test the image against the structure of the poem, we find that it does indeed fit although, unlike the example from Dante, such an interpretation is not essential to some understanding of the poem. And perhaps we might take a final example of this kind of semantic enrichment by means of literary reference. It is the last stanza of Lydgate's lyric 'As a Mydsomer Rose':

> It was the Roose of the bloody feeld,
> Roose of Iericho that greuh in Beedlem;
> The five Roosys portrayed in the sheeld,
> Splayed in the baneer at Ierusalem.
> The sonne was clips, and dirk in euery rem,
> Whan Christ Ihesu five wellys list vncloose
> Toward Paradys, callyd the rede strem,
> Of whos five woundys prent in your hert a roos.[1]

There are two references here which are not evident to the modern reader. The reference to the rose of Jericho is explained by Norton-Smith by reference to Rabanus Maurus's *Allegoria in Sacram Scripturam*:

> Rosa est coetus martyrum, ut in libro Ecclesiastici (24, 18) 'Quasi palma exaltata sum in Cades et quasi plantatio rosae in Jericho'.[2]
>
> [*The rose is the company of martyrs as in the Book of Ecclesiasticus (24, 18); 'I am exalted like a palm tree in Cades and as the setting of a rose in Jericho'.*]

The other is the equation of the wounds of Christ with the rivers of Paradise which explains why the wounds are referred to as 'wells'. Norton-Smith writes of this passage:

> The poetic activity which translates the natural rose, symbol of organic decay, into the highest expression of martyrdom through

---

[1] John Lydgate, *Poems*, edited by J. Norton-Smith (Oxford, 1966), No. 7, p.24. For the two versions of the text, see pp.136–8.
[2] *Lydgate* (1966), p.142.

the traditional symbolism of Christ, the rose of Jericho, and, further, translates the new image into a meditational emblem, is original and unparalleled elsewhere in medieval poetry.[1]

The praise is just but does not explain anything. The passage is, in fact, an admirable example of semantic enrichment. What the poet has done is to bring into relationship with each other a number of discrete elements. Firstly, taking over the rose as an image of martyrdom and suffering, in itself a conventional image, he places it in juxtaposition with a biblical reference which effectively embodies the same image but enables him to suggest a paradox, 'Roose of Jericho that greuh in Beedlem'; this involves a certain emotional disengagement. The rose then turns into the heraldic rose but contains, too, the image of the rose as a symbol of suffering and wounds. But there is already, perhaps, a suggestion of the closer focusing of the rose image, a close focus which is evident in the last line, where the rose becomes visually more precise when, not merely its blood colour, but a five-petalled shape, is suggested by its identification with the five wounds of Christ, the blood from which streams out like the rivers of Paradise, radiating from a common centre but, unlike the rivers of Paradise, from earth to heaven. But these lines suggest another image too, the image of the Christ-knight with his shield and banner, five roses, his five wounds, as his coat of arms. Then briefly, the poet takes us back to the literal level of reference, 'The sonne was clips and dirk in euery rem' before once again moving to the metaphorical level and finally to the deictic 'prent in your hert a roos'. It is by taking the traditional figures, the rose as a symbol of suffering and bringing it into conjunction with other conventional contexts, the Christ-knight and the rivers of Paradise that Lydgate has been able to create that 'ordered complexity of metaphysical allusion that distinguishes medieval religious poetry at its best'.[2]

Let us turn now to my final example. We have already discussed the literary reference as formula, giving rise to sub-

---

[1] *Lydgate* (1966), p.138.   [2] Kaske (1959), p.654.

merged imagery and the literary reference as contextual enrichment, illustrating the first from Old English and the second from Middle English. I have chosen these two areas simply as representative models, although the two types in practice overlap. I now want to deal with the most difficult area of all, the area of the literary commonplace. And, for the sake of convenience, I shall illustrate it mainly from *Pearl*. It is the area of the conventional theme rather than conventional diction or conventional imagery. This poses some interesting theoretical problems as to the nature of 'literary tradition' and when it is legitimate to assume that the poet has exploited such tradition, even though we cannot prove sources, and when it is not. It is perhaps not unreasonable to assume that there are certain conventional themes and forms which rouse certain kinds of expectation in the reader, in the way, for example, that a 'Western' rouses certain expectations in regard to characters, situation and plot. The possibility of parodying certain conventions seems to substantiate the idea that such conventional themes are part of the literary context of a work and thus potentially part of its structure.[1] The opening scene of *Sir Gawain and the Green Knight* would afford an example. This opening, for all its dramatic brilliance, is essentially conventional. There are numerous romances in which the story opens with a challenge of this kind. Such an opening is a 'topic' and must have roused certain expectations in the medieval reader (or listener) as to what kind of tale he was to expect. That the story does not develop entirely along conventional lines is part of its ironic implications. Gawain is not so much an anti-hero[2] as the poem an anti-romance and an anti-romance, like the mock-epic, implies the existence of a concept of literary form. In the same way, the temptation scenes derive much of their effectiveness from the individual treatment of common formulae. The author could have found in *The Romance of Horn* a model for a scene in which a lady makes advances to a

[1] See p.9.
[2] Cp. Spearing (1966), p.307; S. Bercovitch, 'Romance and Anti-romance in *Sir Gawain and the Green Knight*', *PQ*, xliv (1965), 30–7.

knight in this way, but the real effect of the scene comes from the expectation that this will be yet another temptation scene from which the knight will emerge victorious. Now the thesis I want to explore is that the author of *Pearl*, by exploiting conventional themes, creates a structure peculiarly suited to the purpose of the poem. Let us now look at this in detail.

It would perhaps be well to remind ourselves of the poem and its critical history. The poet, it will be remembered, loses his pearl in a garden and falls asleep, overcome with the fragrance of the herbs. As he sleeps, he has a vision of a maiden, adorned with pearls, whom he recognises to be his daughter. The meeting takes place in an earthly paradise but he is separated from the maiden by a stream. A debate follows and the poet eventually is allowed a vision of the heavenly Jerusalem. There have been many opinions as to the form and meaning of this poem. The earliest view was that it was an elegy. According to the first editor, Richard Morris, 'the author evidently gives expression to his own sorrow for the loss of his infant child, a girl of two years old'.[1] Other, and more fanciful, biographical particulars were inferred from the poem in the manner of the time. Later criticism, beginning with Schofield in 1904, regarded the poem, on the other hand, as allegory.[2] More recent critics have placed emphasis rather on imagery and symbolism than on allegory in the more limited sense. Thus R. M. Garrett saw the pearl as an eucharistic symbol;[3] Sister Madeleva thought the poem to be 'a very beautifully wrought account of an experience in interior desolation'.[4] The pearl is thus a symbol of the soul; J. B. Fletcher, by an elaborate analysis and collation of the imagery, attempted to

---

[1] R. Morris, *Early English Alliterative Poems*, E.E.T.S. 1 (2nd edn., 1869), xi.

[2] W. H. Schofield, 'The Nature and Fabric of *The Pearl*', *PMLA*, xix (1904), 154–215; 'Symbolism, Allegory, and Autobiography in *The Pearl*', *PMLA*, xxiv (1909), 585–675. Cp. G. G. Coulton, 'In Defence of *Pearl*', *MLR*, ii (1906), 39–43.

[3] R. M. Garrett, '*The Pearl*': *An Interpretation* (Seattle, 1918).

[4] Sister Mary Madeleva, '*Pearl*': *A Study in Spiritual Dryness* (New York, 1925), p.89.

demonstrate that the poem was about the Virgin Mary.[1] D. W. Robertson thought that the poem was to be interpreted on the traditional four levels. Thus the pearl is literally a jewel, allegorically those members of the Church who will be among the hundred in the celestial procession, the perfectly innocent, tropologically a symbol for the soul which attains innocence through true penance; and anagogically the life of innocence in the heavenly city.[2] Other critics have sought to elucidate the poem by an analysis of the symbolism of the pearl imagery. R. Wellek thought the pearl to be a shifting symbol representing the earthly child; the child in heaven, who, as the Bride of the Lamb, wears the pearl on her breast; and the pearl of great price, which is beatitude. He thus concludes that the symbol shifts from the earthly meaning of possessiveness to the heavenly symbol of grace.[3]

The obvious weakness of much of this criticism is that it focuses exclusively upon the symbolism of the pearl and ignores other aspects of the poem, such as the debate element, and the role of the dreamer. More recent criticism has attempted to rectify this one-sided approach. For example, in 1955, J. Conley suggested that the *Pearl* was a Christian *consolatio* analogous in theme, situation and treatment to Boethius. The theme of the poem is thus the nature of true happiness.[4] Moorman investigated the role of the narrator in *Pearl*[5] and other critics have applied modern techniques of analysis to a consideration of the imagery and symbolism of the poem.[6] This sustained

[1] J. B. Fletcher, 'The Allegory of the Pearl', *JEGP*, xx (1921), 1–21.

[2] D. W. Robertson, 'The Pearl as a Symbol', *MLN*, lxv (1950), 155–61.

[3] R. Wellek, '*The Pearl*: An Interpretation of the Middle-English Poem', *Prague Studies in English*, iv (1933), 5–33.

[4] J. Conley, '*Pearl* and a lost tradition', *JEGP*, liv (1955), 332–47; cp. V. E. Watts, '*Pearl* as a *consolatio*', *Medium Aevum*, xxxii (1963), 34–6.

[5] C. Moorman, 'The Role of the Narrator in *Pearl*', *MP*, liii (1956), 73–81.

[6] See W. S. Johnson, 'The Imagery and Diction of *The Pearl*: towards an Interpretation', *ELH*, xx (1953), 161–80; Stanton de Voren Hoffman, 'The *Pearl*: Notes for an Interpretation', *MP*, lviii (1960), 73–80; A. C. Spearing, 'Symbolic and Dramatic Development in *Pearl*', *MP*, lx (1962), 1–12; P. M. Kean, *The Pearl* (London, 1967).

critical debate has thrown up so many erudite and interesting suggestions about the poem that it may seem wasted effort to discuss it further. In fact, what I want to say does not pretend to be entirely new but I propose to look at the poem from a particular point of view, its exploitation of the literary tradition. This, I believe, will not be entirely unprofitable. I would indeed agree with Spearing that 'the whole force and poignancy of the poem derives from its basic structure as an encounter involving human relationship; and it is through the synthesis of symbol with drama that the writer of *Pearl* conveys his meaning, and not, I believe, through any concealed layers of allegory'.[1]

Yet I would not agree that the meaning of the poem is entirely conveyed through the imagery as Spearing suggests, although, as will appear, I agree with him in many respects. The mechanism appears to me to be rather a manipulation and evocation of traditional commonplaces and themes. Let us look at this a little more closely. When the dreamer sees the pearl-maiden on the other side of the stream, he laments the fate which has parted them. To his lamentation, the maiden replies:

> Sir, ȝe haf your tale mysetente,
> To say your perle is al awaye,
> Þat is in cofer so comly clente
> As in þis gardyn gracios gaye,
> Hereinne to lenge for euer and play,
> Þer mys nee mornyng com neuer nere.
> Her were a forser for þe, in faye,
> If þou were a gentyl jueler.
>
> Bot, jueler gente, if þou schal lose,
> Þy ioy for a gemme þat þe watȝ lef,
> Me þynk þe put in a mad porpose,
> And busyeȝ þe aboute a raysoun bref;
> For þat þou lesteȝ watȝ bot a rose
> Þat flowred and fayled as kynde hyt gef.
> Now þurȝ kynde of þe kyste þat hyt con close
> To a perle of prys hit is put in pref
> And þou hatȝ called þy wyrde a þef,
> Þat oȝt of noȝt hatȝ mad þe cler;

---

[1] Spearing (1962), p.3.

Þou blameȝ þe bote of þy meschef,
Þou art no kynde jueler.[1]

Here certainly we have brought into juxtaposition the two
dominant images of the poem, the jewel imagery and the
imagery from vegetable life; for, in the words of W. S. Johnson,
'the imagery of the poem can in the main be divided into two
groups; on the one hand, images out of the world of growing
things, images of the garden and the vineyard which are associated with the dust of the earth; on the other, images of
light and of brilliant, light-reflecting gems, free of any spot'.[2]
But there is more than imagery in question. The poet is also
manipulating commonplaces, for the images are part of traditional themes. To understand this we must look more closely at
two scenes in the poem; first the garden in which the poet loses
the pearl and falls asleep and then the earthly paradise in which
he finds her again. These are both literary commonplaces. Let
us look at them in turn and consider what clues the text can
provide as to the traditions in question.

The poet, we are told in the first stanza, loses his pearl in an
erbere, 'a garden'. The loss of the precious pearl, that jewel so
beloved of the aristocratic world of the fourteenth century, and
the fact that the man who loses the pearl is one whose business
is to evaluate precious jewels, a jeweller, suggests that we are in
the realm of courtly literature and that the garden is the
familiar romance setting. The *erbere* has many features in
common with these idyllic courtly settings. There is, for example, the mysterious music which comes to the poet after the
loss of the pearl. Within the conventions of the love garden, this
could suggest the song of birds which formed, according to
Libanius, one of the six charms of landscape,[3] a commonplace
neatly adapted to the five senses in Matthieu de Vendôme's
Ars Versificatoria:

> Flos sapit, herba viret, parit arbor, fructus abundat,
> Garrit avis, rivus murmurat, aura tepet.

---

[1] *Pearl*, edited by E. V. Gordon (Oxford, 1953), ll.257–76.
[2] Johnson, p.165.   [3] See Curtius, p.197.

Voce placent volucres, umbra nemus, aura tepore,
Fons potu, rivus murmure, flore solum.
Gratum murmur aquae, volucrum vox consona, florum
Suavis odor, rivus frigidus, umbra tepens.
Sensus quinque loci praedicti gratia pascit,
Si collative quaeque notata notes.
Unda juvat tactum, gustum sapor, auris amica
Est volucris, visus gratia, naris odor.
Non elementa vacant, quia tellus concipit, aer
Blanditur, fervor suscitat, humor alit.[1]

[*The flower breathes forth fragrance, the grass is green, the tree burgeons,
the fruit abounds, the bird twitters, the stream murmurs, the air is warm.
The birds please with their voices, the grove by its shade, the air by its warmth,
the fountain by its water, the stream by its murmuring, the ground by the
flower. Agreeable is the murmur of the water, harmonious the voice of the
birds, sweet the scent of the flowers, cool the stream, and warm the shade.
Observe but all together those things which we have treated severally, and
the beauty of this place feeds the five senses. The wave gratifies the touch,
flavour the taste, the bird is a friend to the ear, beauty to the sight, scent to
the nose. The elements are not idle, for the earth conceives, the air caresses,
the heat draws up, moisture nourishes.*]

Many examples of this theme occur in courtly literature from
The Romance of the Rose in the thirteenth century and *Phyllis and
Flora* in the twelfth,[2] right through to the courtly poems of the
late Middle Ages. When Dunbar walks out on a May morning,
he still hears the song of the birds and so does Lydgate (not to
mention Charles of Orleans). This supposition is, of course,
merely conjecture. The reference is too allusive to be susceptible
of a certain explanation. But the next indication is clearer. The
garden is full of flowers conventionally described as 'yellow,
blue and red' and the plants are named as

Gilofre, gyngure and gromylyoun,
And pyonys powdered ay bytwene.[3]

---

[1] Matthieu de Vendôme, *Ars Versificatoria*; E. Faral, *Les arts poétiques du
xiie et du xiiie siècle* (Paris, 1924), p.149.
[2] Chaucer, *The Romaunt of the Rose*, ll.655–68; *Phyllis and Flora*, stanzas
61–4 in *Carmina Burana*, I, 2; No. 92; 101.
[3] *Pearl*, ll.43–4.

It was Gollancz who first called attention to the influence of
The Romance of the Rose on *Pearl*.[1] In Love's Garden:

> There was eke wexyng many a spice,
> As clowe-gelofre, and lycorice,
> Gyngevre, and greyn de parys,
> Canell, and setewale of prys.[2]

There are flowers too:

> There sprang the vyolet al newe,
> And fressh pervynke, riche of hewe,
> And floures yelowe, white and rede.[3]

Now this may seem little enough upon which to build a theory,
yet, in a sense Robertson is right when he says that 'it may be
that art and literature have "languages" made up of conventions of expression which we should learn to "read" just as we
learn to read an earlier language or a foreign language'.[4]
Many scholars would disagree with the conclusions which
Robertson draws from this premise. Nevertheless, although, in
my view, he is mistaken both in assuming that there is a key
field, namely that of biblical exegesis and in his indifference to
the syntactic field in which words operate, he is in a sense right.
To understand Chaucer's *Nun's Priest's Tale* for example, one
has not merely to look up 'cock' and 'fox' in a patristic index.
One must, on the contrary, consider the configuration of the
work in question. In the case of the *Nun's Priest's Tale*, it is
evident that the configuration is that of the mock epic. With
regard to *Pearl*, the case is certainly more complex. Yet it is
probable, in my view, that the poet, by the conjunction of the
erbere, perhaps bird song, and the spices and flowers, is presenting the reader with a configuration which evokes the expectation of a romantic garden. This expectation is confirmed

---

[1] *Pearl*, edited by I. Gollancz (London, 1891), p.108; cp. H. Pilch, 'Das
mittelenglische Perlengedicht: sein Verhältnis zum Rosenroman', *Neuphilologische Mitteilungen*, lxv (1964), 427–46.

[2] Chaucer, *The Romaunt of the Rose*, ll.1367–70.

[3] Chaucer, *The Romaunt of the Rose*, ll.1431–3. Cp. E. G. Kern, 'The
Gardens in the *Decameron* Cornice', *PMLA*, lxvi (1951), 505–23.

[4] D. W. Robertson, *A Preface to Chaucer* (Princeton, 1963), p.6.

to some extent by the use of terms such as *luf-daungere*, which would also fit into such a configuration.[1]

Yet when we return to the first stanza of the poem we notice that the poet is using a technique of carefully calculated ambiguity. The associations of the pearl were various in the fourteenth century. It was a status symbol. It is pearls which Marco Polo takes with him as capital when he sets off on his travels. Then, like other jewels, they were used to image the beauty of women. The poet indeed gives some indication of the context within which the pearl is placed. He tells us that the pearl is 'plesaunte to prynces paye',[2] an indication of the social and courtly associations of the pearl. The word *luf-daungere* in the same stanza could imply, either that the pearl is a girl with whom he is in love, or merely that the pearl was as precious to him as a lady is to her lover. Ambiguity is created, both by the pronoun *her* in line 4, and the description, in lines 5–6, of the pearl as

> So rounde, so reken in vche araye,
> so smal, so smoþe her sydeȝ were.

When the dreamer sees the pearl-maiden in his vision, she too is described as 'so smoþe, so smal, so seme slyȝt' and it has been thought that the almost identical wording in the first stanza indicates that the pearl is to be understood from the very first stanza to be a girl. Rather, the first stanza of the poem appears to be designedly ambiguous, a riddle which the reader will have to solve. It illustrates admirably the exploitation of ambiguities of meaning within a carefully controlled context. We are not to assume that, at each point in the stanza, the total semantic potential of the words is part of the poetic effect,

---

[1] For some examples of the configuration in Old English compare J. L. Rosier, 'The Uses of Association: Hands and Feasts in *Beowulf*', *PMLA*, lxxviii (1963), 8–14; '*Heafod* and *Helm*: Contextual Composition in *Beowulf*', *Medium Aevum*, xxxvii (1968), 137–41; for the traditional nature of the image configurations in *Pearl* see especially Kean, *passim*.

[2] There has been considerable controversy about this line. Some editors have taken it to mean simply 'pleasing to a prince's delight'. So, for example, E. V. Gordon, Gollancz, Schofield; but others, such as Osgood and Fletcher, see a reference to Christ.

but only in so far as the words fit into the total semantic field
of the stanza. In other words, the aesthetic effect of the stanza
is not the sum total of our possible responses to it but the
stanza is rather a structure which conditions, or, if we read
attentively, should condition, our response to it.

The same careful manipulation of context can be seen in the
rest of this section of the poem. Into this conventional garden,
the poet introduces another note. The description of the
garden is connected with the passage from *John*, xii, 24:
'Except a corn of wheat fall into the ground and die, it
abideth alone; but, if it die, it bringeth forth much fruit.' The
pearl is equated both with a grain of wheat, the symbol of
resurrection, and with the seed from which spring up the
flowers and spices of the garden. We thus have a blending of
traditions, religious and secular. Some critics have supposed the
reference to the spices to be a reference to the Virgin Mary.
Osgood, for example, pointed out that the Feast of the Assumption has a lection from *Ecclesiasticus* (xxiv, 20) in which spices
symbolise the virtues of the Virgin Mary and, if one accepts
the view that the 'high festival' is the Assumption of the Virgin,
on the fifteenth of August, this seems an attractive suggestion.[1]
But spices are used to give sumptuous richness to many kinds
of paradise; from the love garden in *The Romance of the Rose*
or Claudian, to the Eden of Bernard Silvestris.[2] The definition
of the season of August as the time when the corn is cut 'wyth
croke3 kene' has also been seen as a covert reference to the

---

[1] Cp. C. H. Osgood, *The Pearl* (Boston, 1906), p.56. It has also been
suggested that the festival might be the Transfiguration; see W. J. Knightley,
'*Pearl*: The "hy3 seysoun" ', *MLN*, lxxvi (1961), 97–102; or Lammas; see
Pearl, edited by I. Gollancz (2nd edn., London, 1921), pp.118–19; James P.
Oakden, 'The Liturgical Influence in "Pearl" ', in *Symposion für Schirmer*,
p.350.

[2] Chaucer, *The Romaunt of the Rose*, ll.645–1438; Claudian, *Epithalamium
De Nuptiis Honorii Augusti*, edited by J. Koch (Leipzig, 1893), ll.93–6;
Bernard Silvestris, *De Mundi Universitate*, edited by C. S. Barach and J.
Wrobel (Innsbruck, 1876), I, 3, 315–30; Hildebert, *De Ornatu Mundi*,
PL, clxxi, cols. 1235–8; cp. M. P. Hamilton, 'The Meaning of the
Middle English *Pearl*', *PMLA*, lxx (1955), 812–18; C. A. Luttrell, '*Pearl*:
Symbolism in a Garden Setting', *Neophilologus*, xlix (1965), 160–76.

Last Judgement or the Resurrection.[1] If such suggestions are acceptable, it can only be because the poet has already made it evident by his reference to the concept of resurrection that the passage has a religious area of reference as well as a secular one. And this is, of course, reinforced in the last stanza in which the poet tells us that 'kynde of Kryst' gave him comfort; that is to say, that the divine nature of Christ gave him assurance of resurrection. Thus, in the first section of the poem, we see the poet entering the garden in which he, the jeweller, has lost his pearl. In one sense the garden is the objective correlative of the poet's emotion. He enters the garden rebellious and sad as 'the lover' of the lost pearl, who, it has already been implied, is a person. Yet the garden has also religious implications. The spices suggest to him the promise of resurrection and the life to come. It should perhaps be noted that at this stage in the poem the duality of interpretation is, in effect, only in the dreamer's mind. It is natural that, in his grief, he should recollect the biblical image of the corn of wheat, the central metaphor of the Christian belief in resurrection. Just as the dreamer in the dream allegory exists to give actuality to the vision, so here, in a sense, the dreamer gives unity to the imagery.

We then pass to the paradisical garden in which the poet sees the vision of the pearl. Here again we find a carefully manipulated context, designed to reflect the dreamer's mind. This is no longer an *erbere*. We have moved into another area of reference. Here there are no suggestions of death, but only oι life. The poet, as his spirit enters the visionary realm, describes the landscape which meets his gaze:

> . . . I knew me keste þer klyfeȝ cleuen;
> Towarde a foreste I bere þe face,
> Where rych rokkeȝ wer to dyscreuen.
> Þe lyȝt of hem myȝt no mon leuen,
> Þe glemande glory þat of hem glent;

---

[1] Cp. Schofield, p.189; Knightley, *passim*; Johnson (p.167) sees a reference to the circle of life and death. A. R. Heiserman ('The Plot of *Pearl*', *PMLA*, lxxx (1965), pp.164, 166) points out that August was the season of troublesome dreams whose interpretation was difficult.

For wern neuer webbeȝ þat wyȝeȝ weuen
Of half so dere adubbemente.

Dubbed wern alle þo downeȝ sydeȝ
Wyth crystal klyffeȝ so cler of kynde.
Holtewodeȝ bryȝt aboute hem bydeȝ
Of bolleȝ as blwe as ble of Ynde;
As bornyst syluer þe lef on slydeȝ,
Þat þike con trylle on vch a tynde.[1]

The crystal cliffs, as Patch has pointed out,[2] are characteristic of visions of the other world. The trembling leaves may indicate that the dreamer has entered a numinous grove as Dante does when he meets Matilda in the earthly paradise:

Vago già di cercare dentro e dintorno
   la divina foresta spessa e viva,
   ch'a li occhi temperava il novo giorno,
sanza piú aspettar, lasciai la riva,
   prendendo la compagna lento lento
   su per lo suol che d'ogni parte auliva.
Un'aura dolce, sanza mutamento
   avere in sé, mi fería per la fronte
   non di piú colpo che soave vento;
per cui le fronde, tremolando pronte,
   tutte quante piegavano a la parte
   u'la prim'ombra gitta il santo monte.[3]

[*Now eager to search around and within the divine forest, dense and verdant which to my eyes was moderating the new day, without waiting more I left the mountain side, very slowly crossing the plain, over the ground, which gave forth fragrance on every side. A gentle wind, itself invariable, struck my brow with no greater force than a soft breeze, on account of which the leafy branches, responsively quivering, were all bending towards the place where the holy mountain cast its first shadow.*]

---

[1] *Pearl*, ll.66–78. The translation of the last two lines is uncertain. I am assuming the sense 'slides over'. Cp. E. V. Gordon's edition. Or possibly *aslideȝ* means 'slips away' as Hillmann suggested (M. V. H. Hillmann, *The Pearl* ([Convent Station], 1961). Both these interpretations are open to objection, but seem to fit the general sense of moving leaves implied by the following line.

[2] H. R. Patch, *The Other World* (Cambridge, Mass., 1950), *passim*.

[3] Dante, *Purgatorio*, xxviii, ll.1–12.

The dreamer then sees a jewelled stream,

> Þe grauayl þat on grounde con grynde
> Wern precious perleȝ of oryente.[1]

Later in the account of the earthly paradise we are told of
another stream whose banks shone like gold and were of
beryl and each pebble in the bottom of the river was of
emerald, sapphire and other jewels. We are in another world,
an essentially romantic world. For the jewelled streams do not
necessarily indicate the supernatural. We are told in Marco
Polo and in Prester John, for example, of streams which contain
jewels.[2] Nor is it necessarily a Christian paradise. In *Huon of
Burdeux*, the hero comes to a marvellous fountain, the fountain
of youth, in which the gravel at the bottom is all of precious
stones and, later on, the same motif is used again:

> when he was enteryd into this streme he sawe ye goodlyest presyous
> stonys that euer he sawe, they were so fayre and so rych that the
> value coude not be estemyd; the grauell of the streme that issuyd
> out of the fountayne were all precyous stonys, and they cast such
> lyght that al the mountayne and rocke dyd shyne therof, whereof
> Huon had great maruayle.[3]

On the other hand, the motif occurs in descriptions of Eden.
Just as in the biblical Garden of Eden the rivers are associated
with precious metals and stones, gold, bdellium, and onyx; so
in the medieval Edens are jewels and water associated. Thus
for example Avitus:

> Hic fons perspicuo resplendens gurgite surgit.
> Talis in argento non fulget gratia, tantam
> Nec crystalla trahunt nitido de frigore lucem.

---

[1] *Pearl*, ll.81–2.

[2] Marco Polo, *Travels*, III, xix, edited by H. Yule (3rd edn., London,
1921), II, 360; F. Zarncke, *Der Priester Johannes*, Abhandlungen der Phil.-
hist. classe der K. Sächsischen Gesellschaft der Wissenschaften, vii (1879),
912.

[3] *Huon of Burdeux*, edited by S. L. Lee, E.E.T.S. (ES) ,04 41 (1882–3),
pp.433–4, 439. Although the English romance *Huon of Burdeux* is later than
Pearl in all probability, the French source from which it is translated is
from the thirteenth century.

Margine riparum virides micuere lapilli,
Et quas miratur mundi jactantia gemmas,
Illic saxa jacent.[1]

[*Here rises a fountain resplendent with a shining spring. Silver does not shine so bright, nor icicles radiate such a light from the shining cold. Green jewels shone on the edge of the banks and whatever jewels are praised by the boastful world are found there as rocks.*]

Other motifs are equally ambiguous. The fragrant fruits and the beautiful birds feature in many earthly paradises, worlds romantically idealised. Other worlds in medieval literature were of many kinds; the romantic East of Marco Polo; the magic world across the water, the enchanted land, part Celtic, part Christian, of the *Voyage of St. Brendan*; the earthly paradises of the religious writers, such as Bernard Silvestris, Avitus, or Hildebert of Lavardin;[2] such a world could be a prelude to a love vision. And, as the vision proceeds, the poet subtly hints at all these, suggesting the uncertainty of the dreamer himself, as well as the dreamlike quality of blended fantasy and reality, characteristic of a dream. For example, the colour of the trees would seem to be partly fantasy, for we are told that the trunks are blue and the leaves like silver; but there is a hint of reality here too. The trees are blue like the woods on far away hills in the summer when they take upon them the blue haze of distance. The implication is thus one of light and of distance. And this hint of reality is reinforced, I think, by the fact that the poet tells us that the leaves are 'like silver' and not that they are silver. But they too have this dual dreamlike quality. They appear to be quivering in the breeze and in the sun, so that their colour is both natural and supernatural.[3]

It may be thought that these romantic details, which could be indefinitely multiplied, are merely examples of the use, by all these writers, of a vastly popular *topos*, the *topos* of the *locus*

[1] Avitus, *De Initio Mundi*, PL, lix, col. 329.
[2] For the origins of these paradises in fact and legend see Lars-Ivar Ringbom, 'Paradisus Terrestris', *Acta Societatis Scientiarum Fennicae: Commentationes Humanarum Litterarum*, NS C (1) (1958).
[3] Cp. I. Bishop, *'Pearl' in its Setting* (Oxford, 1968), p.89.

amoenus. In one sense this is true, but a *topos*, since it is only a schema, must be fitted into its context and derives its implications from it. It seems to me significant that, in *Pearl*, the earthly paradise, in spite of overlapping details, is treated differently from the garden and from the final vision of paradise. The details of the *erbere* are a semantic configuration suggesting both a romantic garden and also, to the owner of the lost pearl, a prefiguration of the life to come. At the same time, it contains essential motifs to be developed later, the pearl, the garden, the future life. The earthly paradise, on the other hand, though clearly supernatural, yet has not the definitively Christian associations of the Heavenly Jerusalem. This is, of course, partly that it is *not* heaven but merely an ante-chamber to it, where mortal and immortal can communicate. But its ambiguity is also, I believe, a reflection of the dreamer's own mind. And this same ambiguity remains when he sees the maiden.

There has been much debate as to the symbolism of the maiden's appearance. She has all the splendour of an earthly princess, befitting her appearance in this land of fantastic beauty. Her garments are all set with pearls and her crown too has pearls. Her countenance is as white as ivory, her hair is like shining gold. Yet this jewel imagery, like the garden imagery, is not without its ambiguities. For on her breast is a large pearl, a pearl of great price:

> A manneȝ dom moȝt dryȝly demme,
> Er mynde moȝt malte in hit mesure.
> I hope no tong moȝt endure
> No sauerly saghe say of þat syȝt,
> So watȝ hit clene and cler and pure,
> Þat precios perle þer hit watȝ pyȝt.[1]

Some scholars have attempted to see elaborate references to the Virgin Mary in this description. Fletcher, for example, has drawn attention to the parallels between the imagery in *Pearl*, and in the *De Laudibus Mariae Virginis* of Albertus Magnus.[2] Rather, I believe, the poet is combining two traditional

---

[1] *Pearl*, ll.223–8.   [2] Fletcher, pp.7–12.

associations of the pearl, the courtly and the religious and this dual role of the pearl image is essential for his purpose.

What then is his purpose? The gradual evolution of the imagery from the ambiguously secular and religious, from the romantic to the sacred is, in my view, a mirror of the progress of the dreamer's understanding. Let us look at the poem from a slightly different point of view. There is, as we have said, a linking of the imagery of the garden and the earthly paradise. But there is, also, a link between the earthly paradise and the debate section of the poem since it is here that the maiden and the dreamer meet on the two levels reflected in the imagery. If for example we consider the account of the earthly paradise, we discover that the earthliness of the dreamer's understanding is shown by what he sees; he apprehends its earthly rather than its heavenly implications:

> 'O perle,' quod I, 'in perleȝ pyȝt,
> Art þou my perle þat I haf playned,
> Regretted by myn one on nyȝte?
> Much longeyng haf I for þe layned,
> Syþen into gresse þou me aglyȝte.
> Pensyf, payred, I am forpayned,
> And þou in a lyf of lykyng lyȝte,
> In Paradys erde, of stryf vnstrayned.
> What wyrde hatȝ hyder my iuel vayned,
> And don me in þys del and gret daunger?
> Fro we in twynne wern towen and twayned,
> I haf ben a joyleȝ juelere.'[1]

The maiden reproves him for not realising that his pearl is safe for ever, yet he still misunderstands:

> I trawed my perle don out of daweȝ
> Now haf I fonde hyt, I schal ma feste,
> And wony wyth hyt in schyr wod-schaweȝ.[2]

'I thought my pearl to be destroyed. Now I have found it I shall rejoice and dwell with it in these woods.' The maiden

---

[1] *Pearl*, ll.241–52; for the landscape as the mirror of the dreamer's mind cp. Spearing (1962), 4.

[2] *Pearl*, ll.282–4.

reproves him and tells him that, to rejoin her, he must first die. But the dreamer is still thinking in terms of earthly enjoyment of his pearl. He rejoins:

> What serueȝ tresor, bot gareȝ men grete
> When he hit schal efte wyth teneȝ tyne?
> Now rech I neuer for to declyne,
> Ne how fer of folde þat man me fleme.
> When I am partleȝ of perle myne,
> Bot durande doel what may men deme?[1]

Thus in this first section of the debate we see the jeweller regarding the earthly paradise with the eyes of earthly cupidity, as a place where he can again enjoy his pearl. It is to be noted that the refrain of this section with its play on the word 'jueler' underlines the theme, for the jeweller *possesses* his jewels. In the second part of the debate, the dreamer is again presented to us as rebellious against the will of God. Thus when the dreamer sees the Pearl placed high in the heavenly hierarchy he thinks that she has been unjustly preferred.

> That cortaysé is to fre of dede,
> Ȝyf hyt be soth þat þou coneȝ saye.
> Þou lyfed not two ȝer in oure þede;
> Þou cowþeȝ neuer God nauþer plese ne pray,
> Ne neuer nawþer Pater ne Crede;
> And quen mad on þe fyrst day![2]

But the Pearl tells him that in God's Kingdom there is no question of more or less and, in any case, the innocent must be saved: In one sense the dreamer is only the familiar allegorical figure, whose function in the poem is merely to enable the allegorical personages to declaim, usually at the dreamer's expense. But the poet of *Pearl*, with characteristic skill, has transformed the witless dreamer into a real person whose apparent stupidity reveals his character. And it is to be noted that, in the debate section, the images, some of which we have met before, the jewel and the jeweller, the rose and the coffer, the parable of the vineyard, the pearl of great price, are now objects of discussion. Thus in section five the jeweller is lamenting the loss of his

---

[1] *Pearl*, ll.331–6. [2] *Pearl*, ll.481–6.

jewel. The maiden tells him that if he were truly a noble jeweller he would rejoice to see it in the casket of paradise:

> Sir, ȝe haf your tale mysetente,
> To say your perle is al awaye,
> Þat is in cofer so comly clente
> As in þis gardyn gracios gaye,
> Hereinne to lenge for euer and play,
> Þer mys nee mornyng com neuer nere.
> Her were a forser for þe, in faye,
> If þou were a gentyl jueler.[1]

He thinks that the joy of the beautiful paradise involves possession; his judgement is at fault and the theme of judgement is developed in the following section by the play on *deme* in the concatenation; a play on the ideas of man's judgement and God's ordaining. Similarly in the parable of the vineyard we are concerned with money and the value of money. In man's eyes payment should be proportionate to the work done. But the Pearl tells him that such judgements are irrelevant in the world in which she now lives and she urges the dreamer to buy the immaculate pearl of peace and joy; that is to say, change his values from earthly ones to heavenly ones:

> I rede þe forsake þe worlde wode
> And porchace þy perle maskelles.[2]

It is possible that the terms in which the dreamer addresses the maiden, with its suggestions of the world of romance, is intended to imply the dreamer's point of view:

> Pymalyon paynted neuer þy vys,
> Ne Arystotel nawþer by hys lettrure
> Of carped þe kynde þese properteȝ.[3]

This commonplace image, frequent in romance writers from Chrétien onwards to describe the courtly heroine, is a natural reflection of the dreamer's earthly vision. Thus the dreamer appears to be still uncomprehending when he attains the vision of the Heavenly Jerusalem.

Here, it seems to me, we pass to another level of interpretation. In the garden we had the natural level of understanding,

---

[1] *Pearl*, ll.257–64.   [2] *Pearl*, ll.743–4.   [3] *Pearl*, ll.750–3.

the dreamer's apprehension of the spiritual significance of the natural world and his inability to accept its message. In the earthly paradise and the debate, we have two levels of understanding, the earthly and the heavenly, the natural and the supernatural. Here the imagery is still ambiguous, pointing, on the one hand, to the world of romance which is the level of the dreamer's understanding and the divine which is its true significance. In the debate section we have the dual interpretation of the preceding scene. But in the final section, the revelation which is to enlighten the dreamer's understanding, we have the supernatural only and this contrast seems to justify our interpretation of the nature of the imagery in the rest of the poem. Thus the jewelled city has no suggestion of ambiguity; the river is not a natural river, nor could it be, for it flows from the throne of God; the trees are supernatural, for they bear fruit every month. Further, the chivalric imagery which appears ambiguously elsewhere in the poem, here is unambiguously applied to the mystical marriage and the Brides of the Lamb. Thus the images from the natural world, from jewels, and from the chivalric world, all apply unambiguously to divine things. So great is the dreamer's longing for the Heavenly City that he tries to dash across the stream and awakes. For the last time, in the concluding section, we have the pearl imagery. In the opening stanzas the pearl is a precious jewel for the delectation of princes; in the last, the pearl is those who live humbly in submission to the will of God. It is surely not chance that the refrain in the last section is built up on the words *Prynces paye* echoed from the first stanza. As the imagery evolves and devolves so we have the progress of the dreamer's mind from the earthliness, or cupidity, of the natural man to humility and spirituality.

So the *Pearl* poet's manipulation of conventional material has enabled him to create a richly evocative poem in which the use of different semantic fields of reference are made to mirror a dual attitude to the events of the poem. Just as we have tried to suggest that the refrain *Quia amore langueo* in the lyric of that title, draws its force from a dual reference, the exploitation of two semantic fields, conditioned by the shape of the poem itself, so in *Pearl* the author has aroused certain kinds of literary expectation, depending upon the existence of conventional schemata.[1] This view is recommended by the fact that it enables us to see the place of the debate in the poem as a whole, for it is the debate which forms the pivot on which the poem turns from an ambiguous to an unambiguous use of the imagery of the poem.

We have tried to show, in this chapter, some of the ways in which conventional language and imagery is exploited in medieval poetry. The literary matrix which gives life to the embryonic associations of words can be of various kinds; the formulaic matrix of verbal and phrasal associations; the matrix of biblical typology and the liturgy; the matrix of the literary and rhetorical commonplace. The formulaic style depends for its effects upon the creation of variant sets, such as *lindhæbbende, randhæbbende, scyldhæbbende* and so on. And we have tried to show how the introduction of new members into these sets can create an effect, not unlike that of imagery, in which two hitherto unassociated ideas are brought into conjunction. But the formulaic style also depends upon the commonplace and to this extent it resembles the poetry of the later period. These commonplaces are, in effect, structural patterns, schemata whose effectiveness is a function of the schema and its realisation in a particular work of art. It differs from iconography in that iconography depends upon an association of ideas within an historical context and such a configuration depends upon knowledge. To identify the two figures standing beside a cross as St. John and the Virgin one has to be in the possession of certain facts, just as one has to identify Gideon's fleece with the Virgin. This gives an intellectual dimension to works using this kind of imagery. A schema is simply a diagrammatic representation of a person, scene or object which can be filled in at will and as appropriate. There are more senses than one in which Memory is the mother of the Muses.

[1] For the schema see E. H. Gombrich, *Art and Illusion* (3rd end., London, 1968), *passim*.

CHAPTER FOUR

The Romance Mode

Grau, teurer Freund, ist alle Theorie,
Und grün des Lebens goldener Baum.

[Dear friend, all theory is grey, and green the golden tree of life.]

I have chosen to begin my observations on the Middle English romances with these famous lines by Goethe because I believe that they may serve as a model for romance writing. The evocative quality of these lines lies, it has been thought, in the logical contradiction of the last line, a tree which is at once green and gold. The image is effective just because it works on two levels of apprehension; on the one hand, we apprehend the natural image of the tree intuitively;[1] that is to say, as an object of sense perception; on the other hand, the adjectives 'gold' and 'grey' are apprehended as metaphors. Trees are green but theory cannot be grey in any literal sense. Thus the use of the adjective 'grey', in the first line implies the double use, literal and symbolic, of 'green' in the second line. But the second adjective, 'gold' is also metaphorical and reinforces the symbolic implications of 'green'. The word order, moreover, implies that green is the dominant word in the second line and its position underlines its parallelism with 'grey'. The excitement which the reader experiences in reading the line comes very largely from this combination of the literal and the metaphorical, the shock of surprise at finding that the literal image of the green tree, itself a metaphor of the vitality of life, as later in Rilke, is symbolic in a wider sense and is linked with other colour words which do not function at the literal level at all. Our pleasure,

[1] Cp. Urban, pp.147-8, for a somewhat different analysis.

in fact, arises not only from the pattern of the line, though this is, no doubt, important, but even more from the paradox of the two levels of apprehension, that of intuitive sense perception and the intellectual level of metaphor or symbol.

I believe that the romance way of writing operates in an analagous fashion. Many writers have commented with varying degrees of sympathy or antipathy upon the remoteness of romance writing from common experience. 'Enchantments, quarrels, battles, challenges, wounds, wooings, loves, torments and other impossible nonsense' was Cervantes's definition of the romances of his day.[1] The judgement of Hurd, writing in 1762, was perhaps kinder but not dissimilar:

> Thus at length the magic of the old romances was perfectly dissolved. They began with reflecting an image indeed of feudal manners, but an image magnified and distorted by unskilful designers. Common sense being offended with these perversions of truth and nature . . . the next step was to have recourse to *allegories*. Under this disguise they walked the world a while; the excellence of the moral and the ingenuity of the contrivance making some amends, and being accepted as a sort of apology, for the absurdity of the literal story. Under this form the tales of faery kept their ground, and even made their fortunes at court . . . but reason, in the end . . . drove them off the scene, and would endure these *lying wonders*, neither in their own proper shape, nor as masked in figures.[2]

Even the apologists for this kind of writing have emphasised its essential lack of reality. Addison speaks of

> a kind of writing, wherein the Poet quite loses sight of Nature, and entertains his Reader's Imagination with the Characters and Actions of such Persons as have many of them no Existence, but what he bestows on them. Such are Fairies, Witches, Magicians, Demons, and departed Spirits. This Mr. *Dryden* calls *the Fairie way of Writing*, which is, indeed, more difficult than any other that

---

[1] Cervantes, *Don Quixote*, translated by J. M. Cohen (London, 1950), p.32.

[2] Richard Hurd, *Letters on Chivalry and Romance*, edited by Edith J. Morley (London, 1911), pp.153–4; cp. A. Johnston, *Enchanted Ground* (London, 1964), pp.60–74, 195–218.

depends on the Poet's Fancy, because he has no Pattern to follow in it, and must work altogether out of his own Invention.[1]

Indeed, some have seen such fictions as a special gift of the creative mind. For Sidney the creative power of the poet was to be seen in the ability to 'grow' into another nature: 'in making things either better than nature bringeth foorth, or quite a new, formes such as never were in nature: as the *Heroes, Demigods, Cyclops, Chymeras, Furies,* and such like'.[2] Dryden too praised Shakespeare's invention because in Caliban he seems to have created 'a person which was not in nature', even though he moderated his praise by claiming that 'I am certain, that the poet has most judiciously furnished him with a person, a language, and a character, which will suit him, both by father's and mother's side.'[3] The critical problem implied by these comments is particularly relevant to the romance which, as Northrop Frye has said, is a way of writing having the quality of 'disengagement', detachment, distance.[4] Although in many cases, it reflects contemporary manners, its mirror is, as Hurd observed, a distorting one. On the one hand, as has often been claimed, the romances are a mirror of medieval social life;[5] on the other, they are essentially unreal. Much misunderstanding has arisen from this dichotomy and the arguments which have followed from it. If the romances are, however strange to us, a mirror of contemporary life, then we may expect that their mode of writing will be mimetic and here they apparently fail in the majority of cases; not merely the cruder

[1] Joseph Addison, *The Spectator 419,* edited by D. F. Bond (Oxford, 1965), III, 570.

[2] Sir Philip Sidney, *The Defence of Poesie,* edited by A. Feuillerat (Cambridge, 1923), p.8.

[3] John Dryden, *Essays,* edited by W. P. Ker (Oxford, 1900), I, 219; cp. Abrams, pp.272–85.

[4] Frye, p.37

[5] Compare, for example, S. F. Barrow, *The Medieval Society Romances* (New York, 1924); R. W. Ackerman, 'The Knighting Ceremonies in the Middle English Romances', *Speculum,* xix (1944), 285–313; M. A. Gist, *Love and War in the Middle English Romances* (Philadelphia, 1947); M. A. Owings, *The Arts in the Middle English Romances* (New York, 1952).

specimens of the minstrel's art, but the self-conscious produc-
tions of a Chrétien de Troyes or a Chaucer. The world of the
romances, like the world of folk-tale, is a world without depth,
the figures that move in it are, if not without environment,
without an inner world and without genuine relationships with
the people around them. Each episode and each character is
encapsulated and exists without relationship to anyone or
anything else. The folk-tale is, in terms of later narrative
techniques, unmotivated, unrealistic, repetitive.[1] And in varying degrees the same is true of the romance. Yet the problem is,
in a sense, unreal. As I hope to show, the romance world can
more usefully be regarded as exploiting a particular combination of the sensible and the unfamiliar, showing us trees which
are, at once, green, as in nature, and gold as in the world of
analogy. This way of writing, in fact, depends upon a contrast
between different levels of comprehension; it is a world in which
people are magnified and formalised so that they are at once
familiar and unfamiliar. That this is not merely, as Hurd
suggested, due to 'unskilful designers' is indicated by its relevance even to the works of the greatest writers in this kind.

In a now classic delineation of epic and romance, W. P. Ker
wrote,

> The Sagas, which in many things are ironical or reticent, do not
> conceal their standard of measurement or value, in relation to
> which characters and actions are to be appraised. They do not,
> on the other hand, allow this ideal to usurp upon the rights of
> individual characters. They are imaginative, dealing in actions
> and characters; they are not ethical or sentimental treatises, or
> mirrors of chivalry.[2]

There is no doubt that the romances, as Ker implies, are, in many
cases, 'mirrors of chivalry' and reflect a world conditioned by those
contemporary or, at least, broadly medieval, if not precisely contemporary, views of the functions and ideals of the aristocratic

---

[1] Cp. M. Lüthi, *Das europäische Volksmärchen* (2nd edn., Bern, 1960); cp.
also B. K. Martin, '*Sir Launfal* and the Folktale', *Medium Aevum*, xxxv
(1966), 199–210.

[2] W. P. Ker, *Epic and Romance* (2nd edn., London, 1908), p.206.

H

class, which we loosely term 'chivalry'. It is possible to distinguish two strands of development. On the one hand, we have the influence of the old aristocratic ideal as seen in the *chansons de geste* or Old English poetry. The idealisation of loyalty and courage, so central to Old English poetry, is still evident in the poetry of the later period. Indeed, Marc Bloch has suggested that the conditions of near chaos which followed the splitting up of the Carolingian empire resulted in ever increasing emphasis on the protection of the individual by an over-lord and upon the loyalty between lord and vassal.[1] Thus we find in some romances an ethic not unlike that of the earlier heroic poetry, an ethic which clearly reflects feudal actualities. Thus, for example, we find a vendetta pattern in Malory and it can be illustrated from other romances. In *The Foure Sonnes of Aymon*, the whole plot is motivated by a feud arising from the slaying of the King's nephew, Berthelot by one of Aymon's sons. Again, when at last Charlemagne comes into the hands of the sons of Aymon they consider whether they shall slay him. Richard, who has suffered most, thinks they should. But Reynawde disagrees:

> My bredern, ye know well that charlemayn is our soverain lorde; and of thother parte, ye see how rowland, the duke naimes, oger the dane, the bysshop turpyn, and also escouff, the sone of oedon, are wythin for to make our poyntment wyth Charlemagn; for they know well that we ben in the right, and the kyng in the wrong. And thus yf we kylle hym, be it with ryghte or wyth wrong, all the worlde sholde renne vpon vs; nor never, as longe as we lyve, we shall not be wythoute werre.[2]

A concept of honour, not very different from what one can see in *Beowulf*, could be illustrated from the same text. When the four sons find themselves ambushed on the Plain of Valcoloures, Reynawde encourages them to fight well and to die honourably:

> Recomende our self to our lorde and thynke for to deffende vs well

---

[1] Marc Bloch, *Feudal Society*, translated from the French by L. A. Manyon with foreword by M. M. Postan (2nd edn., London, 1962), pp.160–2.

[2] William Caxton, *The Foure Sonnes of Aymon*, edited by O. Richardson, E.E.T.S. (ES) 44, 45 (1884–5), 402–3.

and feere not the dethe for our worshyp. For ones we must deye
wythoute faylle. But it is goode to gete worshyp.[1]

The point could again be illustrated from *Huon of Burdeux*.
When Charlemagne banishes Huon for slaying Duke Amaury,
he is motivated partly by the slaying of his son Charlot. Duke
Naymes protests against the sentence:

> Syrs, ye that be here present and haue well herde the grete
> vnresonablenes that the kynge do too one of oure peres, the
> whyche, as ye knowe well, it is agaynst ryght and reason, and a
> thynge not to be sufferyd. But that by cause we knowe serteynly
> the kynge is our souerayn lord, we muste suffer his plesour. But
> fro hense forthe, sens he wyl vse hym selfe and to do thynges
> agaynst reason and honour, I wyll neuer abyde an oure lenger
> with hym.[2]

These aristocratic themes of feudal loyalty and rebellious barons,
evident in the *chansons de geste*, were evidently thought sufficiently interesting to a fifteenth-century English audience for
the French texts to be translated; and no doubt they were as
topical in the time of the Wars of the Roses as they were
to the French society of their origin. In lesser ways, too, the
romances mirror the aristocratic outlook of the period. Pride
of birth would be a case in point. Thus the wild man, Orson,
impresses, for all his savagery, by his nobility of appearance.
Octavian, the noble boy brought up by the butcher, enrages
his supposed father by the acquisition of horse and weapons
thus revealing his noble birth. Ipomedon's noble blood is revealed by his generosity; on the other hand his apparent
absorption in field sports to the exclusion of chivalric under-
takings is regarded as discreditable. In these and many other
ways, the subject matter of the romances underlines the aristocratic and warlike ethos which underlies them.

Yet the romances reflect not merely the broader aspects of
medieval aristocratic life, whether it be in the eighth century, the twelfth or the fifteenth. The period which we most
particularly associate with the 'romance' has characteristics which mark it off from the earlier period. In particular

---

[1] Caxton, *The Foure Sonnes of Aymon*, p.231.   [2] *Huon of Burdeux*, p.48.

the romancers and lyric poets were no longer content merely to recount men's deeds; they made a serious, if somewhat awkward, attempt to analyse their feelings . . . in many of his characteristics, the man of A.D. 1200 or thereabouts, in the higher ranks of society, resembled his ancestor of earlier generations . . . but in two respects he differed profoundly from his predecessor. He was better educated. He was more self-conscious.[1]

This better education is shown by an increasing association of knighthood with concepts of courtesy, an association clearly seen in the works of the *Gawain* poet. In *Sir Gawain* the concept is indicated, not only by the use of the term itself, but by the range of meaning given to its opposite, villainy. This ranges from the most superficial discourtesy, as when Gawain asks that he may leave the table 'wythoute vylanye'[2] to the 'vylany and vyse' which destroy virtue with which he charges the Green Knight at the end of the poem.[3] More often, this association of courtesy with the idea of knighthood results in a more superficial emphasis on the trappings of aristocratic life. This is sometimes joined, as notably in Chrétien de Troyes, with sophisticated standards of style, evident in the rhetorical *descriptio* familiar in Chaucer, or the soliloquy found in Chrétien, in Chaucer and in other courtly romance writers. These rhetorical devices often serve to emphasise the aristocratic setting. Thus descriptions of ladies abound and of clothes and armour. The authors of even the more naïve examples of the genre seem to feel a need for these descriptions, and Chaucer seems to imply that this was part of the romance convention:

> Sire Thopas wax a doghty swayn;
> Whit was his face as payndemayn,
>   His lippes rede as rose;

---

[1] Bloch, p.106.

[2] *Sir Gawain and the Green Knight*, l.345; for the development from the 'heroic' to the 'knightly' to the 'courtly', cp. K. F. Lippmann, *Das ritterliche Persönlichkeitsideal in der me. Literatur des 13 u. 14 Jahrhunderts* (Meerane, 1933); for a recent survey with useful bibliography see R. Barber, *The Knight and Chivalry* (London, 1970).

[3] *Sir Gawain and the Green Knight*, l.2375.

His rode is lyk scarlet in grayn,
And I yow telle in good certayn,
   He hadde a semely nose.

His heer, his berd was lyk saffroun,
That to his girdel raughte adoun;
   His shoon of cordewane.
Of Brugges were his hosen broun,
His robe was of syklatoun,
   That coste many a jane.[1]

These descriptions are not always of people and clothes. For example, we have the description of tapestries in *Blanchardyn and Eglantine*,[2] of a splendid cup in *Ipomedon*,[3] reflections of courtly customs and amusements in the picture of the page serving his lady in *Ipomedon*[4] and in the same romance of the hunting and brittling of the deer[5] as also in *Partonope*[6] and *Guy of Warwick*.[7] Extended descriptions of tournaments, or single combats, appear in *Melusine*,[8] in *Ponthus and Sidone*,[9] *Libeaus Desconus*,[10] *Guy of Warwick*[11] and in *Partonope*.[12] Occasional descriptions of low life as in *Havelok*,[13] or the rough and tumble of a London street as in *Bevis of Hampton*[14] are exceptional. On the

---

[1] Chaucer, *The Canterbury Tales*, B². ll.724–35.

[2] William Caxton, *Blanchardyn and Eglantine*, edited by L. Kellner, E.E.T.S. (ES) 58 (1890), 14–16.

[3] Stanzaic *Ipomedon*, edited by E. Kölbing (Breslau, 1889), ll.2648–65.

[4] Stanzaic *Ipomedon*, ll.415–511.

[5] Stanzaic *Ipomedon*, ll.612–739.

[6] *Partonope of Blois*, edited by A. Trampe Bödtker, E.E.T.S. (ES) 109 (1912), ll.524–87; 2227–88.

[7] *The Romance of Guy of Warwick*, edited by J. Zupitza, E.E.T.S. (ES) 42 (1883); 49 (1887), (Auchinleck MS.) ll.6715–68.

[8] *Melusine*, edited by A. K. Donald, E.E.T.S. (ES) 68 (1895), 80–5.

[9] *Ponthus and Sidone*, edited by F. J. Mather, *PMLA*, xii (1897), 40-61; 138–40.

[10] *Lybeaus Desconus*, edited by M. Mills, E.E.T.S., 261 (1969), 170–9.

[11] *The Romance of Guy of Warwick*, ll.837–1012.

[12] *Partonope of Blois*, ll.9513–12122.

[13] *Havelok the Dane*, edited by W. W. Skeat, revised by K. Sisam (2nd edn., Oxford, 1915), ll.857–1066.

[14] *Sir Beues of Hamtoun*, edited by E. Kölbing, E.E.T.S. (ES) 48 (1886), ll.4339–532 (Auchinleck MS.).

whole, it is true to say that romances, where they describe people and scenes, reflect the aristocratic life of the times, albeit a life heightened and idealised.[1]

But that increasing sophistication, of which Bloch speaks, is perhaps most clearly seen in the development of what has been called 'religious chivalry'.[2] From the second half of the eleventh century, texts begin to mention ceremonies for the making of a knight. This ritual consisted of several acts. Firstly, an older knight hands the arms symbolic of the postulant's future status; in particular he girded on the sword. Then the sponsor administered a blow with the flat of his hand on the young man's neck or chest, the *paumée* or *colée*. The symbolism of this is uncertain, though it was observed that it was the only blow which a knight must always receive and never return.[3] The ceremony often concluded with some kind of athletic display such as tilting at the quintain. More fully-developed knighting ceremonies are represented by the liturgical texts in which a full-scale symbolism was gradually developed. By means of these the ceremony is firmly implanted in the liturgy. This liturgical development, no doubt, is to be associated with the function of the knightly class as it was understood both then and later. Langland expresses it thus:

> Kynges and kniʒtes . shulde kepe it bi resoun,
> Riden and rappe down . in reumes aboute,
> And taken *transgressores* . and tyen hem faste,
> Til treuthe had ytermyned . her trespas to the ende.

---

[1] Gist has pointed out the underlying realism of the romances in their view of the position of women and in their view of war; but it must also be noted how often this realism is a foil to the idealisation of the characters. Most significantly, she points out that, in the treatment of the theme of war, the authors of the romances often show an awareness of the ideals of the theorists (pp.113–36).

[2] S. Painter, *French Chivalry* (Baltimore, 1940), pp.65–94; cp. W. O. Evans, ' "Cortaysye" in Middle English', *Mediaeval Studies*, xxix (1967), 143–57.

[3] Cp. Bloch, p.312; cp. also L. Gautier, *Chivalry*, edited by J. Levron; translated by D. C. Dunning (London, 1965), pp.118–19.

> And that is the professioun appertly . that appendeth for
>   kny3tes,
> And nou3t to fasten a Fryday . in fyue score wynter;[1]

This is merely the repetition of a commonplace, expressed already, for example, in John of Salisbury:

> Sed quis est usus militiae ordinatae? Tueri Ecclesiam, perfidiam impugnare, sacerdotium uenerari, pauperum propulsare iniurias, pacare prouinciam, pro fratribus (ut sacramenti docet conceptio) fundere sanguinem et, si opus est, animam ponere.[2]

> [*But what is the office of the duly ordained soldiery? To defend the Church, to assail infidelity, to venerate the priesthood, to protect the poor from injuries, to pacify the province, to pour out their blood for their brothers (as the formula of their oath instructs them), and, if need be, to lay down their lives.*]

This religious ideal of knighthood was no doubt in Chaucer's mind when he drew his portrait of the knight in *The Canterbury Tales.*

This aspect of knighthood was later sophisticated by the introduction of elaborate symbolism, the precedent for which was the liturgy itself. One of the more remarkable examples of this is a work by the thirteenth-century mystic Ramón Lull, who also wrote a religious romance, *Blanquerna,* which like the *Queste del Graal* contrasts earthly with heavenly chivalry, both curious examples of the blending of the religious and the secular in the Middle Ages. The work of Lull was translated into French and then into English by Caxton in 1484, under the title *The Book of the Ordre of Chyualry or Knyghthode.*[3] The work is full of elaborate symbolism. We are told that the sword is made in the shape of a cross to remind the knight that as Christ

---

[1] Langland, *Piers Plowman*, B. i, ll.94–9.

[2] John of Salisbury, *Policraticus*, Bk. VI, cap. viii; II, 23; translation by J. Dickinson, *The Statesman's Book of John of Salisbury* (New York, 1927), p.199.

[3] William Caxton, *The Book of the Ordre of Chyualry*, edited by A. T. P. Byles, E.E.T.S., 168 (1926); cp. A. T. P. Byles, *Medieval Courtesy Books and the Prose Romances of Chivalry*, in E. Prestage, *Chivalry* (London, 1928), pp.183–206.

vanquished death on the cross so he must defeat the enemies
of the cross

> and therfore is the swerd made cuttynge on bothe sydes to
> sygnefye that the knyght ought, with the swerd, mayntene
> chyualrye and Iustyce.[1]

The spear signifies truth, the helmet, dread of shame, the
hauberk is a defence against vice, the leg-pieces signify a
knight's duty to punish malefactors, the spurs swiftness and
diligence, the gorget obedience, the mace strength and courage,
the dagger trust in God. The shield symbolises the office of
knighthood and the gauntlet thankfulness and avoidance of
false oaths and evil deeds, the saddle courage and responsibility,
the horse nobility of courage, the bridle signifies 'that a knyghte
oughte to refrayne his tongue and holde that he speke no
fowle wordes ne false'.[2] Some of the virtues might seem un-
suitable for a knight. Thus

> The hatte of steel or yron is gyuen to the knyght to sygnefye
> shamefastnes, for a knyȝt withoute shamefastnesse maye not be
> obeyssaunt to thordre of chyualrye; and al thus as shamefastnes
> maketh a man to be ashamed and causeth to caste doune his eyen
> ayenst the erthe, in lyke wyse the hatte of yron deffendeth a man to
> loke vpward on hyhe and maketh hym to loke toward the ground.[3]

Yet this association of the knight with the virtue of humility
appears also in Chaucer's portrait of the knight:

> And though that he were worthy, he was wys,
> And of his port as meeke as is a mayde.
> He nevere yet no vileynye ne sayde
> In al his lyf unto no maner wight.
> He was a verray, parfit gentil knyght.[4]

Thus it came about that the knight was expected to show, not

---

[1] Caxton, *Ordre of Chyualry*, p.77.

[2] Caxton, *Ordre of Chyualry*, pp.77–84. For the symbolism of armour cp.
also Elspeth Kennedy, 'Social and Political Ideas in the French Prose
Lancelot', *Medium Aevum*, xxvi (1957), 90–106.

[3] Caxton, *Ordre of Chyualry*, pp.77–8.

[4] Chaucer, *The Canterbury Tales*, A. ll.68–72; there is no need to assume
that Chaucer's knight reflects Chaucer's interest in Lollardry. Cp. R. S.
Loomis, 'Was Chaucer a Laodicean?', *Essays and Studies in Honor of Carleton
Brown* (New York, 1940), pp.129–48.

only courage, but piety, a piety, without which, it has been pointed out, Philip Augustus considered that a knight was no true *prudhomme*.[1] He must go to mass every day, or at least frequently, and he must fast (*pace* Langland) on a Friday. This blending of chivalry and morals is picturesquely illustrated in the *Epistle of Othea to Hector*,[2] or in *Sir Gawain and the Green Knight* in the hero's strict observance of his religious duties. Such a blend does not in any way suggest that the poet is portraying anything more than the conventional ideal of knighthood.

Thus the new ideal of knighthood blended fundamental and traditional concepts of courage and loyalty, with the aristocratic ideals of courtly refinement, and with a purely religious concept by which his sword must be used, not only to protect himself and his lord, but, in particular, Holy Church, the widow, the orphan and the poor. This last ideal is summed up in this prayer from the twelfth-century Besançon Pontifical:

Deus, qui trinos gradus hominum post lapsum Adae in toto orbe constituisti, quo plebs tua fidelis immunis ab omni impetu nequitie secura et quieta permaneret: adesto supplicationibus nostris et hunc ensem, quem inuocatione tui nominis benedicimus, ita famulus tuus, cui eum te largiente concedimus et accingimus, utatur, quatenus et hostes ecclesiae dei insidiantes reprimat et seipsum ab omni fraude inimici tua protectione potenter defendat.[3]

[*God who, after the fall of Adam, didst institute three orders of men in the whole world, by which thy faithful people might remain safe and at peace from all attack of wickedness; give heed to our supplications and grant that thy servant may use this sword, which we bless with the invocation of thy name, and which we give and bind on to him by thy grace, so that he may suppress the crafty foes of the church of God and powerfully defend himself by thy protection from every deceit of the enemy.*]

These actual ideals were not far from the ideals of chivalry summarised in the romance of *Partonope*:

> Drawe yow to armes and knygthode,
> And loke there lacke ynne yow no manhode.

---

[1] Cp. Bloch, p.318.

[2] See *Scrope's Epistle of Othea*, edited by C. F. Bühler, E.E.T.S., 264 (1970).

[3] A. Franz, *Die Kirchlichen Benediktionen im Mittelalter* (Freiburg im Breisgau, 1909), II, 294.

Loke ȝe be large and geuyth faste.

. . . .

Any worthy knygthtys thorow the londe.
In alle the haste loke that ye fownde.

. . . .

Loke thatt ye be gentyll, lowly, and meke,
And geuyth to hem gode clothys eke.
Alle-so of speche beyth fayre and lowlyche
As wele to the pore as to the Reche.
Affter my cowncel loke thatt ye wyrke,
And louyth welle God and holy chyrche.
Ye mowe notte fayle of hye cheualrye
Yff ȝe loue God and owr lady.[1]

And for the blending of the two ideals, religious and secular, we could not do better than consider the following passage from the late romance *Ponthus and Sidone*:

So he was in office welbeloued and dred; for if ther wer any dyscen-sion betwen the barounes and the knyghtes, he wold sett theym in peace, and acorde theym. He kepyd the ryght of Bretayn withoute dooyng wrong to any man. He was loued of all men. He iustyd and made festes and revellys. He was ryght plesaunt to grete and small, and in especiall among ladies and gentil-wommen. He was curtes . . . he wold here the pouere, and doo theym ryght . . . he loued Gode and the chirche. He herd euery day thre messes at the leste. He loued woddes and ryvers and all honest dissportes. If he come into a toune, he wolde send for ladyes and gentylwomen and make theym to daunce and syng. All dissportes and ioy come ther as he was; for he wold make to theym dynnars and sopers. He was beloued of mony fair ladies and gentylwomen, that shewed to hym mony fair draghtes of loue, bot he neuer disired loue of ladies ne of gentylwomen othre wys then to their worschip, for any cher that they made hym.[2]

Yet, although the world of chivalry, as presented in the romances, is by no means an entirely unreal world nor, indeed, entirely different from the heroic world from which sprang the epic and heroic works of the Old English period, the typical romance does differ from the typical epic; or to put the matter less tendentiously, there are works like the *Orlando Furioso* which, as literary works, are felt to be different from other

[1] *Partonope of Blois*, ll.2405-22.   [2] *Ponthus and Sidone*, pp.33-4.

works, such as the *Chanson de Roland*, which we should term epic. And this difference lies in part in the treatment of actuality. The characteristic romance procedure can be illuminated by an example from the *Roman de Thèbes*. Owings remarks that, amongst the buildings familiar from romances and real life alike, are the pavilions and tents so often described by romance writers.[1] There is no doubt that Owings is correct in saying that, in one sense, these pavilions are elements of realism in the romances. They were, no doubt, familiar to the contemporary reader. Yet, when we look at them more carefully, some interesting facts emerge. Let us take, for example, the pavilion described in the *Roman de Thèbes*.[2] The pavilion is made of 'pourpre alixandrin':

> De pourpre fu, ynde et vermeille;
> dedenz ot paint meinte merveille.

[*It was of purple, blue and red; within was painted many a marvel.*]

And it has painted upon it a map of the world, the twelve months of the year, the history of the kings of Greece and numerous animals. It is resplendent with precious stones

> Emalvaldes, jappes, sardoines,
> berinz, [sardes] et cassidoynes,
> et jagonces et cristolistes,
> et thompaces et ametistes,
> a tant en l'or qui l'avironnent,
> contre soleill grant clarté donent.

[*Emeralds, jaspers, sardonyx, beryl, sard, calcedony, jacinths, and chrysolites, topaz and amethysts which encompass it there, set in gold, are so numerous that they give great radiance against the sun.*]

Now Faral has pointed out that this description is partly inspired by Ovid,[3] and itself may be compared with passages on the same theme in the *Roman d'Alexandre*, *Doon de Nanteuil*

---

[1] Owings, pp.133–4.

[2] *Le Roman de Thèbes*, edited by Guy Raynaud de Lage (Paris, 1966), ll.4217–302 (S.A.T.F. ll.3979–4068).

[3] E. Faral, *Recherches sur les sources latines des contes et romans courtois de moyen âge* (Paris, 1913), pp.65–9.

and *Athis et Prophilias*.[1] We have in fact here a literary tradition rather than a realistic one. It may be objected that this is an unreal distinction. Themes such as the *Three Living and the Three Dead* have both a literary tradition and a visual tradition which can be realised in actual murals. The existence of a literary tradition does not necessarily exclude a literary description from the realms of actuality. This is so and we shall presumably never be in the position to say that the romance writer of the *Roman de Thèbes* is merely 'romancing'. But this is not really the essential point. The essential point is surely that, in describing something which, if it ever existed, must have been extraordinary, in the strict sense of the word, the poet is converging on the unfamiliar, unknown. The superlatives of the romance technique of necessity and indeed, by design in all probability, remove the narrative from the realm of common experience in a way that is different from the epic. And as they move from the realms of common experience the romance writers, of necessity, move into the realms of analogy; those realms in which, as in the realms of religious experience, actuality can be described only by metaphor. We are therefore, as it were, balanced between a realm of experience, the sensible, and a realm which has to be interpreted by means of the sensible. One has only to consider the medieval representations of a Charlemagne, or a St. Louis, to see the truth of this. Behind the historical figure we have always the shadow of the saint, familiar from a thousand conventional saints' lives. The tendency thus, even in the case of historical figures, is to move away from the naturalistic and historical to the extraordinary, from the present actuality to the unfamiliar and idealised. As D. M. Hill has observed 'Romance writing is essentially conventional. It operates largely, that is, through the employment of symbols whose meanings have been established by continuous corporate use.'[2]

Nowhere is this movement away from the immediate and sensible more evident than in the use made of the supernatural

---

[1] Faral (1913), p.65.

[2] D. M. Hill, 'The Structure of *Sir Orfeo*', *Mediaeval Studies*, xxiii (1961), 140.

in the romances. Historically, the rise of the romance genre
is significantly co-eval with the flood of exotic material which
transformed such classical works as the *Thebaid* of Statius,
Virgil's *Aeneid* or the Trojan Histories of Dares and Dictys into
the *romans d'antiquité*, *Le Roman de Thèbes*, *Le Roman d'Eneas* and
Le Roman de Troie.[1] Faral drew attention to the classical roots
from which the *roman d'antiquité*, in his view, sprang, but he
abundantly illustrates also the taste for the marvellous which
characterised these works.[2] These sources of exotic material are
in general well known. In 1136 Geoffrey of Monmouth produced his *Historia Britonum*[3] and towards the end of the century
a Norman, Beroul, wrote on the legend of Tristan.[4] Curious
confirmation of the taste for Celtic marvels is to be seen in the
De Nugis Curialium[5] of Walter Map or in the strange adventures
of the *Navigatio Brendani*, rendered into Anglo-Norman by a contemporary of Walter Map.[6] Crusades and pilgrimages also contributed marvellous matter for the writer of romances. From the
time of the first crusade at the end of the eleventh century,
until the fourth crusade at the beginning of the thirteenth
century, a large body of material passed from the East into
Europe, including tales of all kinds. If one compares, for
example, some of the early itineraries to the Holy Land, such
as the *Itinerarium a Burdigala Hierusalem usque* (A.D. 333) or
the slightly later *Peregrinatio Aetheriae*,[7] famous antecedents of
Mandeville, with later travel descriptions, such as the exotic

---

[1] See Faral (1913), pp.307–88.

[2] See especially Faral (1913), pp.391–419; for the English literary court
circle, see R. R. Bezzola, *Les origines et la formation de la littérature courtoise
en Occident (500–1200)* (Paris, 1963), III, 1, 3–311.

[3] Geoffrey of Monmouth, *Historia Regum Britanniae*, edited by A. Griscom
(London, 1929).

[4] Béroul, *Tristan*, edited by E. Muret (5th edn., Paris, 1957).

[5] Walter Map, *De Nugis Curialium*, edited by T. Wright (Camden Society
(OS), 50, 1850); tr. F. Tupper and M. B. Ogle (London, 1924).

[6] *The Anglo-Norman Voyage of St. Brendan*, edited by E. G. R. Waters
(Oxford, 1928).

[7] See *Itinera Hierosolymitana Saeculi IIII–VIII*, edited by P. Geyer (Corpus
Scriptorum Ecclesiasticorum Latinorum, XXXIX (1898)), 1–33; *Itinerarium
Egeriae*, edited by O. Prinz (Heidelberg, 1960).

letter of Prester John,[1] known perhaps to Chaucer, or the travels of the Franciscan, Odoric of Pordenone (c. 1330),[2] or, most famous of all, the travels of Marco Polo, a Venetian born in about 1254, one is indeed moving into a different world. The essentially romantic quality of this travel book is well defined by John Masefield in his introduction to the Everyman translation of Marco Polo. 'It is difficult to read Marco Polo, he writes, 'as one reads historical facts. One reads him as one reads romance; as one would read, for instance, the *Eve of St. Mark* or *The Well at the World's End*.'[3] Faral's study of the sources of descriptions in the earliest French romances suggests that this world of marvels was already part of the literary scene in the twelfth century. Indeed, *The Wonders of the East* had already been translated into English at the end of the eleventh century[4] and the later Middle Ages had a well-developed pictorial tradition deriving from these.[5] The opening up of a whole new world of stories and scenes in the eleventh and twelfth centuries no doubt stimulated the growth of interest in romantic wonders in the narrative works of the period. In these works, monsters and marvels abound and the putative 'wilderness of dragons' of the *Beowulf* poet's world becomes indeed a reality. But while the dragon in *Beowulf* is there, so to speak, to be slain by the hero, the dragons of romance exist in their own right to amaze and horrify the reader. But it must be emphasised that these marvels need not be supernatural. They consist not only of magic but of mechanical marvels which are

---

[1] *Prester John*, edited by Zarncke. Cp. also M. Letts, 'Prester John', *NQ*, clxxxviii (May–June, 1945), 178–80, 204–7, 246–8, 266–8; clxxxix (July, 1945), 4–7; *TRHS*, (4) xxix (1947), 19–26; C. E. Nowell, 'The Historical Prester John', *Speculum*, xxviii (1953), 435–45. For the possible influence on Chaucer's *Hous of Fame* see J. A. W. Bennett, *Chaucer's 'Book of Fame'* (Oxford, 1968), p.130.

[2] Odoric of Pordenone, *Les Voyages en Asie*, edited by H. Cordier (Paris, 1891).

[3] *The Travels of Marco Polo* (London, 1908), p.xii.

[4] *Three Old English Prose Texts*, edited by S. Rypins, E.E.T.S., 161 (1924).

[5] R. Wittkower, 'Mavels of the East. A Study in the History of Monsters', *JWCI*, v (1942), 159–97.

not supernatural.[1] An admirable example of these is the splendid tomb of Floris and Blanchefleur described in the French romance:

> En la tombe ot quatre tuiaus,
> A quatre cors bien fez et biaus
> Es quieus li quatre vent feroient
> Chaucuns issi conme il ventoient;
> Quant li venz les enfanz tochoit,
> L'un beisoit l'autre et acoloit
> Si disoient par nigromance
> Tretout lor bon et lor enfance.
> Ce dit Floires a Blancheflor:
> 'Beisiez moi, bele, par amor.'
> Blancheflor respont en besant;
> 'Ge vous aim plus que rien vivant.'[2]

[*In the tomb were four pipes with four horns well made and fair into which the four winds passed whenever they blew; when the wind touched the children they kissed each other and embraced and mentioned through magic, all their happiness and childhood. Thus speaks Floris to Blaunchefleur: 'Kiss me, fair love,' and in kissing Blanchefleur replies, 'I love you more than any living thing.'*]

It is interesting to compare this account with Mandeville's reference to such mechanical contrivances in his *Travels*:

> And þere weren jn þat place many a dyuerse thinges and manye dyuerse storyes, and of bestes and of bryddes þat songen full delectabely and meveden be craft, þat it semede þat þei weren quyke.[3]

Mandeville displays the same cool and sceptical note in regard to other marvels of the Old Man of the mountain:

> And whan þat ony gode knyght þat was hardy and noble cam to see this rialtee, he wolde lede him in to his paradys and schewen him þeise wonderfull thinges to his desport and the merueyllous and delicious song of dyuerse briddes and the faire damyseles

---

[1] See M. Sherwood, 'Magic and Mechanics in Medieval Fiction', *SP*, xliv (1947), 567–92; G. Brett, 'The Automata in the Byzantine "Throne of Solomon"', *Speculum*, xxix (1954), 477–87. Cp. also Faral (1913).

[2] *Floire et Blancheflor*, edited by M. M. Pelan (Paris, 1956), ll.580–91.

[3] Mandeville, *Travels*, edited by P. Hamelius, E.E.T.S., 153 (1919), 185.

and the faire welles of mylk of wyn and of hony plentevous rennynge. And he wolde let make dyuerse jnstrumentes of Musik to sownen in an high tour so merily þat it was ioye for to here and noman scholde see the craft þere of. And þo he seyde weren aungeles of god and þat place was paradys þat god had behight to his frendes seyenge: *Dabo vobis terram fluentem lacte et melle.*[1]

The romance writer is concerned to tell us that the mechanical contrivance is magical, Mandeville to show his scepticism; and if it be objected that the romance writer is merely showing typical medieval credulity, it may be pointed out that Mandeville is not the only medieval writer who displays a sceptical attitude to these marvellous tales. Brunetto Latini, for example, following Cicero, distinguishes between fable, history and 'argument'. He writes:

> Et certes fables, est une conte ke l'en dit des choses ki ne sont pas voires ne voirsamblables, si comme li fable de la nef ki vola parmi l'air longuement. . . .[2] argumens c'est a dire une chose fainte ki ne fu pas, mais ele pot bien estre.
>
> [*And indeed a fable is a narrative which is told concerning things which are neither true nor verisimilitudinous such as the fable of the ship which flew through the air for a long time . . . 'argument' is something feigned which did not happen but which could have done.*]

Even more emphatic are William of Newburgh's well-known comments, made towards the end of the twelfth century, on the subject of Geoffrey of Monmouth's *Historia Britonum*:

> Gaufridus hic dictus est, agnomen habens Arturi, pro eo quod fabulas de Arturo, ex priscis Britonum figmentis sumptas et ex proprio auctas, per superductum Latini sermonis colorem honesto historiae nomine palliavit; qui etiam majori ausu cujusdam Merlini divinationes fallacissimas, quibus utique de proprio plurimum adjecit, dum eas in Latinum transfunderet, tanquam authenticas et immobili veritate subnixas prophetias, vulgavit.[3]

---

[1] Mandeville, *Travels*, pp.185–6.

[2] Brunetto Latini, *Li Livres dou Tresor*, p.353; cp. De Bruyne, II, 19.

[3] William of Newburgh, *Historia Rerum Anglicarum* (Rolls Series, London, 1884), p.12; One might compare also the remarks of Peter of Blois on the fictitious nature of the Arthurian legend. See *De Confessione*, PL, ccvii, col. 1088.

[*This man is called Geoffrey, nicknamed* Arturus, *because he dressed up fables of Arthur, taken from primitive fictions of the Britons and added to by himself, adorned with the Latin tongue, in the honest name of history; with even greater audacity, he propagated most deceitful prophecies of a certain Merlin, to which he added much of his own, these being translated into Latin and put forth as authentic prophecies sustained by immutable truth.*]

Brunetto Latini defines the fable as something which is neither true nor verisimilitudinous. But the essential dividing line is between, on the one hand, *istores et argumens*, on the other *fables*. By *istores* is meant *les ancienes choses ki ont esté veraiement*, and by *argumens*, *une chose fainte ki ne fu pas, mais ele pot bien estre*.[1] The province of the *fables* is the fantastic whether it be in fact true, a mechanical contrivance; or false, a pure fiction. It is in contrast to both *istores* and *argumens*.

Let us now consider this distinction in relation to some passages in Middle English which make use of supernatural motifs. I should like to begin by considering Malory's account of the passing of Arthur.

Than sir Bedwere returned agayne and toke the swerde in hys honde; and yet hym thought synne and shame to throw away that noble swerde. And so effte he hyd the swerde and returned agayne and tolde the kynge that he had bene at the watir and done hys commaundement.

'What sawist thou there?' seyde the kynge.

'Sir,' he seyde, 'I sy nothynge but watirs wap and wawys wanne.'

'A, traytour unto me and untrew,' seyde kyng Arthure, 'now hast thou betrayed me twyse! Who wolde wene that thou that hast bene to me so leve and dere, and also named so noble a knyght, that thou wolde betray me for the ryches of thys swerde? But now go agayn lyghtly; for thy longe taryynge puttith me in grete jouperté of my lyff, for I have takyn colde. And but if thou do now as I bydde the, if ever I may se the, I shall sle the myne owne hondis, for thou woldist for my rych swerde se me dede.' Than sir Bedwere departed and wente to the swerde and lyghtly toke hit up, and so he wente unto the watirs syde. And there he bounde the gyrdyll aboute the hyltis, and threw the swerde as farre into the watir as

---

[1] Brunetto Latini, *Li Livres dou Tresor*, p.353.

he myght. And there cam an arme and an honde above the watir, and toke hit and cleyght hit, and shoke hit thryse and braundysshed, and than vanysshed with the swerde into the watir.[1]

I have chosen this as the epitome of the successful use of a supernatural motif in romance. Something of the nature of romance can be seen, if we compare this, the tragic climax of Arthur's career, with the death of Beowulf. Here there is nothing of the supernatural only sober appraisal:

> Ic on earde bad
> mælgesceafta, heold min tela,
> ne sohte searoniðas, ne me swor fela
> aða on unriht.[2]

[*I have spent my allotted time in the world, ruled my people well; I have not sought treacherous quarrels, nor sworn many oaths unjustly.*]

He thanks God that he has won treasure for his people:

> Ic ðara frætwa Frean ealles ðanc,
> Wuldurcyninge wordum secge,
> ecum Dryhtne, þe ic her on starie,
> þæs ðe ic moste minum leodum
> ær swyltdæge swylc gestrynan.
> Nu ic on maðma hord mine bebohte
> frode feorhlege, fremmað gena
> leoda þearfe; ne mæg ic her leng wesan.[3]

[*With words I thank the Lord, the King of glory, the eternal Lord, for everything, for the treasures which I here gaze upon, and that before the day of my death I could win such treasure for my people. Now that I have sold for the hord of treasures my old life, care for the need of the people. I can not stay here longer.*]

He thinks of his funeral rites, he gives his armour to Wiglaf:

> Þu eart endelaf usses cynnes,
> Wægmundinga; ealle wyrd forsweop,
> mine magas to metodsceafte,
> eorlas on elne; ic him æfter sceal.[4]

[*Thou art the last of our race, the Wægmundingas. Fate has swept all my kin to death, valiant men; I must follow them.*]

---

[1] Malory, *Morte Darthur*, pp.1239–40. [2] *Beowulf*, ll.2736–9.
[3] *Beowulf*, ll.2794–801. [4] *Beowulf*, ll.2813–16.

So the hero dies and his soul seeks *soðfæstra dom*. How different is the death of Arthur! Much of this difference lies in the supernatural motif of the reception of Excalibur by the Lady of the Lake. Whereas the death of Beowulf, if not its cause, is treated as a purely human scene, in which attention is focused on the ethos of the hero, in the *Morte Darthur*, our attention is directed towards the supernatural event which lies outside the realm of the true or the verisimilitudinous. I use the term 'verisimilitudinous' rather than 'probable' because 'probable' implies a judgement as to what is possible; 'verisimilitudinous' on the other hand, merely implies that something is within our range of experience, and I have been trying to suggest that the latter rather than the former is the relevant consideration in regard to the fantastic in the romance way of writing. The medieval reader may have believed in arms coming out of lakes, but I doubt that he had ever seen such a thing. What he believed to be possible is less relevant that what he had actually experienced. The episode, by its fabulous nature, contributes to the removal of Arthur's death from the tragic to the romantic. The action is removed by its presence from the stresses of human immediacy to the realm of the analogous. Our green tree has become gold.

Much has been made of the 'willing suspension of disbelief' as a prerequisite of successful writing in the supernatural kind, but, in regard to medieval literature at least, I think this rests upon a misunderstanding. It is not a question of belief or disbelief. Such a dichotomy assumes the mimetic mode of writing and the engagement of assent which this mode of writing implies. It is interesting in this connection to look a little more closely at the passage from Malory. The supernatural here is, as so often in Malory, contrasted with the matter of fact nature of the human detail. Characteristically the king complains that Bedivere, by his avarice, has put him in 'grete jouperté' of his life 'for I have takyn cold'. The descriptive detail is spare, as usually in Malory, although as vivid as in an Old Testament narrative. When Bedivere comes back from the lake, he tells the king that he saw nothing but the waters lapping and the dark wave. The silence and the dark waters could not be better described than in this brief description, as stark as anything in Old English poetry, yet vividly evocative of a precise sense impression. We are reminded of the Maid of Astolat's boat as it 'rubbed and rolled too and fro a grete whyle or ony man aspyed hit'.[1] Now it might equally be claimed that the arm emerging from the lake, which took the sword and 'cleyght hit, and shoke hit thryse and braundysshed', is effective by virtue of just such detail. But detail as such does not necessarily recommend the unfamiliar.

Let us make another comparison; the comments of Malory upon the final scene in the passing of Arthur with the same scene as treated by Laȝamon.

> Thus of Arthur I fynde no more wrytten in bokis that bene auctorysed, nothir more of the verry sertaynté of hys dethe harde I never rede, but thus was he lad away in a shyp wherein were three quenys; that one was kynge Arthur syster, quene Morgan le Fay, the tother was the quene of North Galis, and the thirde was the quene of the Waste Londis. Also there was dame Nynyve, the chyff lady of the laake, whych had wedded sir Pellyas, the good knyght; and thys lady had done muche for kynge Arthure. . . . Now more of the deth of kynge Arthur coude I never fynde, but that thes ladyes brought hym to hys grave, and such one was entyred there whych the ermyte bare wytnes that sometyme was Bysshop of Caunturbyry. But yet the ermyte knew nat in sertayne that he was veryly the body of kynge Arthur; for thys tale sir Bedwere, a knyght of the Table Rounde, made hit to be wrytten. Yet som men say in many partys of Inglonde that kynge Arthure ys nat dede, but had by the wyll of oure Lorde Jesu into another place. . . . Yet I woll nat say that hit shall be so, but rather I wolde sey; here in thys worlde he chaunged hys lyff.[2]

Leaving aside the problem of what precisely Malory meant by the concluding lines, the precision of this is undeniable. Yet I do not think that the effect of this precision is to increase the reader's acceptance of the supernatural event. The three ladies may have magical antecedents, yet the overprecise identification of them induces scepticism in the reader rather than ac-

---

[1] Malory, *Morte Darthur*, p.1095.   [2] Malory, *Morte Darthur*, p.1242.

ceptance. Even more so the intrusion of the Archbishop oi Canterbury. Yet why should this be so? I think comparison with the passage from Laȝamon perhaps provides the answer as well as indicating another dimension of the problem:

'And Ich wulle uaren to Aualun, to uairest alre maidene,
To Argante þere quene, aluen swiðe sceone,
And heo scal mine wunden makien alle isunde,
Al hal me makien mid haleweiȝe drenchen.
And seoðe Ich cumen wulle to mine kineriche
And wunien mid Brutten mid muchelere wunne.'
Æfne þan worden þer com of se wenden
Þet wes an sceort bat liðen, sceouen mid vðen,
And twa wimmen þerinne wunderliche idihte,
And heo nomen Arður anan and aneouste hine uereden,
And softe hine adun leiden and forð gunnen hine liðen.
Þa wes hit iwurðen þat Merlin seide whilen:
Þat weore unimete care of Arðures forðfare.
Bruttes ileueð ȝete þat he bon on liue
And wunnien in Aualun mid fairest alre aluen.[1]

Here we are presented with an actual scene, nothing violates our sense experience. Yet the king's reference to the queen of the elves and to Avalon hints at a magic reality lying behind and beyond the scene before our eyes, the boat coming across the water, the weeping queens. We are told of Arthur's 'departure', a significantly ambiguous word, and the delicate balance is maintained by the phrase 'Bruttes ileueð', removing the scene, with its magical undertones, to a remote past. In Malory, by contrast, we are brought up sharply by the collision of the here and now, the individuality of the references with the remoteness from sense of the topic. Such precision transposes the topic into the realm of history and truth thus becomes an issue. But romance is not concerned with truth but with a balance between fiction and verisimilitude and to introduce the verifiable is to destroy this delicate balance between two modes of comprehension upon which the romantic mode rests.

[1] Laȝamon's *Brut; Early Middle English Verse and Prose*, edited by J. A. W. Bennett and G. V. Smithers (2nd edn., Oxford, 1968), X, ll.307–21.

It does not seem to me therefore that the introduction of circumstantial detail in itself serves to give credibility to the supernatural. On the contrary, the supernatural is most effective when it effects, as it were, a change of key from that which is intuitively apprehended by the senses to that which is strictly outside this field of reference. Such a shift is effected by the author of *Sir Orfeo* when he describes the fairy hunt with its mixture of the actual, the supernatural and the ambiguous:

> He miȝt se him bisides
> (Oft in hot vnder-tides)
> Þe king o fairy wiþ his rout
> Com to hunt him al about
> Wiþ dim cri and bloweing,
> And houndes also wiþ him berking;
> Ac no best þai no nome,
> No neuer he nist whider þai bi-come.[1]

This I believe to be essentially different from, for example, Dante's descriptions of Heaven, Purgatory and Hell where the immaterial is made tangible by means of imagery. The supernatural of the romances is essentially a way of making the familiar unfamiliar and remote.[2] Where the ice of reality is so thin we are always aware of the dark waters beneath and the familiar world becomes strange. We suspend expectation of the natural rather than disbelief in the supernatural. When we return to the earlier passage from the *Morte*, which we quoted at the beginning of our discussion, we discover why the earlier scene is so much more effective than the later one and also why Malory needed this episode as more than a mere thematic

---

[1] *Sir Orfeo*, edited by A. J. Bliss (2nd edn., Oxford, 1966), ll.281–8, (Auchinleck MS.); cp. Hill, pp.136–8.

[2] A special aspect of this is the function of the adventure in the romance. On this Max Wehrli has commented: 'Die religiöse Geschichte *Parzivals* ist keineswegs ein Heiligenleben, sondern echtester Roman. Die Offenbarungswahrheit wird nicht als göttliche Führung oder gar als direktes Wunder deutlich, sondern als Ergebnis eines Abenteuers, als problemisches Bemühen um den Sog. Gral.' (*Roman und Legende* in *Worte und Werte: Bruno Markwardt zum 60 Geburtstag*, edited by G. Erdmann und A. Eichstaedt (Berlin, 1961)), p.439.

balance. The borderline between reality and unreality is used by Malory in a distinctive way. The book is a recreation of the past, a past which is exemplary and ideal. The shifting border between the natural and the supernatural is a part of this recreation of an ideal past, a past which is concrete and immediate, yet, at the same time, remote and unreal. Malory's mode of writing is essentially romantic, as I have tried to define it. He creates a world in which the actual recedes into a background of the unreal, and the supernatural breaks into the everyday world. It seems to me therefore that, while in Laȝamon and *Sir Orfeo* we find the natural interpenetrated with the supernatural, so that we cannot always tell which is which, in the sword episode in Malory the actual is withdrawn into the fabulous. But again, in the final scene, since we know that the Archbishop of Canterbury does not live in fairyland, the reference to him seems an improbability and does not, in fact, serve to give substantiality to the theme of Arthur's return.

This then would seem to me to be one of the main functions of the marvellous in the romances. It serves to disengage the emotions and to project the tale into an unreal world by virtue of its exploitation of essentially analogous modes of apprehension. I suspect that the *Gawain* poet uses the supernatural theme for the same purpose. That a poet with such a keen eye for human nature and the human scene should choose such an improbable story for his poem might, at first sight, seem odd. Could not his knight have been better put to the test in a fully human world?[1] No doubt the function of the Green Knight is partly to provide the misleading clue for Gawain,[2] for he is ostensibly faced with

---

[1] For an attempt to explain the magical motivation by reference to the hagiographic tradition cp. E. von Schaubert, 'Der englische Ursprung von *Syr Gawayn and the Grene Knyȝt*', *Englische Studien*, lvii (1923), 330–446; T. McAlindon, 'Magic, Fate and Providence in Medieval Narrative and *Sir Gawain and the Green Knight*, RES, xvi (1965), 121–39.

[2] It is also to be noted that the ambiguous identity of the Green Knight is one reason why Gawain falls into the trap of accepting the girdle. According to the laws of 'nurture' he must conceal a love token. *La Diffinission de Amurs* states this commonplace neatly: 'qui que ne saet celer amur, nurture lui faut'. But this obligation would presumably have been nullified had he

a supernatural challenge of the conventional kind, a conventionally perfect knight placed within a conventional romance situation, and apparently to be subjected to conventional tests of courage and virtue. Yet the test turns out other than he had expected and his virtues likewise. But I think the Green Knight has another function. The poem has been described as an 'ironical romance' and the ironic detachment is partly created by the use of supernatural.

Let us now turn to another aspect of the romances. We have tried to show how the marvellous and the exotic could be used to create a romance world in which normal human expectations are short-circuited. This is effected by bringing together objects of sense perception and objects of apprehension in such a way that the familiar and the unfamiliar merge into each other. But there are other ways in which the romance world is created. Of these, the treatment of people is not the least important, and it is here, perhaps, that the modern reader feels that the romances chiefly fail to qualify as part of 'the great tradition'. For the figures of romances are typical figures acting in a typical manner.[1] If the improbable happens, it happens to the hero of romance rather than because of him.

Some light is thrown upon the medieval concept of character painting by Matthieu de Vendôme's *Ars Versificatoria*:[2]

> Est autem forma elegans et idonea membrorum coaptatio cum suavitate coloris. Item matronae debet attribui rigor severitatis, remotio petulantiae, fuga incontinentiae sive libidinis. . . . Similiter ceterae proprietates circa diversitatem personarum diverso modo debent assignari vel observari, scilicet ut 'singula quaeque locum teneant sortita decenter' (Horace, *Poet.* 92). . . . Et quia in peritia describendi versificatoriae facultatis praecipuum

---

known the lady's advances were not, in fact, secret. He took the girdle to save his life but he concealed it to save his honour, or part of his honour. Cp. P. Studer, 'Une Définition d'Amour', *Mélanges de Philologie et d'Histoire offerts a M. Antoine Thomas* (Paris, 1927), pp.433–6.

[1] Cp. Frye, pp.304–5.

[2] Matthieu de Vendôme, *Ars Versificatoria*; Faral (1924), pp.134–5; cp. also pp.118–19.

constat exercitium, super hoc articulo meum consilium erit ut,
si quaelibet res describatur, in expressione descriptionis maximum fidei praetendatur nutrimentum, ut vera dicantur vel veri
similia.

[*Moreover, elegant and appropriate form is a congruence of parts combined
with beauty of colour. For example, to a matron should be attributed a
firm severity, an absence of petulance, avoidance of incontinence or passion* ...
*similarly, the remaining qualities, with regard to diversity of persons,
should be assigned or observed in diverse ways; that is to say, in the words
of Horace, 'Let each thing keep fittingly the place allotted to it'* ... *and
because descriptive skill especially constitutes the poetic faculty, my advice
will be concerning this point so that, whatever is described, the greatest
credibility may be produced in the description, so that, either what is real,
or what gives the appearance of reality, may be described.*]

Precisely what is in Matthieu de Vendôme's mind appears
from what follows. He goes on to explain that a description of a
person can be of two kinds, external or internal. An external
description is where external appearance only is described; internal when characteristics such as *ratio, fides, patientia, honestas*
(reason, loyalty, patience, probity) are described.[1] It is instructive to note how Matthieu de Vandôme goes about constructing
his person. The distinctive quality of a person, he says, consists
of his attributes and there are eleven personal attributes: name,
nature, milieu, fortune, condition, occupation, disposition,
judgement, situation, actions, speeches. The author then has to
assign a topic, or subject, to a matter, or person, by means of
his attributes; that is to say, he must consider what kind of impression he wishes the character to convey, whether he wishes
to praise or blame, and choose the details in accordance with
this theme.[2] Thus the figure of Beroe will be repulsive by virtue
of her personal attributes, that of Helen, attractive. Reality, in
a literary sense, thus appears to be a function of the attributes
and the theme, the result of a 'congruence of parts' by which I
would assume Matthieu to mean that, since a young woman's
most characteristic attribute is beauty, for example, it is in

[1] Matthieu de Vendôme, *Ars Versificatoria*; Faral (1924), p.135.
[2] Matthieu de Vendôme, *Ars Versificatoria*; Faral (1924), p.136.

these terms that she should be described. In other words, description is understood in terms of *differentiae* and thus in terms of the generic.

Matthieu de Vendôme is concerned rather with descriptions of people, than with characterisation as we understand the term. Yet the passage throws an interesting light on the characters in medieval romance. In relation to some of the lesser romances it is perhaps too obvious to be useful and will seem to the modern reader merely to explain their inadequacies. The virtues of a Guy of Warwick or a Bevis of Hampton are too tediously obvious to require explanation. But when we come to more sophisticated examples of the genre, the matter is different, since their evident sophistication invites the modern reader to look for the kind of characterisation which might be expected in a nineteenth-century novel. An admirable example of the way in which the theory functioned can be found in the rendering of Virgil's Camilla in the *Roman d'Eneas*. Here are the two passages, the first from Virgil, the second from the *Roman d'Eneas*:

> Hos super advenit Volsca de gente Camilla
> agmen agens equitum et florentis aere catervas,
> bellatrix, non illa colo calathisve Minervae
> femineas adsueta manus, sed proelia virgo
> dura pati cursuque pedum praevertere ventos.
> Illa vel intactae segetis per summa volaret
> gramina nec teneras cursu laesisset aristas,
> vel mare per medium fluctu suspensa tumenti
> ferret iter celeris nec tingeret aequore plantas.
> Illam omnis tectis agrisque effusa iuventus
> turbaque miratur matrum et prospectat euntem,
> attonitis inhians animis ut regius ostro
> velet honos levis umeros, ut fibula crinem
> auro internectat, Lyciam ut gerat ipsa pharetram
> et pastoralem praefixa cuspide myrtum.[1]

[Besides these there came from the Volscian nation Camilla, leading a train of cavalry, squadrons splendid with bronze; a warrior maiden, her

---

[1] Virgil, *Aeneid*, VII, ll.803–17.

*woman's hands unaccustomed to Minerva's distaff or the wool baskets;
but a girl accustomed to endure fierce battles and, in swiftness of foot
to surpass the winds. She might have skimmed along the blades of standing
corn without so much as bruising the tender ears as she ran; she might have
made her way through the midst of the sea, suspended over the swelling
wave, without so much as wetting the swift soles of her feet. From dwellings and fields the young men all poured out and a crowd of mothers
marvels and gazes at her as she passes, gaping in rapturous astonishment
to see how regal splendour clothed her smooth shoulders in purple, how
the gold clasp binds up her hair, how she carries a Lycian quiver and the
(spear shaft of) pastoral myrtle tipped with steel.*]

Beside this we may put a part of the description of Camilla in
the *Roman d'Eneas*. A limited exerpt only must serve:

> Enprés i vint une meschine,
> qui de Vulcane estoit reïne;
> Camille ot nom la damoissele,
> a mervoille par estoit bele
> et molt estoit de grant poeir;
> ne fu feme de son savoir.
> Molt ert sage, proz et cortoise
> et molt demenot grant richoise;
> a mervoille tenoit bien terre;
> el fu toz tens norrie an guerre
> et molt ama chevalerie
> et maintint la tote sa vie.
> Onc d'ovre a feme ne ot cure,
> ne de filer ne de costure;
> mialz prisoit armes a porter,
> a tornoier et a joster,
> ferir d'espee et de lance:
> ne fu feme de sa vaillance,
> Lo jor ert rois, la nuit raïne;
> ja chanberiere ne meschine
> anviron li le jor n'alast,
> ne ja la nuit nus hom n'entrast
> dedanz la chanbre ou ele estoit;
> tant sagement se contenoit
> n'en darriere ne en davant,
> que ne en fet ne en sanblant
> i peüst an noter folie,
> ja tant n'eüst vers li envie.

De biauté n'ert o li igaus
nule feme qui fust mortaus;
lo front ot blanc et bien traitiz,
la greve droite an la vertiz,
les sorciz noirs et bien dolgiez,
les ielz rianz et trestoz liez;
biaus ert li nes, anprés la face,
car plus blanche ert que nois ne glace;
entremellee ert la color
avenalment o la blanchor;
molt ot bien faite la bochete,
n'ert gaires granz, mes petitete,
menu serrees ot les denz,
plus reluisent que nus argenz.
Que diroie de sa bialté?
An tot lo plus lonc jor d'esté
ne diroie ce qu'en estoit,
de la biauté que ele avoit,
ne de ses mors, de sa bonté,
qui vallent mielz que la bialté.
Molt par ert bele la raïne.
Vers l'ost chevalche la meschine;
chevous ot sors, lons jusqu'as piez,
a un fil d'or les ot treciez.[1]

[*Then there came a young girl who was queen of Vulcania. The maid was named Camilla, she was wondrously beautiful and had great power; no other woman was so learned. She was very wise, brave, and chivalrous and had very great wealth; she governed her country marvellously well. She was ever accustomed to war and greatly loved chivalry and upheld it as long as she lived. She never busied herself with women's work neither with spinning nor sewing; she preferred to bear arms, to joust and break lances, to strike with sword and lance. There was no woman with courage equal to hers. By day she was king and by night queen. There was no lady-in-waiting or serving maid near her by day, nor at night had any man the right to enter her room; so wisely did she comport herself in private as well as in public that neither in fact nor in appearance could any folly be noted in her, not even by the envious. No mortal woman was her equal in beauty. Her*

---

[1] *Eneas*, edited by J.-J. Salverda de Grave (Paris, 1964), ll.3959–4010; cp. E. Auerbach, *Literary Language and its Public*, translated by K. Manheim (London, 1965), pp.183–91; cp. J. Norton-Smith, 'Auerbach on Literary Language', *Medium Aevum*, xxxvi (1967), 159–67.

*forehead was white and beautifully shaped, her head sat straight on her
neck (her hair parted straight over her spine?), her eyebrows were black
and delicately drawn, her eyes were laughing and very gay; fair was the
nose in her face, for it was whiter than snow or ice; her rosy colouring
was pleasantly blended with the white. The mouth was very well-shaped,
and small rather than large; her teeth were close together, gleaming brighter
than silver. What shall I say of her beauty? The longest summer day
would not suffice for me to speak of the beauty that was hers, nor concerning
her character and her goodness, which are more precious than beauty.
The queen was very beautiful; the virgin rode with the army; her hair was
blond and reached to her feet; through it she had woven a golden thread.*]

Auerbach has characterised the second passage as being typically in the middle style. It is our concern rather to note that,
whereas Virgil's portrait is full of motion and related to the
context, that of the French writer is static and detachable.
Not only has he omitted the rhetorical hyperbole designed to
give poetic form to the description of Camilla's fleetness of foot,
but the particular details of the quiver and spear, and the selective use of the colours purple and gold, have been lost. The
alterations might be subsumed under two main headings.
On the one hand, the French passage is much longer than that
of Virgil because the French author has given a complete
portrait of Camilla. He adds a formal description of her appearance, her clothes, her horse, saddle and trappings with, as
Auerbach puts it, 'marvellous, exotic splendor .. the dominant
note'.[1] These lengthy descriptive passages are interspersed with
passages of moralising. The effect of this is to remove the connections between the description and the context in which it
occurs. Whereas in Virgil we see Camilla riding swiftly by, as
she might have appeared to the bystanders, the Camilla of the
French author waits for us to take an inventory. The effect of
this is inevitably that, although in one sense it is a detailed
portrait, it is not part of a realistic whole. Many such portraits
could be found in medieval romance; for example, the portraits
in the alliterative *Destruction of Troy*,[2] those in Benoit's *Roman*

[1] Auerbach (1965), p. 189. The translation is also his.
[2] *The Destruction of Troy*, edited by G. A. Panton and D. Donaldson,
E.E.T.S., 39 (1869), ll.3741–4028.

de Troie[1] or most notably the portraits of Criseyde, Diomede and Troilus in Chaucer's *Troilus and Criseyde* which, by virtue of their detached completeness, paradoxically contribute to our feeling that the characters are receding into the distance.[2]

In the second place, we notice that the description in the French has a quality of generality lacking in Virgil. Camilla is a *mervoille . . . bele et molt estoit de grant poeir.* Instead of Camilla *agmen agens equitum et florentis aere catervas,* with its emphasis on action, and its vivid image, we are given general adjectives and the immediate action, Camilla coming into the sight of the bystanders, is replaced by a consuetudinal present: *fu toz tens norrie an guerre et molt ama chevalerie et maintint la tote sa vie.* Even where we seem to have a detailed inventory of her charms, the details are typical and serve not to individualise her, but to indicate her perfection. The whole passage is a sustained superlative. The total effect is one of richness and brightness. There is about it a kind of shimmer, resulting from the author's choice of epithets. The colours are ballad-like in their vividness, black, white, red. The images are simple and vivid, snow, ice, silver. Her gold hair is contrasted with the gold thread with which it is bound. Even her laughing eyes contribute to this effect of sparkle and flashing light. The passage has charm but its generality removes it from the sphere of the immediate to the sphere of the exemplary. Its paradigmatic quality gives it an intellectual dimension which detracts inevitably from its sensuous impact.

This comparison of two passages describing the Amazon maiden Camilla focuses conveniently one aspect of the treatment of people in the romance way of writing. In talking about structure we have already mentioned the function of typical characters in certain kinds of literary structure. This same spectrum of particularity and generality can be seen in the treatment of characters in narrative fiction. At the one extreme,

[1] *Le Roman de Troie*, edited by L. Constans, S.A.T.F. (1904), I, ll.5093–5582.

[2] M. W. Bloomfield, 'Distance and Predestination in *Troilus and Criseyde*', *PMLA*, lxxii (1957), 14–26.

one might place certain details used by Dickens in portraying Mrs. Gamp. Her frequent injunctions to 'leave the bottle on the chimley piece' that she may put her lips to it when she 'is so dispoged' indicate her membership of a class of people whose drunkenness was notorious in Dickens's day. Betsey Prigg's weakness for cucumber, on the other hand, though shared by Lady Bracknell, is just an individual trait. The characters in Chaucer's Prologue to the *Canterbury Tales* have given rise to much discussion as to their place in the spectrum. Some details, once thought to be purely individualising traits, such as the Wife of Bath's gat-tooth, have now been shown to be indicative of a type of personality.[1] Others, such as her broad-brimmed hat and her red stockings, remain unexplained, and may indeed be intended to individualise her. But it is probably significant that the more the portraits in the Prologue are investigated, the less they appear individual and the more they appear to represent types, though types very sharply and minutely delineated. The point could be made more cogently by reference to a much-quoted passage from *Gawain*:

> Þus laykez þis lorde by lynde-wodez euez
> And Gawayn þe god mon in gay bed lygez,
> Lurkkez quyl þe dayly3t lemed on þe wowes,
> Vnder couertour ful clere, cortyned aboute;
> And as in slomeryng he slode, sle3ly he herde
> A littel dyn at his dor, and dernly vpon;
> And he heuez vp his hed out of þe cloþes,
> A corner of þe cortyn he ca3t vp a lyttel,
> And waytez warly þiderwarde, quat it be my3t.
> Hit watz þe ladi, loflyest to beholde,
> Þat dro3 þe dor after hir ful dernly and stylle
> And bo3ed towarde þe bed; and þe burne schamed
> And layde hym doun lystyly, and let as he slepte.
> And ho stepped stilly and stel to his bedde,
> Kest vp þe cortyn and creped withinne,
> And set hir ful softly on þe bed-syde
> And lenged þere selly longe to loke quen he wakened.

---

[1] W. C. Curry, 'More about Chaucer's Wife of Bath', *PMLA*, xxxvii (1922), 45–6.

Þe lede lay lurked a ful longe quyle,
Compast in his conscience to quat þat cace myȝt
Meue oþer amount – to meruayle hym þoȝt.[1]

This delights the modern reader by its truth to nature. But it is indeed truth to nature in a particular way. It is particular rather than individual. It marks no progress in the development of Gawain's character; nor does it mark him off from the generality of other knights about to undergo trials. The reader does not exclaim 'But only Gawain could have done that!' but rather, 'But I might have done that!' It is a minutely observed, and vividly realised, Everyman that we are watching; and, properly so, for this is not a tale in which the theme is expressed in terms of a developing character, but one in which, as in Chaucer's *Knight's Tale*, the theme is inherent in the pattern of the story. Even the apparent development of the Green Knight is expressed, not in terms of his own personality, for this rumbustious fellow has no real personality, but by the magical change of scene. As the tale progresses his character appears to change but, in fact, character was all there from the beginning. The change is a trick by which we are made to feel that our stationary train is moving.

Nowhere, perhaps, in medieval literature has the rationale of the typical character been more radically misunderstood than in *The Knight's Tale*. The frantic searches of modern critics to differentiate the personalities of the two knights is indicative of this misunderstanding. The modern reader wonders why Chaucer, who shows himself a master of realistic detail in *Troilus and Criseyde*, should choose to present his theme in this work by means of these two pasteboard figures. The answer is surely that the work is a romance and that the pathetic and not the tragic is its proper tone. The love of the two heroes is idealised, their fate a schematic one. Emily is a shadowy figure and rightly so; for she is only a dream, a projection of an ideal. If she sings like an angel, it is because, for the two lovers, she was angelic, a being of a higher order than man. She gathered a

---

[1] *Sir Gawain and the Green Knight*, ll.1178–97.

garland of flowers because she was identified with spring and with love. The description of her is conventional and generalised because she is the type of beautiful maidens with whom men fall in love. Chaucer, in fact, is not trying to show us what Emily was like but what she appeared like to the two young men. He has chosen a particular topic of praise. Thus the poem is not telling us so much about the fortunes of three individuals as about love and death and the noble life, as it was then understood. The poem speaks, less to our emotions than to our understanding. Its aim is perhaps the inculcation of wisdom, that blend of feeling, understanding and experience. It has, indeed, something of the feelings of a Botticelli picture, beautiful, etherial, and, in spite of its detail, unreal; and, like so much of Chaucer's work, it has a painterly quality. It is an example of the romance way of writing at its best.

In the treatment of character, the romance way of writing is concerned with the general and the typical and this is one reason why the mode is an essentially unrealistic one. It has a certain flatness because, although the writer of romances is not averse from numbering 'the streaks of the tulip', the detail is superficial. But there is another aspect of the romance genre to be considered; the way in which emotions are presented in some of the romances. There is indeed only one emotion which receives any extensive analysis in the romances, namely love. Other emotions, such as wonder and fear, are expressed fleetingly in relation to particular events but the emotion of love is not infrequently the subject of exhaustive analysis, albeit in an almost entirely stereotyped form. Discussion of the origins of 'courtly love' would here be out of place, but it is necessary to consider the language of love in some of its manifestations in medieval writing.

The literary stereotypes arose in the twelfth century. This was an era of intensive study of Ovid and, whatever weight is attached to the influence of the Provençal lyric or Arabic philosophy,[1] or to an anticlerical gesture at the court of William

---

[1] Cp. A. J. Denomy, 'An Inquiry into the Origins of Courtly Love', *Mediaeval Studies*, vi (1944), 175–260; *'Fin' Amors:* The Pure Love of the

of Poitiers, there can hardly be any doubt that Ovid was immensely important in providing the vocabulary of love.[1] When the lover in *The Romance of the Rose* was initiated into the Commandments of Love he was told:

> But hyde thyne harm thou must alone,
> And go forth sool, and make thy mone.
> Thou shalt no whyle be in o stat,
> But whylom cold and whilom hat;
> Now reed as rose, now yelowe and fade.
> Such sorowe, I trowe, thou never hade;
> Cotidien, ne quarteyne,
> It is nat so ful of peyne.
>
> . . . .
>
> And whanne the nyght is comen, anoon
> A thousand angres shall come uppon.
> To bedde as fast thou wolt thee dight,
> Where thou shalt have but smal delit;
> For whanne thou wenest for to slepe,
> So full of peyne shalt thou crepe,
> Sterte in thi bed aboute full wide,
> And turne full ofte on every side;
> Now dounward groff, and now upright,
> And walowe in woo the longe nyght;
>
> . . . .
>
> Such hevynesse, and such wakyng,
> Makith lovers, withouten ony wene,
> Under her clothes pale and lene.
> For Love leveth colour ne cleernesse;
> Who loveth trewe hath no fatnesse.[2]

This is the conventional love sickness suffered by lovers from Chrétien to Chaucer and after. And it is all in Ovid, the epi-

---

Troubadours', *Mediaeval Studies*, vii (1945), 139–207; 'The *De Amore* of Andreas Capellanus and the Condemnation of 1277', *Mediaeval Studies*, viii (1946), 107–49; *The Heresy of Courtly Love* (New York, 1947); T. Silverstein, 'Andreas, Plato and the Arabs: Remarks on Some Recent Accounts of Courtly Love', *MP*, xlvii (1949), 117–26; Bezzola, II (Paris, 1960), 292–316.

[1] Cp. J. M. Steadman, '*Courtly Love* as a Problem of Style', in *Symposion für Schirmer*, pp.1–33; for courtly love as convention, cp. J. Stevens, *Music and Poetry in the Early Tudor Court* (London, 1961), pp.147–229.

[2] Chaucer, *The Romaunt of the Rose*, ll.2395–402; 2553–62; 2682–6.

thets *aeger, languidus, malum, pallor,* the oxymoron of love *jucundum malum, incendia mitia,* together with the whole metaphor of love as a disease. Canace in the *Heroides* does not speak in terms very different from a love-sick heroine in Chrétien or Boccaccio:

> Ipsa quoque incalui, qualemque audire solebam,
> Nescioquem sensi corde tepente deum.
> Fugerat ore color, macies adduxerat artus,
> Sumebant minimos ora coacta cibos;
> Nec somni faciles et nox erat annua nobis,
> Et gemitum nullo laesa dolore dabam;
> Nec, cur haec facerem, poteram mihi reddere causam,
> Nec noram, quid amans esset; at illud eram.[1]

[*I too was inflamed by love; I felt some god in my glowing heart, and knew him from what I used to hear he was. My colour had fled from my face wasting had shrunk my frame; I scarce took food, and with unwilling mouth; my sleep was never easy, the night was a year for me and I groaned though stricken with no pain. Nor could I render myself a reason why I did these things; I did not know what it was to be in love – yet in love I was.*]

This stereotype was used by countless authors in the Middle Ages. The oxymoron of love is a striking example of a rhetorical trope from classical sources which medieval authors were never tired of repeating. It appears, for example, in the *De Planctu Naturae* of Alanus de Insulis:

> Pax odio, fraudique fides, spes juncta timori,
> Est amor, et mistus cum ratione furor.
> Naufragium dulce, pondus leve, grata Charybdis,
> Incolumis languor, et satiata fames.
> Esuries satiens, sitis ebria, falsa voluptas,
> Tristities laeta, gaudia plena malis.[2]

[*Love is peace joined with hatred, faith with fraud, hope with fear and fury mixed with reason; pleasant shipwreck, light heaviness, welcome Charybdis, healthy sickness, satisfied hunger, famished satiety, drunken thirst, deceptive delight, glad sorrow, happiness full of evils.*]

---

[1] Ovid, *Heroides,* edited by A. Palmer (Oxford, 1898), xi, ll.25–32; translation by G. Showerman (London, 1921), p.135; for the influence of Ovid, cp. E. K. Rand, *Ovid and his Influence* (London, 1926).

[2] Alanus de Insulis, *De Planctu Naturae,* PL, ccx, col. 455.

Petrarch does not disdain to use this time-honoured trope to describe his own 'lusty sorrow' in the *Trionfi*.[1] Alain Chartier is still using it in the fifteenth century:

> Triste plaisir et doulereuse joie,
> Aspre doulceur, reconfort ennuyeux,
> Ris en plourant, souvenir oublieux,
> M'accompaignent, combien que seul je soie,
>
> Embuchez sont, afin qu'on ne les voie,
> Dedens mon cuer en l'ombre de mes yeulx.
> *Triste plaisir . . . . ennuyeux.*
>
> C'est mon tresor, ma part et ma monjoie,
> De quoy Dangier est sur moy envieux.
> Bien le sera, s'il me voit avoir mieulx,
> Quant il a dueil de ce qu'Amours m'envoie.
> *Triste plaisir . . . seul je soie.*[2]

[*Sad pleasure and grievous joy, bitter sweetness, burdensome consolation, weeping laughter, forgetful memory, all accompany me, however long I am solitary; that one may not see them, they lurk in my heart in the shadow of my eyes; it is my treasure, my prize and my peak of joy; for this, Danger is envious of me. Well may he be, if he sees me more fortunate, when he grieves at that which Love sends me.*]

Readers of the pseudo-Chaucerian poems of the fifteenth century will be familiar with its use in English and, indeed, the sixteenth-century lover continued to languish and shake and toss on his sleepless bed much as his twelfth-century counterpart had done. For the Petrarchan tradition only perpetuated this particular stereotype. In other ways, too, the Ovidian fashion was reflected in romantic writings of the Middle Ages. Especially was this the case with the rhetorical and introspective monologue, so evident in the works of Chrétien and Boccaccio, which was modelled, in some degree, at least, on the sentimental monologues of Ovid's *Amores* and *Heroides*.

If I have laboured this point, it is because I believe that 'courtly love' is, primarily, in English literature at least, a

[1] Petrarch, *I Trionfi*, edited by P. Lecaldano (Milan, 1956), *Trionfo d'Amore* iv, 143–53.

[2] *One Hundred Ballades, Rondeaux and Virelais from the late Middle Ages* edited by Nigel Wilkins (Cambridge, 1969), No. 78, pp.98–9.

conventional way of writing about romantic love. Such love is essentially a refined emotion, a self-conscious emotion and one for which there is a traditional rhetorical language, befitting its significance and centrality in the experience of a courtly person. The range and fluidity of the concept is evident from the abundant discussion on the topic of love in the twelfth and thirteenth centuries. One has only to call to mind such works as Andreas Capellanus,[1] or the *Anti-Nasonem* of William of St. Thierry with its obvious reference to Ovid's *Ars Amatoria* and *Remedia Amoris*:

> Nam et fedus amor carnalis feditatis sue olim habuit magistros, in eo quo corrupti erant et corrumpebant tam perspicaces, tam efficaces, ut ab ipsis feditatis amatoribus et sociis, doctor artis amatorie recantare cogeretur, quod intemperantius cantaverat; et de amoris scribere remedio, qui de amoris carnalis scripserat incendio.[2]

> [*For formerly the filthy love of the flesh also had masters of its filthiness; they professed corruption and so acutely and so effectively did they corrupt, that the master of the erotic art was compelled, by the very lovers and companions of filthiness, to recant that which he had more intemperately sung and to write of the remedy of love, he who had written of the fire of carnal love.*]

One has only to call to mind the work of the Victorines, especially Richard of St. Victor,[3] and above all the work of St. Bernard.[4] Nor should it be forgotten that at this period too, the *De Amicitia* of Cicero was known and studied; witness the work of Peter of Blois,[5] witness the treatise on spiritual love by Ailred of Rievaulx[6] and its counterpart in the English *Ancrene*

---

[1] Andreas Capellanus, *De Amore*, edited by E. Trojel (Copenhagen, 1892): translated by J. J. Parry, *The Art of Courtly Love* (New York, 1941).

[2] William of St. Thierry, *De Natura et Dignitate Amoris*, edited by M.-M. Davy (Paris, 1953), p.72.

[3] Richard of St. Victor, *De Quatuor Gradibus Violentae Caritatis.*

[4] Bernard, *De Diligendo Deo; Opera*, III (1963), 111–54. Cp. E. Gilson, *The Mystical Theology of St. Bernard*, translated by A. H. C. Downes (London, 1940).

[5] Peter of Blois, *De Amicitia Christiana et de Charitate Dei et proximi.*

[6] Ailred of Rievaulx, *De Spiritali Amicitia*, edited by J. Dubois (Bruges & Paris, 1948).

Wisse.[1] Evidence of this debate is also seen in such texts as *L'amistiés de vraie amour* of the thirteenth century or the text *Hec sunt duodecim signa* on the signs of love. The former is particularly interesting in its presentation of two opposing views of love. To quote its editor:

> l'auteur de cet Art d'aimer oppose deux conceptions de l'amour, *concordances de diverses volontés* . . . et *derverie de pensée*, et opte pour la première, qui est empruntée à l'amitié.[2]

The concept of love which developed from this debate, even in a secular context, was susceptible of many definitions.[3] It included the adulterous love of a Lancelot and Guinevere or a Tristan and Isolde; it included the married love of Chrétien's *Erec et Enide*; it included the passionate love of a William of Poitiers or the platonic love of Dante for Beatrice which, by a platonic ladder, could lead the poet up to heaven. Yet this diversity of concept is presented in imagery which is markedly uniform and conventional, the imagery of the Ovidian stereotype. In England this stereotype appears early, not only in the *Harley Lyrics*, but, for example, in the romance of Guy of Warwick, where the love of that tough warrior Guy for the maiden Felice, whom he subsequently married, is narrated in just the terms of the convention:

> At Felice he tok his leue þo,
> & in his way he goþ apliȝt.
> Vnto his chamber he went ful riȝt,
> & wepe & made grete wo,
> For he loued þat maiden so.
> His men axed him on hy,
> Why þat he was so sori?

---

[1] *Ancrene Wisse*, pp.19–30.

[2] J. Thomas, 'Un art d'aimer du xiiie siècle', *Revue belge de philologie et d'histoire*, xxxvi (1958), 791.

[3] Cp. M. Lazar, *Amour courtois et 'Fin Amors' dans la littérature de xiie siècle* (Bibliothèque française et romane, ser. C. Études littéraires, No. 8. Paris, 1964).

He hem answerd sone anon,
Þat swiche iuel is comen him on
Þat he weneþ his liif forgon,
Bote no tit him neuer non.[1]

Thereafter he becomes so ill that physicians are sent to diagnose the nature of his illness. After swooning frequently, he seeks out Felice in a garden and tells her he loves her to the point of death and, after more swooning, Felice agrees to grant her love if he is made a knight. And so the story is motivated. A classic statement of the theme is to be found in the stanzaic *Ipomedon*:

Whate myghte þat be, but derne love,
That all ways wyll be above
To them, that shall it havnte?
All othere thynges men davnte may,
But, sertenly, be no waye
Love wille not be davnte!
Who presus ofte to serue hytte,
Worse schall have his gurdovn quyte,
For he be loves seruante.
Who entrys in to lovys scolys,
The wyseste is holdyn moste foolys,
Fro that they haue graunte.[2]

or again

'The blame ys thyne owne, Imayne,
That love dothe the so mekyll payne,
Woundes wyth outen spere!
Nay, it is turment, as men tellis!
Hit is love – what is hit ellys? –
That peas hathe turnyd to werre!'
Vp she ryses and downe she fallis,
And on love playnly she callys;
'Why dost thou me this dere?'[3]

---

[1] *The Romance of Guy of Warwick* (Auchinleck MS.), ll.258–68.
[2] Stanzaic *Ipomedon*, ll.797–808.
[3] Stanzaic *Ipomedon*, ll.7143–51.

or again

> Love is so mekyll of myghte,
> That is will davnte bothe kyng and knyght,
> Erle and bold barowne;
> They, that wyseste is of witte,
> Fro tyme they be takyne wyth it,
> Hit takythe from them there reasowne.[1]

Yet the romances vary widely in their concept of love. The faithful love of the warrior Guy, who serves his lady by chivalric enterprise for many years, is then knighted and marries her, is far from the romance of *Partonope*, for example. Beauty and chastity, according to this author, do not agree:

> For beaute loveth all gentilnesse,
> Honour noble, and largesse,
> Faire speche, and þerto full of plesaunce,
> Lovyng boþe pley, to sing and daunce.
> Chastite putteth beaute oute of array.
> She will neuer suffre hir be fresshe and gay,
> But shadowes hir euer with mournyng chiere;
> Of hir she hath a full lewde fere.
> For beaute desyreth to haue þe colour
> Of þe faire fresshe rose floure,
> And loveth also to lyve in Iolyte,
> Desyryng to haue hye prosperite.
> But þat foule þat may not haue
> To hir love noþer knyght ne knave,
> Gentilman ne yeman of no degree,
> Lette hir þan lyve in chastite.[2]

Yet again, the very courtly romance of *Ponthus and Sidone* praises its hero for clean and stable love. Certainly, it seems likely that those romances which treat their love theme without breach of morals would have had the support of not a few contemporaries. The lady of La Tour Landry has no illusions as to the value of the postures of love so familiar from lyric and romance writers:

> . . . many gentylle men whiche ben so fals and deceyuable, that they requyre euery gentylle woman that they may fynde, and to

---

[1] Stanzaic *Ipomedon*, ll.7346–51.   [2] *Partonope of Blois*, ll.7654–69.

them they swere that they shalle kepe to them their feythe, and
be trewe to them, and shalle loue them without falshed or
deceyuaunce, and that rather they shold deye, than to thynke
ony vylonye or dyshonoure, and that they shalle be the better
preysed for the loue of them, and that, yf they haue ony good and
worship, it shalle come by them, and thus they shalle shewe and
saye to them so many reasons and abusions, that a grete meruaylle
is to here hem speke. And yet more they gyue oute of theyr
brestes grete and fayned syghes, and make as they were thynkynge
and Melancolyous, and after they cast a fals loke, and thenne
the good and debonayr wymmen that sene them, supposen, that
they be esprysed of trewe and feythfull loue.[1]

To these warnings the Knight replies:

Lady ye be moche hard & euyll, in as moche that ye wyll not suffre
that your doughters be amerouse; and yf so came that somme
gentyl knyght, worshipful, myghty, and puyssaunt ynough after
theyre degree, had sette his herte on one of them, and be wyllynge
to loue her, and take her to his wyf, why shalle she not loue hym?[2]

But the anxious mother explains that, though some men ask
their paramours to be their wives, others do not, and she adds
the warning that 'many wymmen haue lost theyr maryage, by
cause of theyr amerous loke and fayr semblaunt',[3] an echo
perhaps of *The Romance of the Rose*.

Gower too inveighs against the worldly knight who pursues
wealth and women:

O, cur sic miles mundi sibi querit honores,
Cuius honor mundi stat sine laude dei,
Vulgi vaniloqui sermones miles honorem
Credit, et hos precio mortis habere cupit?
Nil tamen ipse cauet dum vincitur a muliere,
Quo reus ante deum perdit honoris opem.
Quid sibi vult igitur audacia sic animosa

---

[1] William Caxton, *The Book of the Knight of the Tower*, edited by M. Y.
Offord, E.E.T.S. (SS) 2 (1971), 166; cp. N. K. Coghill, 'Love and *Foul
Delight*', in *Patterns of Love and Courtesy*, edited by J. Lawlor (London, 1966),
pp.141–56.
[2] Caxton, *The Book of the Knight of the Tower*, p.167.
[3] Caxton, *The Book of the Knight of the Tower*, p.168.

Militis in vacuum, que racione caret?
Laus caniter frustra, nisi laudis sit deus auctor;
Dedecus est et honor qui sonat absque deo.
Nescio quid laudis cupit aut sibi miles honoris,
Dum deus indignum scit fore laudis eum.[1]

[*O why does a knight whose worldly honour remains without God's esteem
seek such honors for himself? Why does he believe that the words of the
prattling mob are an honour, and wish to possess them at the price of
death? Then too he fears nothing when he is overcome by a woman, whereby
he, guilty before God, loses a wealth of honour. What does a knight's so
dauntless courage, lacking rationality, vainly desire. The knight's praises
are sung in vain, unless God is the author of them. And that honour
which is noised abroad apart from God is a disgrace. A knight is eager
for any kind of praise or honour, when God knows he is unworthy of it.*]

Gower uses the term *fin amour* to express the love of God, not of
man. It is thus evident that behind the similarity of presentation there is a diversity of moral concepts in the treatment of
love in secular works. Such works may assume an immoral
stance, but neither Gawain's rejection of the lady's advances nor
the epilogue to *Troilus and Criseyde* are, I believe, in themselves
uncourtly.

The stereotyped expression of this passion, which we find
in the romances, is not then due to a monolithic concept of the
passion but to a literary schema. The schema represents a for-
malising of the passion of love, but the circumstances and the
moral stance may be widely different from text to text. Just as
chivalry and aristocratic life, as seen in the romances, rest upon
a social actuality, so the passion of love as presented in these
texts rests upon a psychological actuality. Both are removed
from reality in so far as they are expressed in a conventional
manner. The apparent uniformity arises, not from the expression of a theory of love, common to all texts which write in this
way, but from a commonplace of expression. The manner
however does imply a certain social background and certain

---

[1] John Gower, *Vox Clamantis* V, **v.** ll.281–92; *Complete Works, IV*, edited by
G. C. Macaulay (Oxford, 1902); English based on E. W. Stockton, *The Major
Latin Works of John Gower* (Seattle, 1962), p.202; cp. J. A. W. Bennett,
'Gower's *Honeste Love*', in *Patterns of Love and Courtesy*, pp.107–21.

shared preconceptions, as is implied by the words of the royal
tersel:

> Thanne oughte she be myn thourgh hire mercy,
> For other bond can I non on hire knette.
> For nevere for no wo ne shal I lette
> To serven hire, how fer so that she wende.[1]

Nicholas is presumably aping his betters in words, if not in
deeds, when he exclaims:

> 'Ywis, but if ich have my wille,
> For deerne love of thee, lemman, I spille'.
> And heeld hire harde by the haunchebones,
> And seyde, 'Lemman, love me al atones,
> Or I wol dyen, also God me save!'[2]

No doubt his philosophy, in fact, would have been that of the
duck 'There been mo sterres, God wot, than a payre'.[3] That
continued debate about the nature of love, which the nineteenth
century called 'courtly love', is often expressed in terms as
formal as those of a scholastic disputation. Sensitivity, fidelity,
high seriousness are generally accepted virtues in a lover as they
must be in any romantic concept of love. But essentially it is a
debate rather than a theory, although the formal and traditional nature of its expression has blinded critics to this fact.

Just as the use of the strange and exotic give remoteness and
strangeness to the romances, so too, in many cases, the stereotyped vocabulary, and the conventional postures of the love
themes, serve, not only to make the action and the characters
remote, but also to generalise them. Even though the characters
of a romance by Chrétien or Boccaccio may appear to analyse
their emotions in lengthy monologues, their formulation of the
passion is essentially the same. Whether the subject be the
passion of a Soredamors, Troilus or Madonna Fiammetta, the
symptoms and the metaphors which express them represent the
formalisation of a common passion, the idealisation of a

---

[1] Chaucer, *The Parlement of Foules*, ll.437–40.
[2] Chaucer, *The Canterbury Tales*, A. ll.3277–81.
[3] Chaucer, *The Parlement of Foules*, l.595.

primary emotion. Yet it would be a mistake to assume that the emotions, because formalised, are not to be taken seriously. It is not a question of the actuality or otherwise of the emotion expressed by the heroes and heroines of romance. Their emotion and its symptoms may be very similar in a romantic and a realistic medium; yet the formal style of the romantic mode will differ from that of the more realistic medium. A comparison of two passages from Boccaccio will illustrate the point. The one is from the *Elegia di Madonna Fiammetta*. The nurse discovers the passion of Fiammetta:

> Ecco che li cresciuti ornamenti, gli accesi sospiri, li nuovi atti, li furiosi movimenti, la perduta quiete, e l'altre cose in me per lo nuovo amore venute, tra gli altri domestici familiari a maravigliarsi mossero una mia balia, d'anni antica e di senno non giovane, la quale, già seco conoscendo le triste fiamme, mostrando di non conoscerle, più fiate mi riprese de' nuovi modi. Ma pure un giorno me trovando sopra il mio letto malinconosa giacere, vedendo di pensieri carica la mia fronte, poi che d'ogni altra compagnia ci vide libere, così cominciò a parlare.[1]

> [*Lo, how my increased adornments, my burning sighs, my unwonted gestures, my furious movements, my lost peace, and those other things in me which came through my new love, moved, amongst the other familiar servants, a nurse of mine to marvel. She was old in years and not young in wisdom and she, already recognising the sorrowful flames, but feigning not to recognise them, many times reprehended me for my new conduct. But, indeed, one day, finding me lying melancholy on my bed, seeing my brow laden with thoughts, when she saw no company with me but herself, she thus began to speak.*]

The nurse then proceeds to extract a confession from the amorous girl. The setting is traditional with the figure of the nurse going back to Virgil, the phrasing is conventional and so is the situation. A different kind of effect is given in a similar situation in one of the tales of the *Decameron*. Here it is a young man who is afflicted with the pains of love. His family call a doctor, a practical measure which in itself sets the tone. The doctor takes

[1] Giovanni Boccaccio, *Elegia di Madonna Fiammetta*, edited by P. P. Addoli (Milan, 1962), p.30.

steps to cure him. He feels his pulse and at this moment the young man's beloved enters the room:

La quale come il giovane vide, senza alcuna parola o atto fare, sentì con più forza nel cuore l'amoroso ardore, per che il polso più forte cominciò a battergli che l'usato: il che il medico sentì incontanente e maravigliossi, e stette cheto per vedere quanto questo battimento dovesse durare. Come la Giannetta uscì della camera, e il battimento ristette; per che parte parve al medico avere della cagione della infermità del giovane; e stato alquanto, quasi d'alcuna cosa volesse la Giannetta addomandare, sempre tenendo per lo braccio lo'nfermo, la si fé chiamare. Al quale ella venne incontanente; né prima nella camera entrò che'l battimento del polso ritornò al giovane, e lei partita, cessò.[1]

[*Whom when the young man saw, without any word or deed, he felt the amorous ardour stronger in his heart, wherefore his pulse began to beat more vigorously than usual, which the doctor immediately feeling, he marvelled and remained quiet to see how long this beating would last. When Giannetta left the room the beating subsided too, and accordingly the doctor thought he knew the reason for the young man's infirmity; and after a little while, as though wishing to ask Giannetta for something, still holding the sick man by the arm, he had her called. At which she came immediately; and no sooner had she entered the room than the beating of the pulse returned to the young man, and when she had left, it ceased.*]

The difference in tone between the two passages is immediately apparent. In the one, we have generalities; in the other, precision and careful, matter-of-fact detail. The remoteness of the first passage is due not to the unreality of the emotion expressed, but to the generality and formality with which it is stated; a generality which inevitably gives an intellectual dimension which for the modern reader conflicts with the expectations of an intuitive experience such as he will receive from a tale in a realistic mode.

I propose finally to consider briefly characterisation in Malory. E. A. Baker has written of Malory that

The *Morte Darthur* is not a novel, but it shows a distinct advance towards the future novel. Attention is turned, more than in any

---

[1] Giovanni Boccaccio, *Decameron*, II, 8, edited by V. Branca (2nd edn., Firenze, 1960), I, 262.

of the antecedent stories that went to its making, upon the inner world of character and motive. Especially is this so after the coming of the Grail; from that point onwards the characters are more firmly and distinctly limned, and the causation of events depends more intimately upon the conduct of the actors.[1]

The fallacy here, I think, lies in the equating of an interest in people with 'the inner world of character and motive'. The French *Mort Artu* is not analytical in the way that Henry James is analytical, but is as deeply concerned as Malory with the results of action. Indeed, Malory might be said to have more affinities with the epic than with the novel in that his interest in people is social rather than psychological. The same is true of a poem such as the alliterative *Morte Arthure*. The diversity of characteristics attributed to Arthur are all related to his social function as king and leader.[2] Many attempts have been made to demonstrate the character development and motivation of the characters in Malory. For example, P. E. Tucker has seen the fatal flaw in Lancelot's character as instability.[3] R. H. Wilson has drawn attention to what he considers the development of Lancelot's character. Malory, he claims, has developed Lancelot's character more than the French. He has emphasised his modesty, his unselfish devotion to the queen, his kindness and consideration to young knights such as Gareth, his generosity to his opponents and so on.[4] In a similar vein, Lumiansky has suggested that the character of Bors is systematically built up, especially after the Grail Quest.[5] The character of Bors is pictured less as that of an individual than as that of a man having a particular function in a social context. Thus, for ex-

---

[1] E. A. Baker, *The History of the English Novel* (New York, 1924), I, 193.

[2] Cp. J. Finlayson, 'The Concept of the Hero in *Morte Arthure*,' in *Symposion für Schirmer*, pp.249–74.

[3] P. E. Tucker, 'The Place of the "Quest of the Holy Grail" in the *Morte Darthur*', *MLR*. xlviii (1953), 391–7. Cp. 'Chivalry in the *Morte*', in *Essays on Malory* edited by J. A. W. Bennett (Oxford, 1963), pp.88–93.

[4] R. H. Wilson, *Characterisation in Malory* (Chicago 1934).

[5] R. M. Lumiansky, 'Malory's Steadfast Bors', *Tulane Studies in English*, viii (1958), 5–20; cp. C. Moorman, 'Malory's Treatment of the Sankgreall', *PMLA*, lxxi (1956), 496–509.

ample, Lumiansky points out that he plays an active part in the wars against Lucius although he does not appear in the source. He is mentioned as one of the knights who goes on an embassage to the emperor Lucius. But this only establishes him as an important character in the Arthurian circle, not as an individual. From the tale of Tristram onward he assumes even greater importance. He seems to be contrasted with Lancelot in the story of the begetting of Galahad, in that, whereas Lancelot begets the Grail winner under compulsion and the influence of magic, Bors, at this point, is vouchsafed a vision of the Grail. In this Grail section Bors is presented in contrast with his brother Lionel 'whych ys dry withoute vertu . . . for he ys a murtherer and doth contrary to the Order off Knyghthode'.[1] And he is one of the heroes to achieve the Grail ship. In the final books, as Lumiansky points out, there are numerous significant scenes, particularly those in which he tries to modify the jealous imprudence of the queen. When the queen is 'nygh ought of her mynde for wratthe' when she hears that Lancelot has worn the 'rede slyve of the Fayre Maydyn of Astolat' it is Bors who reproves and pacifies her.[2] It is Bors, as Lumiansky says, who warns Lancelot against the trap set by Agravain and his kin to entrap Lancelot and the Queen. Again when Guinevere is impeached as a result of the poisoned apple incident, Bors reproves her, but in the end agrees to fight for her, if no better man can be found. Most interesting of all is a passage, at the beginning of Book XVIII, where Bors reproves Lancelot, to the significance of which Lumiansky has again drawn attention:

> 'Fayre sir,' seyde Bors de Ganys, 'ye shall departe oute of thys londe by myne advyce, for ye muste remembir you what ye ar, and renomed the moste nobelyst knyght of the world, and many grete maters ye have in honde. And women in their hastynesse woll do oftyntymes that aftir hem sor repentith. And therefore, be myne advyce, ye shall take youre horse and ryde to the good ermytayge here besyde Wyndesore, that somtyme was a good

---

[1] Malory, *Morte Darthur*, p.968.
[2] Malory, *Morte Darthur*, pp.1080–1.

knyght, hys name ys sir Brascias. And there shall ye abyde tyll that I sende you worde of bettir tydynges'.[1]

This passage is apparently an addition by Malory and it has been thought significant for this reason in assessing how Malory understood the character of Bors. Yet when we look more closely at the figure of Bors, as presented to us by Malory, we are struck by the lack of motivation in the figure. As Lumiansky claims, he is certainly a contrast with Lancelot, stable, faithful, virtuous, a pillar of society and above all loyal and reasonable. We all know such people. In that sense he is real. But he is not real in the sense that we are ever told anything of his 'inner world', why he acts as he does or what he thinks of the events in which he is involved, except in the most general way. The same might be said of the figure of Gawain. R. H. Wilson has attempted to show that Malory has tried to reconcile the two traditions of Gawain which he met in his sources;[2] the good man, the right hand man of Arthur, as in the Vulgate Merlin, the alliterative *Morte Arthure*, the Vulgate Lancelot, the *Mort Artu* and, on the other hand, the worldly and treacherous Gawain of the *Tristram* and the *Queste*. Only in *The tale of Lucius*, does he remain a purely epic hero. Malory's stress on the theme of the Pellinore feud, and the related theme of the feud with Lancelot, means that he mainly conceives of Gawain as an irascible and vindictive character. Thus we are told at the end of the tale of Gareth that 'he wythdrewe hymself fro his brother sir Gawaynes felyship, for he was evir vengeable, and where he hated he wolde be avenged with murther; and that hated sir Gareth'.[3] This picture is reinforced by the comments of the other characters in the book. In *The book of Tristram*, we hear several times of the feud between Gawain and his family and the family of Pellinore. Palomides judges that Sir Lamorak was slain 'felounsly, unto all good knyghtes grete damage',[4] and, later,

---

[1] Malory, *Morte Darthur*, p.1047.

[2] R. H. Wilson, 'How many books did Malory write?' *Texas Studies in English*, xxx (1951), 13–15.

[3] Malory, *Morte Darthur*, p.360.

[4] Malory, *Morte Darthur*, p.688.

as this act of treachery echoes through *The book of Tristram*, we hear other criticisms of Gawain. Tristram says to Agravain and Gaheris

> hit is shame . . . that sir Gawayne and ye be commyn of so grete blood, that ye four bretherne be so named as ye be: for ye be called the grettyste distroyers and murtherars of good knyghtes that is now in the realme of Ingelonde.[1]

It has also been pointed out how Malory remodelled the Ettard and Pelleas story in order to project a picture of a lascivious and treacherous Gawain.[2] In the Quest of the Grail, Malory keeps, on the whole, the picture of Gawain as the secular man untouched by the spiritual realities of the Grail Quest. When he is told to do penance by the hermit he refuses.

> 'Nay,' seyd sir Gawayne, 'I may do no penaunce, for we knyghtes adventures many tymes suffir grete woo and payne.' 'Well,' seyde the good man, and than he hylde hys pece.[3]

But the French is more explicit and perhaps gives us the implications of this 'well'.

> Et li pruedome le let a tant, que plus ne li dit, car il voit bien que ses amonestemenz seroit peine perdue.[4]

> [*And the good man leaves it at that, for he well sees that his admonition would be effort wasted.*]

And the last we see of Gawain in the Quest is his riding away from a hermit who reproves him for his evil life.

> 'Sir,' seyde sir Gawayne, 'and I had leyser I wolde speke with you, but my felow sir Ector ys gone and abithe me yondir bynethe the hylle.' 'Well,' seyde the good man, 'thou were better to be counceyled.' Than departed sir Gawayne and cam to sir Ector, and so toke their horsis and rode tylle that they com to a fosters house, which herberowde them ryght welle. And on the morne

---

[1] Malory, *Morte Darthur*, p.691.

[2] F. Whitehead, 'On Certain Episodes in the Fourth Book of Malory's *Morte Darthur*', *Medium Aevum*, ii (1933), 199–208.

[3] Malory, *Morte Darthur*, p.892.

[4] *La Queste del Saint Graal*, edited by A. Pauphilet (Paris, 1923), p.55.

departed frome hir oste and rode longe or they cowthe fynde ony adventure.[1]

Now whether we regard these descriptions of Gawain as the product of a single scheme, designed for a single book, or whether we think of them as the product of eight different sources combined at random, the fact remains that, as in the case of Bors, they do not give us either singly, or as a whole, any explanation, except the baldest, of Gawain's motives for his actions. That he acted from a desire for vengeance in a family feud, that he was lascivious, and that he was not a religious man, is all we really know of him. Like Bors, he has no inner life and it is a distortion of Malory's work to look for one. Even his repentance is perhaps more important for its justification of Lancelot than as a psychological revelation. But in Lancelot and Guinevere, at least, we seem to have fully realised characters. Yet is this really the case? Like Bors, Lancelot stands out as a credible person. He is brave, considerate, courteous, flawed only, if it be a flaw, by his love for Guinevere. P. E. Tucker has argued that the fatal flaw in his character is instability and that the story of Lancelot is the story of a failure in loyalty. He claims that, as the *Morte* proceeds, right is increasingly seen as having precedence over love.[2] Yet I think it significant that we become aware of this instability in Lancelot mainly through the mouth of the hermit in the *Quest* and that this is not a sustained characteristic nor maintained as an inner conflict. The motivation is obvious but not subtle. And Guinevere remains a shadowy figure throughout the work except perhaps in the last books. Even in these last books her words and actions are only reflections of her situation, the words and actions of 'everywoman' in such a situation, and we never have a clear picture of her as we have of Chaucer's Criseyde.

Wherein then lies the undoubted strength of the work? Does the impact of the characters really depend upon such details as that of Lancelot leaving the Grail ship? I do not believe so. The

[1] Malory, *Morte Darthur*, p.949.

[2] P. E. Tucker, 'Chivalry in the *Morte*', in *Essays on Malory*, pp.101–2; cp. p.260, n. 3.

story of the *Morte* is the rise and fall of the Round Table and in particular of Lancelot, its great hero, whose love lays him open to the scheming of his enemies, and whose downfall is lamented even by his greatest enemy, Gawain, who eventually sees in his vindictive pursuit of the feud the cause of it all. The aim of the story is not the exploration of character but the presentation of a theme. And the theme is a social one; on the one hand, the tragic conflict between Lancelot's loyalty to Arthur and to Guinevere and, at the same time, the picture of an ideal past. And the way in which this is presented can be seen, in miniature, in the treatment of the love of Lancelot and Guinevere. It is well known that Malory seems to take up an equivocal position in regard to this love. On the one hand, in the final eulogy on Lancelot, it is presented as good. Here we are told that Lancelot was 'the trewest lover, of a synful man, that ever loved woman'[1] and of Guinevere that 'whyle she lyved she was a trew lover, and therefor she had a good ende'.[2] At times, he is curiously reluctant to admit the adulterous nature of their relationship. For example:

> For, as the Freynshhe booke seyth, the quene and sir Launcelot were togydirs. And whether they were abed other at other maner of disportis, me lyste nat thereof make no mencion, for love that tyme was nat as love ys nowadayes.[3]

And yet later, in the story of the Knight of the Cart, we hear explicitly of Lancelot's adultery and, in the Quest of the Grail, he is censured for his adultery with the queen. It seems likely that Malory, while taking over much of the material of his sources, where he would have found both the glorification of love, its tragic consequences and the Church's censure of its adulterous nature, probably added the concept of stable love as characteristic of love in the good old days which he is trying to depict. The concept can be found, as R. T. Davies points out, as far back as Chrétien's *Ywain*, but a more apposite example, perhaps, is a passage in Lydgate's *Reson and Sensuallyte*. Lydgate

---

[1] Malory, *Morte Darthur*, p.1259.   [2] Malory, *Morte Darthur*, p.1120.

[3] Malory, *Morte Darthur*, p.1165. On this cp. S. J. Miko, 'Malory and the Chivalric Order', *Medium Aevum*, xxxv (1966), 215-6.

is describing how, in King Arthur's time, Diana had many
friends and the knights of Britain loved only for honour:

> The myghty famous werriours,
> Lovede the dayes paramours,
> Gentilwymmen of high degre,
> Nat but for trouthe and honeste,
> And hem self to magnyfye,
> Put her lyf in Iupartye
> In many vnkouth straunge place,
> For to stonde more in grace
> Of ladyes, for ther high empryse.
> And al they mente in honest wyse,
> Vnleful lust was set a-syde,
> Women thanne koude abyde,
> And loveden hem as wel ageyn
> Of feythful herte hool and pleyn,
> Vnder the yok of honeste,
> In clennesse and chastite,
> So hool that Venus, the goddesse,
> Hadde tho noon Interesse.
> That wer so feythful and so stable
> To knyghtis that wer honourable,
> Chose out for her ovne stoor
> To love hem best for euer moor;
> Wher so as her sort was set,
> The knot never was vnknet.
> Their choys was nat for lustynesse,
> But for trouth and Worthynesse,
> Nor for no transitorie chaunce
> Nor, shortly, for no fals plesaunce,
> How ofte that they wer requered;
> Of my scole they wer so lered
> To love hem that wer preved best,
> And in armys worthyest,
> Many sithe and nat oonys,
> That wer chose out for the nonys,
> In high prowesse hem self to avaunce
> Throgh her long contynywaunce. . . .[1]

---

[1] Lydgate, *Reson and Sensuallyte*, edited by E. Sieper, E.E.T.S. (ES) 84
(1901), ll.3179–214; cp. R. T. Davies, 'The Worshipful Way in Malory',
in *Patterns of Love and Courtesy*, p.167.

It is Diana who speaks in favour of the chaste and stable love of the days of King Arthur and I think the point is significant for Malory. The contrast is surely between the love which is virtuous, namely which chooses its object for worth and not for physical desire and which, having chosen, remains faithful, and a false love, which is based on physical desire, and which is promiscuous, a love which is not 'pour cause de mieulx en valoir, ne pour vertu: mais seulement pour la delectation que ton corps en a ou espere avoir'.[1] The perspective is different from what we expect. Of course, fornication and adultery were sins in the eyes of the Church. The Quest of the Grail makes this clear and, of course, Malory understood this. It is even possible that the words of 'moral Gower' echoed in his ears:

> Gallica peccata, nuper quibus hii ceciderunt,
> Clamant iam nostras intitulare domos:
> Nunc licet alterius sponsam quod quisque frequentet
> Est status ingenui, dicitur illud amor.
> Non erit hoc laicis vicium set gracia magna,
> Dum sit adulterio magnificatus homo,
> Dummodo sponsa stuprum perquirit adultera donis:
> Soluet ob hoc sponsus, qui luet illud opus.
> Sic se nunc homines vendunt, quasi sint meretrices,
> Prospera dum Veneris larga sit illa manus.[2]

> [*The sins of the French, who have recently fallen prey to them, now clamour to take possession of our households. Now is it permissible for every man to dance attendance upon another man's wife, and this is called the noble rank's love. This is not a vice for laymen, but a great mark of esteem, for a man becomes distinguished through adultery, while his adulterous wife courts dishonor for the sake of gifts. The husband who will himself have to atone for that sin will therefore absolve her. Thus men and women now sell themselves as if they were whores, while Venus' generous hand is propitious.*]

---

[1] *Le livre des faicts du bon messire Jean le Maingre, dit Boucicaut*, edited by J. F. Michaut and [J. J. F.] Poujoulat (Nouvelle collection des mémoires pour servir à l'histoire de France, II, Paris, 1836), p.221. Cp. R. T. Davies, 'The Worshipful Way in Malory', in *Patterns of Love and Courtesy*, p.163.

[2] Gower, *Vox Clamantis*, VII, iii, ll.157–66; Stockton, p.258. Cp. also *Vox Clamantis*, V, caps. i–viii, on the conflict of chivalry and courtly love; Stockton, pp.196–208.

But there is also a worldly perspective which, while condemning excess of passion, especially when it leads a man into conflict with his feudal obligation, does not necessarily condemn adulterous love as such. Guinevere's love for Lancelot is good in so far as it is inspired by Lancelot's knightly prowess, and not merely by idle lust, and in so far as it is stable. That it is adulterous is, in itself, less important than the fact that it brings Lancelot into conflict with King Arthur who is his feudal superior.[1] For Lancelot is guilty of a breach of 'fellowship' and this leads to disaster. The essence of the dilemma is put by Bors: 'Whether ye ded ryght othir wronge hit ys now youre parte to holde wyth the quene.'[2] It is perhaps worth noticing in this connection the oaths and ordinances of the knights of the Round Table, a curious text printed by Sandoz. We notice in particular the following items:

> Le v^m de porter foy de loyaulte a leurs compaignons et garder leur honneur et profit en leur absence et presence. Et combatre en tous lieux pour soubstenir lonneur lun de lautre et dommage eschiver. Et ne devoient combatre lun contre lautre si mescongnoissance ne le faisoit fere.
>
> Le vingtiesme quilz ne devoient prandre ne toucher nulle Dame ne damoiselles proposant quilz leussent conquise de force darmes *si elle ny prenoit plaisir et que elle y fut consentante.*[3]

> [*The fifth is to keep loyal faith with their companions and to preserve their honour and profit in absence and presence. And in all places to fight to preserve each other's honour and to avoid harm. And they should not fight each other unless mistaken identity bring it about. The twentieth is that they should not take or touch any lady or maiden, supposing that they have conquered them by force of arms, unless she take pleasure in it and consent thereto.*]

or in the words of Gawain 'Þrete is vnþryuande in þede þer I lende'.[4]

---

[1] Cp. Miko, pp.211–30; R. T. Davies, 'Malory's Launcelot and the Noble Way of the World', *RES*. vi (1955), 356–64; W. L. Guerin, ' "The Tale of the Death of Arthur"; Catastrophe and Resolution', in *Malory's Originality*, edited by R. M. Lumiansky (Baltimore, 1964), pp.269–74.

[2] Malory, *Morte Darthur*, p.1171.

[3] E. Sandoz, 'Tourneys in the Arthurian Tradition', *Speculum*, xix (1944), 401–2.

[4] *Sir Gawain and the Green Knight*, l.1499.

In the eyes of the Church Lancelot's love for Guinevere is a sin; in the eyes of the chivalric world not necessarily so. As C. S. Lewis pointed out, Malory has a three-storeyed mind.[1] On the other hand, Agravain and Gawain, as Gawain in the end admits, have offended against *foy de loyaulte a leurs compaignons*. I believe that Malory's intention in the presentation of his characters is not the analysis of character but the presentation of a theme. The characters are not individualised but draw their vitality almost entirely from their social milieu. It is in relation to their social milieu that they have meaning. We might say of them as has been said of the Chaucer's characters that they 'do not change or develop under the impact of experience; they display various aspects of an established set of characteristics as the progress of the narrative places them in varying circumstances'.[2] But above all they illustrate for Malory the virtues of an ideal past. As such they are shadows on a wall, seen from a distance, part of a heroic past. They are romance itself.

We have tried to point out some of the characteristics of romance but the reader will no doubt have observed how fluid the limits of romance are. It is doubtful whether the romance can be indeed regarded as a genre at all. There is much to be said for the view that the romance genre is the creation of the Renaissance critics who designed it as an escape route for Ariosto.[3] The romance is in origin merely a narrative in the vernacular[4] and the texts that we call romances merely a somewhat arbitrary selection from medieval narrative. It might seem possible to make a distinction between the literature of entertainment and the tales used for exemplary purposes but there is certainly evidence that in the Middle Ages at least, in spite

[1] See C. S. Lewis's review of E. K. Chambers, *Sir Thomas Wyatt and Some Collected Studies*, *Medium Aevum*, iii (1934), 239.

[2] A. Mizener, 'Character and Action in the Case of Criseyde', *PMLA*, liv (1939), 68.

[3] See Weinberg, pp.954–1073.

[4] R. Hoops, 'Der Begriff "Romance" in der Mittelenglischen und früh-neuenglischen Literatur', *Anglistische Forschungen*, lxviii (1929), 1–46.

of the moralist's condemnation of minstrels and their wares,[1] the term *romanz* could even cover such tales as the Life of Christ.[2] It seems preferable to speak of a romance mode. I have tried to suggest some of the ways in which this romance mode achieves the sense of remoteness from life, often in spite of a basis in social actuality.[3] In the next chapter, I want to look at some medieval narratives which it seems to me are written in a different mode. But it should be said in conclusion that, in some degree, the texts which we have subsumed under the vague heading of romances owe their characteristic tone to the simple fact that they are medieval narratives. That is, essentially they belong to the 'mythical' way of writing in which the story is primary, and motivation is not demonstrated through analysis of individual character, but people exist for action. It is a world where action is more important than motive, and judgement perhaps more significant than understanding. They might most truly be called 'mirrors', for they 'show things as they are and as they ought to be, in terms of exemplary ideas'.[4]

On the other hand, the distinction between romance, chronicle and autobiography is also a shifting one. This is well illustrated by the 'chivalric biography'. The deeds of the Black Prince, Marshal Boucicaut, Jacques Lalain, or Bayart, the knight *sans peur et sans reproche*,[5] are all based on fact but, not only

---

[1] Cp. John of Salisbury, *Policraticus* I, 8; I, 46–9; Langland, *Piers Plowman*, Prologue, ll.33–7; B. x, ll.27–50; B. xiii, ll.422–57; G. R. Owst, *The 'Destructorium Viciorum' of Alexander Carpenter* (London, 1952), pp.27–8; for the Penitential of Thomas of Cabham see E. K. Chambers, *The Medieval Stage* (Oxford, 1903), II, 262–3; cp. also I, 23–86; for a general survey see A. C. Baugh, 'The Middle English Romance', *Speculum*, xlii (1967), 1–31.

[2] See D. Mehl, *The Middle English Romances of the Thirteenth and Fourteenth Centuries* (London, 1968), pp.13–22; p.266, n. 43.

[3] The use of alliterative vocabulary to give such effects is discussed by Marie Borroff, *Sir Gawain and the Green Knight: A Stylistic and Metrical Study* (Yale Studies in English, 152, New Haven, 1962), pp.52–90; L. D. Benson, *Sir Gawain and the Green Knight* (New Brunswick, 1965), pp.117–43.

[4] Cp. Sister Ritamary Bradley, 'The *Wife of Bath's Tale* and the Mirror Tradition', *JEGP*, lv (1956), 624; 'Backgrounds of the Title *Speculum* in Medieval Literature', *Speculum*, xxix (1954), 100–15.

[5] See The Chandos Herald, *The Life of the Black Prince*, edited by M. K. Pope (Oxford, 1910); Georges Chastellain, *Chronique de Jacques de Lalain*,

do they shade off into fiction, but the presentation of the characters is essentially idealised.[1] These works mirror ideals but ideals which were actual, not fictitious. For example, the prologue to *Le livre des faicts du mareschal de Boucicaut* speaks of knowledge and chivalry as the two pillars of society:

> Et comme homme ne puisse bien vivre sans loy, et seroit retourné comme en beste, avec ce le royaume ou contrée là où deffence de chevalerie cesseroit, l'envieuse convoitise des ennemis, qui rien ne craindroit, tost à confusion le mettroit.[2]

> [*And as man could not live without law, but would return as to a beast, in the same way, the kingdom or country in which the protection of chivalry ceased would quickly be brought to confusion by the envious covetousness of enemies who would fear nothing.*]

This is a picture of chivalry in its ideal aspect, but a view common to life and to fiction. On the other hand, some of the more romantic episodes in the chivalric biography appear to be based on fact. Thus, for example, the elaborate tournaments in Georges Chastellain's *Chronique de Jacques de Lalain* appear to be derived from the *procès verbaux* drawn up by Lefebvre de Saint-Remy, the first king-at-arms of the Order of the Golden Fleece.[3]

The romance and chronicle, or biography, have indeed this in common, that 'al is wryton for our doctryne'.[4] This claim is made by Caxton for works which we should term romances;[5]

---

edited by J. A. Buchon (Collection des chroniques nationales françaises du treizième au seizième siècle, Paris, 1825); [Le loyal Serviteur], *Histoire du Seigneur de Bayart, le Chevalier sans paour et sans reprouche*, edited by O. H. Prior (Paris & Cambridge, 1927); for Boucicaut see Bibliographical Index *sub Le Livre des faicts du mareschal . . . de Boucicaut.*

[1] For an interesting study of sources see Camille Monnet, *Bayart et la Maison de Savoie* (Paris, 1926); J. Letonnelier, *Étude critique sur le Loyal Serviteur et son Histoire de Bayart* (Grenoble, 1926).

[2] *Le Livre de Boucicaut*, p.215.

[3] See Chastellain, *Chronique*, pp.393–4.

[4] Caxton's Preface to *Le Morte Darthur*; cp. *The Prologues and Epilogues of William Caxton*, edited by W. J. B. Crotch, E.E.T.S., 176 (1928), 95.

[5] Cp., for example, the Prefaces to *Blanchardyn and Eglantine* and *Charles the Grete* and the Epilogue to *The Order of Chyualry*; see Caxton's *Prologues and Epilogues*, pp.104–5; 95; 82–4.

equally, it is made for works, such as the Chronicle of Froissart, which we should term history. Indeed, the commonplace can hardly be more forcibly put than by Froissart himself and by Berners:

> To thentent that the honorable and noble aventures of featis of armes, done and achyved by the warres of France and Inglande, shulde notably be inregistered and put in perpetuall memory, whereby the prewe and hardy may have ensample to incourage them in theyr well doyng, I syr John Froissart, wyll treat and recorde an hystory of great louage and preyse.

Berners is more explicit and his Preface to Froissart could stand as an appropriate comment on romance and chronicle alike:

> What condygne graces and thankes ought men to gyve to the writers of historyes, who with their great labours, have done so moche profyte to the humayne lyfe? They shewe, open, manifest and declare to the reder, by example of olde antyquite, what we shulde enquere, desyre, and folowe; and also, what we shulde eschewe, avoyde, and utterly flye: for whan we (beyng unexpert of chaunces) se, beholde, and rede the auncyent actes, gestes, and dedes, howe and with what labours, daungers, and paryls they were gested and done, they right greatly admonest, ensigne and teche us howe we maye lede forthe our lyves.[1]

---

[1] *The Chronicle of Froissart* translated out of French by Sir John Bourchier, Lord Berners, with an introduction by W. P. Ker (London, 1901), I, 17, 3.

CHAPTER FIVE

Medieval Realism

'The poetic reflection of reality cannot be mechanical or photographic.' Thus wrote the Hungarian critic Lukács.[1] He had in mind primarily the novels of Balzac, Zola and Tolstoy and he was concerned to designate a truly socialist realism depending for its vitality on roots thrust deep into social realities. Nevertheless, the opinion calls to mind a not dissimilar judgement of Auerbach on the art of the fifteenth century:

> While the old order declines, there is nothing in Franco-Burgundian realism to announce the rise of a new one. This realism is poor in ideas; it lacks constructive principles and even the will to attain them. It drains the reality of that which exists and, in its very existence, falls to decay; it drains it to the dregs, so that the senses, and the emotions aroused by them, get the flavor of immediate life; and, having done that, it seeks nothing further. Indeed, the sensory itself, for all the intensity of the expression, is narrow; its horizon is restricted.[2]

Here again we have posed, in another context, the fundamental problem of artistic imitation, its means and its function. Since the rediscovery of Aristotle's *Poetics* in the fifteenth century, the term 'imitation' has been a commonplace of critical vocabulary. But the critical concept was somewhat different in the early Middle Ages. John of Salisbury, for example, in speaking of the use made of the *artes* by literary authors, describes how

> Illi enim per diacrisim, quam nos illustrationem siue picturationem possumus appellare, cum rudem materiam historie aut

---

[1] Georg Lukács, *Studies in European Realism*, translated by Edith Bone (London, 1950), p.168.

[2] Auerbach (1953), p.259.

argumenti aut fabule aliamue quamlibet suscepissent, eam tanta disciplinarum copia et tanta compositionis et condimenti gratia excolebant, ut opus consummatum omnium artium quodammodo uideretur imago.[1]

[*The authors by* diacrisis, *which we may translate as 'vivid representation' or 'graphic imagery' when they would take the crude materials of history, arguments, narratives and other topics, would so copiously embellish them by the various branches of knowledge, in such charming style, with such pleasing ornaments, that their finished masterpiece would seem to image all the arts.*]

The pictorial image is commonplace in medieval writing about the art of poetry. Thus Alanus de Insulis clearly regards rhetoric as a painting of language and, like painting, it is the language of colour.

Claudit eam uestis que, picturata colore
Multiplici, gaudet uarios inducta colores.
Hic pictoris ope splendet pictura coloris
R[he]torici, sic picturam pictura colorat.[2]

[*A garment encloses her which, painted with manifold colours, rejoices, dressed in various colours. Here, with the work of the painter, shines a picture of rhetorical colour; so the painting colours what is painted.*]

Such a view seems to be quite at variance with modern views, which decry such 'colour' as 'inorganic ornament'. Yet we find it again in Matthieu de Vendôme, for example, who writes echoing Augustine:

Est autem forma elegans et idonea membrorum coaptatio cum suavitate coloris[3]

[*Elegant and fitting form is, moreover, propriety of parts with beauty of colour.*]

---

[1] John of Salisbury, *Metalogicon*, I, xxiv; edited by C. C. I. Webb (Oxford, 1924), p.54; translation by D. D. McGarry, *The Metalogicon of John of Salisbury* (Berkeley & Los Angeles, 1955), pp.66–7. Mr. Harbert has suggested to me, however, that *diacrisis* here may mean rather the construction of an elaborate treatment of the material by dividing it into as many components as possible.

[2] Alanus de Insulis, *Anticlaudianus*, edited by R. Bossuat (Paris, 1955), III, 166–9; cp. Marbod of Rennes, *De Ornamentis Verborum*, PL, clxxi, col. 1687.

[3] Matthieu de Vendôme, *Ars Versificatoria*; Faral (1924), p.134.

Or again:

Siquidem, sicut in constitutione rei materialis ex appositione alicujus margaritae vel emblematis totum materiatum elegantius elucescit, similiter sunt quaedam dictiones, quae sunt quasi gemmarum vicariae, ex quarum artificiosa positione totum metrum videbit festivari.[1]

[*So indeed as in the disposition of a material substance, the whole material receives lustre from the addition of a pearl or ornament, so are certain verbal figures, which are, as it were, the substitutes for jewels, from the artful disposition of which the whole poem will seem to be adorned.*]

Yet these writers were not unmindful of the role of imitation in art. Again we may quote Matthieu de Vendôme:

Et quia in peritia describendi versificatoriae facultatis praecipuum constat exercitium, super hoc articulo meum consilium erit ut, si quaelibet res describatur, in expressione descriptionis maximum fidei praetendatur nutrimentum, ut vera dicantur vel veri similia.[2]

[*And because descriptive skill especially constitutes the poetic faculty, my advice will be concerning this point so that, whatever is described, the greatest illusion of reality may be produced in the description; so that either what is real, or what gives the appearance of reality, may be described.*]

The often quoted (and often misunderstood) tag of Horace *ut pictura poesis* is the basis of much medieval poetic theory.

We tried to suggest in the last chapter that there are certain modes of writing in which particularity is combined with abstraction, with a certain removal of the subject matter of the tale from the particular to the general. In proportion as the image with which the reader is presented moves from the individual and particular to the typical or general, so the mind of the reader has to grasp concepts and the less evident is the imitation of nature. And yet, in another sense, the more we move to the particular, the further we move from the common human experience. Thus it happens that a modern reader who can enjoy a folk-tale is repelled by the rendering of what is virtually the same tale in a medieval romance; for the medieval

---

[1] Matthieu de Vendôme, *Ars Versificatoria*; Faral (1924), p.154.
[2] Matthieu de Vendôme, *Ars Versificatoria*; Faral (1924), p.135.

romance projects an image of a world which has passed away. And so, one imagines, such as Chaucer is shall Dreiser be. It is indeed true that 'nothing can please many, and please long, but just representations of general nature. Particular manners can be known to few, and therefore few only can judge how nearly they are copied.' We have tried to suggest some of the ways in which medieval narratives can be removed from the world of sense to the world of idealised fantasy, a world in which, however serious the underlying theme, the image presented is a fantastic one and the characters, acting within this world of fantasy, are essentially typical and unmotivated. That the subject matter of many romances is contemporary society, does not destroy their fantastic nature. There is all the difference in the world between H. G. Wells's *The First Men in the Moon* and watching astronauts on television.

To avoid begging the question of 'realism', I have adopted for the detailed and sensibly immediate description the term 'picturation' although I have used 'realism' and 'realistic' in more general contexts. The process of 'picturation' is clearly not peculiar to what may be called 'realistic' modes of writing, such as the fabliau. In turning to the topic of 'realism' in medieval literature we shall not therefore necessarily be turning away from the romance genre. As we have already pointed out, this pictorial technique is notably found in the *Romans d'anti-quité*. We have already mentioned the elaborate accounts of people and objects in the *Roman de Thèbes* and the portraits in the *Roman de Troie*. We have also pointed out the ways in which such descriptions are removed from actuality. It is now time to look at them in another perspective and to ask ourselves the question, 'Granted that these pictures are generalised and stereotyped, how does the detail function?' or, put in another way, 'Why is it that these pictures are at once detailed and unreal, and what is the relationship of such portraits to other medieval pictures, in Chaucer's fabliaux, for example, which strike the modern reader as real?' And, lastly, 'How far, in medieval literature, do such picturations create, as writers on rhetoric tend to assume that they do, a sense of reality?'

Let us begin this exploration with a simple and familiar example. Among the analogues of Chaucer's *Merchant's Tale* is a short Latin story from the fables of Aesop.[1] Like *The Merchant's Tale*, its subject is a jealous old man and his young wife, who cuckolds him in a pear tree. The story opens with a description of the old man:

> Cecus erat quidem habens uxorem perpulcram, qui cum cruciatu mentis uxoris castitatem observabat, zelotipus namque fuerat.

> [*There was a blind man who had a very beautiful wife and, with anguish of mind, he watched over his wife's chastity; for he was a jealous man.*]

His jealousy is presented to us by a simple and single action. When his wife climbs the pear tree, the old man clasps the tree to prevent any lover approaching. The wife is even less realised. She merely illustrates the wiles of women. But the story is neatly and effectively told. It illustrates its point succinctly. It focuses interest, not by 'picturation', but merely by the grotesque feature of the pear tree, a 'machine' which attracts attention by its very grotesque randomness. The visual content of the story is at a minimum, the personages (they are hardly characters) illustrate a point. They have no life of their own. Even their conversation is impersonal and functional. The story is characteristic of many medieval tales in its purely illustrative character, which holds the attention, not by an absorbing imitation of life but by some novelty, a pun, an outrageous joke, a miracle, a fantasy. The immediate appeal to the sense is minimal, and the shape of such tales is not the shape of reality but, often, as in Chaucer's *Man of Law's Tale*, a pattern of balance and repetition. The point of focus may even be a simple verbal joke as in *La Male Honte*,[2] or in the tale of the obedient

---

[1] Most easily accessible in W. F. Bryan and G. Dempster, *Sources and Analogues of Chaucer's Canterbury Tales* (Chicago, 1941), pp.354–5. It is also printed by Thomas Wright, *A Selection of Latin Stories* (Percy Society, 1842), No. xci.

[2] *De La Male Honte; Fabliaux*, edited by R. C. Johnston and D. D. R. Owen (Oxford, 1957), pp.51–5.

wife in *The Book of the Knight of the Tower*.[1] Such tales may be realistic in their themes but are not realistic in their presentation of these themes, if by 'realistic' we mean 'presented in a life-like manner'. This is as true of the fabliau as of the fable of the pear tree.

With the fable we may compare the version in the *Cento Novelle Antiche*.[2] We immediately observe a difference. There is effectively no 'picturation' in the sense of descriptive detail. Nevertheless, we have moved into a more 'realistic' world. In the first place, we observe that the tale has been given a time dimension lacking in the fable. The time sequence in the fable is minimal, and corresponds strictly with the rationale of the tale. It might be summarised as follows: 'There was a blind man who had a beautiful wife whose chastity he scrutinised with anguish of mind; for he was a jealous man.' The action then proceeds. It happens one day that, as they sit in their garden, the wife wishes to climb the pear tree to collect pears. To guard the wife, the old man clasps the tree but the lover is already there. So the story goes on with each significant step in the action, the entering the garden, the climbing of the tree, the union of the lovers, the husband's hearing of the noise and his prayer to receive his sight and the wife's quick excuse which pacifies the husband; all are essential for the projection of the theme and each has a correlative in the time sequence.

In the *novella*, this is changed. In the first place, we are not presented at the beginning with the *datum* of the story. Instead there is an additional time dimension. That is to say, the blindness of the husband, an essential and symbolic part of the story, is narrated in two stages:

A uno tempo era uno riccho homo, ed avea una molto bella donna per molglie; et questo homo le volea tutto il suo bene, ed erane molto geloso. Or avenne, chome piacque a Dio, che questo homo li venne uno male nelgli occhi, donde aciechò, sicchè non vedea lume.[3]

---

[1] Caxton, *The Book of the Knight of the Tower*, pp.35-7.
[2] Bryan and Dempster, pp.341-3.
[3] Bryan and Dempster, p.342.

[*Once upon a time there was a rich man and he had a very beautiful woman as wife; and this man set great store by her and he was very jealous of her. Now it happened, as it pleased God, that an affliction of the eyes came upon this man, whence he became blind so that he could not see the light.*]

The *novella* also prepares us for the lover in the tree. Instead of his appearing in the tree at the moment when the action requires it, without any previous preparation for this, the writer of the *novella* adds circumstantial detail at the expense of surprise. To do this he adds a new sequence of events: 'Ora avenne che uno homo della contrada invaghío di questa donna.'[1] [Now it happened that a man of the district fell in love with this lady.] The lover is dying of love for the lady and, out of pity for his plight, she tells him what to do. The writer thus casts his story in, as it were, three acts, each having an action of its own. The story loses its pungency but gains in narrative diversity since we have a narrative which is not entirely congruent with its theme and which thus assumes a certain independent vitality. In short, what it loses in intensity it gains in verisimilitude.

But there are other ways in which the *novella* is instructive. We notice an attempt to assign motives to the characters. In the fable, the whole motivation is implicit in the opening words *nam zelotipus erat*. The only other occasion when the writer suggests a motive, is when the husband clasps the tree, and this is necessary to explain an otherwise inexplicable action. But the writer of the *novella*, when he has told us that the lady is never allowed to leave home, adds 'per tema ch'ella no lli facesse fallo' [for fear that she should deceive him].[2] The reason why the lady grants her favours to the lover is explained as pity, even though this weakens the satiric impact of the story. Interesting, too, is the re-motivation of the *novella*. In the fable, the husband himself realises that he has been betrayed by the wife. But in the *novella* it is only when God grants him sight that he learns the truth. This gives a curious moral dimension to the tale and it is perhaps worth noting that at this point we have an authorial intervention. Moreover, the writer has tried to make the tale credible by inventing a long tube by means of

[1] Bryan and Dempster, p.342.   [2] Bryan and Dempster, p.342.

K

which the lady communicates with the lover, a ludicrous detail forced upon the writer by his attempts to explain what had better have remained unexplained, the appearance at the appropriate moment of the lover in the tree. For the writer of the fable, why the lover is in the tree is irrelevant. It makes no difference to the illustration of his theme. To the writer of the *novella*, with his concern for verisimilitude, it clearly does matter and he is prepared to achieve verisimilitude even at the expense of probability.[1]

In yet another respect the writer of the *novella* shows this concern for verisimilitude. This is in the introduction of dialogue. In the fable, direct speech, with its emphatic force, is used only in relation to the climax of the tale, when the husband hears the noise in the tree. Then he shouts to the wife and prays to Jove to give him sight. The wife's reply is also in direct speech, as is fitting, since it is the climax of the tale. In the *novella*, on the other hand, we have the lady speaking to the lover in direct speech: 'Tue vedi chome io posso, chè questi non si parte mai da me.'[2] [You see my situation for this man never leaves me.] She tells him how to meet her in the garden. Thus there is a little scene between the lover and the lady. In the same way, we have a conversation between the husband and the wife in the garden. He tries to prevent her from climbing the tree. 'Call someone,' he says, 'who will pick pears for you.' Then we have the author's attempt to visualise the scene. When the lovers encounter in the tree, the pears begin to fall as the tree shakes. In the fable, the noise from the tree reveals to the husband what is happening, but here the detail of the falling pears is not functional, but merely a realistic detail which leads to further dialogue between husband and wife. The comic little scene between God and St. Peter is again marked off as a separate scene by the immediacy of the dialogue form in which it is presented.

The writer of the *novella* has thus moved away from the

---

[1] Booth's remarks (pp.9–16) on Boccaccio's narrative technique are interesting in this connection.

[2] Bryan and Dempster, p.342.

mythic simplicity of the fable, in which the action is a mirror of the theme, towards a greater verisimilitude, where the projection of a life-like image is of more importance than the theme itself. The writer even shows himself uneasy about the improbability of the plot; a different point, of course, for a very improbable plot can be presented in a very life-like manner, and an entirely probable story can be presented in the mythic mode. *Sir Gawain and the Green Knight* would serve as an example of the first situation and some of the tales of Valerius Maximus of the second. It should incidentally be clear that I am not suggesting that the *novella* is 'better' than the fable. In some ways it is a less effective narrative. Verisimilitude can have diminishing returns as some of the versions of the Orpheus story demonstrate. It is, however, different and this difference, in my view, lies in the addition of a time dimension, dialogue, editorial comment and motivation. All these devices bring the story into closer focus and create an illusion of participation.

When we turn to Chaucer, we find that to these he has added a device not present in the *novella*, that of description. Not only is the story more leisurely, the authorial participation more evident[1] (or rather that of the *persona* of the Merchant), the dialogue more extensive, soliloquies frequent, motivation displayed, but, for the first time since Boccaccio handled the story in the *Ameto*, we see the people. Take, for example, the picture of January on the morning after his wedding.

> He was al coltissh, ful of ragerye,
> And ful of jargon as a flekked pye.
> The slakke skyn aboute his nekke shaketh,
> Whil that he sang, so chaunteth he and craketh.
> But God woot what that May thoughte in hir herte,
> Whan she hym saugh up sittynge in his sherte,
> In his nyght-cappe, and with his nekke lene;
> She preyseth nat his pleyyng worth a bene.[2]

---

[1] Cp. J. S. P. Tatlock, 'Chaucer's *Merchant's Tale*', *MP*, xxxiii (1936), 367–81; G. G. Sedgewick, 'The Structure of the *Merchant's Tale*', *University of Toronto Quarterly*, xvii (1948), 337–45.

[2] Chaucer, *The Canterbury Tales*, E. ll.1847–54.

This picture, like the similar one in Boccaccio, represents yet another feature not present in the fable or the *novella*; that is to say, the realisation of one of the characters in pictorial terms. And there are further points to be noticed about it, I think. It is in contrast with, for example, the portrait of Camilla, which we have already discussed in the last chapter. Clearly, the subject matter is of a different kind. In rhetorical terms it is a portrait of the Beroe class and not of the Helen of Troy class.[1] This is obvious and obviously important. But there is a less obvious difference in that, because the picture of Camilla, which we took as an example of a picture which was detailed but unrealistic, was presented in what might be called a consuetudinal mode, it described her appearance *sub specie aeternitatis*; in Chaucer, on the contrary, the portrait is firmly localised in its context. One might compare the portrait of Morgan le Fay in *Gawain*, in a sense undeniably realistic and yet in a sense also consuetudinal, front facing rather like some stiff Velasquez Infanta. But January, as he sits up in bed, though there are consuetudinal features (the scraggy neck, for example), is wearing his nightcap and his nightshirt because he is in bed, and he is 'ful of jargon' because it is the day after the wedding night. Moreover, we might notice the technique of focusing details, a Rembrandt-like shaft of light which falls upon the scraggy neck, the nightshirt and the nightcap to light up for a moment the elderly lover. The portrait is a contextual and selective one quite unlike the flat and static portrait of Camilla. It is essentially painterly. We notice, also, the particularity of the description. Whereas in the Camilla portrait the images were of a general kind, gold, silver and so on, here we find images such as the 'flekked pye', a concrete, particular image. This concern for the particular can be seen everywhere in the tale. For example, we are told that, as the garden is kept carefully locked, May takes an impression of the key in wax or again that May pushes the letter for Damian under his pillow. Yet when we look at the later versions in relation to the

---

[1] Matthieu de Vendôme, *Ars Versificatoria*; Faral (1924), pp.129–32.

fable all is not on the credit side. The *novella*, by its development
of the scene between the lovers, upsets the balance of the tale.
Whereas the fable, after quickly setting the scene, concentrates
upon the pear-tree episode, which is its *raison d'être*, in Chaucer,
though the immediacy of presentation is enormously enhanced,
it is questionable whether the dramatic impact of the story is
increased. And there are details essential to the story which are
submerged in the circumstantiality. Such a detail is January's
blindness, which is not introduced until the beginning of the
pear-tree story. Blurred, also, is the conclusion, in which May
first claims that she has cured January's blindness but then
drops the claim and suggests that January's eye-sight is at
fault, a dramatic shift, but one that blurs the satiric impact.
There is indeed a contradiction between the story, designed to
illustrate a satirical point, and the 'picturation' which, in its
particularity, suggests that figures who are essentially and
necessarily types are, in fact, individuals. I think we may,
therefore, regard *The Merchant's Tale* as an example of a type
of medieval realism, which uses a kind of 'picturation' differing
from the 'picturation' of the *Roman de Thèbes* in its greater
particularity, but which retains a type of narrative and a type
of character which properly belong to the mythic rather than
the mimetic type.

Let us now consider some examples of 'picturation' from two
different genres, the romance and the fabliau.[1] It is a commonplace of Chaucer criticism that the portrait of Alisoun in *The
Miller's Tale* is modelled on that of Emelye in *The Knight's Tale*.
Like that, it is a conventional *descriptio*, but one in a satirical
vein. Now it is true that of all Chaucer's so-called fabliaux it is
The Reeve's Tale and *The Miller's Tale* which reflect most clearly
Chaucer's application of the rhetorical style to stories of low
life. Indeed, a reader familiar with the French fabliaux alone,
would be ill-prepared for what he would find in Chaucer's

[1] Cp. L. A. Haselmayer, 'The Portraits of Chaucer's *Fabliaux*', *RES*, xiv
(1938), 310–14; R. M. Lumiansky, 'Benoit's Portraits and Chaucer's
General Prologue', *JEGP*, lv (1956), 431–8; E. T. Donaldson, 'Idiom of
Popular Poetry in the *Miller's Tale*', *English Institute Essays* (1950), 116–40.

tales. Boccaccio's *Decameron* and, to a lesser extent, the other *novelle* are more like Chaucer, but even these lack the extensive rhetorical descriptions of Chaucer's fabliaux. More appropriate analogies with French literature can be drawn with works such as Deschamps' *Miroir de Mariage* than with the fabliaux proper. What is striking in Chaucer, is the amount of rhetorical amplification, especially in the tales of the Reeve and the Miller. These tales are, therefore, interesting as examples of 'picturation', generally lacking in the genuine fabliau, but 'picturation' in a middle or low style, and they provide us with examples of the technique applied to a popular theme.[1]

It has often been pointed out that the imagery in the portrait of Alisoun is all drawn from the farmyard, as is fitting for the heroine of this low-life tale. Thus she is constituted a kind of anti-heroine. In other words, the epithets applied to Alisoun are drawn from a different semantic field from those applied to Emelye in the companion description. One could, again, compare the description of Simkin with that of Lycurgus in *The Knight's Tale*. Both are close-ups in the rhetorical manner. But the field of reference is quite different. It might be said that Lycurgus, like Simkin, is 'a bruiser'. We note

> His lymes grete, his brawnes harde and stronge,
> His shuldres brode, his armes rounde and longe.

But we see this athletic figure standing on a 'chaar of gold' led by four white bulls. True he wears a bear-skin 'col-blak for old' but the description is firmly kept in its appropriate context by the comment that this was 'in stede of cote-armure' and that it was over his harness 'with nayles yelewe and brighte as any gold', and that his black hair is encircled by a gold wreath set with fine rubies and diamonds.[2] Simkin, on the other hand, has homely talents:

> Pipen he koude and fisshe, and nettes beete,
> And turne coppes, and wel wrastle and sheete.[3]

---

[1] See note on p.283.

[2] Chaucer, *The Canterbury Tales*, A. ll.2128–54.

[3] Chaucer, *The Canterbury Tales*, A. ll.3927–8; for the meaning of *turne coppes*, cp. R. A. Pratt, 'Symkyn koude *turne coppes*', *JEGP*, lix (1960), 208–11.

His weapons are homely too. A cutlass in his belt, a small dagger in his pouch and a large knife in his hose; plainly, a quarrelsome man as Chaucer goes on to point out. In contrast with the aristocratic features of Lycurgus, the miller has a round head, a flat nose and a bald head. This is clearly consonant with the familiar tone of dialogue and the immoral stance of the fabliau.

Thus has Chaucer transferred the rhetorical close-up of the high style, by a brilliant stroke of originality, to the matter of the fabliau. Here, in the words of John of Salisbury, has Chaucer taken the crude material of a fable and embellished it by vivid representation and graphic imagery. The characteristic rhetorical *descriptio* has been transposed into terms drawn from everyday life. But is there more to it than this? Are the fabliaux merely a comic, satirical transposition of the romance genre? We have shown how a fable could be transposed from a mythic to a realistic form of narrative. Could the aristocratic romance itself be so transposed? I should like to consider this point a little in relation to *The Knight's Tale* and the tales of the Miller and the Reeve. In particular, I should like first to consider a little further the matter of the set descriptions. It seems to me that we have here a matter, partly of the relationship of the picture to its context, and partly of the form of the picture itself. Let us begin with the first. If, for example, we take the love theme in *The Knight's Tale* and in the fabliaux we notice at once that they all in some degree make use of the language of love service. But whereas the love of Palamon and Arcite is noble and idealised that of *hende* Nicholas and Absolon is not. Put in another way, the love of Palamon is expressed in conventional terms within a conventional framework, which gives the characters themselves a typical form. This typicality is enhanced by the association of the one lover with Mars and the other with Venus. That is to say, their characteristics are expressed, not by action or description (in fact they never are described), but through something else. The gods and their temples are symbols of the types to which the lovers belong and those parts of the story which are most vividly realised in terms of sense impression are just those parts of the story which carry the typical and symbolic implications. Moreover, even the detail may often be used primarily to make a general point, if we accept Curry's view that the portraits of Lycurgus and Emetreus are representations of the Saturnial and of the Martian man.[1] In exactly the same way the sentiments of the lovers are expressed in terms of the utmost generality. Inevitably they love a typically beautiful maiden, a dream which they pursue and who, even if she assumes a touching humanity when she embraces (as we must suppose she does) the dying Arcite, never assumes an individuality. And it is characteristic that we are not *told* that she does embrace him. On the other hand, when Chaucer puts into the mouth of *hende* Nicholas and of Absolon the language of love service, the context is such that it becomes a personal trait. 'Of deerne love he koude and solas' we are told of Nicholas and his language is consonant with his pretension. The same is true of Absolon as he sings in a voice 'gentil and smal'

> Now, deere lady, if thy wille be,
> I praye yow that ye wole rewe on me.[2]

Here the characters do not illustrate a theme as in *The Knight's Tale* but exist for their part in the story. Let us take another example. As Arcite is dying he exclaims:

> What is this world? what asketh men to have?
> Now with his love, now in his colde grave
> Allone, withouten any compaignye.[3]

He is uttering a commonplace. He is speaking of his lot in terms of the common lot of man. His singular fate is put in the

---

[1] W. C. Curry, *Chaucer and the Medieval Sciences* (2nd edn., London, 1960), pp.130–7.

[2] Chaucer, *The Canterbury Tales*, A. ll.3361–2; cp. A. 4236–9 and R. E. Kaske, 'An Aube in the *Reeve's Tale*', *ELH*, xxvi (1959), 295–310; 'January's Aube', *MLN*, lxxv (1960), 1–4; 'The Aube in Chaucer's *Troilus*', in *Chaucer Criticism*, edited by R. J. Schoeck and Jerome Taylor (Notre Dame, 1960–1), II, pp.167–79; for a contrary view see M. Copland, '*The Reeve's Tale*: Harlotrie or Sermonyng?', *Medium Ævum*, xxxi (1962), 14–32.

[3] Chaucer, *The Canterbury Tales*, A. ll.2777–9.

general context of man's lot. And it is this generality which gives the passage its impact. It is a 'just representation of general nature'. Just as the conventional nature of the love theme places the two young men in the genus 'lover', so this farewell to Emily places Arcite in the genus of 'mortal man'. But when we are told, in *The Miller's Tale*, of *hende* Nicholas that

> A chambre hadde he in that hostelrye
> Allone, withouten any compaignye,
> Ful fetisly ydight with herbes swoote,[1]

there is no such general implication. It is not necessarily man's lot to be alone. Nicholas is alone, perhaps, because he was 'sleigh and ful privee'. Put in more general terms, if I say 'he was alone in his grave' I am stating the obvious; if I say 'he was alone in his room' I am not. Again we have the difference between a consuetudinal and an indicative mode of writing. When the two lovers of *The Knight's Tale* speak in terms of an idealised love, this is in a sense a tautology. They speak as we expect them to speak, as they must speak. When Nicholas or Absolon speak in these terms, this tells us something about them as individuals in a particular situation. Again we have the difference between the consuetudinal and the indicative, the general and the particular.

Another example might be taken from the account of the temple of Mars to illustrate a further point. In the midst of the examples of savagery and disaster, we come to the seemingly domestic example of the carter run over by his cart. This comes in a series in which misfortune overtakes men in the pursuit of their avocations:

> The hunte strangled with the wilde beres;
> The sowe freten the child right in the cradel;
> The cook yscalded, for al his longe ladel.
> Noght was foryeten by the infortune of Marte

---

[1] Chaucer, *The Canterbury Tales*, A. ll.3203–5. For the description of Absolon and Nicholas and the possible motivation of detail, cp. Paul E. Beichner, 'Chaucer's Hende Nicholas', *Mediaeval Studies*, xiv (1952), 151–3; 'Characterisation in *The Miller's Tale*', in *Chaucer Criticism*, I, 117–29.

> The cartere overryden with his carte:
> Under the wheel ful lowe he lay adoun.[1]

Does this not look like Chaucer giving us the kind of realistic detail for which he has often been praised? But compare the carter with this passage from *The Friar's Tale*:

> They saugh a cart that charged was with hey,
> Which that a cartere droof forth in his wey.
> Deep was the wey, for which the carte stood.
> The cartere smoot, and cryde as he were wood,
> 'Hayt, Brok! hayt, Scot! what spare ye for the stones?
> The feend,' quod he, 'yow fecche, body and bones,
> As ferforthly as evere were ye foled,
> So muche wo as I have with yow tholed!
> The devel have al, bothe hors and cart and hey!'[2]

We see immediately that a reference to domestic or low life does not in itself create a realistic style. In the passage from *The Knight's Tale*, the carter is not realised pictorially or dramatically and rightly so. For he, like Pride falling from his horse, is merely exemplary and such a realisation would have detracted from its effectiveness. Its function is not verisimilitude but illustration. How different is the little scene in *The Friar's Tale*! Although the carter has an essential function in the economy of the story, the details are contextual not exemplary. It is filled out with colloquial speech and with action which, though simple, is appropriate to the occasion. Thus we see that subject matter alone does not create the low style but the style is a function of the image within its context.

But there is I think a further aspect of the matter, namely that of point of view or perspective. If we look carefully at the portraits of Lycurgus and Emetreus we notice that the details of these companion pieces are so arranged as to correspond to each other. In both cases we have reference to the eyes and hair and the complexion, in each case we have a description of the armour. Both the kings wear a crown and each is accompanied by an appropriate hunting symbol, the wolfhounds in the case

---

[1] Chaucer, *The Canterbury Tales*, A. ll.2018–23.

[2] Chaucer, *The Canterbury Tales*, D. ll.1539–47.

of Lycurgus and an eagle in the case of Emetreus. Just as the plot of the tale is designedly symmetrical, so the portraits are given an artificial symmetry. The portraits in the fabliaux, on the other hand, have a random air, as though they were being observed for the first time.[1] Chaucer uses the same technique in the Prologue to *The Canterbury Tales*. Whatever the significance of the details, and opinions have varied about these,[2] they are presented in a random and not an orderly fashion, presumably so as to give the impression of natural observation. Yet another use of the technique can be observed in the work of the *Gawain* poet. If we take, for example, the description of the two ladies we find that, although this is, in one sense, a conventional rhetorical close-up, yet it is not arranged symmetrically in the same way as the portraits in *The Knight's Tale*; but is not withstanding carefully selected. What is stressed in the description of the young lady is her beauty and this is clearly intended to draw the hero's love. On the other hand, the old woman is not given the characteristics of the stately matron that we might have expected, and I suspect that her ugliness is meant to put us on our guard against her; and rightly so, for she is Morgan le Fay, the evil genius of the poem. The details are therefore functional as predicting something of the role which the characters will play in the story. Yet there is here a certain ambiguity in the use of the conventional *descriptio*. On the one hand, we have the conventional properties of the romance, the temptress and the wicked witch but, on the other hand, as Gawain supposes, real people whom he greets with the courtesy due to their age and station. And there is yet a further point to be noticed, I think. What the poet has described is what would first strike Gawain as the ladies advanced towards him. His first impression is a general one. The younger lady is more

---

[1] Cp. Robertson, pp.257–9; Salter (1969), pp.16–32.

[2] In many cases, details have been thought to have a moral significance; for example, the miller's bagpipes may indicate gluttony and luxury; cp. E. A. Block, 'Chaucer's Millers and their Bagpipes', *Speculum*, xxix (1954), 239–43; cp. G. F. Jones, 'Wittenwiler's *Becki* and the Medieval Bagpipe', *JEGP*, xlviii (1949), 209–28; K. L. Scott, 'Sow-and-Bagpipe Imagery in the Miller's Portrait', *RES*, xviii (1967), 287–90.

beautiful than Guinevere, the knight thinks. His impression of the first lady is merely that she is someone of importance for she is 'heȝly honowred with haþeleȝ aboute'. Thus, as we see the party of ladies drawing near, the poet registers the impressions of Gawain as well as indicating the *argumentum* of the passage. As the two ladies advance, the knight's attention is fixed on their necks and throats, perhaps a suggestion of the incipient temptation, but a temptation hardly yet perceptible to the knight himself. As he looks at them he forgets the honour due to the older lady and is repelled by her. Then by a neat reversal of theme the poet implies but does not state the sexual attractions of the younger one:

> Hir body watz schort and þik,
> Hir buttokez balȝ and brode,
> More lykkerwys on to lyk
> Watz þat scho hade on lode.[1]

As Renoir has pointed out, this kind of effect is used by the poet in some of the most dramatic scenes.[2] As an example, he cites the beheading scene. First we have a general uniformly illuminated view; Gawain rises up and kneels before the king, takes up his weapons and goes towards the Green Knight; they exchange terms. This is followed by a series of individual pictures in which we see Gawain stroking his axe and the Green Knight baring his neck for the blow. First Gawain strikes the naked flesh so that his sharp axe sunders the bone and, sinking into the white flesh, sunders it so that the edge of the axe bites the ground. The head falls to the earth so that the courtiers spurn it with their feet. The blood spurts from the body and shone against the green. Then we have the final enlarged view of the decapitation as the knight picks up his head and rides away. Similar observations have been made by Spearing, con-

---

[1] *Sir Gawain and the Green Knight*, ll.966–9.

[2] Alain Renoir, 'Descriptive Technique in "Sir Gawain and the Green Knight"', *Orbis Litterarum*, xiii (1958), 126–32; cp. 'The Progressive Magnification, an instance of psychological Description in "Sir Gawain and the Green Knight"', *Moderna Språk*, liv (1960), 245–53; D. Mehl, 'Point of View in Mittelenglischen Romanzen', *Germanisch-Romanische Monatsschrift*, xiv (1964), pp.35–46; Borroff, pp.120–9; Benson, pp.167–206.

cerning the treatment of the storm scene in *Patience*. 'The storm begins', he writes, 'conceived largely as a structure of noise and movement, but with a single vivid glimpse of the visual effect, a red glare beneath huge storm-clouds. From the display of the divine power we are suddenly directed to its effect on the men in the boat, shouting and throwing their goods overboard. The closing-in effect is characteristic of the skill of the *Gawain*-poet in manipulating perspective, moving in imagination through the space of his poem.'[1]

A related but distinct technique is that of focus and to this we must now turn. We have already discussed the ideas of focus and impact in our introductory chapter[2] but it is now time to look at them more closely. A consideration of the literary portrait brings certain points to the fore. If one is to delineate a person (or a scene) what are the principles on which the picture can be organised? There would seem to be at least three. Firstly, one can transfer a schema onto the pages as it stands. Thus, one can begin at the head and work downwards but, contrary to what is usually supposed, this is not commonly done. On the other hand, one can shape the scene in some way or other; particularly either in relation to the significance of the detail, or, secondly, in relation to the onlooker, as in the example which we quoted from *Sir Gawain and the Green Knight*. As an example of the second, I would instance the descriptions of Lycurgus and Emetreus where it seems that attention has been directed to those details which indicate their planetary significance. Focus is, however, a matter of detail. The close-up, or *descriptio*, is a close focus technique not unlike the pictorial enlargements used in medieval art to emphasise the most important figures without regard to perspective. The length of the description and the density of detail both tend to give this emphasis but it is the detail alone which gives the focus. Density of detail gives the impression of close focus, sparse detail the impression of distant focus. But the kind of words used also contribute to this effect. The more precise a word the

---

[1] Spearing (1966), pp.317–18·
[2] See pp.15–16, 17–20.

more it gives the impression of close focus. Thus 'he went' is a word of distant focus, 'he hurried' closer focus and 'sword' is a word of less focus than 'bright sword', which is no doubt why the Gawain poet, in his description of the beheading, refers to 'the bright steel', as the sword accomplishes the decapitation. 'The serpent-patterned sword' gives us even closer focus. On the other hand, abstractions are less sharply focused (which is not the same as saying that they have less impact) than common nouns. The difference between 'focus' and 'impact' can be illustrated from proper names. When Chaucer begins *The Miller's Tale* with the words 'Whilom ther was dwellynge at Oxenford'[1] or *The Reeve's Tale* with the words 'At Trumpyngtoun, nat fer fro Cantebrigge'[2] it has far more impact for the English reader than the opening of *The Knight's Tale*:

> Whilom, as olde stories tellen us,
> Ther was a duc that highte Theseus;
> Of Atthenes he was lord and governour. . . .[3]

But the focus is almost identical except that Chaucer puts *The Knight's Tale* into the past by 'as olde stories tellen us'. Otherwise, in each poem we learn in the opening lines the trade, name and dwelling of one of the main characters in the story. But the impact of the first two is greater to the English reader and greatest of all to anyone familiar with Oxford, or Cambridge. Impact is thus a variable as between nation and nation or generation and generation or between one individual and another. Thus, for example, abstractions such as 'patriotism', 'loyalty' have less impact now than they did in the nineteenth century. But focus implies the impression of visual distance and sharpness of delineation; the dilation (or amplification) or contraction (abbreviation) of a scene; whereas impact implies the emotional response and the vividness of association which the words have for the reader. Surely, the use of particularity in Chaucer portraits is designed to achieve this kind of close focus. It does not necessarily imply that Chaucer had a parti-

---

[1] Chaucer, *The Canterbury Tales*, A.13187.
[2] Chaucer, *The Canterbury Tales*, A.1.3921.
[3] Chaucer, *The Canterbury Tales*, A.11.859–61.

cular person in mind, although he may have done so. I should not therefore think it necessarily reasonable to suppose for example that, because Chaucer mentions the *lord of Palatye* and Turkey in his picture of the knight, that he must be describing an individual known to him.[1]

As well as varying the focus of a scene the writer can, in an analogous way, change the speed of his narration. Thus we can see an action taking place slowly when the verbal structure is enlarged or a quickening of speed when the verbal structure is contracted as in Chaucer's description of the tournament:

> In goon the speres ful sadly in arrest;
> In gooth the sharpe spore into the syde.
> Ther seen men who kan juste and who kan ryde;
> Ther shyveren shaftes upon sheeldes thikke;
> He feeleth thurgh the herte-spoon the prikke.
> Up spryngen speres twenty foot on highte;
> Out goon the swerdes as the silver brighte;
> The helmes they tohewen and toshrede. . . .[2]

The anaphora, of course, gives emphatic force to the repeated verbs but the speed is largely due to the predominance of verbs in the description and the way they are piled rapidly one after the other and underlined by the alliteration.

Let us now consider more carefully the descriptions in Chaucer. When we look more closely at the portraits of Lycurgus and Emetreus we notice that each item of the description consists of a basic frame of noun and adjective. Thus

> Blak was his berd, and manly was his face;
> The cercles of his eyen in his heed,
> They gloweden bitwixen yelow and reed,
> And lik a grifphon looked he aboute,
> With kempe heeris on his browes stoute.[3]

If the description is followed through it will be found that this pattern persists to the end. The adjectives are commonplace; mostly colours or adjectives of size or strength. There is very

[1] Cp. J. R. Hulbert, 'Chaucer's Pilgrims', *PMLA*, lxiv (1949), 823–8.
[2] Chaucer, *The Canterbury Tales*, A. ll.2602–9.
[3] Chaucer, *The Canterbury Tales*, A. ll.2130–4.

little movement. The most common verb is the colourless 'was' but even this is often omitted in the interests of compression:

> His lymes grete, his brawnes harde and stronge,
> His shuldres brode, his armes rounde and longe.[1]

The other verbs are correlatives of adjectives such as 'gloweden yelow and reed', 'as any ravenes fethere it shoon forblak'; or the verb is consuetudinal as 'to hunten at the leoun or the deer'; or else they are verbs of minimal movement such as 'looked', 'stood', 'ybounde', 'armed' or of minimal semantic content such as 'wenten', 'folwed'. If there is a point at which the camera may be said to have moved a little closer it is when the poet notes the dogs which accompany Lycurgus:

> with mosel faste ybounde,
> Colered of gold, and tourettes fyled rounde.[2]

And this too is entirely static.

Many of the traits of the rhetorical portrait, as we have already noted, have been carried over into the fabliaux portraits, and into those in the Prologue to *The Canterbury Tales*. But the treatment is by no means uniform. If, for example, we look at the portrait of the Prioress, we notice that it is entirely 'out of context'. Many of the things which we are told about her are 'consuetudinal' such as her table manners, her manner of speaking French and so on;[3] whereas we are not told anything about Lycurgus and Emetreus which an onlooker could not have observed. They are static but they are entirely indicative in aspect. The portrait of the Prioress, for all its detail, is not 'realistic' in this way. The same might be said of the portrait of Alisoun. To some extent we have a portrait with perspective. The picture begins with her waist and her bosom, described in relation to her clothes. By degrees we work down to her feet. But we are given some inside information, we are 'told' and not 'shown'.

---

[1] Chaucer, *The Canterbury Tales*, A. ll.2135–6.
[2] Chaucer, *The Canterbury Tales*, A. ll.2130–54.
[3] For the Prioress cp. R. J. Schoeck, 'Chaucer's Prioress: Mercy and Tender Heart', *Chaucer Criticism*, I, 245–58.

But of hir song, it was as loude and yerne
As any swalwe sittynge on a berne.
Therto she koude skippe and make game,
As any kyde or calf folwynge his dame.[1]

We are equally told things about Nicholas and Absolon which only the privileged narrator could know and in this context this gives the portraits a sense of immediacy, of people known to the narrator and thus possibly known to us.[2] Thus Chaucer gives his characters a context of a kind. They have at least a past, as well as a present and, by implication, a future too. They are not timeless like the portraits in *The Knight's Tale*. Sometimes, of course, the narrator breaks in overtly as when he comments on the characters in the Prologue 'and I said that his opinion was good'. Thus the portraits in these realistic modes of writing create the impression of actuality because they have a time dimension.

This technique of 'telling', the use of aspect, is reinforced by a perspective technique, that of 'the random shot'.[3] In many of Chaucer's portraits it is as if the camera and not the human eye with its concomitant, the categorising or schematising brain, were following the person. Suddenly some small detail is lit up, Alisoun's brooch or eyebrows, the Wife of Bath's stockings, Absolon's hair.[4] In many cases, it has been shown that these apparently random details have a physiological significance; the details are not meaningless but they give an impression of individuality because of the way in which they are suddenly thrust at us. Sometimes the sense of abruptness is made by a

[1] Chaucer, *The Canterbury Tales*, A. ll.3257-60.

[2] For the *persona* of Chaucer, cp. B. Kimpel, 'The Narrator of the *Canterbury Tales*', *ELH*, xx (1953), 77-86; cp. E. Talbot Donaldson, 'Chaucer the Pilgrim', *PMLA*, lxix (1954), 928-36.

[3] W. H. Clawson ('The Framework of *The Canterbury Tales*', *The University of Toronto Quarterly*, xx (1951), 137-54) observes that 'No small part of the realism of these portraits is their informality, their lack of regular order.'

[4] Cp. Paul E. Beichner, 'Absolon's Hair', *Mediaeval Studies*, xii (1950), 222-33; G. B. Pace, 'Physiognomy and Chaucer's Summoner and Alisoun', *Traditio*, xviii (1962), 417-20.

sudden shift of subject as though the camera had been jerked
in the hand. This is often underlined by rhyme:

> She was ful moore blisful on to see
> Than is the newe pere-jonette tree,
> And softer than the wolle is of a wether.
> And by hir girdel heeng a purs of lether.[1]

That this technique is deliberate seems to be suggested by the
way in which Chaucer, when he chooses, can, as we have
already pointed out, give an admirably painterly description
with its own perspective, like the famous one in *The Summoner's
Tale*:

> And fro the bench he droof awey the cat,
> And leyde adoun his potente and his hat,
> And eek his scrippe, and sette hym softe adoun.[2]

or from *The Merchant's Tale*:

> He lulleth hire, he kisseth hire ful ofte;
> With thikke brustles of his berd unsofte,
> Lyk to the skyn of houndfyssh, sharp as brere –
> For he was shave al newe in his manere –
> He rubbeth hire aboute hir tendre face.[3]

or the picture in the *Man of Law's Tale*, unforgettably illustrating 'the pale Drede':

> Have ye nat seyn somtyme a pale face,
> Among a prees, of hym that hath be lad
> Toward his deeth, wher as hym gat no grace,
> And swich a colour in his face hath had,
> Men myghte knowe his face that was bistad,
> Amonges alle the faces in that route?[4]

Yet in the portraits in the comic vein he chooses to break, as it
were, the rhetorical mould by giving the impression of a

---

[1] Chaucer, *The Canterbury Tales*, A. ll.3247–50.
[2] Chaucer, *The Canterbury Tales*, D. ll.1775–7.
[3] Chaucer, *The Canterbury Tales*, E. ll.1823–7; it is perhaps worth noticing
parallels with the art of the period. P. Mroczkowski ('Mediaeval Art and
Aesthetics in *The Canterbury Tales*', *Speculum*, xxxiii (1958), 211–12) points
out parallels between January portraits and *The Franklin's Tale*, ll.1250–5.
[4] Chaucer, *The Canterbury Tales*, B¹. ll.645–50.

random selection of detail, as well as a random combination of authorial knowledge and observation, physiological traits, and, as far as our knowledge goes, individual oddities. It is one of the marks, I think, of the formal *descriptio* that, although the writer may indicate attributes which are not observable, he does not intrude his voice. Even when he is 'telling' us he appears to be 'showing' us. It is one thing to tell the reader that a beautiful woman is also good. This is so much part of a stereotype that we hardly notice the author's voice. It is quite another thing to tell us that the character is a carpenter, a barber, a scholar when these facts are not an essential part of his character stereotype. And this perhaps explains the different effect of the consuetudinal aspect in the description of Camilla, in the fabliaux, or in the portraits in Chaucer's Prologue. For the portraits in the Prologue are different again from the portraits in the fabliaux, in that, whereas the portraits in the fabliaux are, on the whole, individual, the characters in the Prologue are not, for all the sharply focused detail.

But before concluding our discussion of this topic, I want to turn to a particularity of quite a different kind.[1] We have already tried to suggest that the 'realism' or otherwise of a passage is not entirely a question of subject matter or semantic field of reference, nor yet of density of detail. We noted in discussing the Chaucer texts that the same image or phrase could be used in different contexts with quite a different effect. We also noted the different functions of perspective, focus and aspect. The second class of descriptions which I want to consider are interesting here because they are drawn from religious writings and therefore, though both in subject matter and presentation they have affinities with our previous category, they are not comic. But before looking at them in detail it might be helpful to say something of the history of these writings, since their context is not unimportant for an understanding of their characteristics.

[1] But not entirely unconnected perhaps. Cp. Auerbach (1953), pp.165–173.

Otto Pächt has written

> In reality, it was the new ascetic movement of the eleventh century (of which Anselm was one of the greatest exponents) with its urge towards introspection, its emphasis on affective feeling and pious compassion, that fermented visual imagination and led to new artistic experiences which ultimately had a humanising effect on the imagery of Christian art. Anselm's prayers and meditations are the great document of the new piety which R. Southern in his penetrating analysis of Anselmian spirituality has aptly called affective piety.[1]

This is a story which has often been told. Ever since Émile Mâle indicated the debt, as he saw it, of late medieval art to the Pseudo-Bonaventuran *Meditations on the Life of Christ*, it has been understood that a new realism came into medieval art during and after the thirteenth century.[2] It is with the history of this movement that we are concerned.

It is now generally recognised that the movement is considerably anterior to Pseudo-Bonaventura or even to Anselm. In so far as an historical movement can be said to have a beginning, it may be said that the movement can be traced back to the period of Gregory VII. His sensational quarrel with Emperor Henry IV and the dramatic scene at Canossa in 1077 have obscured in popular imagination his stature as a reforming pope. Yet the revival of asceticism with which he was associated was as significant in the life of the Church as his constitutional and legal reforms. The eremitical movement has indeed been traced back to Lorraine in the ninth century, to the influence of a certain Grimlaic, who lived a hermit's life in Lorraine and who left a rule.[3] In the second half of the tenth century

---

[1] O. Pächt, 'The Illustrations of St. Anselm's Prayers and Meditations', *JWCI*, xix (1956), 82; cp. also R. Southern, *St. Anselm and his Biographer* (Cambridge, 1963), pp.42–7.

[2] E. Mâle, *L'Art religieux de la fin du Moyen Age en France* (3rd edn., Paris, 1925), pp.1–34, 85–154; cp. E. Gilson, 'Saint Bonaventure et l'iconographie de la passion', *Revue d'histoire franciscaine*, i (1924), 405–24.

[3] *Grimlaici Presbyteri Regula Solitariorum*, PL, ciii, cols. 573–664. Oliger dates this rule as ninth century. See *Speculum Inclusorum*, edited by P. L. Oliger, *Lateranum*, iv (1), (1938), 9.

another eremitical movement appears, associated with St. Romuald (d. 1027) and he was followed by a more illustrious successor, St. Peter Damian (d. 1072), who wrote a life of St. Romuald.[1] St. Peter Damian was especially associated with the eremitical settlement at Fonte Avellana in central Italy, as Dante tells us:

> 'Tra' due liti d'Italia surgon sassi,
>   e non molto distanti a la tua patria,
>   tanto, che 'troni assai suonan piú bassi,
> e fanno un gibbo che si chiama Catria,
>   di sotto al quale è consecrato un ermo,
>   che suole esser disposto a sola latria.
>
> . . . .
>
>   Quivi
>   al servigio di Dio mi fe' sí fermo,
> che pur con cibi di liquor d'ulivi
>   lievemente passava caldi e geli,
>   contento ne'pensier contemplativi.
> Render solea quel chiostro a questi cieli
>   fertilemente; e ora è fatto vano,
>   sí che tosto convien che si riveli.
> In quel loco fu'io Pietro Damiano. . . .'[2]

[*Between two shores of Italy rise rocks and not far from thy fatherland, so that the thunders further down sound loudly enough; and they make a hump which is called Catria, below which is consecrated a hermitage which formerly was given to the service of God alone . . . here in the service of God I made myself so resolute that I easily endured heat and cold, satisfied with the oil of olives alone, content with contemplative thoughts. That cloister used to render ample fruits to the heavens; but now it has become idle so that soon must it be revealed. In that place was I Peter Damian.*]

He too wrote a rule for hermits[3] but more important than this, from the point of view of his later influence, is his popularisation of devotion to the humanity of Christ. Often, he tells us, was the crucifixion, in all its horrible details, present to his spiritual

---

[1] *Vita Sancti Romaldi*, PL, cxliv, cols. 953–1008.

[2] Dante, *Paradiso*, xxi, ll.106–21.

[3] *De Ordine Eremitarum* and *Ad Stephanum Monachum de Suae Congregationis Institutis*, PL, cxlv, cols. 327–36, 335–64.

sight, but he leaves to others the contemplation of the majesty of God's glory:

> quia dum tam profunda redemptionis humanae mysteria pene-trare non possumus, quasi ori nostro digitum superponimus, ut divinitatis Christi celsitudinem majoribus relinquentes, de sola tantum ejus cruce tractemus.[1]

> [*for while we cannot penetrate such deep mysteries of human redemption we lay as it were a finger on our lips, that leaving to others the lofty theme of the divinity of Christ, we may treat of his cross alone.*]

Thus we find already in Peter Damian a tradition of prayers and meditations which are both highly dramatic as projecting the emotions of the speaker and, in many cases, highly realistic in their realisation of the details of the suffering of Christ. We find many examples of an exclamatory and rhetorical style in the prayers and meditations attributed to St. Anselm,[2] and in similar works attributed to St. Bernard. Two examples may serve to illustrate this dramatic, exclamatory style and the emphasis on closely focused detail. The first is from the *Liber Meditationum* attributed to Anselm although the meditation is in fact possibly by a disciple of Bernard:[3]

> Dulcis Jesus in inclinatione capitis et morte, dulcis in extensione brachiorum, dulcis in apertione lateris, dulcis in confixione pedum clavo uno. Dulcis in inclinatione capitis; inclinans enim caput in cruce, quasi dilectae suae dicere videtur: "O dilecta mea, quoties desiderasti frui osculo oris mei, nuntians mihi per sodales meos, *osculetur me osculo oris sui.*" Ego paratus sum, caput inclino, os porrigo, osculare quantumlibet; nec dicas in corde tuo: Illud

---

[1] See *Opuscula*, 32, viii; PL, cxlv, col. 557; cp. also A. Wilmart, 'Les Prières de saint Pierre Damien pour l'adoration de la Croix', *Auteurs spirituels du Moyen Age latin* (Paris, 1932), pp.138–46; J. Leclercq, F. Vandenbroucke, L. Bouyer, *La Spiritualité du Moyen Age* (Paris, 1961), p.146.

[2] See *S. Anselmi Meditationes*, PL, clviii, cols. 709–820; for Jean de Fécamp see A. Wilmart, 'La Tradition des Prières de Saint Anselme', *Revue Bénédictine*, xxxvi (1924), 52–71; Wilmart, 173–201; J. Leclercq and J-P. Bonnes, *Un maître de la vie spirituelle au xie siècle, Jean de Fécamp* (Paris, 1946).

[3] See Wilmart, p.194.

osculum non quaero, quod est sine specie et decore; sed illud gloriosum, quo semper frui desiderant angelici cives.[1]

[*Jesus sweet in the bowing of his head and in death, sweet in the extension of his arms, sweet in the opening of his side, sweet in the piercing of his feet by a single nail, sweet in the bowing of his head; for, inclining his head on the Cross, it is as though he did say to his beloved, 'Oh, my beloved how often hast thou desired to enjoy the kiss of my mouth, speaking to me through my companions, let him kiss me with the kiss of his mouth.' I am ready, I bow my head, I offer my mouth to kiss as much as you please; say not in thy heart: I seek not that kiss which is without beauty or comeliness; but that kiss is glorious which the angels ever long to enjoy.*]

In the same vein is our second example, taken from Pseudo-Bernard, *Lamentatio in Passionem Christi*:

O lacrymae, ubi vos subtraxistis, ubi estis, fontes lacrymarum? Humectate maxillas meas, irrigate genas meas, fluite super faciem. Heu me miserum! omnis creatura compatitur Christo, et turbatur de morte sua, sed miserum cor meum non compatitur Creatori suo morienti pro ipso. Flete me, coelum et terra; lugete me, omnes creaturae. Melius esset me non esse creatum, quam sic induratum cor meum remanere de tanta morte. O Domine! quantum humiliasti te! Sed per mortem tuam, cui tam fuit chara anima mea, Jesu bone, libera me ab iniquitatibus meis, et per passionem tuam fuga impietatem meam.[2]

[*O tears, whither have you withdrawn, where are you fountains of tears? Wet my face, moisten my cheeks, flow over my face. Alas, wretch that I am! Every creature suffers with Christ and is distressed by his death, but my wretched heart suffers not with its Creator dying for it. Weep for me heaven and earth; mourn for me all creatures. Better had I never been created than that my heart should remain so stony at such a death. O Lord! how didst thou humiliate thyself! But by thy death to whom my soul was so precious, good Jesus, free me from my sins and by thy passion put to flight my impiety.*]

---

[1] PL, clviii, col. 761.

[2] Pseudo-Bernard, *Lamentatio in Passionem Christi*, PL, clxxxiv, col. 772; cp. Pseudo-Bede, *De Meditatione Passionis Christi*, PL, xciv, cols. 561–8; Bernard, *Liber de Passione Christi*. On Pseudo-Bede see Pseudo-Bonaventura, *Meditaciones de Passione Christi*, edited by M. J. Stallings, The Catholic University of America: Studies in Medieval and Renaissance Latin Language and Literature, XXV (1965), pp.17–19.

We have also from the eleventh century, perhaps from the pen of Jean de Fécamp, a passage the English translation of which well illustrates the continuing tradition of some eleventh-century writers into the later Middle Ages.

> Candet nudatum pectus. rubet cruentum latus. tensa arent viscera. decora languent lumina. regia pallent ora. procera rigent brachia. crura dependent marmorea, rigat terebratos pedes beati sanguinis unda.

> Wyth was hys nakede brest and red of blod hys syde,
> Bleyc was his fair handled, his wnde dop ant wide,
> And hys armes ystreith hey up-hon þe rode;
> On fif studes on his body þe stremes ran o blode.[1]

Such then were the antecedents to the movement which lay behind the more well-known movement of the thirteenth century, associated with the familiar figures of St. Francis and St. Bonaventura. The distinctive nature of this movement and its particular interest for our purpose is that it achieves a vivid realisation of the story of the Gospels and especially the Passion narratives by all the devices of realistic narrative. We have already pointed out the dramatic nature of some of the meditations and prayers written in this tradition but, in fact, the dramatisation of the Passion narrative goes further than this. Already, probably fairly early in the medieval period, certainly before the Pseudo-Bonaventura,[2] we have the Pseudo-Anselm *Dialogus Beatae Mariae et Anselmi de Passione Domini*[3] in which the Virgin and St. Anselm appear as spectators at the crucifixion. A similar rendering of the facts of the Passion story into a dramatic narrative is the famous *Donna del Paradiso* of the mid-thirteenth century by Jacopone da Todi. The story is narrated to the Virgin by a messenger who has witnessed the

---

[1] Pseudo-Augustine, *Liber Meditationum*, PL, xl, col. 906; *Religious Lyrics* (1952), No. I, p.1; cp. also Leclercq and Bonnes, p.44 and fn. 1; R. Woolf, *The English Religious Lyric in the Middle Ages* (Oxford, 1968), pp.28–30.

[2] See Pseudo-Bonaventura, *Meditaciones*, pp.20–2.

[3] PL, clix, cols. 271–90. Dr. A. M. Hudson has kindly called my attention to a vernacular version in MS. Laud Misc. 38.

event which he describes. The horror of the Passion is described and the emotions of the Virgin displayed in a dialogue form:

Nunzio Donna, la man gli è presa
E nella croce stesa,
Con un bollon gli è fesa:
Tanto ci l'han ficcato.

L'altra mano si prende,
Nella croce si stende;
Et lo dolor s'accende
Che più è moltiplicato.

Donna, li piè se prenno
E chiavellansi al legno;
Ogni giuntura aprendo
Tutto l'han disnodato.

Vergine E i'comencio il corrotto.
Figliuolo, mio diporto,
Figlio, chi mi t'ha morto,
Figlio mio dilicato?

Meglio averieno fatto
Che'l cor m'avesser tratto,
Che nella croce tratto
Starci descilïato.[1]

[The Messenger: *Lady, his hand is taken and stretched on the cross; it is rent with a nail – so have they fixed him there. The other hand is taken, is stretched on the cross and the pain, greatly intensified, increases. Lady, the feet are held and nailed to the tree and, every joint torn apart, they have wholly dislocated him.* The Virgin: *Now I begin my lament. Oh my beloved son, my joy, my delicate son, who has slain thee for me? Better had they torn my heart from me than (that I should see thee) placed on the cross, all torn.*]

This is but one aspect of the increasing concentration on the identification with, and the contemplation of, the humanity of Christ and His sufferings in this world. There resulted from it the dramatisation of the biblical characters, especially the Virgin,

[1] See *The Oxford Book of Italian Verse*, edited by St. John Lucas (2nd edn., revised by C. Dionisotti, Oxford, 1952), No. 11, p.23.

a dramatisation seen in the lyric tradition of the *planctus* and ultimately in the drama itself.[1] How intense this emotional concentration becomes by the end of the Middle Ages is well illustrated by Ludolphus of Saxony's account of the sorrows of the Virgin:

> Flebat illa lacrymis irremediabilibus. Ipsius lacrymarum tanta ubertas fluebat, ut caro cum spiritu in lacrymis resolvi putaretur. Rigabat lacrymis faciem et extinctum Filii sui corpus, et perfundebat undique plagas ejus. Lapidem quoque quo corpus ejus positum et locatum fuerat, lacrymis madebat, in quo ejus lacrymae adhuc apparere dicuntur, qui nunc in ingressu ecclesiae Sancti Sepulchri esse memoratur. Lavit et tersit vulnera ejus cruentata, et osculabatur ea, et faciem ejus sacratissimam. Aspiciebat vulnera corporis, et vultum ejus et caput, videbat spinarum puncturas, depilationem barbae, faciem ex sputis et sanguine deturpatam; et de sic aspiciendo et flendo non poterat satiari.[2]

> [*She wept with irremediable tears. Her tears flowed in such profusion that flesh and spirit could have been thought to be dissolved in tears. With tears she bedewed her face and the dead body of her son, and everywhere flooded with tears his wounds. The stone also on which his body had been placed and laid down, she wetted with tears, on which stone, now said to be at the entrance to the church of the Holy Sepulchre, her tears are said still to be evident. She washed and dried his bloody wounds and kissed them, and his most blessed face. She beheld the wounds of his body and his face and head, she saw the punctures of the thorns, the depilation of his beard, and the countenance defiled with spittle and blood; and she could never so gaze and weep enough.*]

It is well known that the dissemination of this kind of devotion was considerably the work of the Franciscans, who, in many spheres, popularised the presentation of the bible narrative, just as they did the lyric and the art of preaching.[3] But, above all, the stigmata showed, in a dramatic form, the significance of a

---

[1] For the *Planctus* see Woolf (1968), pp.239–73 and references.

[2] Ludolphus of Saxony, *Vita Jesu Christi*, Pt. II, cap. lxv, 5, edited by L. M. Rigollot (Rome, 1878), IV, 144.

[3] See R. H. Robbins, 'The Earliest Carols and the Franciscans', *MLN*, liii (1938), 239–45; 'The Authors of the Middle English Religious Lyrics', *JEGP*, xxxix (1940), 230–8.

life devoted to the imitation and contemplation of Christ's earthly life.

And, after all, it was the Franciscan, Bonaventura, the official, although not the earliest, biographer of the saint, who represented most fully to the later Middle Ages the technique of realistic presentation of the gospel narratives. Not that the idea behind the famous Pseudo-Bonaventuran *Meditations* was entirely new. The practice of intensive meditation on the Gospel narrative, a practice familiar to a later period from the Religious Exercises of St. Ignatius Loyola, had already been recommended by St. Edmund in his *Speculum Ecclesiae*. He indicates the theme and scope of devout meditation thus:

> Of his manhede, sall þou thynke thre thyngeȝ: þe meknes of his Incarnacyone, þe swetenes of his conuersasione, and þe grete charite of his passione. Bot þis may þou noghte do all att anes, and þare-fore hafe I twynned the thaym by þe seuene houres of þe daye þat þou saise in þe kyrke, swa þat nane houre passe the þat þou ne sall be swetely ocupyede in þi herte. . . . Now, dere frende, before matyns sall þou thynke of þe swete byrthe of Ihesu Cryste alþer-fyrste, and sythyne eftyrwarde of his passione. Of his byrth, sall thou thynke besyly þe tyme, and þe stede, and þe houre þat oure lorde Ihesu Criste was borne of his modir Marie. Þe tyme was in myd-wyntter, whene it was maste calde, þe houre was at mydnyghte, þe hardeste houre þat es, þe stede was in mydwarde þe strete, in a house with-owttene walles.[1]

But the opening of the Pseudo-Bonaventura *Meditations* is perhaps the classic statement of the aim of such religious exercises. The author writes:

> Inter alia virtutum et laudum praeconia de sanctissima virgine Caecelia legitur, quod Evangelium Christi absconditum semper portabat in pectore. Quod sic intelligi debere videtur, quod ipsa de vita Domini Jesu in Evangelio tradita, quaedam sibi devotiora praeelegeret, in quibus meditabatur die ac nocte, corde puro et integro.
>
> [*Among other noteworthy virtues and excellences of the most holy virgin Cecilia, we read that she always carried the Gospel of Christ concealed*

---

[1] *The Myrrour of Seynt Edmonde*, edited by C. Horstman, *Yorkshire Writers* (London, 1895), I, 235.

in her bosom; which we apparently must understand to mean that she meditated, day and night, with pure and sincere heart, upon certain things recorded in the Gospel concerning the life of Jesus Christ which she had chosen as, for herself, most congenial to piety.]

The writer goes on to explain how such meditation steadies the mind, fortifies the will, and instructs in the avoidance of vice. Then he significantly concludes:

Non autem credas, quod omnia quae ipsum dixisse, vel fecisse constat, meditari possimus, vel quod omnia scripta sint: ego vero ad majorem impressionem, ea sic, ac si ita fuissent, narrabo, prout contingere vel contigisse credi possunt, secundum quasdam imaginarias repraesentationes, quas animus diversimode percipit.[1]

[*However, you must not believe that we can meditate upon all those things which it is certain that he said or did, or that all things are in writing; but, for the sake of greater impressiveness, I shall narrate them thus, as they may be thought to happen or have happened, according to certain imaginary representations which my mind perceives in various ways.*]

The writer is thus deliberately taking the bare Gospel narrative (and various apocryphal narratives such as the Childhood of Christ) and clothing them in realistic detail in order to make them immediate to the reader. This may serve as an example of his method:

Hic modum crucifixionis diligenter attende. Ponuntur due scale, una retrorsum, alia ad sinistrum brachium, super quas malefici ascendunt cum clavis et martellis. Ponitur eciam alia scala ex parte anteriori, attingens usque ad locum ubi debebant pedes figi. Conspice nunc bene singula; compellitur Dominus Iesus crucem ascendere per hanc scalam parvam; ipse autem sine rebellione et contradiccione facit humiliter quidquid volunt. Cum igitur in superiori parte illius parve scale pervenit ad crucem, renes vertit, et illa regalia aperit brachia, et extendens manus pulcherimas, in excelsis eas porrigit suis crucifixoribus.[2]

---

[1] Bonaventura, *Opera Omnia*, XII, edited by A. C. Peltier (Paris, 1868), p.510–11. Cp. Pseudo-Bonaventura, *Meditations on the Life of Christ*, edited by I. Ragusa and R. B. Green (Princeton, 1961), pp.1–5.

[2] Pseudo-Bonaventura, *Meditaciones*, p.112; Pseudo-Bonaventura, *Meditations*, pp.333–4; for the Passion cp. also the vernacular version of Nicholas Love, *The Mirrour of the Blessed Lyf of Jesu Christ*, edited by L. F. Powell (Oxford, 1908).

[*Here pay diligent attention to the manner of the Crucifixion. Two ladders are set in position, one of them at the back, another at the left arm, which the evildoers ascend holding nails and hammers. Another ladder is placed also in front reaching where the feet were to be affixed. Look well now at each thing: the Lord Jesus is compelled to ascend by this small ladder. Yet without rebelliousness or gainsaying he humbly does whatever they wish. When therefore he reaches the cross at the top of that small ladder he turns himself around, opens those royal arms and, extending his most beautiful hands, stretches them out on high to his crucifiers.*]

How dramatic this technique is in its effect can be seen by noting its exact translation into dramatic terms in the drama of the late Middle Ages. Indeed one must feel that Émile Mâle's instinct was right when he saw a connection between affective piety, late medieval realism and the medieval drama.[1] Compare, for example, this from the play by the Wakefield Master in the Towneley Plays:

Primus Tortor:	Lo, here I haue a bande,
	If nede be to bynd his hande;
	This thowng, I trow, will last.
Secundus Tortor:	And her oone to the othere syde,
	That shall abate his pride,
	Be it be drawen fast.
Tertius Tortor:	Lo, here a hamere and nales also,
	For to festen fast oure foo
	To this tre, full soyn.[2]

Even closer in detail is the comparable passage from the York cycle:

Tertius Miles:	And sties also are ordande þore,
	With stalworthe steeles as mystir wore,
	Bothe some schorte and some lang.
Primus Miles:	For hameres and for nayles,
	Latte see sone who schall gang.
Secundus Miles:	Here are bragges þat will noght faile,
	Or irnne and stele full strange.[3]

---

[1] Mâle, pp.35–84.

[2] *The Towneley Plays*, edited by G. England and A. W. Pollard, E.E.T.S. (ES) 71 (1897), 260.

[3] *The York Plays*, edited by L. Toulmin Smith (Oxford, 1885), p.340.

and as we proceed to the crucifixion itself, we see, in horrible detail, the punishment in progress. Yet the dramatic immediacy is not greater than in many of the graphic descriptions of the meditations in the affective tradition. As has been observed 'The apogee of medieval realism is reached in the crucifixion, which represents the final and complete transformation of the universal symbolism of the liturgical office into the literal particulars of drama.'[1] One has only to compare the Christ of the Old English *Dream of the Rood* as he strips himself for the contest and as, confident of triumph, he mounts the cross, with the figure of the meek and suffering Christ of late medieval plays and meditations, despoiled of his clothes and cruelly tormented by his enemies, to perceive the nature of late medieval realism, the close focus combined with a technique of audience participation, in the plays inevitable, but in the meditations created by the use of the deictic aspect. A Peter Damian may exclaim 'Video te interioribus oculis, Redemptor meus, crucis clavis affixum'[2] [I see the with the eyes of the mind, my Redeemer, pierced with the nails of the Cross] but the writer of the *Meditations* does not leave this inward vision to chance. He is ever pointing to the details; 'See now', 'Imagine now' he constantly urges his reader, whose eyes are ever directed to the physical details of Christ's life. It is perhaps instructive to look again at *The Dream of the Rood*. The author of this poem also is watching the crucifixion:

> Hwæðre ic þær licgende lange hwile
> beheold hreowcearig Hælendes treow,
> oððæt ic gehyrde þæt hit hleoðrode.[3]

[*Yet I, lying there for a long time, sorrowful beheld the tree of the Saviour, until I heard it speak.*]

But how different from Rolle's account of how he saw the same event:

---

[1] W. F. McNeir, 'The Corpus Christi Passion Plays as Dramatic Art', *SP*, xlviii (1951), 621.

[2] *Oratio* xxvi: PL, cxlv, col. 927.

[3] *The Dream of the Rood*, ll.24–6, edited by M. J. Swanton (Manchester, 1970).

A, Lord, þi sorwe, why were it not my deth? Now þei lede þe forthe nakyd os a worm, þe turmentoures abowtyn þe, and armede knyȝtes; þe prees of þe peple was wonderly strong, þei hurled þe and haryed þe so schamefully, þei spurned þe with here feet, os þou hadde been a dogge. I se in my soule how reufully þou gost: þi body is so blody, so rowed and so bledderyd; þi crowne is so kene, þat sytteth on þi hed; þi heere mevyth with þe wynde, clemyd with þe blood; þi lovely face so wan and so bolnyd with bofetynge and with betynge, with spyttynge, with spowtynge; þe blood ran þerewith, þat grysyth in my syȝt; so lothly and so wlatsome þe Jues han þe mad, þat a mysel art þou lyckere þan a clene man. Þe cros is so hevy, so hye and so stark, þat þei hangyd on þi bare bac trossyd so harde.[1]

We notice, in the first place, that the author of the Old English poem has shown us the action at one remove by making the cross the speaker. In the second place, not only is the event shown in its theological rather than its human implications, as has often been pointed out, but the human implications are presented by imagery, the imagery of the retainer who is compelled to be the *bana* of his lord. It is thus the emotional implications of the suffering which are presented to us rather than the suffering itself. And even where the physical aspects of the event are referred to they are seen indirectly:

> Hwæðre ic þurh þæt gold ongytan meahte
> earmra ærgewin, þæt hit ærest ongan
> swætan on þa swiðran healfe. Eall ic wæs mid sorgum gedrefed.
> Forht ic wæs for þære fægran gesyhðe. Geseah ic þæt fuse beacen
> wendan wædum ond bleom; hwilum hit wæs mid wætan bestemed,
> beswyled mid swates gange, hwilum mid since gegyrwed.[2]

[*Yet through that gold I could perceive the former strife of wretched men, in that it first began to bleed on the right side. I was all overcome with sorrows, fearful was I because of that fair sight. I saw that shining symbol,*

---

[1] Richard Rolle, *Meditations on the Passion*, in *English Writings of Richard Rolle*, edited by H. E. Allen (Oxford, 1931), p.21.
[2] *The Dream of the Rood*, ll.18–23.

change hangings and colours; sometimes it was bedewed with moisture, defiled with flowing blood; sometimes adorned with treasure.]

In the Old English poem we see Christ's humanity and Christ's divinity in a paradoxical juxtaposition:

> Geseah ic weruda God
> þearle þenian. Þystro hæfdon
> bewrigen mid wolcnum Wealdendes hræw,
> scirne sciman; sceadu forð eode,
> wann under wolcnum.[1]

[*I saw the Lord of Hosts terribly extended. Shades of night had covered the body of the Lord with clouds, the fair radiance; shadow went forth, dark beneath the clouds.*]

But we do not see the Man of Sorrows, as the later Middle Ages pictured him, in the context of everyday life.

Nevertheless, this close focus is not concerned only to create a photographic reflection of reality. There is in the Rohan Book of Hours a *Pietà* in which St. John stands in the centre with the cross in the background. He holds the Virgin in his arms and she leans towards her dead son lying on the ground across the bottom of the picture. She sees only the dead and blood-stained Christ, but St. John, his head twisted backward and upward, sees behind and above him the figure of God the Father leaning out of a blue background of angels' wings, His hand raised in blessing.[2] This is a perfect comment on these realistic forms. They are only close-ups in the drama of salvation. And, indeed, even the horrors of the crucifixion can be so closely focused that they cease to be realistic at all. The second text of Rolle's *Meditations on the Passion* well illustrates this:

> Efte, swet Jhesu, þy body is like to a dufhouse. For a dufhouse is ful of holys, so is þy body ful of woundes. And as a dove pursued of an hauk, yf she mow cache an hool of hir hous she is

---

[1] *The Dream of the Rood*, ll.51–5.

[2] Cp. Ekbert of Schönau's prayer *Respice Domine* in which God the Father is called on to witness the death of His Son. Anselm, *Meditationes*, ix, col. 756. I owe this reference to the kindness of Dr. A. M. Hudson. For the authorship, see Wilmart, p.194.

siker ynowe, so, swete Jhesu, in temptacion þy woundes ben best refuyt to us. Now, swet Jhesu, I beseche þe, in euche temptacion graunt me grace of some hoole of þy woundes, and lykynge to abide in mynd of þy passioun.[1]

Also, swete Jhesu, þi body is like to a honycombe. For hit is in euche a way ful of cellis, and euch celle ful of hony, so þat hit may nat be touched without yeld of swetnesse. So, swet Jhesu, þy body is ful of cellys of devocion, þat hit may nat be touched of a clene soule without swetnesse of lykynge. Now, swet Jhesu, graunt me grace to touche þe with criynge mercy for my synnes, with desyre to gostly contemplacion, with amendynge of my lyf and contynuynge in goodnes, in stody to fulfille þy hestes and delicatly to abyde in mynd of þy passioun.

In the same way, the wounds of Christ are compared to the stars of heaven, Christ's body to a net, for a net, like Christ's body, is full of holes, to a book written in red ink for 'so ys þy body al written with rede woundes'.[2] The text is an admirable example of Auerbach's observation that as the physical portrayal of the Passion grows more brutal the 'sensory and mystic power of suggestion grows stronger'.[3] For the writer passes from the simple contemplation of an actual scene, vividly imagined in all its horrifying physical detail, to a series of poetic images which serve as a link with a series of prayers. The images are configurational rather than evocative. Some of these images are emotionally neutral, such as the image of the book, or the net, and, like the shield image in the *Ancrene Wisse*, they have an intellectual character. Others, like the stars, or the honeycomb, or the dove-cot, appear to be more evocative, but it is noteworthy that, in most cases, the connection with the following petition is purely verbal. A comparable example may be taken from the *Revelations* of Juliana of Norwich. In the eighth shewing she sees a vision described in the longer version as 'the last petiuous peynes of Criste deyeng, and discoloryng of his face and dreyeng of his flesh'.[4] The basis of the

[1] For this, cp. E. Colledge, *The Mediaeval Mystics of England* (London, 1962), pp.11–12.

[2] Rolle, *Meditations on the Passion*; *The English Writings*, pp.35–6.

[3] Auerbach (1953), p.247.

[4] The text is taken from MS. Sloane 2499 of the longer version, f. 13–13ᵛ.

L

vision is the process of physical death. Yet it goes beyond a purely sensuous record of decomposition. The details are no longer part of an actual context. We no longer have the moment by moment account of the event but the focus enlarges so that what we see assumes an unreal dimension. The whole vision, in the longer version, is built round the four pains:

> For that eche tyme that our Lord and blissid savior deyid upon the rode it was a dry harre wynde and wond colde as to my sigte, and what tyme the pretious blode was blede oute of the swete body that migte passe therfro yet there dwellid a moysture in the swete flesh of Criste as it was shewyd. Blodeleshede and peyne dryden within and blowyng of wynde and cold commyng fro withouten metten togeder in the swete body of Criste; And these iiij tweyn withouten and tweyn within dryden the fleshe of Criste be process of tyme.

Throughout the passage Juliana plays upon these ideas. She tells us first how the face is dry and bloodless with pale dying and 'sithen more pale dede langoring, and then turnid more dede, mo blew and sithen more browne blew,[1] as the flesh turnyd more depe dede'. Then she briefly focuses upon the parts of the face:

> For his passion shewid to me most propirly in his blissid face, and namly in his lippis there I saw these iiij colowres, tho yt were aforn freshe redy and likyng to my sigte. This was a swemful chonge to sene this depe deyeng, and also the nose clonge and dryed to my sigte, and the swete body was brown and blak al turnyd oute of faire lifely colowr of hymselfe on to drye deyeng.

And this vision with its echoing repetition of the words *deep*, *dead*, *pale*, *dry*, *dying*, moves briefly from the scrutiny of the dying form to the 'blowyng of wynde and cold commyng fro withouten', but it is a wind which can only be seen in the drying of the dying body, for it has no context apart from this. And, as Juliana turns again to the figure on the cross, she describes the slowness of the process of dying. Not, however, by the addition

---

[1] The manuscript appears to have *browne* deleted before *blew* but the apparent deletion is in fact from the heavy scoring out of a word on the other side of the page.

of graphic detail, for no new details are added, but by a paradox:

> This longe pynyng semyd to me as if he had bene seven night ded,
> deyand at the poynt of out passing awey, sufferand the last peyne;
> And than I said it semyd to me as if he had bene seven night dede,
> it menyth that the swete body was so discoloryd, so drye, so clongen,
> so dedely, and so petevous as he had be seven night dede, con-
> tinuly deyand. And me thowte the deyeng of Crists flesh was the
> most peyne and the last of his passion.

Juliana is remarkable for her graphic similes, which have often
been praised. Thus she sees with her 'bodyly sight' great drops
of blood 'like pellots' whose plenteousness was 'like to the
dropys of water that fallen of the evys after a greate showre of
reyne', 'and for the roundhede it were like to the scale of heryng,
in the spreadeing on the forehead'.[1] And of the four manners
of dryings: 'the first was blodeless; the secund was payne
folowyng after, the thred hangyng up in the eyr as men hang a
cloth to drye'.[2] But vivid though these simple images are, her
realism is very different from the rhetorical 'picturation' which
we were discussing at the beginning of this chapter. It is a
realism rooted in an actual experience. Not unlike those lyrics
which are rooted in the liturgy, it is a realism which must always
be seen in a living context. Its function is to rouse compassion.
As the writer of the *Stimulus Amoris* puts it:

> ȝif þou wolt haue compassion on Crist crucifyet furst schape þe
> ȝif þu mai to bi oned to him þorw feruent disyre. For whi, þe
> more feruentli þou louest him þe more pite schalt þou haue of
> his passion and þe more compassion þat þou felest þe more schal
> þi loue be.[3]

Have we then passed out of the realm of realism? The time
has perhaps come that we should stand back and review our

---

[1] MS. Sloane 2499, f. 6.

[2] MS. Sloane 2499, f. 14.

[3] Vernon MS. f. 319[v], col. 2. *The Goad of Love*, translated by Clare
Kirchberger (London, 1952), p.55; a particular aspect of this is the *Andachtsbild*; cp. T. Wolpers, 'Zum Andachtsbild in der mittelenglischen religiösen
Lyrik', *Symposion für Schirmer*, pp.293–336; Woolf (1968), pp.184–238;
389–91.

progress. In our opening paragraph we presented the reader with two contrasts; the contrast between a 'mechanical or photographic' reflection of reality and a true realism rooted in social reality, a contrast calling in question the very nature of truth to life; on the other hand, a contrast between the raw material of literature, the fable, the plot, and the finished work, a narrative or description which is realised in a particular way, a piece of writing in which the author's *diacrisis* becomes apparent in its particular realisation. Our example of the fable of the blind man and the pear-tree, demonstrated what is meant by the different realisations of a tale and showed some of the different ways in which medieval writers might make their choice. As we have tried to suggest in the course of the last two chapters, the realisation of a story, in medieval terms, can be in the direction of the general or in the direction of the particular. Of the generalised tale, the narratives usually termed 'romances' by modern critics, afford numerous examples. The characters are generalised, the subject matter tends towards fantasy, the descriptions are formal, conventional and static. The *descriptio*, essentially a 'close up', has none the less, generalising features. I think it is probably true to say that the subject matter and sentiment in such tales will usually be elevated and aristocratic. On the other hand, the realisation of a narrative can be in the direction of the particular. Here two unexpected facts emerge. On the one hand, the subject matter need not be 'low' or 'comic' for the work to be particularised. Clearly it is so in Chaucer's fabliaux, but the tradition of religious meditations, as well as the drama, show that this need not be the case. Here we have a style which is minutely particular and vividly realised. Yet it is noble in sentiment and ever ready to tip over into poetic imagery or biblical typology.

At the beginning of this chapter we asked how far 'pictura-tions' create a sense of reality. This question must now be briefly considered. We have said that the people of romances are characteristically typical. Yet are the people in Chaucer's *Canterbury Tales*, so minutely particularised, individuals? In regard to the Prologue to *The Canterbury Tales*, opinion has ranged from those critics who have supposed that real people were behind the portraits to those who have supposed them to represent abstractions such as the Seven Deadly Sins;[1] some, taking up a middle position, have supposed that they represent simply classes of people, while Curry's work has tended to emphasise that many of the apparently individual details are present in order to place the people within a physiological type.[2] The same kind of ambiguity reigns in regard to the tales. For example, opinion has diverged as to whether the portrait of Emetreus in *The Knight's Tale* represents a physiological type as Curry thought, or whether, on the other hand, it represents Richard II as Manly tentatively suggested, or the Earl of Derby, as Cook suggested.[3]

There seems to me no doubt that, in one way, the people who move through the *Canterbury Tales* are simply types.[4] Anyone familiar with medieval anti-clerical satire, from the twelfth century onwards, cannot but perceive that the clerical characters in the Prologue are compounded of traits which are commonplace in this satire. As we have tried to suggest, the knight, although his rusty armour may be a detail taken from the *Teseida*, on the whole conforms to the stereotype of the Christian knight. The Prologue is above all a survey of society of a kind familiar to readers of estates literature. In the same way, the characters in the fabliaux are typical figures. Sometimes, as

[1] Cp. J. M. Manly, *Some New Light on Chaucer* (London, 1927); cp. F. Tupper, 'The Pardoner's Tavern', *JEGP*, xiii (1914), 553–65; 'Chaucer and the Seven Deadly Sins', *PMLA*, xxix (1914), 93–128; 'The Quarrels of the Canterbury Pilgrims', *JEGP*, xiv (1915), 256–70; 'Chaucer's Bed's Head', *MLN*, xxx (1915), 5–12; 'Chaucer's Sinners and Sins', *JEGP*, xv (1916), 56–106; J. L. Lowes, 'Chaucer and the Seven Deadly Sins', *PMLA*, xxx (1915), 237–371.

[2] Cp. R. Mohl, *The Three Estates in Medieval and Renaissance Literature* (New York, 1933); Curry, *passim*. Individual studies are too numerous to be itemised.

[3] Cp. Robinson's note, in his edition of Chaucer, on lines 2155–86; pp.678–9.

[4] Cp. Donaldson (1954); R. K. Root, *The Poetry of Chaucer* (Boston, 1906), pp.161–3; for the successful blending of the type with the individual, cp. G. G. Sedgewick, 'The Progress of Chaucer's Pardoner, 1880–1940', *MLQ, I* (1940), 431–58; Hulbert.

in *The Merchant's Tale*, they have names which give away their status: Placebo and Justinus, the complacent and judicious friends, May and January the young bride and the old husband. Ironically, only the most shadowy of them all, Damian, has an individual name. In the other fabliaux we again have basically stereotypes, the jealous husband, the amorous scholar, the flighty maiden and so on. Anti-clerical satire forms the basis of the tales of the Summoner and the Friar. Even the Wife of Bath's Prologue is a magnificent embroidery on a conventional anti-feminist satire. Yet is this the whole story? Is not the tale of the jealous husband who kills his wife a stereotyped tale? Was not the revenge tragedy a literary stereotype when Shakespeare wrote? Was not the tale of Lear a folk tale of a very improbable kind? Certainly it is true that a conventional figure, an improbable tale, a literary stereotype, does not in itself prevent the realisation of characters as individuals. But it is essential, I think, that the individual traits should be sharply focused representations of general characteristics. Art is, after all, illusion, as Gombrich has reminded us, and the nature of this illusion is a coincidence of the general and the particular. When we learn that Cordelia's voice is 'low and tender' this is a particular which is not essential for an understanding of the function of Cordelia in the action. It is in terms of the story an 'accident'. Yet it is a physical trait which we feel to be consonant with her character. It is a concrete universal, a particular realisation of a general expectation. Just as the details of a plot must give the illusion of a time–space continuum, so characters to be individuals must combine into a credible whole and this can only happen when 'general nature' suffuses the detail. But the characters in the comic works of Chaucer do not, I think, have this wholeness except, perhaps, the Wife of Bath. Some of the most vivid touches in Chaucer's portraits, such as Absolon's hair in *The Miller's Tale*, or Nicholas's taste for music, seem to be a kind of *trompe d'œil* to convince us that the puppets are real. They are particulars with no root in reality. They are purely 'photographic'. The merchant and his wife in *The Shipman's Tale* talk like real people, but they are only the means by which the story is propelled. In other words, the story is primary and the characters are secondary; the characters exist for the story and not the story for the characters. Characterisation for its own sake is only rarely a medieval concern.

Thus we find that medieval 'picturations' do not necessarily produce a work that is realistic. They are, in a sense, a 'photographic representation of reality', and how far they project real people and situations is dependent upon the way in which they are used. As we have seen, it is possible, on the one hand, to use such 'picturation' to project the formal, typical figures of *The Knight's Tale* in the romance mode; on the other, the informal but still typical portraits of the Prologue to *The Canterbury Tales*: used in a different way again, they can project the intensely serious subject matter of the writings in the tradition of affective piety, or the low-life portraits of the fabliaux which tend to be purely photographic. Lukács has observed that 'the live portrayal of the complete human personality is possible only if the writer attempts to create types'.[1] Yet only in the unique events of the life of Christ does the medieval writer really create a unique person and a unique situation. In other cases, serious themes tend to be expressed in generalities or, when detailed, in the consuetudinal aspect, with symmetry rather than perspective as their structural principle. On the other hand, the comic forms tend towards the indicative aspect, towards a use of detail which is without a basis in any general concept; or else the detail tends towards a tautological relationship with the underlying general concept; that is, towards the typical.

So far we have been considering mainly modes of writing in which the author engages our interest or sympathy by the use of 'picturation'. Before leaving the topic of 'realism' I propose to consider two examples of the use of the deictic mode. As we noted, in considering the development of the story of the blind man and the pear tree, the deictic mode is one device by means of which an author can give his story immediacy comparable to the close focus of the 'picturation'. We have also noted its use in the tradition of affective piety. It would seem therefore

[1] Lukács, p.8.

fitting to conclude with some examples of this device in other genres. The first example is that of medieval satire. It has been claimed that the Middle Ages have no genuine satire but only complaint.[1] Now it is certainly true that much medieval satire is 'normative'. An admirable example would be the work of Gower. J. H. Fisher has pointed out that the concept of universal order lies behind all three major works of Gower.[2] The nature of this satire can be clearly seen in the Prologue to the *Confessio Amantis* in which Gower laments the decline of the world:

> If I schal drawe in to my mynde
> The tyme passed, thanne I fynde
> The world stod thanne in al his welthe:
> Tho was the lif of man in helthe,
> Tho was plente, tho was richesse,
> Tho was the fortune of prouesse,
> Tho was knyhthode in pris be name,
> Wherof the wyde worldes fame
> Write in Cronique is yit withholde;
> Justice of lawe tho was holde,
> The privilege of regalie
> Was sauf, and al the baronie
> Worschiped was in his astat;
> The citees knewen no debat,
> The poeple stod in obeissance
> Under the reule of governance,
> And pes, which ryhtwisnesse keste,
> With charite tho stod in reste:
> Of mannes herte the corage
> Was schewed thanne in the visage;
> The word was lich to the conceite
> Withoute semblant of deceite:
> Tho was ther unenvied love,
> Tho was the vertu sett above
> And vice was put under fote.

---

[1] John Peter, *Complaint and Satire in Early English Literature* (Oxford, 1956), pp.1–103.

[2] J. H. Fisher, *John Gower: Moral Philosopher and Friend of Chaucer* (London, 1965), especially pp.135–203.

Now stant the crop under the rote,
The world is changed overal,
And therof most in special
That love is falle into discord.[1]

Here the satirical mode is akin to the romance mode in that it involves the posing and exemplification of a standard against which actuality is to be measured. Anti-curial satire is essentially of the same kind, in that it tends to imply a contrast between the life of court and the simple life of honesty and contentment. When Aeneas Silvius writes 'Virtutes enim . . . foelicis uitae sunt effectrices; quae a principum domiciliis exclusae' [For the virtues of the happy life are efficacious; which are excluded from the dwellings of princes][2] he is uttering a commonplace; a commonplace implying a norm from which the life at court deviated. In different ways the same concept can be seen in anticurial literature from the *Policraticus* of John of Salisbury to the *Curial* of Alain Chartier or the court poems of Dunbar.[3] Yet this view is a one-sided view of medieval satire. It is perhaps true that the kind of satire represented by the work of Dryden or Pope is not commonly found in the Middle Ages; satire, that is, which consists of a personal attack on individuals. Yet examples even of this are not unknown. French examples are found in the personal attack on King John, for the loss of Poitou and Touraine, written probably after 1214, by Bertrand de Born,[4] or the two *sirventes* written against Henry III by Bernard de Rovenac.[5] There were many poems on individual occasions, often showing personal animosity either to individuals or nationalities. Such would be the poems on the arrest and

---

[1] John Gower, *Confessio Amantis*, Prologus, ll.93–121; *The English Works*, edited by G. C. Macaulay (Oxford, 1901).

[2] Aeneas Silvius, *De Curialium Miseriis*, edited by W. P. Mustard (Baltimore, 1928), p.23.

[3] Cp. Caxton, *The Curial made by maystere Alain Charretier*, edited by P. Meyer and F. J. Furnivall, E.E.T.S. (ES) 54 (1888); William Dunbar, *Poems*, edited by W. M. Mackenzie (London, 1932), Nos. 13, 21, 29.

[4] T. Wright, *Political Songs of England* (Camden Society (OS) 6, 1839), pp.3–6.

[5] *Political Songs*, pp.36–42; cp. S. M. Tucker, *Verse-Satire in England before the Renaissance* (New York, 1908), pp.48–9.

death of the Duke of Suffolk[1] in 1450; the poem on the execution of Sir Simon Fraser in 1306[2] or the poems manifesting popular feeling against Philip, Duke of Burgundy after the siege of Calais in 1436.[3] Minot's hatred of the French and the Scots would illustrate the same point.[4] From the later period one might again note the poems on the execution of Gaveston listed by A. G. Rigg in the Glastonbury Miscellany.[5] Miss Legge has drawn attention to the practice of the lampoon in Anglo-Norman.[6] It seems fair to say that the tradition of lampoon and personal invective was practised throughout the thirteenth, fourteenth and fifteenth centuries in England. Nevertheless, it is perhaps true that two other kinds of satire are more common and certainly of more literary significance. The first of these is the tradition of invective against classes of people. The anti-clerical satire of the Wycliffite writings and of Langland immediately spring to mind. But anti-clerical satire is as chronic in the Middle Ages as the corruption of the church.

> Propter Sion non tacebo,
> set ruinas Rome flebo

[*I will not be silent concerning Sion but I will weep the ruins of Rome.*]

writes Walter of Châtillon in the twelfth century,[7] and many of his contemporaries did the same. One has only to look through Thomas Wright's collection of poems attributed to Walter Mapes[8] to see the range of anti-clerical satire, from the gro-

---

[1] R. H. Robbins, *Historical Poems of the xivth and xvth Centuries* (New York, 1959), Nos. 75, 76, pp.186–9.

[2] *Historical Poems*, No. 4, pp.14–21.

[3] *Historical Poems*, Nos. 28–30, pp.78–89.

[4] Lawrence Minot, *Poems*, edited by J. Hall (2nd edn., Oxford, 1897), *passim*.

[5] A. G. Rigg, *A Glastonbury Miscellany of the Fifteenth Century* (Oxford, 1968), Nos. XLI, XLII, pp.87–8.

[6] M. D. Legge, *Anglo-Norman Literature and its Background* (Oxford, 1963), pp.351–7; cp. I. S. T. Aspin, *Anglo-Norman Political Songs*, A.N.T.S., 11 (1953).

[7] *The Oxford Book of Medieval Latin Verse*, No. 196, ll.1–2; p.282.

[8] *The Latin Poems commonly attributed to Walter Mapes*, edited by T. Wright (Camden Society (OS) 16, 1841); for a useful survey of the medieval satirical tradition see A. R. Heiserman, *Skelton and Satire* (Chicago, 1961), *passim*.

tesque poems associated with Bishop Golias to the poems, such as those of Walter of Châtillon, which reflect the influence of classical authors like Juvenal. Parody too exists alongside invective and it is interesting to note how texts such as *The Gospel according to St. Mark*, or *The Tale of the Adulterous Monk*, survived in manuscripts from the thirteenth to the fifteenth centuries.[1] How popular these satirical texts were can be seen also from their inclusion in the Glastonbury Miscellany.[2] Satirical technique in these works is widely varied. It can include allegorical machinery as in some of the Goliardic poetry; it includes the ironical exploitation of literary texts as in the use of the Bible in parodies such as *The Tale of the Adulterous Monk*; or traditional themes as in the outrageous 'comic fantasy' of *The Land of Cokaygne*.[3]

Something of the different authorial voices possible in satire can be summarised briefly by comparing the two portraits of a pardoner in Chaucer and Langland:

> Þere prechide a pardoner as he a prest were;
> Brouȝte forþ a bulle wiþ bisshopis selis
> And seide þat hymself miȝte assoile hem alle
> Of falsnesse of fastyng and of auowes broken.
> Lewide men leuide hym wel and likide his speche;
> Comen vp knelynge to kissen his bulle.
> He bunchide hem wiþ his breuet and bleride here eiȝen
> And rauȝte wiþ his rageman ryngis and brochis.
> Þus ȝe gyuen ȝoure gold glotonis to helpe
> And leniþ it loselis þat leccherie haunten.
> Were þe bisshop yblissid and worþ boþe hise eris,
> His sel shulde not be sent to disseyue þe peple.[4]

If we compare this picture with the portrait of the Pardoner in the Prologue to *The Canterbury Tales*, it is evident that the technique of portraiture is different in the two authors. In Langland

---

[1] Cp. P. Lehmann, *Die Parodie im Mittelalter* (Stuttgart, 1963), pp.183–8, 224–31; cp. J. A. Yunck, *The Lineage of Lady Meed* (Notre Dame, 1963).

[2] Rigg, *A Glastonbury Miscellany*, Nos. II, IV, V, VIII, XIII, XXII, XXX, XXXI.

[3] See Bennett and Smithers, *Early Middle English Verse and Prose*, pp. 136–144.

[4] Langland, *Piers Plowman*, A. *Prologue*, ll.65–76.

we have a dramatic moment chosen to reveal the Pardoner. He is like Faux Semblant, in that we see only those parts of the character which are immediately relevant to the satire. He appears briefly lit up in the act of deceit but, unlike Frate Cipolla, we do not hear him speak. In Chaucer, on the other hand, the detail is abundant. We do not have the sudden spotlight turned upon the man in a typical action, but Chaucer's camera apparently wanders at random over the unattractive figure until gradually we find that our physical repulsion has a moral justification. Yet the difference between the two portraits is not entirely a matter of difference in focus or perspective. The author's tone of voice, also, contributes to the different effect; that of Langland is earnestly drawing the moral from the brief *exemplum* presented to the audience; that of Chaucer is cool, detached, reminiscing: 'I trowe he were a geldyng or a mare'.[1] The voice of Langland is that of the preacher; that of Chaucer the voice of the story-teller. Chaucer allows himself the privilege of the historian and of the prophet:

> with thise relikes, whan that he fond
> A povre person dwellynge upon lond,
> Upon a day he gat hym moore moneye
> Than that the person gat in monthes tweye;
> And thus, with feyned flaterye and japes,
> He made the person and the peple his apes.[2]

Yet both these satirical portraits, so different in their technique, are essentially portraits of a class of people and not of individuals, and thus illustrate from another mode, using other means, the combination of the typical and exemplary with the particular in a characteristically medieval fashion.

In the last two chapters, we have tried to distinguish between two modes of writing, a mode of disengagement, a generalised mode, tending towards the typical, and the more realistic modes which are particularly associated, in the comic mode with the fabliau, and, in the tragic mode, with affective piety and the drama. We have also considered the different functions

---

[1] Chaucer, *The Canterbury Tales*, A. l.691.
[2] Chaucer, *The Canterbury Tales*, A. ll.701–6.

of the 'picturation' or rhetorical portrait in these modes of writing. There is, moreover, another mode of 'realism' seen in the satire of the period and especially in the writings of Chaucer; that of the speaking voice, the scorn of the satirist or the ironic intervention of a Chaucer; an exploitation, in fact, of the deictic mode. We cannot leave this topic without some considera-tion of Chaucer's *Troilus and Criseyde*, an interesting and appo-site illustration of medieval exploitation of the different modes of writing, combining the romance and the realistic genres with the appropriate levels of style. The poem contrasts the lofty sentiments of the lovers and the lofty theme of the fall of Troy with the plebeian commonsense and cynical realism of Pan-darus; aureate diction with a racy proverbial style; the con-ventional attitudes and phraseology of 'courtly love', with the pragmatic sexuality of a Pandarus or a Diomede; the philoso-phical questionings of a Troilus, with the self-sufficiency of Diomede. On the other hand, characters, in a sense already familiar from *The Knight's Tale*, assume a dramatic actuality. The shadowy figure of Emelye becomes the flesh and blood figure of Criseyde, watching Troilus from her window, debat-ing, like any heroine of romance, whether she shall accept the love of Troilus, sitting in her paved parlour reading a romance of Thebes; and the shadowy figures of Palamon and Arcite are transformed into Troilus, debating with Pandarus, singing with Criseyde, riding back from the wars; the action is focused by means of concrete objects, the brooch, the smoky rain, the chimney-piece in Criseyde's bedroom; the figures act with realistic vitality. We see Pandarus peeping under the bed-clothes, running for the cushion, teasing Troilus. Just as, in our comparison of *The Merchant's Tale* with the Latin fable, we noted the devices by means of which Chaucer realised the tale in an immediate and dramatic form and gave it a superficial realism, so here in *Troilus and Criseyde* we seem to have a fully realised dramatic narrative. And, indeed, in some degree this is true and it is easy to see why the poem has been compared with the psychological novel.

Yet that this view is an oversimplification is evident from the critical battle which has raged over the epilogue. And it is surely much nearer the truth to regard the poem as incorporating a number of different perspectives, a 'pun-like ambiguity of focus'.[1] The poem indeed is a great debate on the nature of love, rather than a psychological novel. As has been noted, the poem is, in a sense, an extension of that debate begun in *The Parlement of Foules* with Troilus for the royal tercel and Pandarus for the duck. The substance of the debate, or at least one side of it, is to be found in the *Vox Clamantis* of 'moral Gower':

> Milicie pars vna petit mulieris amorem,
> Altera quod mundi laus sonet alta sibi.
>
> . . . .
>
> Si laudem mundi cupiat, tunc copia Cresi
> Defluit, vt donis laus sonet alta suis:
> Tunc aurum, vestes, gemmas et equos quasi grana
> Seminat, vt laudis crescat in aure seges.
> Set sibi femineum si miles adoptet amorem,
> Carius hunc precio tunc luet ipse suo:
> Quod sibi natura, sibi vel deus attulit omne,
> Corpus, res, animam, tot dabit inde bona.
> Cum tamen ipse sui perfecerit acta laboris,
> Laus et vtraque simul perfida fallat eum,
> Cum nec fama loquax mundi peruenit ad aures,
> Nec sibi castus amor reddit amoris opem,
> Tunc deceptus ait, 'Heu, quam fortuna sinistrat!
> Cum labor a longo tempore cassus abit.'
> Tardius ipse venit, qui sic sibi plangit inepte,
> Cum sibi non alius causa sit ipse doli.[2]

[*One part of the knightly estate seeks after woman's love, and another, what the world's lofty praise may extol to it. . . . If he wishes worldly praise, then he pours out the wealth of Croesus in order that his lofty praise may be sounded, because of his gifts. Then he sows gold, clothes,*

---

[1] R. M. Jordan, 'Chaucer's Sense of Illusion: Road-side Drama Reconsidered', *ELH*, xxix (1962), 21; cp. Bloomfield; C. Muscatine, *Chaucer and the French Tradition* (Berkeley & Los Angeles, 1957), p.129; R. M. Jordan, 'The Narrator in Chaucer's *Troilus*', *ELH*, xxv (1958), 237–57; D. Bethurum, 'Chaucer's Point of View as Narrator in the Love Poems', *PMLA*, lxxiv (1959), 511–20; cp. E. T. Donaldson, 'The Ending of Chaucer's *Troilus*', in *Early English and Norse Studies*, pp.26–45.

[2] Gower, *Vox Clamantis*, V, v, ll.251–72; Stockton, pp.201–2.

gems and horses like grain, in order that a crop of praises may grow in his ear. But if a knight chooses a woman's love for himself, then he will pay for it more dearly than with his wealth. He will give up so many good things for it – his body, his soul, his property, everything that Nature or God has imparted to him. Nevertheless, when he shall have done with his troublesome doings, yet at the same time every fickle compliment deceives him, and when neither the prattling talk of the world reaches his ears nor virtuous love bestows its treasures upon him, then the dupe will say, 'Alas, how wicked Fortune is! For all my labor turns out fruitless after such a long time.' The man who laments for himself in this foolish way is too late, for he himself is the cause of his suffering, and not another.]

On the other side of the debate is that noble and stable love which Criseyde herself praises:

> For trusteth wel, that youre estat roial,
> Ne veyn delit, nor only worthinesse
> Of yow in werre or torney marcial,
> Ne pompe, array, nobleye, or ek richesse
> Ne made me to rewe on youre destresse;
> But moral vertu, grounded upon trouthe,
> That was the cause I first hadde on yow routhe!
>
> Eke gentil herte and manhod that ye hadde,
> And that ye hadde, as me thoughte, in despit
> Every thyng that souned into badde,
> As rudenesse and poeplissh appetit,
> And that youre resoun bridlede youre delit.[1]

Now, as in *The Parlement of Foules* we have two contrary views of love reconciled by a third,[2] so in *Troilus* we have opposed to the noble love of Troilus the worldly practical views of Pandarus and Diomede. It is, of course, this dialectic which explains the abrupt changes of tone in the poem. For example, Troilus is cut short in a long speech in a courtly and elevated strain by Pandarus's curt

> thow wrecched mouses herte,
> Artow agast so that she wol the bite?[3]

---

[1] Chaucer, *Troilus and Criseyde*, IV, ll.1667–78.

[2] For *The Parlement of Foules*, cp. R. W. Frank, 'Structure and Meaning in the *Parlement of Foules*', *PMLA*, lxxi (1956), 530–9.

[3] Chaucer, *Troilus and Criseyde*, III, ll.736–7.

and at the most solemn climax of the love of Troilus and Criseyde, Pandarus is fussing about with a cushion. This contrast of
views is, of course, sometimes explicit, most notably in the
discussion between Troilus and Pandarus after the news of the
exchange of Criseyde and Antenor. Pandarus suggests that
Troilus shall carry her off, but Troilus refuses to countenance
such a plan. Now this may seem to amount merely to saying that
Pandarus and Troilus are different kinds of people. But, if we
assume that the tale is directed purely towards the tragedy of
the hero, then it is hard to see why the love upon which he sets
such store, and for which he suffers, should be decried in the
epilogue. Are we to suppose merely that the noble Troilus has
been a miserable sinner all along? To engage our sympathies
and then, as it were, to throw the whole thing back in our faces,
seems aesthetically naïve.

Now, I think that the answer to the problem lies largely in
the person of the narrator. Jordan has suggested that in the
epilogue we have not the narrator, but the poet himself,
speaking.[1] But I believe this view to be mistaken. I think that
what Chaucer has done in the poem is to build into it as a
narrator, a Theseus-like figure, who regards the lovers with a
certain sympathetic but ironical detachment. He is the *dramatis
persona* who finally adjudicates between the different points of
view.[2] If we look carefully at the appearances of the narrator,
I think this becomes more credible. At the beginning of the
poem he seems to suggest that he, like the hero of the *Confessio
Amantis*, is 'unlikely' for love, yet he has deep sympathy with
lovers and for their sake will he tell the tale of *Troilus and
Criseyde*. Yet, as the poem progresses, we can see a change in
attitude in the narrator. In the consummation scene there is a
comment curiously reminiscent of Gower. The narrator exclaims
of the love of Troilus and Criseyde: 'Why nad I swich oon with

[1] Jordan (1958), pp.253–4; for general discussion see especially S. B.
Meech, *Design in Chaucer's 'Troilus'* (Syracuse, 1959), pp.370–85; Ida L.
Gordon, *The Double Sorrow of Troilus* (Oxford, 1970), pp.93–129.

[2] Cp. G. T. Shepherd, 'Troilus and Criseyde', in *Chaucer and Chaucerians*,
edited by D. S. Brewer (London, 1966), pp.65–87.

my soule ybought?'[1] An even more remarkable intervention by the narrator occurs as Criseyde pins on Troilus's shirt the precious brooch which was to become the emblem of her fickleness. Can any miser, the narrator asks, ever have such joy in his wealth as these two had in their love? No, he replies, avarice is a vice, and love a virtue, though men regard it as foolish. There must be irony in the context of this parenthesis; it raises at the climax of the poem the very problem with which the poem is concerned. Why else should the poet choose to phrase his praise of Criseyde's generosity in such negative and defensive terms? The sense that the narrator is an onlooker is increased by his disclaimers in the art of love. In the proem to Book II, he fears that he will speak of love *unfelyngly* 'without experience', for 'A blynd man kan nat juggen wel in hewis'.[2] When he describes himself in the proem to Book III as love's clerk, I doubt that he means any more than that he is a student of love but one, it would appear from other parts of the poem, who has not himself experienced it. In the same way, his frequent references to the book, though serving other functions, also serve, in part, to give this sense of a man describing something with which he is not entirely familiar. As we pass through the events of the fifth book, the narrator appears, as has often been noted, to present the feelings and actions of Criseyde more and more at second hand. This has the effect of giving a certain dramatic credibility to the narrator's final disclaimer:

> Ne me ne list this sely womman chyde
> Forther than the storye wol devyse.
> Hire name, allas, is punysshed so wide,
> That for hire gilt it oughte ynough suffise.
> And if I myghte excuse hire any wise,
> For she so sory was for hire untrouthe,
> Iwis, I wolde excuse hir yet for routhe.[3]

Now, if the story is purely exemplary, then clearly Chaucer ought to blame her; otherwise he is making nonsense of his

---

[1] Chaucer, *Troilus and Criseyde*, III, l.1319.
[2] Chaucer, *Troilus and Criseyde*, II, l.21.
[3] Chaucer, *Troilus and Criseyde*, V, ll.1093-9.

story. But the story is only exemplary in the sense that it presents a number of different points of view in themselves irreconcilable. And later on Chaucer withdraws yet further from any posture of blame. Women too have been betrayed, he says. His poem is not intended to attach blame exclusively to women. But as the narrator seems about to bow himself out, he turns to the epilogue. And that the epilogue is spoken by the narrator seems to be suggested by the fact that it includes the final stage of the action of the poem: Troilus's ascent to the heavens and his transformed perspective on earthly matters. It is to be noted that this new perspective does not imply that his love for Criseyde was sinful by its sexual nature, so much as that it was sinful by virtue of its cupidity and its vanity. And so the narrator in his final comment on the action supplies the final perspective: love as an ennobling passion; love as lust, love as vanity. Like the lover at the end of the *Confessio Amantis*, he turns from earthly love to heavenly love. This is the final comment on the whole debate; even Criseyde's fickleness is irrelevant when earthly love is seen in its true perspective. We have not here Chaucer giving judgement on his own creation, but a concluding judgement in a sustained debate. Chaucer's point of view we shall probably never know. The poem perfectly exemplifies that tension which gives poignancy to so much medieval literature; the tension between the beauty of earthly nobility and the sense of the vanity of human things. Only an acute sense of such beauty can explain the violence with which it was rejected.

Thus we see that in *Troilus and Criseyde* Chaucer has perfectly blended the romance genre, the high style, with the fabliau figure of Pandarus, the unrealistic with the realistic in order to project a concept upon different planes. But most interesting of all perhaps is the function of the narrator, a figure already familiar from *The Canterbury Tales* and the *Bok of the Duchese*. He it is who links together the whole poem and prepares us for the *volte face* of the epilogue. The poem is a brilliant exploitation of the deictic mode.

We have looked in this chapter at two aspects of 'realistic writing' in medieval literature; on the one hand, the use of the 'picturation'; on the other the use of the deictic mode. In conclusion we might briefly look at the matter in a slightly different perspective. Obsession with the theme of death has sometimes been cited as an example of medieval 'realism'. Some of the modes of representation of this theme well illustrate the different 'realistic' techniques which we have briefly surveyed in this chapter. Let us consider first the closely focused treatment in the Soul and Body Poem from the Worcester Fragments:

> þonne þe licame ond þe sowle. soriliche todæleþ.
> þonne biþ þet wræcche lif. iended al mid sori siþ.
> þonne biþ þe feige. iflut to þen flore.
> he biþ eastward istreiht. he biþ sone stif.
> he coldeþ also clei. hit is him ikunde.
> Mon hine met mid one ȝerde. ond þa molde seoþþen.
> ne mot he of þære molde. habben nammore.
> þonne þet rihte imet. rihtliche tæcheþ.
> þonne liþ þe clei clot. colde on þen flore.
> ond him sone from fleoþ. þeo he ær freome dude.
> nulleþ heo mid honden. his heafod riht wenden.
> heom þuncheþ þet hore honden. swuþe beoþ ifuled[1]

Here the theme is projected by the use of realistic details, the cooling of the body, the measuring for the grave, the defilement of death. Yet the theme of death can be projected in a different way; in a mode which may be called admonitory as in *The Dance of Death*:

> ȝe riche marchaunt ȝe mote loke hiderwarde
> That passed haue ful many dyuerse londe
> On hors on fote hauyng moste rewarde
> To lucre and wynnynge as I vndurstonde
> But now to daunce ȝe mote ȝeue me ȝowre honde
> For al ȝowre laboure ful litel availeth now
> A-dieu veyneglorie bothe of fre and bonde
> None more coueite than thei that haue ynow.
>
> Be many an hille and many a straunge vale
> I haue trauailed with my marchaundise

---

[1] *The Worcester Fragments*, B. ll.28–39; *Selections from Early Middle English* edited by J. Hall (Oxford, 1920), I, pp.2–3.

> Ouer the see do carye many a bale
> To sundri Iles mo than I can deuyse
> Myn herte inwarde ai frette with couetise
> But al for nowght now dethe dothe me constreyne
> Be whiche I seie be recorde of the wise
> Who al embraceth litel schal restreyne.[1]

The image here is not made meaningful by a structure of physical details but by the dramatic and deictic aspect. It is a structure which depends not upon what is essentially, in spite of some authorial comment, a picture, but upon a speaker. If it is deemed 'realistic' it must be in virtue of its theme and not in virtue of its picture which is generalised and conventional. What then are we to think of the following?

> Nixt him in dans come Cuvatyce,
> Rute of all evill and grund of vyce,
> That nevir cowd be content;
> Catyvis, wrechis, and ockeraris,
> Hud-pykis, hurdaris and gadderaris,
> All with that warlo went:
> Out of thair throttis thay schot on udder
> Hett moltin gold, me thocht a fudder,
> As fyreflawcht maist fervent;
> Ay as thay tomit thame of schot,
> Feyndis fild thame new up to the thrott
> With gold of allkin prent.[2]

This, in comparison with the previous example, gives the impression of being more 'realistic'. Yet if by 'realistic' we mean 'individual', this is not so. The effect of immediacy is created by closeness of texture and by the use of words of a certain register. Thus the lines 'ockeraris, / Hud-pykis, hurdaris, and gadderaris' with its splendidly robust effect, in fact, means approximately 'usurers', 'misers', 'hoarders' and 'gatherers'. The terms are general and repetitive, not unlike the terms of opprobrium used in a flyting. None of these passages can be said to be 'a photographic representation' of reality; indeed no art can be this,

---

[1] *The Dance of Death*, edited by Florence Warren and Beatrice White, E.E.T.S., 181 (1931) (Ellesmere MS.), ll.329–44.

[2] Dunbar, *The Dance of the Sevin Deidly Synnis*, ll.55–66.

for a photograph can only give an image. The subject matter of all three is death. Yet none I think can be said to be more realistic than the other in the sense of giving the 'flavour of immediate life'. But, in different ways and by different means, they all attempt to present the topic with a certain degree of particularity, or illusion of particularity; the first by the exploitation of the intuitive; the second by the use of the deictic mode and the third by closeness of texture. Lukács should perhaps have the last as well as the first word in this chapter: 'true realism (is) the great writer's thirst for truth, his fanatic striving for reality – or, expressed in terms of ethics: the writer's sincerity and probity'.[1]

[1] Lukács, p.11.

CHAPTER SIX

Mannerism and Renaissance

Fraunceys Petrak, the lauriat poete,
Highte this clerk, whos rethorike sweete
Enlumyned al Ytaille of poetrie.[1]

In 1341, perhaps a few years before the birth of Chaucer, on
the Capitol at Rome, a Campidoglio not yet adorned with the
Piazza del Campidoglio of Michelangelo, yet venerable for its
antiquity and for its associations, a scene took place of profound
significance for the literature of Western Europe. On April 8,
in the audience hall of the Senatorial Palace, Petrarch, wearing
a robe of honour, delivered an oration, the theme of which was
the art of poetry, its claims and rewards. Then a senator listed
the eight awards to be given to Petrarch, he was declared
magnum poetam et historicum and *magister*, and a professorship of
poetic art and of history was conferred upon him. Most significant of all, he was crowned with the crown of laurel and received Roman citizenship.[2] This scene is symbolic of a new age,
the age of a new Renaissance, the third renaissance of classical
studies in Europe. In this last chapter, I propose to consider
some examples of late medieval art, an art which was increasingly permeated by classical studies. There are many
strands, not all of which we shall attempt to disentangle. The
pressures upon English literature, as we clearly see in the work
of Chaucer, are both Italian and French and the French too
were deeply influenced by the Italian classical revival centred

---

[1] Chaucer, *The Canterbury Tales*, E. ll.31–3.
[2] Cp. E. H. Wilkins, *Life of Petrarch* (Chicago, 1961), pp.24–9; for the
text of the coronation oration see E. H. Wilkins, *Studies in the Life and Works
of Petrarch* (Cambridge, Mass., 1955), 300–13.

in Petrarch. The Renaissance in France is usually associated with the accession of the Valois branch of the Capetian House, in the person of Philippe VI (1328–50). In the reign of his son, Jean II (1350–64), Pierre Bersuire, well known for his rendering of the *Ovide Moralisé* and a friend of Petrarch at Avignon, in his translation of Livy of about 1356, deliberately created words and neologisms and to the book he appended a chapter entitled *La Déclaration des motz, qui n'ont point de propres françois ou qui autrement ont mestier de déclaration.* Other significant figures were Nicholas Oresme (1310–82), writing in the reign of Charles the Wise (1364–80), who translated into French (1370–77) the *Politics, Ethics* and *Economics* of Aristotle, and the humanist Jean de Montreuil (1354–1418), the secretary of Charles VI, of whom W. F. Patterson writes: 'More deeply than any French humanist since the day of John of Salisbury and the notable twelfth-century Renaissance at Chartres and Orléans Montreuil appreciated the beauty and profundity of antiquity.'[1] But the context of late medieval art does not consist only of the humanist movement. Those characteristic documents of the period, the texts of the Second Rhetoric, are equally part of this context.[2] The earliest and perhaps the most significant is the *Art de Dictier* of Deschamps. Poetry is for him, as for John of Garland, a kind of music:

> L'autre musique est appellée *naturele* . . . et est une musique de bouche en proferant paroules metrifiées, aucunefoiz en *laiz*, autrefoiz en *balades*, autrefoiz en *rondeaulx, cengles* et *doubles*, et en *chançons baladées* . . . que aucuns appellent . . . *virelays*.[3]

> [*The other music is called* natural . . . *and is a music of the mouth, uttering metrical words, sometimes in* lays, *sometimes in* balades, *sometimes in* rondeaux, single *and* double, *and in* chançons baladées . . . *which some people call* virelais.]

---

[1] W. F. Patterson, *Three Centuries of French Poetic Theory*, Pts I & II (Ann Arbor, 1935), 71–4; J. Huizinga, *The Waning of the Middle Ages*, translated by F. Hopman (London, 1924), pp.297–308.

[2] Cp. Patterson, pp.129–75.

[3] Eustace Deschamps, *Art de Dictier; Oeuvres Complètes*, edited by G. Raynaud, S.A.T.F. (1891), VII, p.270.

But the musical aspect of poetry is not the only aspect with which the texts of the Second Rhetoric are concerned. They show a concern for elevation of style and for word play, especially *rime equivoque*. Jean Molinet, for example, gives lists of words which can be used in this way. Thus his *Equivocques a quatre*:

> Voloye; vous loye; voloie, *de voler*: vol oye, *audiat*.
> Sçavoie, *sçavoir*; Savoye, *pays*; sa voye, *via*; sa voie, *verbum*.

An anonymous writer of the same group gives lists of hard words: for example,

> *Bajulacion* est chose portée; *Brutulacion* est chose de rude entendement; *Bartelacion* est chose faulce ou malicieuse; *Balneacion* est chose qui vault autant a dire que baignerie; *Blandicion*, qui vaut autant que flaterie.

> [Bajulacion *indicates something carried;* Brutelacion *indicates something of crude understanding;* Bartelacion *is something false or malicious;* Balneacion *is something which amounts to saying 'bathing';* Blandicion *is as much as to say 'flattery'.*]

and so on through the alphabet.[1] The following *balade* by Deschamps illustrates the use of *rime equivoque*.

> Lasse, lasse, maleureuse et do*lente*
> *Lente* me voy, fors de soupirs et *plains.*
> *Plains* sont mes jours d'ennuy et de tour*mente;*
> *Mente* qui veult, car mes cuers est cer*tains,*
> *Tains* jusqu'a mort et pour celli que j'*ains;*
> *Ains,* mais ne fu dame si fort a*tainte;*
> *Tainte* me voy quant il m'ayme le *mains.*
> *Mains,* entendez ma piteuse com*plainte.*[2]

> [*Wretched, wretched, unhappy and sorrowful, I find myself sluggish except for sighs and laments. Full are my days of vexation and torment. Let he who will lie, for my heart is firm, wretched until death and for him I love; but never was lady so mightily afflicted. I see myself wretched when he loves me least. At least hear my piteous complaint.*]

---

[1] M. E. Langlois, *Recueil d'Arts de seconde Rhétorique* (Paris, 1902), pp.252, 49–50.

[2] Deschamps, *Art de Dictier; Oeuvres*, VII, p.277.

At the same time, old forms took on a new shape. Seznec has written that 'the great allegorical current of the Middle Ages, far from shrinking, flows on in an ever widening channel'.[1] Yet the late Middle Ages sees the development of an allegorical mode which is didactic rather than truly allegorical. Thus, for example, if we look at Machaut's *Fonteinne Amoureuse* we find that, effectively, there is no allegory. The story tells how Machaut, about to fall asleep, hears the complaint of a lover. He gets out of bed and copies down the complaint. He then betakes himself to the lover's lodging and they walk out to a fountain which is adorned with mythological figures. They both fall asleep. Venus appears with the Prince's lady and explains the meaning of the figures on the fountain. They talk about the dream but are interrupted by the servitor who comes to announce their dinner. Many other such allegories are to be found in the works of Machaut, Froissart, Deschamps, poems, that is to say, in which there is no genuine allegorical action but only allegorical pageants, static scenes, such as the pictures round the fountain in *La Fonteinne Amoureuse*, which serve, on the one hand, to give pictorial effects and, on the other, to make didactic points. Lowes pertinently observes of Machaut, 'His pages are thronged with capitalized personifications, but Guillaume de Lorris's caroling, dancing, gaily-robed abstractions, alive and concrete in all save their names, have given place to names alone, with which a clever dialectician conjures.'[2] As a description of late medieval allegory this could hardly be bettered.

Such was the immediate heritage of English literature in the late fourteenth and early fifteenth centuries. It was predominantly a period of new ideas and old themes, of stylistic originality and conventional content. It was, in fact, a mannerist age in which, in spite of new stylistic techniques, the arteries hardened. It was in a sense a Pre-renaissance, in a sense a Renaissance *manqué*, especially in England, where a writer of the brilliant originality of a Rabelais or a Villon was lacking.

[1] Seznec, p.103.
[2] J. L. Lowes, *Geoffrey Chaucer* (Oxford, 1934), p.68.

Clearly, it is impossible to review the whole period of the late fourteenth and fifteenth centuries, the era of Chaucerian and post-Chaucerian literature. I propose, therefore, to look rather closely at some aspects of particular interest for the development of style in the period. I want, in particular, to try to characterise three types of writing: the first is represented by the lyrics of Charles of Orleans; the second by some of the poems of Lydgate, and the third by a group of late medieval allegorists. Obviously these cannot illustrate all characteristics of late medieval style, but I believe they may serve as models for further investigations into this topic.

Let us begin by looking in some detail at one of the English poems of Charles of Orleans:

> The smylyng mouth and laughyng eyen gray,
>   The brestis rounde and long smal armys twayne,
> The hondis smoþe, þe sidis streiȝt and playne,
> Yowre fetis lite – what shulde y ferþer say?
> Hit is my craft when ye are fer away
> To muse þeron in styntyng of my payne,
>   The smylyng mouth and laughyng eyen gray,
>   The brestis rounde and long smal armys twayne.
> So wolde y pray you gef y durste or may,
>   The sight to se as y haue seyne;
>   Forwhi þat craft me is most fayne,
> And wol ben to þe howre in which y day,
>   The smylyng mouth, etc.[1]

This provides an admirable example of what I would call 'the abstract style'. It is fundamentally a musical style (the poem is a rondel) and one which, therefore, depends for its effectiveness rather on patterns than on imagery. The poem is clearly articulated by the refrain and the refrain itself is balanced grammatically. The first half of the first three lines consists of

---

[1] *The English Poems of Charles of Orleans,* edited by R. Steele and M. Day, E.E.T.S., 215, 220 (1941, 1946; reprinted in one volume with bibliographical supplement, 1970), ll.4137–50. For the identification of the English poet with Charles of Orleans, cp. N. L. Goodrich, *Charles of Orleans: A Study of Themes in his French and in his English poetry* (Geneva, 1967), and bibliography.

the definite article, an adjective and a noun, the second half in each case contains a disjunction, *laughyng eyen gray*; *long smal armys twayn*; but the pattern is broken, in the third line, by placing both adjectives after the noun *þe sides streiȝt and playne*. This much is obvious. But there are more interesting and subtle effects, too. In the first place there is semantic balancing, the exploitation of lexical sets. Thus, in the first three lines, we have *smylyng – laughyng*; *rounde – long – smal*; *smoþe – streiȝt – playne*. It is as though the author were modulating the key. In the second place, we have a change of aspect between the first stanza and the second. In the first stanza the poet makes a statement:

> Hit is my craft when ye are fer away,
> To muse þeron in styntyng of my payne –

but in the second he changes aspect: *So wolde y pray yow, gef y durste or may* and *and wol ben to þe howre in which y day*. In the third place, there is a contrast between the first person of the stanzas and the impersonality of the refrain. It is noteworthy too that Charles uses the definite article until the fourth line when he turns to the possessive *yowre fetis lite*. It is as though he is thinking of his lady and then suddenly turns to her; but, seeing her, he begins to speak in his own person. The difference can be clarified by comparing this poem with a poem from *The Harley Lyrics*:

> Wiþ longyng y am lad,
> on molde y waxe mad,
>   a maide marreþ me;
> y grede, y grone, vnglad,
> for selden y am sad
>   þat semly forte se.
> Leuedi, þou rewe me!
> To rouþe þou hauest me rad.
> Be bote of þat y bad;
>   my lyf is long on þe.[1]

In neither poem is there a real picture of the lady. The poet of

[1] *The Harley Lyrics*, No. 5, ll.1–10.

The Harley Lyrics gives a catalogue as conventional as that of Charles of Orleans:

> Lylie-whyt hue is,
> hire rode so rose on rys,
>   þat reueþ me mi rest.[1]

Both poems appear to use, as far as can be judged, words which are in common use. The poet of the Harley lyric, like Charles of Orleans, makes use of figures of repetition, the figure *traductio*: *longyng*: *long* and *rewe, roupe*. But surely the impression that the poem is more direct and passionate than the other is largely owing to the use of the present tense; the predominant use of the first person, and the series of short repetitive patterns made by the sentence structure. There is nothing like the detached, impersonality of the infinitive and the verbal noun in Charles of Orleans' line: 'To muse þeron in styntyng of my payne'. The poem by Charles of Orleans, in fact, is not only a carefully balanced system of repetitions, but one of carefully organised modalities. The two poems, indeed, illustrate some of the differentiae posited by Hugo Kuhn in his discussion of what he calls *symbolic realism* and *symbolic naturalism*.[2] But this would not in itself justify us in speaking of an 'abstract style'. What do we mean by this? The style, to be sure, is abstract in a negative sense, in lacking rhetorical descriptions and it is, to use a bibliographical metaphor, a 'blind' style in lacking ornament of a visual kind. But there is a more fundamental and interesting sense in which it may be called 'abstract'. In this connection we may look next at a poem discussed by Fox in his book on Charles of Orleans:

> Ainsi que chassoye aux sangliers,
> Mon cueur chassoit aprés Dangiers
> En la forest de ma Pensee,
> Dont rencontra grant assemblee
> Trespassans par divers sentiers.

---

[1] *The Harley Lyrics*, No. 5, ll.31–3.
[2] H. Kuhn, 'Stil als Epochen-,Gattungs – u. Wertproblem in der deutschen Literatur des Mittelalters', in *Stil-und Formprobleme*, pp.123–9.

Deux ou trois saillirent premiers,
Comme fors, orguilleux et fiers;
N'estoit ce pas chose effroyee?
Ainsi que chassoye aux sangliers,
Mon cueur chassoit aprés Dangiers
En la forest de ma Pensée.

Lors mon cueur lascha sus levriers,
Lesquelz sont nommez Desiriers;
Puis Esperance, l'asseuree,
L'espieu ou poing, sainte l'espee,
Vint pour combatre voulentiers,
Ainsi que chassoye aux sangliers.[1]

[*Just as I was hunting wild boar, my heart was hunting Dangers in the forest of my Thought and met a great gathering of them going along diverse paths. Two or three leaped out first of all, like strong, proud, fierce animals. Was this not a terrible thing? Just as . . . Then my heart let loose the hounds which are called Desires; then steadfast Hope, with lance held in fist and sword girded on, came to fight willingly, just as . . .*]

This curious reversed allegory[2] in which the literal sense, the poet's thoughts of his beloved and her coldness to him, becomes the allegorical sense, and join in the action with the abstractions, Danger, Desires and Hope seems to suggest the extent to which allegory has ceased to be truly polysemous. And we notice throughout the poetry of Charles of Orleans the use of such metaphors. They are rather structural devices than true allegory. Compare, for example, the use in Langland and Charles of Orleans of the writ or charter figure. The difference is striking. This is how Langland describes the enfeofment of Mede:

Witeth and witnesseth . that wonieth vpon this erthe,
That Mede is y-maried . more for here goodis,
Than for ani vertue or fairenesse . or any free kynde.
Falsenesse is faine of hire . for he wote hire riche;

---

[1] Charles d'Orléans, Rondel cxcvii; *Poésies*, edited by P. Champion (Paris, 1966), p.403; cp. J. Fox, *The Lyric Poetry of Charles d'Orléans* (Oxford, 1969), pp.73-4. The translation is his.

[2] Cp. Goodrich, pp.67-95, and for the hunting allegory J. Wimsatt, *Chaucer and the French Love Poets* (Chapel Hill, 1968), pp.39-48.

And Fauel with his fikel speche . feffeth bi this chartre
To be prynces in pryde . and pouerte to dispise,
To bakbite, and to bosten . and bere fals witnesse,
To scorne and to scolde . and sclaundere to make,
Vnboxome and bolde . to breke þe ten hestes; –
And the erldome of enuye . and wratthe togideres,
With the chastelet of chest . and chateryng-oute-of-resoun,
The counte of coueitise . and alle the costes aboute,
That is, vsure and auarice . alle I hem graunte,
In bargaines and in brokages . with al the borghe of
                                                         theft.[1]

The same allegorical figure is used by Charles of Orleans in the introductory section of *Love's Service* in which Cupid issues a letter patent:

Gyve on the day of seynt Valentyn þe martere,
As in the Castelle of humbille desere.[2]

The 'Castle of Humble Desire' is almost the only example in the poem of the poet's bringing together explicitly the literal and the metaphorical levels. The rest of the poem depends upon an extended fiction in which Cupid ennobles Charles of Orleans and commands his followers:

Him to susteyne in his necessite,
Ageyn daunger and his affynyte,
Cursid daunger and wickid Ielowse
And fals dissayt.[3]

Analogies are indicated by the use of formulae rather than by reference to concrete objects. Instead of the 'Erledom of envye', 'the chastelet of chest' and 'þe conte of coueitise and alle þe costes aboute' we have legal phrases such as 'doyng yow wite':

we haue him assignyd on oure rent,
The fayrist pencioun aftir his entent,
For to enyoy bi oure lettir patent. . . .[4]

The poet leaves his heart 'in morgage'. The letter is given

---

[1] Langland, *Piers Plowman*, B. ii. ll.74–87.
[2] Charles of Orleans, *English Poems*, ll.53–4.
[3] Charles of Orleans, *English Poems*, ll.25–8.
[4] Charles of Orleans, *English Poems*, ll.9–11.

'vndir (Cupid's) seele'.[1] The same kind of structural 'blind'
imagery can be seen elsewhere in the poems. For example, in
Ballade 8, the poet's heart reads to him from the 'romaunce of
plesaunt pancer'[2] and keeps the poet awake by so doing. In
Ballade 37 the poet goes to visit his heart and in the conclusion:

> My sabille hert with hope now blusshith reed
> And for comfort of yow my fayre maystres
> Which haue me promysid of yowre womanhed
> The hool tresoure of louys gret ricches.[3]

This is surely a rhetorical conceit rather than true allegory. It
is a metonymy, a dramatic development of a conventional
thought, common in Charles of Orleans, that the lover loses his
heart. In Ballade 43 his heart has become a hermit,[4] in Ballade
32 he keeps his lady's heart in a coffer of remembrance[5] and so
on. It is perhaps worth noting that these images have a counterpart in the visual arts. Raimond van Marle tells us that the
commonplace image of the Castle of Love was even translated
into real life terms. For a certain Roland Patavin tells us that
in 1214, near Trévise, a kind of symbolic fete took place for
which had to be constructed a castle. This was to be defended
by ladies, whose hearts it represented, while the young men
attacked it with fruit, flowers and perfume.[6] This is neatly
reversed in Charles of Orleans, in Ballade 50, in which we see
the poet fortifying his heart 'Ayens daunger and alle his rude
puysshaunce'.[7] Yet, although the theme is one which had a
visual realisation in the realm of art, Charles makes no attempt
to realise his castle in visual terms. Instead it is described as
'Stondyng vpon the roche of espeyraunce' and:

> In this Castelle ther are thre towris hye,
> Of which the first berith propir name fyaunce,

---

1 Charles of Orleans, *English Poems*, ll.37, 48.
2 Charles of Orleans, *English Poems*, l.415.
3 Charles of Orleans, *English Poems*, ll.1336-9.
4 Charles of Orleans, *English Poems*, ll.1511-47.
5 Charles of Orleans, *English Poems*, ll.1163-90.
6 Raimond van Marle, p.423.
7 Charles of Orleans, *English Poems*, l.1753.

> To haue socoure and that right hastily;
> And the secund is callid remembraunce;
> The thridde is stedfast desyraunce.[1]

The analogy gives a shape to the poem, it is a configuration, an intellectual construct and that is all.

Now, it might be argued that the reason for the apparent disregard for visual effects is a regard for rhetorical propriety in that lengthy descriptions would be out of place in a short form such as the ballade or rondel. That this is not so seems to be indicated by the way in which natural phenomena some-times are treated in the poems. The refrains of two well-known rondels which Panofsky claimed illustrated the 'artificial glitter and pseudo-reality' of the International Style,[2] have been thought by a recent critic to illustrate the courtly nature of Charles's imagery:

> Les fourriers d'Esté sont venus
> Pour appareillier son logis
> Et ont fait tendre ses tappis
> De fleurs et verdure tissus . . .

and

> Le temps a laissié son manteau,
> De vent, de froidure et de pluye,
> Et s'est vestu de brouderie
> De soleil luyant, cler et beau.

[*Summer's harbingers have arrived to make ready his dwelling-place, and have spread out his carpets woven with flowers and greenery . . . the weather has left its cloak of wind, cold, and rain, and has put on embroidery of gleaming sunshine, bright and lovely.*]

He adds 'It would not have occurred to him to liken a singer's voice to that of a bird, but it did occur to him to compare the flitting of birds from branch to branch to the movements of dancers, and birds' song to the harmonious choruses he heard at court:

> Lez oyseaus deviennent danseurs
> Dessuz mainte branche flourie,

---

[1] Charles of Orleans, *English Poems*, ll.1751, 1755-9.
[2] Panofsky, p.69.

Et font joyeuse chanterie,
De contres, deschans et teneurs . . .[1]

[*The birds become dancers over many a flowery branch and make a joyful choir of counter-tenors, descants and tenors.*]

Yet the courtly glitter of these poems is in contrast with the comparative generality of the English poems. Look, for example, at Ballade 88 from *The New Fortune*:

Aftir wyntir the veer with foylis grene,
Aftir the sterry nyght, the morow gray,
Lucyna chaungyng in her hornys shene
The enpese made of many gret affray.
The sondry chaunge of thingis se y may
But ye swet hert so voyde are of pite
That for no thyng y kan yow write or say
The chaunge of yowre mystrust kan y not se.[2]

The effectiveness of this style does not depend upon visual detail. The poetic impact is the result of pattern and contrast, which detail would destroy. In the first place, there is the purely verbal pattern of 'Aftir wyntir the veer . . . aftir the sterry nyght' followed by a repetition of the topic, with a changed verbal pattern, as though a musical theme had been repeated in another key.[3] There is also the contrasting diction of the opening lines, the first with its comparatively unusual words, *veer* and *foylis* and the second with its simple words, and the third with the classical figure. This change of register is used again by Charles of Orleans in Ballade 72:

Whan fresshe Phebus day of seynt Valentyne
Had whirlid vp his golden chare aloft,
The burnyd bemys of it gan to shyne,
In at my chambre where y slepid soft,

---

[1] Fox, p.85. The translations are also his; Charles d'Orléans, *Poésies*, Rondeaux xxx, xxxi, xxxiv; pp.307, 309.

[2] Charles of Orleans, *English Poems*, ll.5436–43.

[3] Cp. Allan Rodway, 'By Algebra to Augustanism' in *Essays on Style and Language*, pp.53–67.

M

> Of which the light that he had with him brought,
> He wook me of the slepe of heuynes
> Wherin forslepid y alle the nyght dowtles,
> Vpon my bed so hard of newous thought.[1]

or again in the lines

> For Crepusculus that revith day his light,
> Gan in the west his clowdy mantel shake.[2]

Here, as in Ballades 88 and 72, we have not only a change of register from the grand, latinate *Crepusculus*, which is even given its Latin ending, to the 'clowdy mantel', but a contrast between the personification, which removes the concept from common experience, and the familiar 'mantle', which elicits a more intuitive response. Finally, we notice again a change of aspect in the sixth line of Ballade 88. Charles leaves the generalisations of the first five lines and turns to address the lady:

> But ye swet hert so voyde are of pite
> That for no thyng y kan yow write or say
> The chaunge of yowre mystrust kan y not se.[3]

Thus even where the subject would have been susceptible of visual realisation, the opportunity is not taken; instead the poetic structure results from changes of aspect and register and the careful juxtaposition of these. The point can perhaps be made more cogently by comparing a poem from Charles of Orleans and one from *The Harley Lyrics* once again. I will take a few stanzas from each.

---

[1] Charles of Orleans, *English Poems*, ll.2455–62.

[2] Charles of Orleans, *English Poems*, ll.5324–5; 'cloudy' can also mean 'dark' in Middle English (see *MED*, s.v. *cloudi*). This is one of the numerous cases in which Charles of Orleans and Lydgate share common phrases. Lydgate has the phrase 'clowdie cope' in *The Serpent of Division*, edited by H. N. MacCracken (London, New Haven, 1911), p.56, l.32. But there is possibly another implication. In his description of Fortune, Charles of Orleans says that the tissue of her mantle 'ran in clowde werk' (l.5002). It seems possible that as well as indicating that her mantle was covered with clouds, symbolising the mutability of fortune, it may refer to some kind of fabric with a cloud-like pattern, not unlike a watered silk. This may be the implication also in the reference to the 'clowdy mantel' of Twilight.

[3] Charles of Orleans, *English Poems*, ll.5441–3.

Lenten ys come wiþ loue to toune,
wiþ blosmen ant wiþ briddes roune,
    þat al þis blisse bryngeþ.
Dayeseȝes in þis dales,
notes suete of nyhtegales,
    vch foul song singeþ,
Þe þrestelcoc him þreteþ oo;
away is huere wynter wo
    when woderoue springeþ.
Þis foules singeþ ferly fele,
ant wlyteþ on huere wynne wele,
    þat al þe wode ryngeþ.[1]

Compare with this the following from Charles of Orleans:

To longe for shame and alle to longe trewly
Myn hert y se thee slepe in displesere;
Awake this day, awake, o verry fy;
Lete vs at wode go geder may in fere
To holde of oure oold custume the manere;
Ther shalle we here the birdis synge and pley
Right as the wood therwith shulde forshyuere
This ioly tyme, this fresshe first day of May.

The god of loue, this worldis god myghti,
Holdith this day his feste to fede and chere
The hertis of vs poore louers heuy
Which only him to serue sett oure desere;
Wherfore he doth affoyle the trees sere
With grene, and hath the soyle y-flowrid gay
Only to shewe his fest to more plesere
This ioly tyme, this fresshe first day of May.[2]

Three points are strikingly brought out by such a comparison;
firstly, the more intuitive nature of the first passage with its
constant reference to things, in many instances very particular
things, is notable; secondly, the sentence structure of the first
is more or less symmetrical. Note, for example, the rhymes

[1] *The Harley Lyrics*, No. 11, ll.1–12.
[2] Charles of Orleans, *The English Poems*, ll.1689–704; for lines 1694–5 cp.
Chaucer, *The Parlement of Foules*, l.493; Lydgate, *The Complaint of the Black
Knight*, ll.45–6; W. W. Skeat, *Supplement to the Works of Geoffrey Chaucer*
(London, 1897), p.246.

formed of verbs. The sentences tend to begin with the subject. This is not so in Charles's poem; thirdly, we have in Charles of Orleans a change of aspect from apostrophe to indicative speech; further, there is a change of register, for example, in the use of the unusual word *affoyle* in conjunction with words like *trees, grene*.

The style of Charles of Orleans is also notable for its frequent use of abstract nouns. Let us take as an illustration the following poem:

> Honure, ioy, helthe and plesaunce,
> Vertu, ricches habundaunt with good vre
> The Lord graunt yow, which hath most puysshaunce,
> And many a gladsom yere forto endure.
> With loue and prays of every creature;
> And for my loue alle prevayle it smalle,
> I gyve hit yow as be ye verry sewre
> With hert, body, my litille good and alle.
>
> And so yow not displese with my desire,
> This wolde y yow biseche that of yowre grace
> Hit like yow, lo, to graunt me alle þis yere,
> As in yowre hert to haue a dwellyng place,
> Al be hit neuyr of so lite a space;
> For which as this, the rente resceyue ye shalle
> Mi loue and seruice as in euery case,
> With hert, body, my litille good and alle.
>
> And syn hit is to yow no preiudice,
> Sum litille prati corner sekis me
> Within your hert, for parde, lo, iustice,
> If y offende hit must your selven be
> To punysshe, liche as ye þe offensis se;
> For y as name nor haue no thing at alle,
> But it is sovl your owen in eche degre,
> With hert, body, my litille good and alle.
>
> What so ye wille, y wil hit so obey,
> For payne or smert how so þat me bifalle;
> So am y yowre, and shal to that y dey,
> With hert, body, my litille good and alle.[1]

---

[1] Charles of Orleans, *English Poems*, ll.6227–54.

There seems to be a contrast between a certain colloquial generality of style and a very carefully organised sentence structure. Thus, for example, we have the direct personal address in such exclamations as 'as be ye verry sewre', 'lo', 'for parde, lo, iustice'. Contrasted with this tone of personal address there is a dignified impersonality in the abstract nouns and the relationship of the sentence structure and the verse pattern. For example, the zeugma of the opening stanza with the abstract nouns as an object preceding the verb, with another object following 'and many a gladsome yere'. The whole stanza depends upon a contrast between the abstract nouns at the beginning, and the personal nouns represented by the poet's heart, body and possessions. This contrast gives the concluding lines both a more personal and a less elevated tone. Moreover, the whole poem is a kind of play on the idea of 'granting'. Thus in the first stanza, the pattern runs: 'may the Lord grant you favours; I shall give you my love; do you grant me to dwell in your heart; I will pay you rent and you shall administer justice.' Thus basically we have again a use of aspect, the device of personal address, together with the exploitation of words of distance, the abstract and the common noun combined with the formality of a rhetorical pattern contrasted with the diction of everyday speech, an exploitation of registers. It is a style in which a personal immediacy is combined with a rhetorical formality of pattern. The themes are realised, not by visual detail, but largely by grammatical means. The effect is a style both dignified and personal and it is a good example of the 'abstract style' effectively used.

But this is not the only kind of abstract style in the period. Better known is the so-called 'aureate style', the style which employs Latinate synonyms for already existing words. We have already called attention to the significance of the works of the Second Rhetoric in this connection. The fashion for learned borrowing is, as is well known, evident in Chaucer and other late fourteenth-century writers. The poet of *Pearl* uses many *calques* on French words, and many unusual words in the alliterative *Morte Arthure* are of French and not English origin.

But the essence of the aureate style is, not only that the words should be new, but that the vocabulary should be ornamental.

As C. S. Lewis has said, 'the long surprising words . . . are in language what the gorgeous armours of tournament were in life; the proper expression for a vision of brightness, largesse, ceremony, exhilaration'.[1] The matter raises some problems of definition. Norton-Smith has pointed out[2] that both the adjective *aureat* and the conception of an aureate style are Lydgate's.[3] Lydgate always speaks of the style in certain metaphors of colour, fragrance, distilling moisture or dew. It seems clear that Lydgate regarded the aureate terms as an aspect of rhetoric, a source of the *epitheton ornans*. Norton-Smith, accordingly, distinguishes between such borrowings as *deambulatorie*, and such as *nebule*:

> In the context of the *Commendation* it is obvious that 'nebule' forms part of a larger attempt to construct an ornate, Latinate liturgical style in English. In the *Troy Book* II Lydgate is merely trying to convey a technically accurate picture of building methods. He himself complains of the lack of such words in English. There is no attempt at any kind or degree of *eloquentia*.[4]

Yet it is not easy, in my view, to maintain this distinction in every case. To take a later example, what is one to make of Caxton's disclaimer in the preface to the *Eneydos*?

> And whan I had aduysed me in this sayd boke, I delybered and concluded to translate it in-to englysshe, And forthwyth toke a penne and ynke, and wrote a leef or tweyne, whyche I ouersawe agayn to corecte it. And whan I sawe the fayr and straunge termes therin, I doubted that it sholde not please some gentylmen whiche late blamed me, sayeng that in my translacyons I had ouer curyous termes whiche coude not be vnderstande of comyn peple,

---

[1] C. S. Lewis, *English Literature in the Sixteenth Century* (Oxford, 1954), pp.75–6.

[2] Lydgate (1966), pp.192–5.

[3] For useful discussion of aureate terms in Lydgate, cp. E. Tilgner, *Die 'Aureate Terms' als Stilelement bei Lydgate* (Berlin, 1936); W. F. Schirmer, *John Lydgate; A Study in the Culture of the XVth Century*, translated by A. E. Keep (London, 1961), pp.73–7.

[4] Lydgate (1966), p.194.

and desired me to vse olde and homely termes in my translacyons. and fayn wolde I satysfye euery man and so to doo, toke an olde boke and redde therin and certaynly the englysshe was so rude and brood that I coude not wele vnderstande it.

He goes on to point out that, since English is certainly always changing, new words are often more comprehensible than old ones and he claims that he has 'reduced and translated this sayd booke in to our englysshe, not ouer rude ne curyous, but in suche termes as shall be vnderstanden, by goddys grace, accordynge to my copye'. Yet, in spite of this claim to moderation, there seems an evident desire to elevate the style, suggested by the tell-tale phrase, 'fayr and straunge termes' and we suspect that Caxton's claim is not entirely disingenuous. What are we to make, for example, of such a passage as the following from Dido's speech to Anna?

'Anne, my suster and frende, I am in ryght gret thoughte strongely troubled and incyted, by dremes admonested, whiche excyte my courage tenquire the maners and lygnage of this man thus valyaunt, strong, and puyssaunt, which deliteth hym strongly to speke, in deuysing the hie fayttes of armes and perillys daungerous whiche he sayth to haue passed, ne-weli hither comyn to soiourne in our countreys. I am so persuaded of grete admonestments that all my entendement is obfusked, endullyd and rauysshed.'[1]

It is difficult to believe that Caxton could not have used the English word *derken* for *obfusked*, the verb *dull* for *endull*. On the other hand, although the verb *monish* is common in Middle English, the corresponding noun is not, although Caxton himself uses the word *monishment*. But no doubt the less common noun *admonestement* had stylistic advantages over the more frequent *monishment*. The criterion of intention, therefore, seems to me difficult to apply. In any case, it is necessary to distinguish between the author's intention and the aesthetic effect. Whatever Lydgate's intention, the effect, of both *deambulatorie*

---

[1] Caxton, *Eneydos*, edited by W. T. Culley and F. J. Furnivall, E.E.T.S. (ES) 57 (1890), 1-3, 41; cp. N. Blake, 'Caxton's Language', *Neuphilologische Mitteilungen*, lxvii (1966), 127; 'Caxton and Courtly Style', *Essays and Studies*, 1968, 29-45.

and of *nebule,* would, in virtue of their novelty, be one of 'unique variation' or 'foregrounding' by the bringing into prominence of some unusual linguistic feature.[1]

A distinction between semantic range and semantic density is perhaps more relevant. The implications of such an approach may be illustrated by a passage from Chaucer:

'Oh God!' quod she, 'so worldly selynesse,
Which clerkes callen fals felicitee,
Imedled is with many a bitternesse!
Ful angwissous than is, God woot,' quod she,
'Condicioun of veyn prosperitee;
For either joies comen nought yfeere,
Or elles no wight hath hem alwey here.

O brotel wele of mannes joie unstable!
With what wight so thow be, or how thow pleye,
Either he woot that thow, joie, art muable,
Or woot it nought; it mot ben oon of tweye.
Now if he woot it nought, how may he seye
That he hath verray joie and selynesse,
That is of ignoraunce ay in derknesse?

Now if he woot that joie is transitorie,
As every joie of worldly thyng mot flee,
Than every tyme he that hath in memorie,
The drede of lesyng maketh hym that he
May in no perfit selynesse be;
And if to lese his joie he sette a myte,
Than semeth it that joie is worth ful lite.'[2]

We have here two lexical sets: *joie, selynesse, felicitee, wele, (prosperitee)* and *unstable, muable, transitorie, brotel.* We might render these approximately in English as *joy, blessedness, felicity, happiness (prosperity); unstable, mutable, transitory, brittle.* It is impossible for a modern reader to judge the precise overtones of these words, but it seems a fair presumption that Chaucer could have written 'O brotel joie of mannes wele muable'. That is to say, the words are approximately synonymous and create

---

[1] Cp. G. N. Leech, *Linguistics and the Figures of Rhetoric,* in *Essays on Style and Language,* pp.144–7.

[2] Chaucer, *Troilus and Criseyde,* III, ll.813–33.

semantic density; or, in textual terms, close texture. Thus, although the variety of near synonyms, made available by linguistic borrowing, enables Chaucer to make use of elegant variation, with, perhaps, subtle semantic shading of the kind observable in the modern approximations, these words have not significantly enlarged his semantic range. In other words, *deambulatorie* widens semantic range, since it has no synonyms, whereas *nebule* increases semantic density. Yet words in either category can be aureate or familiar. The 'aureate' style is a way of 'foregrounding' by means of words of Latin origin. It is, in short, a particular instance of a general stylistic procedure. Aureate terms will have a low statistical frequency or the novelty of a neologism (or both); or perhaps an association with a particular linguistic field connected with these. When Hamlet says 'Absent thee from felicity awhile', he is using elevated language, not because 'felicity' is new, but because it is comparatively rare in certain kinds of familiar context. He is exploiting a particular register. It is, therefore, significant stylistically that the words *felicitee*, *muable*, *transitorie* in the passage from *Troilus* appear to be Chaucerian importations and therefore presumably have a different tone from the more familiar words *joie*, *selynesse*, *wele*. The Chaucer passage indeed, offers a good example of the comparative irrelevance of the source of borrowing to the question of the elevation of style. The word *ioie* is as commonplace in Chaucer as it is now, but the word *muable* is a neologism. Both are from French. Aureation is essentially a matter of register and it is important to notice that, because the words used by aureate poets are of low statistical frequency, they often have limited impact. On the other hand, they are prominent by virtue of their rarity. They can be words which increase semantic range or semantic density, but their effective use will depend upon a just estimation of the category to which they belong. Let us by way of illustration consider the following sequence by Adam of St. Victor:

> Salve, mater salvatoris,
> vas electum, vas honoris,
>   vas caelestis gratiae;

ab aeterno vas provisum,
vas insigne, vas excisum
   manu sapientiae!

Salve, verbi sacra parens,
flos de spina, spina carens,
   flos, spineti gloria!
nos spinetum, nos peccati
spina sumus cruentati,
   sed tu spinae nescia.

Porta clausa, fons hortorum,
cella custos unguentorum,
   cella pigmentaria;
cinnamomi calamum,
myrrham, tus et balsamum
   superas fragrantia. . . .[1]

[*Hail, mother of the saviour, vessel elect, vessel of honour, vessel of divine
grace. Vessel ordained from eternity, noble vessel, vessel shaped by the hand
of wisdom. Hail! sacred parent of the Word, flower from the thorn, lacking
a thorn, flower the glory of the thorn hedge! We are the thorn hedge, we are
bloodstained with the thorn of sin; but thou art without a thorn. Closed
gate, fountain of gardens, storeroom, guardian of spices, storeroom of
unguents; a stick of cinnamon, myrrh, incense and balsam thou dost excel in
fragrance.*]

If we put this beside the following from William of Shoreham
we can see the conventional nature of the imagery.

Þou ert þe coluere of noe,
Þat broute þe braunche of olyue tre,
In tokne þat pays scholde be
   By-tuexte god and manne.
Suete leuedy, help þou me,
   Wanne ich schal wende hanne.

Þou art þe bosche of synay,
Þou art þe rytte sarray;
Þou hast ybrouȝt ous out of cry
   Of calenge of þe fende.
Þou art crystes oȝene drury,
   And of dauyes kende

---

[1] Adam of St. Victor, *Sequence for the Nativity of the Virgin Mary; The
Oxford Book of Medieval Latin Verse*, No. 163, ll.1–18.

Þou ert the slinge, þy sone þe ston,
Þat dauy slange golye op-on;
Þou ert þe ȝerd al of aaron
    Me dreye iseȝ spryngynde.
Wyt-nesse at ham euerechon
    Þat wyste of þyne chyldynge.[1]

These poems essentially are poems of statement. They depend for their effectiveness upon the nature of the imagery, the types of the Virgin which in themselves constitute a kind of poetic diction. Contrast with this Lydgate's *Balade in Commendation of Our Lady*:

O rightest rewl, O rote of holynesse,
And lightsom lyne of pite for to pleyne,
Origynal gynnyng of grace and al goodnesse,
And clennest condite of vertu souerayne,
Modyr of mercy, oure troubyl to restreyne,
Chambyr and closet clennest of chastyte,
And namyd herberwe of þe deyte,

O closid gardeyn, al void of weedes wicke,
Cristallyn welle, of clennesse cler consigned,
Fructif olyve, of foilys faire and thicke,
And redolent cedyr, most derworthly ydynged,
Remembyr of pecchouris unto thee assigned,
Or þe wyckid fend his wrath upon us wreche,
Lantyrn of light be þu oure lyfis leche.

Paradys of plesaunce, gladsom to all good,
Benygne braunchelet of the pigment-tre,
Vinarye envermailyd, refrescher of oure food,
Lycour aȝens langour that pallid may not be,
Blisful bawm-blossum, bydyng in bounte,
Thi mantel of mercy on oure myschef spred,
Or woo awak us, wrappe us undyr thi weed.

Rede rose, flouryng withowtyn spyne,
Fonteyn of fulnesse, as beryl corrent clere,
Some drope of thi graceful dewe to us propyne;
Þu light without nebule, shynyng in thi spere,
Medicyne to myscheues, pucelle withoute pere,
Flawme down to doolful, lyght of thyn influence,
Remembryng thi servant for thi magnificence.[2]

---

[1] *Religious Lyrics*, No. 32, ll.13–30.
[2] Lydgate (1966), No. 8; *A Balade in Commendation of Our Lady*, ll.29–56.

The subject matter and the construction of the passages, although not identical, is essentially the same. In each we have the types of the Virgin arranged in a list-like shape. They all follow the pattern of liturgical intercession. The difference between them is clearly in the diction, in the 'elaboration of the artefact'.[1] *Cristallyn*, a favourite Lydgate word, outside Lydgate seems to have been largely a scientific term. It appears, for example, in Trevisa's *Bartholomeus Anglicus* and in Guy de Chauliac; *vinarye* is a rare word, apparently introduced by Lydgate; *foilys* an uncommon word apparently used partly as a technicality in cooking and *fructif* is also rare;[2] *pigment* and *redolent*, as far as can be judged from the *NED*, are rare. The first citation of *pigment* is from *Bartholomeus Anglicus*; and *braunchelet* and *envermailyd* are *hapax legomena*.[3] But more interesting perhaps is the way in which Lydgate, by means of these words, stretches out the sense. This appears clearly if we compare the English with the Latin upon which it depends.[4] The line 'Cristallyn welle, of clennesse cler consigned', is a variation of *fons signatus*,[5] an epithet of the Virgin. Lydgate has rendered *fons* by *cristallyn welle*, and *signatus* by *clennesse cler consigned*. The introduction of the word 'crystalline' thus enables him to create a close texture, since *crystallyn* is similar in meaning to *cler* and *clennesse*. The relationship might be expressed in the following progression: *Crystallyn* (shining + translucent + white like crystal): *cler* (translucent + pure as in *Pearl* – *gold so cler*): *clennesse* (purity). Now the word 'crystalline' could not be replaced by the word 'shining' for example, since it is linked with the word 'crystal'; that is to say, it implies not only 'bright' but

[1] See Derek Pearsall, *John Lydgate* (London, 1970), p.268.

[2] Or possibly the reading is *fructifying* as in the Sloane manuscript but, since this, though commoner than *fructif*, is not very common, it may be a scribal substitution.

[3] Cp. *MED*, s.v. *cristallin(e* adj., *foil, fructif, braunchelet, envermailed; OED*, s.v. *redolent, pigment, vinery*. It may be noted, however, that *MED* has missed *foylis* in Charles of Orleans, *English Poems*, l.5436.

[4] For the source see Lydgate (1966), pp.143–4; I. Hyde, 'Lydgate's "Halff Chongyd Latyne": an Illustration', *MLN*, lxx (1955), 252–4.

[5] Cp. W. Schirmer, 'Consigned', *Anglia*, lxvii (1944), 339–40.

'translucent' and is often applied to water or dew. It implies, that is to say, a particular texture which could not be rendered by 'shining'. Here the definition of the aureate term as a mere learned synonym seems to break down. Lydgate has used the word *crystallyn* to give an effect similar to that of *rime equivoque*, to give semantic density. *Cristallyn* is 'aureate' only in being a rare word but, by virtue of its synonymity, it creates a close texture. In the hands of a good poet this can be effectively used. The distinction is clear in Lydgate's rendering of the Latin *thalamusque pudoris* in the preceding stanza. Here Lydgate creates a close texture without aureation. The terms *chambyr* and *closet* overlap semantically but neither is aureate; nor, as in the previous example, does the overlap appear significant. Likewise, *chastyte* is semantically close to *clennest* but is not an aureate term. On the other hand, in rendering *lux nubila pellens* by 'thou light without nebule shining in thi spere' Lydgate uses an aureate term without closeness of texture. In the rendering of the words *fons expers limi* 'fountain free of filth' we have in miniature an example of the poem's style. Lydgate's version is

> Fonteyn of fulnesse, as beryl corrent clere
> Some drope of thi graceful dewe to us propyne.

The Latin *fons expers limi* is expressed by *fonteyn of fulnesse . . . clere* in which each element has a distinct semantic function. Lydgate adds a comparison 'as beryl corrent clere', using a fairly common qualifier combined with a neologism *corrent*. The common application of the word *beryl* to water in Middle English poetry may be due to the greenish-bluish colour of the aquamarine, or to the more general sense of 'bright clarity' and 'luminosity'. If the latter meaning predominates, it may partly overlap in meaning with *clere*. The image is sharply focused but, though the register is literary, it is not aureate. On the other hand, *propyne* is a purely aureate term, a rare alternative for the verb 'to pour out'. It appears from these examples that Lydgate's aureate style is not merely a matter of verbal substitution. It consists also of contrasting registers combined with richness of semantic texture. Thus when he writes

'Fructif olyve of foilys faire and thicke' we have, both the contrast of linguistic tone arising from the juxtaposition of the rare *fructif*, *foilys* and the common *faire and thicke*, and the extension of the implications of *fructif* in the second half of the line to create close texture. It is also perhaps worth noting that, compared with Dunbar's *Ane Ballat of Our Lady*, he uses aureate terms of a more concrete kind. Such words are very largely lacking in such lines from the *Ballat* as the following:

> Imperiall wall, place palestrall,
>   Of peirles pulcritud;
> Tryumphale hall, hie trone regall
>   Of Godis celsitud;
> Hospitall riall, the lord of all
>   Thy closet did include;
> Bricht ball cristall, ros virginall,
>   Fulfillit of angell fude.[1]

Here the prominent words, *palestrall*, *pulcritud*, *celsitud* are all abstract.

Thus analysis of some examples of aureate style suggests that the authors are not merely substituting hard and neologistic forms for familiar ones. Indeed, the better the author writes, the less is he likely to do only this. An aureate term is not a kind of fly on the poet's nose, burning, as it were, in a literary hell. We have emphasised the effective conjunction in Lydgate of aureate terms, close texture and contrast of register. Many examples of the same technique could be provided from the lyrics of the fifteenth century, but I propose to consider only a final example from Dunbar, the well-known passage from the opening of *The Goldyn Targe*:

> Ryght as the stern of day begouth to schyne,
> Quhen gone to bed war Vesper and Lucyne,
>   I raise and by a rosere did me rest;
> Up sprang the goldyn candill matutyne,
> With clere depurit bemes cristallyne,
>   Glading the mery foulis in thair nest;

---

[1] Dunbar, *Ane Ballat of Our Lady*, ll.73–80.

Or Phebus was in purpur cape revest
Up raise the lark, the hevyns menstrale fyne
In May, in till a morow myrthfullest.

Full angellike thir birdis sang thair houris
Within thair courtyns grene, in to thair bouris
Apparalit quhite and red wyth blomes suete;
Anamalit was the felde wyth all colouris,
The perly droppis schake in silvir schouris,
Quhill all in balme did branch and levis flete;
To part fra Phebus did Aurora grete,
Hir cristall teris I saw hyng on the flouris,
Quhilk he for lufe all drank up wyth his hete.[1]

The poet is describing sunrise on a spring morning. The theme is entirely conventional. The style is aureate, as is evident from the use of the words *matutyne, revest, purpur,* and, that favourite word of aureate poets, *cristall, cristallyne.* Yet this is not, in itself, sufficient to explain the impression of brilliance and luminosity combined with an enamel-like hardness of finish[2] which the passage gives. Certainly, the imagery contributes to this impression. We notice, further on in the poem, the use of jewels as descriptive words:

The cristall air, the sapher firmament,
The ruby skyes of the orient,
Kest beriall bemes on emerant bewis grene;
The rosy garth depaynt and redolent,
With purpur, azure, gold, and goulis gent[3]
Arayed was.

The roses

War powderit brycht with hevinly beriall droppis,
Throu bemes rede birnyng as ruby sperkis;
The skyes rang for schoutyng of the larkis,
The purpur hevyn, our scailit in silvir sloppis,
Ourgilt the treis, branchis, lef, and barkis.[4]

---

[1] Dunbar, *The Goldyn Targe*, ll.1–18; cp. P. H. Nichols, 'Lydgate's Influence on the Aureate terms of the Scottish Chaucerians', *PMLA*, xlvii (1932), 516–22.
[2] Cp. D. Fox, 'Dunbar's *The Golden Targe*', *ELH*, xxvi (1959), 311–34.
[3] Dunbar, *The Goldyn Targe*, ll.37–41.
[4] Dunbar, *The Goldyn Targe*, ll.23–7.

The use of jewels as descriptive terms is common in medieval poetry and it is interesting to note the difference between the usage here and the use in an earlier poem such as *Annot and John*:

> Ichot a burde in a bour ase beryl so bryht,
> ase saphyr in seluer semly on syht,
> ase iaspe þe gentil þat lemeþ wiþ lyht,
> ase gernet in golde ant ruby wel ryht;
> ase onycle he ys on yholden on hyht,
> ase diamaund þe dere in day when he is dyht;
> he is coral ycud wiþ cayser ant knyht;
> ase emeraude amorewen þis may haueþ myht.
>> Þe myht of þe margarite haueþ þis mai mere;
>> ffor charbocle ich hire ches bi chyn ant by chere.[1]

Or add *Blow, Northerne Wynd*, another poem from *The Harley Lyrics*:

> Heo is coral of godnesse,
> heo is rubie of ryhtfulnesse,
> heo is cristal of clannesse,
>> ant baner of bealte.[2]

The different structure of the earlier and later poems admittedly contributes to a different effect. But the jewel imagery is not unimportant and the difference is surely that, in Dunbar, the jewel words are used, not only to give the generalised sense of something brilliant, beautiful, and precious, but with a particular colour reference. It is not to be presumed from the poems in *The Harley Lyrics*, that the ladies are the colours of the rainbow; but in Dunbar the actual colour of the jewels is significant. The drops of dew are round and white like pearls, and, as they fall, they are pale and shining like silver; the *beriall droppis* are translucent like the pale beryl; the purple heaven, with its silver stripes, gilds the trees. The brilliance of the morning sky, and its reflection on the leaves, is translated into a picture with outline and colour, the air hazy and bright, the upper sky blue, shading into white, and the eastern part

---

[1] *The Harley Lyrics*, No. 3, ll.1–10.
[2] *The Harley Lyrics*, No. 14, ll.47–50.

of the sky red, the leaves green, but shining with the rays of the morning sun. This is not a Turneresque picture but a late medieval miniature in which each shape is clearly defined and without shadow.

Yet the imagery of the poem's opening lines is not entirely responsible for the effect of the description. Other qualities, more immediately related to the aureate style, play their part. In the first place we note, as in Lydgate, the use of semantic density, a certain redundancy of meaning in phrases such as 'clere depurit bemes cristallyne', each component of which belongs to the semantic complex; pure, bright, shining, white; or, by contrast, 'goldyn candill matutyne', where the image of the candle is metaphorically consonant with the word *matutyne* as sharing the idea of brightness, but, contrastive in that candles are not generally used in the morning. Again, in 'bemes rede birnyng as ruby sperkis' we have an exploitation of the semantic complex of 'brightness', 'redness' and 'fire'. This dilation of the image is effected in other ways too. Objects are split up into components, the 'treis, branchis, lef and barkis',[1] 'wyth skippis and wyth hoppis'.[2] If indeed we consider the factual content of the opening line of the poem we find that Dunbar has, indeed, said very little in terms of information. He has arisen one spring morning and gone out and sat down by a rose bush. The birds are singing, the sun is rising, dew and flowers are everywhere. There is a river running through the woods. But just as in the lines

> The roch agayn the rivir resplendent
> As low enlumynit all the leves schene[3]

the learned words *resplendent, enlumynit* serve to dilate the sense, so the whole description is dilated by this semantic density. And again, as in the earlier poets, we note the contrast between the aureate terms and jewel imagery, on the one hand, and the simple terms with which they are contrasted on the other, as well as the artificial simplicity of some of the imagery. The

[1] Dunbar, *The Goldyn Targe*, l.27.   [2] Dunbar, *The Goldyn Targe*, l.19.
[3] Dunbar, *The Goldyn Targe*, ll.44–5.

birds are pictured as sleeping in the trees behind 'courtyns grene', their bowers adorned with a kind of floral wall-paper.[1] In spite of the Chaucerian echo, as the birds sing naturally enough on the 'tender croppis', they turn out to be 'Venus chapell clerkis'.[2] This, as artificial as the sartorial imagery of Charles of Orleans, is one aspect of a more general quality of style. This may perhaps be defined as a style at once dilated and diffused, rich in contrast of register, semantically dense. The point emerges strikingly if we compare Dunbar's passage with a passage from *The Knight's Tale*:

> The bisy larke, messager of day,
> Salueth in hir song the morwe gray,
> And firy Phebus riseth up so bright
> That al the orient laugheth of the light,
> And with his stremes dryeth in the greves
> The silver dropes hangynge on the leves.[3]

The description is not unartful but the scene is only outlined, as is fitting in the context. In spite of common subject matter and phrasing, it entirely lacks the dense texture of Dunbar. Thus it seems to me that the function of the aureate term is not merely decorative, although it is this, but also to make possible a dilation and diffusion of the semantic content. Paradoxically the aureate terms which, on the one hand, tend to the abstract and the semantically shallow, in another sense, in the hands of a good poet, increase the semantic content. And by this means the poets can obtain that richness which was their aim.

It is often claimed that the later Middle Ages is above all an age characterised by a love of allegory and didacticism. That it is an age of true allegorical writing I doubt; rather one might say that as the art of writing allegory declines, the cult of didacticism increases and didacticism to some extent takes the place of allegory. For it would surely be truer to say that the later Middle Ages is above all an age of pageantry. It is the age of the morality and miracle plays, the age of tournaments,

---

[1] Dunbar, *The Goldyn Targe*, ll.11–12.
[2] Dunbar, *The Goldyn Targe*, ll.20–1.
[3] Chaucer, *The Canterbury Tales*, A. ll.1491–6.

of street pageants and mummings,[1] an age when the Court of Burgundy was marked by a taste for the splendid and the ostentatious as perhaps no court had ever been before.[2] Increasing wealth made possible an ever-increasing standard of luxury. The splendour of the tournament contributed not a little to this pageantry. The late medieval character of such pageantry can indeed be over-emphasised. Records for this period are more plentiful on the one hand; on the other hand, what evidence we have suggests that pageantry was not lacking in earlier periods. The ideas of chivalry, and, in particular, the Arthurian story, penetrated and transformed the tournament from the thirteenth century onwards. A. Lane-Poole points out that in 1252 Matthew Paris speaks of 'that knightly game called a Round Table'. This differed from the ordinary tournament in that two combatants jousted or charged each other with levelled lances over a course instead of joining in a general mêlée. The exploitation of the Arthurian legend for political purposes, from the reign of Edward I onwards, formed a ready-made theme for pageantry of all kinds. So in 1279 we hear that 'an innumerable concourse of knights and ladies' attended a Round Table at Kenilworth which Roger Mortimer organised 'at enormous expense'. Already, in the semi-historical ancestral romance of Fulk Fitz-Warin, we hear of a proclamation inviting 'all valiant knights who wished to tourney *pur amurs* to present themselves and the prize was to be the land and the love of a lady'.[3] In 1344, Edward III held a Round Table at Windsor in imitation of Arthurian chivalry.[4] It seems clear that, at least from the thirteenth century onwards,

[1] Cp. Glynne Wickham, *Early English Stages* (London, 1959), I, esp. pp.13–176; 179–253.

[2] Cp. M. Meiss, *French Painting in the Time of Jean de Berry: The Late Fourteenth Century and the Patronage of the Duke* (London, 1967), pp.36–63; Huizinga, *passim*; O. E. W. Cartellieri, *The Court of Burgundy*, translated by M. Letts (London, 1929).

[3] *Medieval England*, edited by A. Lane-Poole (Oxford, 1958), p.623.

[4] Cp. R. S. Loomis, 'Chivalric and Dramatic Imitations of Arthurian Romance', in *Medieval Studies in Memory of A. Kingsley Porter*, edited by W. R. W. Koehler (Cambridge, Mass., 1939), I, 82; 'Edward I,

pageantry such as the *Feast of the Swan* was not uncommon in connection with court occasions.

Nevertheless, as Wickham has pointed out, the later Middle Ages extended the scope of these entertainments by the introduction of pastoral and allegorical motifs such as we find represented in the *Pas de la Bergière* held at Tarascon in 1449.[1] Those who issued challenges to attack the *Pas* were dressed as two shepherds; and the object they offered to defend against all comers, supposedly a shepherdess and her sheep, was Jeanne de Laval, René's second wife. She sat beneath a tree watching over her flock. Attached to the tree were two jousting shields; one white, signifying joy; the other black, signifying noblesse. Further, the white shield signifies those who are happily in love; the black shield those who are not. Each knight is to strike the shield that befits his state. At the end of the lists is a tableau in which the shepherd-challengers' pavilions are made to resemble cottages while the shepherdess herself has a crook 'about six foot long, the metal work being fashioned in fine silver. A little barrel at her side for thirst-quenching drink was also made of silver. Besides these she had a little food basket which was very quaint.' The lady was beautifully dressed:

> La bergière portoit ung vestement
> Qui bien estoit à son corps mesuré,
> Et au costé lassié moult gentement:
> Et si estoit de damas figuré
> Ung très beau gris, non pas trop obscuré,
> Très bien fourré et bordé à l'entour
> De menu vair; mais point n'avoit d'atour,
> Fors ung gentil chapperon de bourgoise
> De rosée, qui bien, comment qu'il voise,
> Lui afferoit au gré de mainte gent.[2]

Arthurian Enthusiast', *Speculum*, xxviii (1953), 114–27; Sandoz; R. H. Cline, 'The Influence of Romances on Tournaments of the Middle Ages', *Speculum*, xx (1945), 204–11.

[1] Wickham, pp.22–4; cp. Le Comte de Quatrebarbes, *Oevres Complètes du Roi René* (Angers, 1844), II, 49–96; cp. also Huizinga, pp.115–23, for late medieval pastoralism.

[2] Roi René, *Oeuvres*, II, 57.

[*The shepherdess wore a garment which fitted her well and was elegantly laced at the side. It was of figured damask, a very beautiful brown, not too dark, very well furred and edged round about with fine* vair. *But she had no headdress except an elegant bourgeois hat of brown cloth which well suited her notwithstanding, in the opinion of many people.*]

The same pastoralism appears in other aspects of court life. Huizinga points out that, at the marriage feasts of Charles the Bold and Margaret of York at Bruges in 1468: 'an *entremets* glorified the princesses of yore as "noble shepherdesses who had formerly tended and guarded the sheep of the *pays de par deça*" '.[1] We may also note the elaborate heraldic pageants of Richard Beauchamp, Earl of Warwick,

And when that he herd that the gaderyng in Fraunce was nat appoynted to come to Caleys, he cast in his mynde to do some newe poynt of chevalry. Wheruppon he lete paynt iij pavises, and in euery pavice a lady, the first harpyng atte ende of a bedstede, with a grate of golde on her lifte sleve, and her knyght called þe grene knyght, with a blakke quarter. And he shulde be redy to Just with eny knyght of Fraunce xij. courses . . . and that knyghtes lettre was sealed with the seale of his Armes: the felde syluer, a Maunche gowlys. The secund Pavys hadde a lady sittyng at a covered borde, worchyng perles, and on her sleve was tached a gloue of plate. And her knyght was called Chevaler vert. And his lettre was sealed with the Armes: the felde sylver, and ij. barres of gowles. . . . The iij^de pavys, a lady sittyng in a gardeyn, makyng a Chapellet. And on her sleve a poleyn with a Rivet. Her knyght was called Chivaler attendant. And he and his felowe must renne x. cours with sharpe speres and without sheldys; his lettre was sealed with golde and gowles quarte, a bordour of vere. Thies lettres were sent to the Kynges Coort of Fraunce.[2]

Glynne Wickham has drawn attention to the symbolism of such pageants.

For Christians of the Middle Ages, the meanings of many colours had been standardized by the rules laid down for their use in vestments in 1198; and the process thus begun was continued by

---

[1] Huizinga, p.123.

[2] *The Pageants of Richard Beauchamp, Earl of Warwick*, edited by William, Earl of Carysfort (Roxburghe Club, Oxford, 1908), Pageants xxvi and xxvii.

those responsible for formulating the codes of Heraldry, due largely to the requirements of the Tournament. Thus colours, besides serving the simple function of distinguishing one armoured combatant from another, could be given an additional allegoric significance.

He draws attention, for example, to sets of equivalents between the nine orders of angels, virtues, precious stones and heraldic colours, and similar analogies between the insignia of royalty, the corresponding virtues and the emblems of nobility.[1] Lydgate's ballads for Mummings well illustrate the taste of the period. Thus the Bishopswood ballad had classical deities such as Flora and Ver,[2] the ballad for the Eltham Mumming, Bacchus, Juno, Ceres,[3] the London Disguising, abstractions such as Fortune and the virtues.[4] In the Triumphal Entry of Henry VI into London on 21 February 1432, we hear that 'all the comunes off the citee rood all clothed in white with sundrye devyses, lyke as the mater here after more pleynly specifieth.'[5] Lydgate's poem describes the 'devices':

> First whanne he passed was the Fabour
> Entryng the Brigge off this noble town,
> Ther was a pyler reysed lyke a tour
> And ther-on stoode a sturdy champeoun.

The sturdy champion turns out to be a giant. On each side is an antelope with the arms of England and France. In the middle of the bridge is a tower with three empresses who represent Nature, Grace and Fortune. They give the king Science, Skill, Strength and Beauty, Prosperity and Wealth. On their right were seven maidens who presented the seven gifts of the Holy Spirit. And in the same way, at other stations, such as Cornhill,

---

[1] Wickham, pp.45–9.

[2] Lydgate, *The Mumming at Bishopswood; The Minor Poems*, edited by H. N. MacCracken, II, E.E.T.S., 192 (1934), No. 40, pp.668–71; cp. Wickham, pp.191–228 for mummings and disguisings; compare also E. Welsford, *The Court Masque* (Cambridge, 1927), pp.42–80; on Lydgate pp.52–61; for the court of Burgundy, pp.65–80.

[3] *A Mumming at Eltham*; Lydgate (1934), No. 41, pp.672–4.

[4] *A Mumming at London*; Lydgate (1934), No. 43, pp.682–91.

[5] C. L. Kingsford, *Chronicles of London* (Oxford, 1905), p.97.

the Conduit, Cheapside, were similar pageants incorporating moralities or ancient worthies.[1] The possible relationship between allegory and pageantry in the late medieval period seems to be suggested by the curious parallel between the pageant presented at the coronation of Richard II and the angel and goliardys episode in the B text of *Piers Plowman*.[2] Indeed it would be surprising, in a period when a wealth of public spectacles, the tournament, the street pageant, the mummings, the *pas d'armes*, and even such details of courtly life as the subtlety, manifest a taste for the visually didactic, the pictorial realisation of ideas and the enrichment of life by every kind of splendour from jewels and rich fabrics to the adornment of aureate language, if this were not reflected in the literature of the period, and especially allegorical and didactic literature.

The concept of disguised symbolism, of which Panofsky speaks in discussing the art of late medieval Flanders,[3] I believe to be relevant to the understanding of late medieval allegorical writing. It is a commonplace that, as the Middle Ages drew to a close, allegory became more formal and more stereotyped. Yet, on the other hand, with the increasing taste for naturalism, so evident in the art of the period, the function of allegory changed.[4] And this change coincided with certain changes in literary taste and fashion. On the one hand the emblematic pictures, the origin and nature of which we have tried to describe in a previous chapter, became increasingly popular through the mythological studies of Holcot, Waleys and Ridevall. But these emblematic pictures blended with another tradition of classical interests, which became increasingly important after the middle of the fourteenth century. The justification of the poetic fiction was already implicit in the works of such writers as John of Garland. His *Integumenta Ovidii* was a revelation of the hidden truths in the *Metamorphoses*.

[1] *King Henry VI's Triumphal Entry into London*, 21 February 1432; Lydgate (1934), No. 32, pp.630–48; Wickham, pp.72–8.

[2] Langland, *Piers Plowman*, B. Prologue, ll.128–42; cp. Donaldson (1949), p.118 and Wickham, pp.54–5.

[3] See pp.2–3.　　　　　　　　[4] Cp. J. Wimsatt, p.36.

Morphosis Ovidii parva cum clave Johannis
Panditur et presens cartula servit ei.
Nodos secreti denodat, clausa revelat
Rarificat nebulas, integumenta canit.[1]

[*The Metamorphoses of Ovid are opened with this little key of John, and this short booklet suffices him. It unlooses the knots of secret matters, unveils hidden matters, disperses clouds, sings hidden things.*]

Yet the fourteenth century had special and widely popular apologists for poetry. Of these Boccaccio and Petrarch, to whom we have already referred, were the most famous, but others, such as Coluccio Salutati, were also influential.[2] Coluccio's programme for the study of literature has, at times, a somewhat modern ring:

... omnia, inquam, que apud poetas fabulosa videntur, oportet vel ad deum vel ad creaturas aut ad aliquid ad hos pertinens debita expositione reduci. Cumque poetarum abdita misticus interpres aperiet, et ad deum, naturam, vel mores singula referens adaptaverit, sine dubitatione reputet se, quamvis incogitatum ab autore dici queat id quod invenerit, in sententiam tolerabilem incidisse. Quod si ad illa que senserit adaptare poterit propriorum nominum rationem, audacter affirmem ipsum sine controversia veram autoris eliciuisse sententiam, aut si forsitan illa non fuerit, et ad id quod autor intendisset nomina non accedant, longe commodiorem sensum quam autor cogitaverit invenisse.[3]

[*All things, I say, which seem to be fictitious in the poets, it is necessary to refer, with fitting exposition, either to God or to creatures or to something else pertaining to these. And whenever the mystical interpreter reveals the hidden things of the poets and shall have adapted them by reference to God, nature or individual habits, without doubt, albiet that which he shall have found may be unthought of by the author, he should consider himself to have fallen upon an acceptable meaning. But if he can adapt the system of proper names to fit his sense, I would boldly affirm that, without doubt, he has elicited the true thoughts of the author, or if perhaps it was not his thought, and the names do not fit what the author intended, he has found a sense far more appropriate than the author had thought of.*]

---

[1] John of Garland, *Integumenta Ovidii*, ll.5–8.

[2] Cp. J. R. O'Donnell, 'Coluccio Salutati on the Poet-Teacher', *Mediaeval Studies*, xxii (1960), 240–56.

[3] Coluccio Salutati, *De Laboribus Herculis*, II, ii, 13–14, edited by B. L. Ullman (Zurich, 1952), p.86.

There were famous literary models, such as Petrarch's adaptation of Berchorius's *De Imaginibus Deorum*, in the *Africa*,[1] which encouraged the use of all kinds of emblematic material, not only in allegory, but in narrative works. And much of this emblematic material was classical or Neoplatonic in origin.[2] And thus it came about that there was an extraordinary enrichment of the imagery of poetry, and, whereas earlier writers of allegory will often present an embodied and realised abstraction, such as the abstractions in the *Romance of the Rose*, later writers tend increasingly to present their ideas, not by abstractions or *figurae*, but through the medium of a *fictio*, often in the form of moralised classical deities. That there was gain as well as loss in this procedure, we hope later to demonstrate.

In this milieu, the art of allegory becomes more and more decorative, and less and less figural, or even truly polysemous, and, in some instances, and Ariosto would be a case in point, the relationship between the narrative and the interpretation become more and more artificial even in 'fictional' writing. On the other hand, there develops a new use of allegorical writing. Voretzsch has remarked that, in Old French literature, from the middle of the fourteenth century, allegory ceases increasingly to be an independent genre.[3] On the contrary, it is used more and more as an ornamental feature, not unlike the use of aureate language, to give semantic depth at certain points in an otherwise unallegorical work. *The Fonteinne Amoureuse*, to which we have already referred, would be an admirable example of this use of allegory. There is a kind of two-way traffic. On the one hand, much of the older allegorical material is used in the morality play, a form only minimally polysemous as we have defined the term.[4] Langland's Four Daughters of God who danced until the day dawned when men rang to

[1] Petrarch, *Africa*, edited by N. Festa (Firenze, 1926), III, ll.136–262.

[2] Cp. Seznec, pp.96–103.

[3] K. Voretzsch, *Introduction to the Study of Old French Literature*, translated by F. M. du Mont (Halle, 1931), p.466.

[4] For the use of Prudentius in the morality play, cp. E. T. Schell, 'On the Imitation of Life's Pilgrimage in *The Castle of Perseverance*', *JEGP*, lxvii (1968), 235 and references.

N

celebrate the Resurrection of Christ,[1] give way to real people representing Mercy, Truth, Justice and Peace in a theatrical 'place'; and the inevitable split between the actual person and place, represented by the actor and stage in a theatrical representation, and the abstractions which they represent, seems to be reflected in an increasing tendency for non-dramatic allegorical figures to speak, as though they *were* on a stage, although in fact, the realisation of their actions and appearance are not provided by the actors, costume and setting. The difference is apparent in the treatment of the theme of the Four Daughters of God in Langland and in *The Court of Sapience*.[2] On the other hand, the dramatisation of material emblematic in the strict sense was necessarily difficult in that the surface image might well be fantastic and the inevitably naturalistic tendency of drama conflicted with such dramatic representation except perhaps in the pageantry of mummings and tournaments. The morality play apparently succeeded in reconciling naturalism with didacticism within an allegorical framework; but it was only allegorical in the limited way in which the animated personifications or abstractions can be allegorical. If we compare the abstraction Everyman with the figural Piers Plowman, we see immediately how the morality, effective and moving though it often is, is not a fully polysemous form. Everyman is a human being of the greatest imaginable degree of generality; Piers Plowman is a human being, who, in virtue of existing within an historical and actual context, can be used to typify certain qualities which he supremely possesses. Everyman's actuality is the actuality of dramatic realisation; Piers's actuality is the actuality of historical realisation in time. The same is true of other *figurae* such as St. Francis in the *Divine Comedy*. It is only in virtue of his historical life that he can act as a *figura*. He is not Everyman although he may serve as an ideal for Everyman. Everyman functions by a process of identification; Francis by a

---

[1] Langland, *Piers Plowman*, B. xviii, ll.406b–25; C. xxi, ll.454–72.

[2] *The Court of Sapience*, edited by R. Spindler (Leipzig, 1927), ll.190–902; cp. Derek Pearsall, 'The English Chaucerians', in *Chaucer and Chaucerians*, pp.230–1.

process of exemplification. On the other hand, both differ from the Everyman of the *Romance of the Rose* who exists only as mirrored in his allegorical context.

This movement towards the morality rather than true personification, that is to say towards an abstraction depending for its realisation on dramatic action and presentation rather than a textual realisation in an allegorical picture, and the related movement towards the fictional rather than the figural, is evident in many late medieval allegories and pseudo-allegories. *The Assembly of Gods* will serve as an example of the latter process. The chief actors in the first part are *idola*, classical gods and goddesses who, at the end of the poem, are elaborately glossed, just as Boccaccio glossed the *Teseida* and the *Madonna Fiammetta*. It is typical that it is Doctrine who gives elaborate explanations. The imprisonment of Eolus, we are told, signifies that wealth increases misrule; the complaint of Diana and Neptune signifies the folly of fools who try to bring the winds to correction and so on. That is to say, we have a *fictio* not a figural narrative. The technique, of course, is not new. The whole tradition of moralisations, from the elaborate and ingenious moralisations of Ovid, to the moralisations of popular tales such as the *Gesta Romanorum*, antedates the period of which we are writing. But it seems consonant with the increasing taste for the naturalistic that a form of allegorical writing should become increasingly popular which favoured the surface consistency at the expense of allegorical subtlety.

It will perhaps be useful to look at *The Assembly of Gods* a little more closely. The poem consists of a number of sections. The theme, like that of *Les Echecs Amoureux* and Lydgate's *Reson and Sensuallyte* is how Reason and Sensuality may be made to accord, and the frame of the action is a dream which came to the dreamer, as he sat alone beside a lake, and, suitably enough, his dream is compered by Morpheus. The first part of the dream is at the courts of Minos and Apollo and the *dramatis personae*, as we have said, are classical gods and goddesses, and abstractions such as Discord, Virtue and Vice. The second scene is a psychomachia, and the third the School and lessons of Doctrine in which Doctrine expounds the previous scenes. On reading the poem we are immediately struck by the split between picture and theme. This is particularly evident in the section presided over by Doctrine. We notice at once that, whereas the discourse of Langland's personifications Wit, Study, Clergy and the like, is constantly drawn from the exemplary detail of everyday life, which gives concrete richness of expression, in *The Assembly of Gods* (or the discourses of Doctrine in *The Pastime of Pleasure* would afford another example) the discourses of Doctrine are without this lively, everyday detail. More significantly, however, we realise that the poem tends to split into two parts; the allegorical picture and the didactic discourse. For example, the pictures are in some cases not allegorical at all:

> Thys Reconsylyacion was the Tyme of Grace,
>> When foundyd was the churche vppon the feyr stoon,
> And to holy Petyr the key delyueryd was
>> Of heuyn; then helle dyspoyled was anoon.
> Thus was mankynde delyueryd from hys foon.
>> And then began the New Testament
>> That the Crystyn pepyll beleue in present.

> Whyche iii tymes, a sondry deuydyd,
>> Mayst thow here see, yef thow lyst beholde.
> The furst behynde the yn pycture ys prouydyd.
>> The second of the lyft hande shewe prophetes olde.
>> The iii^{de} on the ryght hande here hit ys to the tolde.
>> Thus hast thow in vysyon the verrey fygure
>> Of these iii tymes here shewyd in purtrayture.[1]

These pictures also afford an interesting example of an allegorical device used purely for pictorial effect. Thus

> Furst, to begyn, there was in portrature
> Adam, and Eue holdyng an appyll round;
> Now in a shyp; and Abraham hauyng sure
> A flynt stone in hys hand; and Isaac lay bound

---

[1] Lydgate (?), *The Assembly of Gods*, ll.1758–71.

> On an hygh mount; Iacob slepyng sound,
> And a long laddyr stood hym besyde;
> Ioseph in a cysterne was also there that tyde.[1]

The emblematic objects which these people are given have no allegorical functions; nor, as the people are named, have they the practical function, which they would have in the visual arts, of identifying the people in question. This picture illustrates the Old Testament just as on the second wall, Peter with his key, Paul with his sword, James with his scallop and so on represent the New Dispensation. They are actual, historical realisations and not exemplary or allegorical and their emblems have a purely historical basis also. Yet they are not *figurae* because they are purely themselves and not figures of some aspect of themselves. In the *figura*, the historical character is made to stand for some particular aspect of his historical actuality but, at the same time, he functions in the allegorical narrative as a person and not as a personification. It is this combination of the typical and the actual which enables writers using the *figura* to combine the abstract with the personal in the dream vision in a particularly effective way. These figures are not *figurae*, yet even if we compare them with the figures on the wall in *The Romance of the Rose*, which uses the same allegorical device in a different mode, the purely pictorial nature of *The Assembly of Gods* is apparent.

> Another ymage set saugh I
> Next Coveitise faste by,
> And she was clepid Avarice.
> Ful foul in peyntyng was that vice;
> Ful fade and caytif was she eek,
> And also grene as ony leek.
> So yvel hewed was hir colour,
> Hir semed to have lyved in langour.
>
> . . . .
>
> And she was clad ful porely
> Al in an old torn courtepy,

---

[1] Lydgate (?), *The Assembly of Gods*, ll.1520–6.

As she were al with doggis torn;
And bothe bihynde and eke biforn
Clouted was she beggarly.[1]

This is allegorical by virtue of its reference to two different universes of discourse which are related as picture and theme. On the one hand, the abstraction Avarice and, on the other, the person pale, dirty and so on, with whom this vice is linked. As we have already pointed out, personification is not fully polysemous in itself, but as an allegorical device it depends upon this linking of two similar areas of discourse in an allegorical narrative. Now the figures in *The Assembly of Gods*, though actual and not personifications, have no such duality. Adam, representing the age in which he lived, holds an apple, because he ate an apple. There is no implied comparison. And so on for the rest. But, we might ask, how would the figures in *The Assembly of Gods* compare with the apparently comparable figures in the *Purgatorio*? Let us take an example:

L'angel che venne in terra col decreto
de la molt'anni lacrimata pace,
ch'aperse il ciel del suo lungo divieto,
dinanzi a noi pareva sí verace
quivi intagliato in un atto soave,
che non sembiava imagine che tace.
Giurato si saría ch'el dicesse 'Ave!';
perché iv'era imaginata quella
ch'ad aprir l'alto amor volse la chiave;
e avea in atto impressa esta favella
'Ecce ancilla Dei,' propriamente
come figura in cera si suggella.[2]

[*The angel that came to earth with the decree of the so long wept for peace,
which released heaven from its long ban, before us appeared so vividly en-
graved, with gentle mien, that it seemed not like a dumb image. One would
have sworn that it was saying 'Ave'. For there she was fashioned who
turned the key to open the supreme love. And in her attitude were imprinted
these words, 'Behold the handmaid of the Lord', as expressly as a figure is
stamped on wax.*]

---

[1] Chaucer, *The Romaunt of the Rose*, ll.207–23.
[2] Dante, *Purgatorio*, x, ll.34–45.

This, like the picture from *The Assembly of Gods*, is an example of an historical kind, but it is to be noted first that the scene typifies humility. That is to say, we are here in the realm of the *figura*. In the second place, we have a plastic scene complete in itself with light and shade. In the third place, the scene is 'told' not 'shown'. We are drawn into the scene by the author's comment. The comparison highlights the characteristic mode of the late medieval allegory, the tendency to split the narrative into the purely didactic and the purely pictorial. In other words, the intuitive and intellectual elements instead of standing in a metaphorical relation to each other, are almost entirely divorced.

There is, however, another regard in which the late medieval allegory shows increasing shallowness. If we look at an allegory such as *King Hart*, this is immediately apparent. The framework of the poem is allegorical indeed; King Hart lives in a castle, man's body. Yet he is not entirely free, for Nature has provided men to govern and to guide him. The qualities of youth are listed without any attempt at creating an allegorical picture:

> First Strenth, Lust and Wantownnes,
> Grein Lust, Disport, Ielousie and Invy,
> Freschnes, Newgate, Waistgude and Wilfulnes,
> Delyuernes, Fulehardenes; thairby
> Gentrice, Fredome, Price previe I espy,
> Wantwyt, Vanegloir, Prodigalitie,
> Vnrest, Nichtwalk and Full of Glutony,
> Vnricht, Dyme Sicht, with Slicht and Subtiltie.[1]

The castle is under the care of five sentries, the five senses. The allegorical narrative is sustained throughout but there is no pictural development. Even where there is allegorical imagery, it is brief and fleeting like the picture of 3outhheid who

> vpstart and cleikit on his cloik,
> Was browdin all with lustie levis grene;[2]

or Innocence 'Ane mylk quhyt steid, þat ambilit as the wynd'.[3]

---

[1] *The Shorter Poems of Gavin Douglas*, edited by Priscilla J. Bawcutt, S.T.S. (1967), *King Hart*, ll.25–32.   [2] Gavin Douglas, *King Hart*, ll.153–4.
[3] Gavin Douglas, *King Hart*, l.162.

Then we return to abstraction upon abstraction: 'And fresche Delyt raid on Benevolence'.[1] And the cavalcade is met by another crowd of abstractions:

> The king outsent Newgate and Wantownnes
> Grene Luif, Disport, Waistgude, that nocht can lane,
> And with þame freschlie feir, Fule-hardynes.[2]

Dreid of disdane runs on foot beside them, warns them of the results of pride. If we put this cavalcade beside Langland's Mede episode, which superficially it might be thought to resemble, we immediately see the difference. True, Langland's actors are partly abstractions, Simony and Civil (Law). But, as always in Langland, his figural way of writing necessitates his using real people as part of his allegorical machinery. Thus, alongside Simony and Civil we find the rogues of the church in a vivacious crowd which gives vitality, movement and concreteness to the picture. There are, of course, other ways of giving depth and variety to the allegorical picture. We have only to remember some of the more notable chariots of allegory to see how this can be done, the chariot of the liberal arts in the *Anticlaudianus*,[3] for example, or the chariot of the Church in the *Purgatorio*.[4] Although static, these compensate for this by the richness of their visual impact.

Alongside these late medieval allegories we find a number of poems which are not true allegories but narrative or lyrical poems which use allegorical devices as an ornamental feature. These might be called pseudo-allegories. I mean such poems as *The Floure and the Leafe*, *The Island of Ladies*, *The Assembly of Ladies*. Here we see clearly the split between the purely abstract and the purely decorative. For example, in *The Assembly of Ladies* the *dramatis personae* are Loyalty, Largesse, Composure, Diligence, Perseverance, Discretion and so on. Their function is to give tidings of love. There is indeed a description of the

---

[1] Gavin Douglas, *King Hart*, l.163.
[2] Gavin Douglas, *King Hart*, ll.178–80.
[3] Alanus de Insulis, *Anticlaudianus*, II, 363–IV, 244.
[4] Dante, *Purgatorio*, xxix, ll.106–54.

great Lady Attemperaunce, but, interestingly, it is entirely unallegorical:[1]

> I shal yow tell the maner of hyr goune;
> Of cloth of gold full ryche, hyt ys no nay,
> The colour blew of a ryght good fassion,
> In taberd wyse, the slevys hangyng don;
> And what purfyll ther was and in what wyse
> So as I can I shall hyt yow devyse.

> Aftyr a sort the coler and the vent,
> Lyke as ermyn ys made in purfelyng,
> With gret perles full fyne and oryent
> They were couchyd all aftyr oon worchyng,
> With dyamondes in stede of pouderyng;
> The slevys and purfyllys of assyse;
> They were made lyke in every wyse;

> Abowte hir nekke a serpe of fayre rubies
> In white floures of right fyne enemayle;
> Upon hir hede sette in the fresshest wise
> A cercle with gret balays of entaile;
> That in ernest to speke, withouten faile,
> For yong and old and every maner age,
> It was a world to loke on hir visage.[2]

This is pretty, but not allegorical, except perhaps in the particular of the blue gown and the *balays*. The charming poem, *The Floure and the Leafe*, is merely a projection of the courtly cult of the Flower and the Leaf in pseudo-allegorical terms. The poem could well be a court pageant or mumming. Whereas it would be difficult to unite all the physical details of the allegorical figures of Guillaume de Lorris into a visual whole which could appear on a stage, the descriptions here of the followers of the Flower and the Leaf could be so represented, just as it would be possible to represent Attemperaunce in *The Assembly of Ladies*. They are real people dressed up and not allegorical figures at all; that is to say, the particulars of their appearance belong to

[1] But cp. Derek Pearsall, '*The Assembly of Ladies* and *Generydes*', *RES*, xii (1961), 229, for *The Assembly of Ladies* as 'a conventional love allegory'.

[2] *The Assembly of Ladies*, ll.520–39, in *The Floure and the Leafe* and *The Assembly of Ladies*, edited by D. A. Pearsall (London, 1962). The transposition of stanzas does not essentially affect the argument.

a visual whole and not to an underlying pattern of thought. That delicate balance which we find in true allegories between the visually convincing and the intellectually significant has here tipped over into the purely naturalistic. The frame of the poem raises the expectation of allegory but we have not true allegorical action in fact.

Other examples in the same mode would be Lydgate's *Temple of Glass* or Chaucer's *Hous of Fame*. The *Temple of Glass* is essentially a Complaint Poem like the *Bok of the Duchese* or *The Complaint of the Black Knight*. Already in the French writers of the fourteenth century, the theme of the Lover's Complaint was combined with the dream convention and might, as we have said, include allegorical elements. Thus *The Temple of Glass* begins with a seemingly allegorical topic. The poet falls asleep and sees a temple of glass standing on a craggy rock. Inside he sees, predictably, pictures of lovers, although they are listed, in the manner of the lovers in the *Trionfi*, rather than pictured. But the main action is narrative and concerned with the story of an unhappy love. In the same way it seems to me that Chaucer's *Hous of Fame* is to be understood as a mythic narrative rather than a true allegory, although a narrative with allegorical components. The temple of Venus, with which the poem, like Lydgate's, begins, contains examples of love rather than an allegory of love. And the figure of Venus, although based on the *Ovide Moralisé*, as Bennett has pointed out, gives an impression of casualness which suggests that Chaucer did not perhaps take the allegorical components very seriously. The long narration of the story of Dido and Aeneas certainly assumes a greater impressiveness. Nor, in my view, can the second book be regarded as allegorical. Rather, it is, surely, part of the enigmatic dream. An enigmatic dream need not be an allegory. According to Macrobius, the Dream of Scipio exemplifies five types of enigmatic dream.[1] Thus the dream

---

[1] Macrobius, *In Somnium Scipionis*, I, iii, 12, 13; p.11; Stahl, pp.90–1. For the view that Chaucer had not yet read the *Somnium Scipionis* when he wrote *HF*, see M. H. Shackford, 'The Date of Chaucer's *Hous of Fame*', *MLN*, xxxi (1916), 507–8; but cp. Bethurum, p.514 and fn. 8.

was, for example, a universal enigmatic dream, that is, one in which the dreamer dreams that some change has taken place in the sun, moon, planets, or regions of the earth; and therefore in the words of Macrobius it is:

generale quod caelum caelique circulos conversionisque concentum, vivo adhuc homini nova et incognita, stellarum etiam ac luminum motus terraeque omnis situm suspiciendo vel despiciendo concepit.[1]

[*Universal since by gazing up and down he perceived the wonders of the heavens, the great celestial circles, and the harmony of the revolving spheres, things strange and unknown to mortals before this; in addition he witnessed the movements of the stars and planets and the position of the whole earth.*]

So Chaucer in the claws of the eagle is experiencing a *somnium generale* the significance of which is explained to him by the eagle. As for the House of Fame itself, it is again an enigma rather than an allegory, although not without allegorical touches, such as the whirling house and the rock of glass. It is probably significant, however, that these details seem to have been taken from romantic fiction. Their strangeness, as much as any allegorical quality they possess, explains their presence in the poem. And surely the mysterious 'man of gret auctorite' must indicate that the poem was also to be an *oraculum* in which the significance of the dream is explained, as in Scipio's Dream, by a person of oracular dignity. It seems not impossible that Chaucer intended the poem to be an example of the dream types which he feigns in the prologue not to understand. Be that as it may, the poem is a typical late medieval pseudo-allegory and different in genre, for this reason, from *The Parlement of Foules*.

As a final example of this genre I should like to look at *The Testament of Cresseid*. The poem is a narrative, not an allegory, but in Cresseid's dream we have 'pictures' of the gods which

---

[1] Macrobius, *In Somnium Scipionis*, I, iii, 13; p.11; Stahl, p.91.

follow in the allegorical pictural tradition. Take, for example, the picture of Saturn:

> His face fronsit, his lyre was lyke the Leid,
> His teith chatterit, and cheverit with the Chin,
> His Ene drowpit, how sonkin in his heid,
> Out of his Nois the Meldrop fast can rin,
> With lippis bla and cheikis leine and thin;
> The Iceschoklis that fra his hair doun hang
> Was wonder greit, and as ane speir als lang.
>
> Atouir his belt his lyart lokkis lay,
> Felterit unfair, ouirfret with Froistis hoir,
> His garmound and his gyis full gay of gray,
> His widderit weid fra him the wind out woir;
> Ane busteous bow within his hand he boir,
> Under his girdill ane flasche of felloun flanis,
> Fedderit with Ice and heidit with hailstanis.[1]

This is the conventional 'picture' of Saturn, the God of melancholy and cold, the causer of disasters and sorrow.[2] The whole portrait is gray and cold. It could be paralleled from numberless portraits of the god in art and literature. But what I want to call attention to at the moment is the nature of the description in relation to the allegorical mode. It was an evident advantage of the pictures that, in so far as the gods represented certain ideas or states, as Saturn represents melancholy and disaster, their use enabled the poet to present an allegorical portrait which would have the greatest surface consistency. That the pictures did not always achieve this is evident from the illustrations in the *Fulgentius Metaforalis* but, on the other hand, it is evident that such consistency was obtainable.

It is, however, worth noting that, even where the tradition is continuous, in the later renderings of this tradition the spirit

---

[1] Henryson, *The Testament of Cresseid*, ll.155–68.

[2] For discussion of the sources and analysis of this passage, cp. M. A. Twycross, *The Representation of the Major Classical Divinities in the Works of Chaucer, Gower, Lydgate and Henryson* (unpublished thesis, Oxford, 1961), pp. 158–66. The portrait of Saturn in *The Assembly of Gods* illustrates the same point although less completely. Henryson may, of course, have been influenced by Lydgate.

of the pictures changes. Let us take the example of Saturn and compare some traditional renderings of the portrait of this god. Our first example is from the work of Mythographer III, Albricus I:

> Primum deorum Saturnum ponunt. Hunc maestum senem, canum, caput glauco amictu coopertum habentum, filiorum suorum voratorem, falcemque ferentem, draconem etiam flammivomum qui caudae suae ultima devorat, in dextra tenentem, inducunt.[1]

> [*They place Saturn first among the gods. Him they represent as a sad old man, hoary, having his head covered with a grey cloak, the devourer of his sons, carrying a sickle, and also he bears in his right hand a dragon spitting fire, devouring the end of its own tail.*]

A slightly longer version appears in Petrarch's *Africa* and in Berchorius. This is the version in the *Africa*:

> Inde autem incessu gravior tristisque senecta,
> Velato capite et glauco distinctus amictu,
> Rastra manu falcemque gerens Saturnus agresti,
> Rusticus aspectu natos pater ore vorabat;
> Flammivomusque draco caude postrema recurve
> Ore tenens magnos sese torquebat in orbes.[2]

> [*Thereafter, however, more heavy of tread and sad in his old age, with veiled head and set off with a grey cloak, Saturn bearing in his rustic hand a rake and a sickle, rustic-looking the father was devouring his sons, and a fire-spitting dragon twisted himself in great coils, holding in his mouth the tip of his backward curving tail.*]

Very similar is the related description in Berchorius:

> Saturnus pingebatur et supponebatur homo senex: curuus tristis et pallidus. In vna manu falcem tenebat: et in eadem draconis portabat imaginem qui dentibus caudam propriam commordebat: altera vero filium paruulum ad os applicabat: et eum dentibus deuorabat. Caput etiam galeatum amictu coopertum habebat.[3]

---

[1] G. H. Bode, *Scriptores Rerum Mythicarum* (1834), p.153; for the texts cp. also Seznec, p.176; Liebeschütz, pp.58–9.
[2] Petrarch, *Africa*, III, ll.143–8.
[3] Berchorius, *De Formis Figurisque Deorum*, p.5.

[*Saturn was painted and set down as an old man, bent, sad and pale, holding in one hand a sickle and in the same hand he was holding the image of a dragon biting its own tail; with the other, however, he was putting to his mouth a small boy and devouring him with his teeth. Even his helmeted head was covered with a cloak.*]

And finally we have the portrait in the *Libellus de deorum imaginibus*:

Saturnus primus deorum supponebatur. Et pingebatur ut homo senex, canus, prolixa barba, curvus, tristis et palidus, tecto capite, colore glauco qui una manu, scilicet dextera, falcem tenebat et in eadem serpentis portabat ymaginem qui caudam propriam dentibus commordebat. Altera vero, scilicet sinistra, filium parvulum ad os applicabat et eum devorare videbatur.[1]

[*Saturn was placed first of the gods and painted as an old, hoary man with a flowing beard, bent, sad and pale, his head covered, grey in colour, who, in one hand, namely his right, was holding a sickle and in the same hand the image of a serpent who bit his own tail. But with the other, namely the left, he was putting to his mouth a small boy and appeared to eat him.*]

Now Seznec has rightly pointed out that

the difference between the 'first' and the 'second' Albricus is profound, for the spirit has changed. Whereas the *Liber ymaginum* brought together the mythological substance encumbered with the medieval glosses, the *Libellus*, renewing Petrarch, and again separating the images from the allegorical ensemble in which Bersuire had reinserted them, offers us a clear text, determinedly profane and purely iconographical. The same formula recurs in it constantly: 'Pingebatur'. This formula tends to freeze the god in some one typical and immutable attitude and setting, which can be easily studied and endlessly reproduced.[2]

Henryson has made a brilliant selection from the traditional pictures of Saturn to assort with the grey tones with which the poem opens. Yet more interesting is the surface consistency, the naturalistic tone of the portrait. The more grotesque details of the pictures are absent although it is difficult to believe that Henryson did not know them. The description is an admirable

[1] Albricus, *Libellus de deorum imaginibus*, edited by Liebeschütz, p.117.
[2] Seznec, pp.176–7.

example of the use of an iconographical motif in a non-allegorical poem in order to give richness and pictorial variety. Moreover, like the use of aureate diction, it adds a semantic depth and range by virtue of its allegorical implications. It is at once natural and symbolic, a kind of iconographical parallel to the *figura*, but static whereas the *figura* is dramatic. It might stand as a model of the second direction in which late medieval allegory evolved.

What then are we to conclude at the end of this chapter in which we have tried to indicate some of the features of late medieval writing. Much has been omitted, but this was inevitable. Rather than attempt a complete picture we have tried to suggest a few of the ways in which the late medieval period moved in the direction of verbalism. This verbalism sometimes took the form of verbal ornament as with aureate diction and the pictorial tradition. On the other hand, in lyric poetry, it took the form of a 'musical' style in which verbal form was dominant. Sometimes it meant the movement away from polysemy towards other forms of expression. But it must be observed that the late medieval period is not, as is often suggested, merely a period when the old forms were repeated with increasing rigidity and decreasing vitality. It was also a period of increasing verbal subtlety and experiment, a period when the enriched language moved towards new forms of expression. If it sometimes seems frigid it is because it is putting old wine in new bottles. The precarious balance of the late fourteenth century between symbolism and naturalism, colloquial vitality and elaborate rhetoric, may seem frozen, but the leaven of linguistic change is in fact at work.

Conclusion

If anything emerges from this study of aspects of form and style in Old and Middle English it is confirmation of the truism that style is choice. The distinction between literature and non-literature is, as the Middle Ages rightly perceived, largely a distinction between truth and verisimilitude, history and *fictio*; the most indifferent of medieval romances, the most banal of modern novels, is still literature, but literature which lacks an effective style. For style is the creation of a structure related to, but distinguishable from, the linguistic form. The distinction is the distinction between a casual photograph and a painting. And the difference is just that personal vision which creates patterns and relationships. A photograph of a chair signals to our sight and mind an object of perception with which we are familiar, just as the sound or sight of words signals a message to the brain. A chair painted by Van Gogh also suggests to our minds that this is a chair, but a chair related to certain patterns of colour and shape which may also imply an attitude on the part of the painter. The chair as an object may, indeed, be distorted in order to bring out these relationships. A striking example of this truism is to be seen in Van Gogh's copy of Millet's *Cornfield*, in a sense a careful replica of Millet's picture; in a sense unmistakably Van Gogh's own. In Gombrich's words, 'He repeats Millet's statements in his own accent'.[1]

When we spoke at the beginning of the book of 'image' and 'meaning' it was these concepts that we had in mind. The image, the object of apperception, is the verbal message. Implicit in this is the structural pattern we have called 'meaning'. The image of course, has its own structure of relationships, dis-

[1] Gombrich, p.309.

tinguishable from, although related to, stylistic relationships. The phonetic, grammatical, lexical and syntactic features of an author's language are relevant to his style only when there is a choice open to him. Only by examining the linguistic options open to an author, therefore, can we discuss his style. This is not to say that linguistic features are unimportant. In order to discover whether an author is using rhyme or assonance we must know something of his pronunciation;[1] to discover whether he has intended a pun we must know something of contemporary lexical usage; to apprehend his meaning we must understand the syntax and grammar of his period. But these matters are not stylistics, but what might be called proto-stylistics, comparable to the learning of a foreign language as a prerequisite to studying the literature of that language. A grammar of an author's language is not a study of his style. To point out, for example, that a modern author uses the third present singular of verbs in -*s* is not to say anything about his style. He has no choice. The relationship between stylistics and proto-stylistics is well authenticated by a recent study of Old English metrics. Here it is convincingly demonstrated that the Old English poet could give a particular shape to his theme by the utilisation of linguistic and metrical options.[2]

Within the field of choice, grammatical and syntactical choices are perhaps the simplest. The field of lexical choice is more complex. And here we come up against a slightly different aspect of choice. Register, for example, can be a purely dramatic feature associated with the choice of certain kinds of character; on the other hand, it can be a more truly stylistic choice. We have called attention to the use of contrasting registers in the poetry of Charles of Orleans. But these effects can also be contextual. Thus the words 'Pray you, undo this button,' in themselves linguistically unremarkable, take their effect, not so much from what might be called a local linguistic

---

[1] But such sound effects can, of course, be part of stylistics. Cp. W. K. Wimsatt, pp.153–66.

[2] Lydia Fakundiny, 'The Art of Old English Verse Composition', *RES*, xxi (1970), 129–42, 257–66.

choice, as much as from an implied contrast with the aureate language of the earlier part of the play. Moreover, the author's choice involves also his choice of mode, and this can be as significant as his purely verbal choices in a limited area of the text. As we have tried to show, for example, the theme of poverty could be presented in the figure of St. Francis, or as a personification, or in emblematic form. Each choice would have its linguistically distinctive form, in that, according to the author's choice of form, the relationship between picture and theme would be different. Or, in choosing to write in the romance mode, or in a more realistic mode, the author is choosing to present his characters and situations in different ways and in a different linguistic form. We have tried to demonstrate some of these differences at the linguistic level, by an analysis of the use of rhetorical descriptions in romances and in fabliaux. And, in addition to these large modal configurations, the author may exploit also the diachronic aspect of literary language. That is to say, he may operate a process of recall by evoking stock responses. This can be done in a number of ways. In the case of Old English poetry, it is done by the manipulation of lexical sets. As Quirk has pointed out, 'the setting up of lexical expectations is basic in the composition and enjoyment of the early poetry'.[1] But expectations can be of other kinds too. As we have tried to show, this expectation can be also schematic. That is to say, a certain configuration of events can, by a kind of shorthand, recall previous examples of the schema. This is what we imply when we talk of a literary tradition. But the author can also call upon certain conventional images as we tried to show in connection with the Middle English lyric.

Finally, it might be asked how far it is possible to construct a history of styles in Old and Middle English Literature, and what criteria one would apply. I have tried to suggest, in the last chapter, the kind of question which such a study should ask, but it is doubtful whether it is possible to proceed very far

[1] R. Quirk, 'Poetic Language and Old English Metre', in *Early English and Norse Studies*, p.153.

with such an investigation. Some general points could, perhaps, be made. For example, a late medieval taste for the florid and dramatic, as well as for the symmetrical, can be seen by comparing, for example, *A Talkyng of þe Loue of God* with the earlier versions in *On wel swuðe god Ureisun of God Almihti* and *Þe Wohunge of ure Lauerd*.[1] There is, also, as we have tried to suggest, an increasing sense of naturalism, a movement, as it were, in a metaphor from the visual arts, from the 'linear' towards the 'painterly' and from 'closed' to 'open form'.[2] Such a movement might be seen by comparing a stanza by the thirteenth-century trouvère, Jacques de Cambrai, with a possible later rendering. The stanza is as follows:

> Ensi com sor la verdure
> Descent rosée des ciels,
> Vint en vos cors, Virge pure,
> De paradis vos dous Fiels

[*As the dew falls onto the grass from the sky so, fair Maiden, your sweet son enters your body from heaven.*]

Compare with this

> He cam also stille
>   There his moder was,
> As dew in Aprille
>   That falleth on the grass.
> He cam also stille
>   To his moderes bour,
> As dew in Aprille
>   That falleth on the flour.
> He cam also stille
>   There his moder lay;
> As dew in Aprille
>   That falleth on the spray.[3]

---

[1] *A Talkyng of þe Loue of God*, edited by M. S. Westra (The Hague, 1950); *Þe Wohunge of Ure Lauerd*, edited by W. Meredith Thompson, E.E.T.S., 241 (1958).

[2] Cp. H. Wölfflin, *Principles of Art History*, translated by M. D. Hottinger (London, 1932), pp. 18–23, 124–54.

[3] *Early English Lyrics*, edited by E. K. Chambers and F. Sidgwick (London, 1926), pp. 107, 349; cp. Spitzer, 152–63; Barbara C. Raw, 'As Dew in Aprille', *MLR*, lv (1960), 411–14.

The re-organisation of the motif is significant. In the French, the lack of any indication of the basis of the comparison of the incarnation with the falling dew, suggests the artificial nature of the simile. In the English poet, a naturalistic twist is given by the emphasis on the quietness of the falling dew. That this too has a basis in patristic literature does not invalidate the argument. There is a difference between the apparent incongruence of the way in which the image is used in the first poem, and the ambiguously turned image of the second. The second, in fact, may be regarded as moving in the direction of 'disguised symbolism'. At the same time, it may be noted, it has a formally isometric pattern reminiscent of the musical form of the late Middle Ages. Moreover, the metaphor is complicated by the introduction of the term 'Aprille', suggestive, as Miss Raw points out, of the *reverdie* and thus again of the naturalistic implication of the image. This blending of different levels of discourse is again characteristic of 'disguised symbolism' and seems to represent a movement towards 'closed form'. We have noted, too, the way in which a greater flexibility of syntax, and an increasing vocabulary, are reflected in some of the later poetry. There is here a kind of two-way movement; on the one hand, the isometric principle favoured in the late medieval period, the development of repetitive lyric forms such as the *virelai*, the *balade* and the *rondel*; on the other hand, we see in the use of register, aspect and syntax in Charles of Orleans something of a movement from 'multiplicity' to 'unity'.[1] These are perhaps the lines on which a study of the history of medieval styles might be constructed.

A final example. Fierz-Monnier calls attention in her book *Initiation und Wandlung* to the following passages:[2]

> Inde toro pater Aeneas, sic orsus ab alto:
> Infandum, regina, iubes renovare dolorem,
> Troianas ut opes et lamentabile regnum
> Eruerint Danai. . . .

[*Whence father Aeneas, from his lofty couch, 'Inexpressible, o queen, is the*

---

[1] See Wölfflin, pp.155-9.
[2] A. Fierz-Monnier, *Initiation und Wandlung* (Bern, 1951), p.23.

sorrow you bid me recall; how the Greeks utterly destroyed the power of Troy and her woeful realm.']

and

> Enéas sozrit un petit
> Et en apres se li a dit
> 'Dame', fait il, 'ma grand dolor
> Me remembrez et ma tristor.

[*Eneas smiled a little and then said to her, 'Lady,' he said, 'you call to mind my great sorrow and my sadness.'*]

This seems to illustrate briefly the points which we have been trying to make. On the one hand, we notice certain obvious linguistic points. Thus, the disjunction in the French is emphatic but repetitive, whereas in Virgil the separation of *infandum* and *dolorem* is not only emphatic, but implies, by reference to the lexical matrix, a contrastive effect. Aeneas is commanded to speak the unspeakable. On the other hand, the absence of a possessive before *dolorem* gives a certain generality to the tone, lacking in the French, even allowing for the different grammatical structure of the two languages, the one possessing an article and the other not. These, and many other cases of the author's linguistic choice, would have to be analysed in order to give a full account of the difference between the two passages. But there is another way in which the two passages differ. The difference of effect is, after all, not inconsiderably due to the French poet's presenting us with a smiling Eneas. Here we are immediately up against the problem of the linguistic structure of connected discourse. Our understanding of the words *tristor* and *dolor* must be modified by their conjunction with *sozrit*, just as our conception of Aeneas in Virgil is modified by the words *toro . . . ab alto*. Our author's choice is thus a series of concentric circles with ripples of meaning passing more and more widely as the linguistic stone is cast into the water. We have touched upon many matters in this book but in fact the time is not yet ripe for a rigorous and definitive work on this topic. Many proto-stylistic studies must yet be made and this book can only hope to suggest some ways towards the future.

Bibliographical Index

ABRAMS, M. H., *The Mirror and the Lamp*, New York, 1953.

ALANUS DE INSULIS, *Anticlaudianus*, edited by R. Bossuat, Paris, 1955.

ALFRED, *Augustine's Soliloquies*, edited by T. A. Carnicelli, Cambridge, Mass., 1969.

Ancrene Wisse, Parts six and seven, edited by G. Shepherd, London, 1959.

The Anglo-Saxon Minor Poems, edited by E. Van Kirk Dobbie, The Anglo-Saxon Poetic Records, VI, New York, 1942.

ANSELM, *Meditationes*, PL, clviii, cols. 709-854.

ARNULFE OF ORLEANS, *Allegoriae super Ovidii Metamorphosin*, edited by F. Ghisalberti, Memorie del Reale Istituto Lombardo di Scienze e Lettere (Classe di Lettere, Scienze Morali e Storiche), xxiv (1932), 157-234.

AUERBACH, E., *Mimesis: The Representation of Reality in Western Literature*, translated by Willard Trask, Princeton, 1953.

— *Scénes from the Drama of European Literature*, New York, 1959.

— *Literary Language and its Public in late Latin Antiquity and in the Middle Ages*, translated by R. Manheim, London, 1965.

AUGUSTINE, *De Civitate Dei*, edited by B. Dombart, Leipzig, 1905, 1909.

BENNETT, J. A. W. and G. V. SMITHERS, *Early Middle English Verse and Prose*, 2nd edn., Oxford, 1968.

BENSON, L. D., *Art and Tradition in Sir Gawain and the Green Knight*, New Brunswick, 1965.

Beowulf and the Fight at Finnsburg, edited by F. Klaeber, 3rd edn., London, 1950.

BERCHORIUS, PETRUS, *De Formis Figurisque Deorum*, edited by J. Engels etc., Utrecht, 1960.

BERNARD, *Opera Omnia*, edited by J. Leclercq and H. M. Rochais, Rome, 1957 ff.

— *Liber de Passione Christi et Doloribus et Planctibus Matris Ejus*, PL, clxxxii, cols. 1133-1142.

BERNARDO, A. S., *Petrarch, Scipio and the 'Africa'*, Baltimore, 1962.

BETHURUM, D., 'Chaucer's Point of View as Narrator in the Love Poems', *PMLA*, lxxiv (1959), 511–20.

BEZZOLA, R. R., *Les origines et la formation de la littérature courtoise en Occident (500–1200)*, Paris, 1944–63.

BLOCH, M., *Feudal Society*, translated from the French by L. A. Manyon with a foreword by M. M. Postan, London, 1962.

BLOOMFIELD, M. W., 'Distance and Predestination in *Troilus and Criseyde*', *PMLA*, lxxii (1957), 14–26.

BOCCACCIO, GIOVANNI, *Genealogie Deorum Gentilium Libri*, edited by V. Romano, Bari, 1951.

— *Teseida: Delle Nozze d'Emilia*, edited by A. Roncaglia, Bari, 1941.

BONAVENTURA, *Opera Omnia*, Quaracchi, 1882–1902.

BONJOUR, A., '*Beowulf* and the Beasts of Battle', *PMLA*, lxxii (1957), 563–73.

BOOTH, W. C., *The Rhetoric of Fiction*, Chicago, 1961.

BORROFF, M., *Sir Gawain and the Green Knight: A Stylistic and Metrical Study*, Yale Studies in English, 152, New Haven, 1962.

BRODEUR, A. G., *The Art of Beowulf*, Berkeley & Los Angeles, 1959.

BROOKE-ROSE, C., *A Grammar of Metaphor*, London, 1958.

BRUNETTO LATINI, *Li Livres dou Tresor*, edited by F. J. Carmody, University of California Publications in Modern Philology, XXII, 1948.

DE BRUYNE, E., *Études d'esthétique médiévale*, Brugge, 1946.

BRYAN, W. F. and G. DEMPSTER, *Sources and Analogues of Chaucer's Canterbury Tales*, Chicago, 1941.

Carmina Burana, edited by A. Hilka and O. Schumann, Heidelberg, 2 vols., 1930–41.

CAXTON, WM., *The Book of the Ordre of Chyualry*, edited by A. T. P. Byles, E.E.T.S., 168 (1926).

— *The Book of the Knight of the Tower*, edited by M. Y. Offord, E.E.T.S. (SS) 2 (1971).

— *The Foure Sonnes of Aymon*, edited by O. Richardson, E.E.T.S. (ES) 44, 45 (1884–5).

— *The Prologues and Epilogues of William Caxton*, edited by W. J. B. Crotch, E.E.T.S., 176 (1929).

CHARLES D'ORLÉANS, *Poésies*, edited by P. Champion, Paris, 1966.

CHARLES OF ORLEANS, *English Poems*, edited by R. Steele and M. Day, E.E.T.S., 215, 220 (1941, 1946; reprinted with bibliographical supplement, 1970).

CHASTELLAIN, GEORGES, *Chronique de Jacques Lalain*, edited by J. A. Buchon, Collections de chroniques nationales françaises du treizième au seizième siècle, Paris, 1825.

CHAUCER, GEOFFREY, *The Complete Works*, edited by F. N. Robinson, 2nd edn., London, 1957.

Chaucer and Chaucerians, edited by D. S. Brewer, London, 1966.

Chaucer Criticism, edited by R. J. Schoeck and Jerome Taylor, Notre Dame, 2 vols., 1960, 1961.

Chaucer und seine Zeit, see *Symposion für Schirmer*.

Christ, see *The Exeter Book*.

CHRISTINE DE PISAN, *Ballades, Rondeaux and Virelais*, edited by K. Varty, Leicester, 1965.

CHYDENIUS, J., 'The Theory of Medieval Symbolism', *Acta Societatis Scientiarum Fennicae*: Commentationes Humanarum Litterarum, XXVII(2), 1961.

COLERIDGE, SAMUEL TAYLOR, *Miscellaneous Criticism*, edited by T. M. Raysor, London, 1936.

CURRY, W. C., *Chaucer and the Medieval Sciences*, 2nd edn., London, 1960.

CURTIUS, E. R., *European Literature and the Latin Middle Ages*, translated by W. R. Trask, London, 1953.

DANTE ALIGHIERI, *La Divina Commedia*, edited by T. Casini and S. A. Barbi, Firenze, 6th edn., 1923.

DAVIES, R. T., *Medieval English Lyrics*, London, 1963.

DAY LEWIS, C., *The Poetic Image*, London, 1947.

DESCHAMPS, EUSTACE, *Oeuvres Complètes*, Vol. VII, edited by G. Raynaud, S.A.T.F. (1891).

DONALDSON, E. T., *Piers Plowman: The C Text and its Poet*, Yale Studies in English, 113, New Haven, 1949.

— 'Chaucer the Pilgrim', *PMLA*, lxix (1954), 928–36.

DOUGLAS, GAVIN, *The Shorter Poems*, edited by Priscilla J. Bawcutt, S.T.S. (1967).

The Dream of the Rood, edited by M. J. Swanton, Manchester, 1971.

DUNBAR, WILLIAM, *Poems*, edited by W. M. Mackenzie, London, 1932.

DUNNING, T. P., *Piers Plowman: An Interpretation of the A-Text*, Dublin, 1937.

Early English and Norse Studies, Presented to Hugh Smith, edited by A. Brown and P. Foote, London, 1963.

Elene, edited by P.O.E. Gradon, London, 1958.

English Historical Documents, I, edited by Dorothy Whitelock, London, 1955.

English Lyrics of the xiiith *Century*, edited by Carleton Brown, Oxford, 1932.

ENKVIST, N. E., J. SPENCER and M. J. GREGORY, *Linguistics and Style*, London, 1964.

Essays on Malory, edited by J. A. W. Bennett, Oxford, 1963.

Essays on Style and Language, edited by R. Fowler, London, 1966.

Essays on the Language of Literature, edited by S. Chatman and S. R. Levin, Boston, 1967.

The Exeter Book, edited by G. P. Krapp and Elliott Van Kirk Dobbie, The Anglo-Saxon Poetic Records, III, New York, 1936.

FARAL, E., *Recherches sur les sources latines des contes et romans courtois du moyen âge*, Paris, 1913.

— *Les arts poétiques du xii et du xiii siècle*, Paris, 1924.

FELIX, *Life of St. Guthlac*, edited by B. Colgrave, Cambridge, 1956.

FISER, E., *Le symbole littéraire*, Paris, n.d.

FLETCHER, J. B., 'The Allegory of the Pearl', *JEGP*, xx (1921), 1–21.

FOWLER, R., 'Linguistics, Stylistics; Criticism?', *Lingua*, xvi (1966), 153–65.

FOX, J., *The Lyric Poetry of Charles d' Orléans*, Oxford, 1969.

FRANK, R. W., 'The Art of Reading Medieval Personification-Allegory', *ELH*, xx (1953), 237–50.

— *Piers Plowman and the Scheme of Salvation*, Yale Studies in English, 136, New Haven, 1957.

FRYE, NORTHROP, *The Anatomy of Criticism*, Princeton, 1957.

FULGENTIUS METAFORALIS, *see* Liebeschütz.

Genesis A., see *The Junius Manuscript*.

GHISALBERTI, F., 'Giovanni del Virgilio espositore delle Metamorfosi', *Giornale Dantesco*, xxxiv (1933), 3–110.

GIST, M. A., *Love and War in the Middle English Romances*, Philadelphia, 1947.

GLUNZ, H. H., *Die Literarästhetik des europäischen Mittelalters*, Bochum-Langendreer, 1937.

GOMBRICH, E. H., *Art and Illusion*, 3rd edn., London, 1968.

GOODRICH, N. L., *Charles of Orleans: A Study of Themes in his French and in his English poetry*, Geneva, 1967.

GOWER, JOHN, *The Complete Works*, edited by G. C. Macaulay, Oxford, 1899–1902.

The Harley Lyrics, edited by G. L. Brook, Manchester, 1948.

HENRYSON, ROBERT, *Poems and Fables*, edited by H. H. Wood, 2nd edn., Edinburgh, 1958.

HILL, D. M., 'The Structure of *Sir Orfeo*', *Mediaeval Studies*, xxiii (1961), 136–53.

Historical Poems of the xiv^th *and* xv^th *Centuries,* edited by R. H. Robbins, New York, 1959.

HORACE, *Works,* edited by E. C. Wickham, Vol. II, Oxford, 1903.

HUIZINGA, J., *The Waning of the Middle Ages,* translated by F. Hopman, London, 1924.

HULBERT, J. R., 'Chaucer's Pilgrims', *PMLA,* lxiv (1949), 823–8.

Huon of Burdeux, edited by S. L. Lee, E.E.T.S. (ES) 40, 41 (1882–3).

Ipomedon, edited by E. Kölbing, Breslau, 1889.

ISIDORE OF SEVILLE, *Etymologiae,* PL, lxxxii.

JOHN OF GARLAND, *Integumenta Ovidii,* edited by F. Ghisalberti, Messina & Milan, 1933.

JOHN OF SALISBURY, *Policraticus,* edited by C. C. I. Webb, Oxford, 1909.

JOHNSON, W. S., 'The Imagery and Diction of *The Pearl*: towards an Interpretation', *ELH,* xx (1953), 161–80.

JORDAN, R. M., 'The Narrator in Chaucer's *Troilus*', *ELH,* xxv (1958), 237–57.

JULIANA OF NORWICH, *Revelations of Divine Love:* MS. Sloane 2499; modernised version by Dom Roger Hudleston, 2nd edn., London, 1952.

The Junius Manuscript, edited by G. P. Krapp, The Anglo-Saxon Poetic Records, I, New York, 1931.

KASKE, R. E., 'Langland's Walnut-Simile', *JEGP,* lviii (1959), 650–4.

KATZENELLENBOGEN, A., *Allegories of the Virtues and Vices in Mediaeval Art,* London, 1939.

KEAN, P. M., '*The Pearl*': *An Interpretation,* London, 1967.

KLIBANSKY, R., E. PANOFSKY, and F. SAXL, *Saturn and Melancholy,* London, 1964.

KNIGHTLEY, W. J., '*Pearl*: The "hyȝ seysoun"', *MLN,* lxxvi (1961), 97–102.

LANGLAND, WILLIAM, *The Vision of Piers the Plowman,* edited by W. W. Skeat, Oxford, 1886.

— *Piers Plowman : The A Version,* edited by G. Kane, London, 1960.

LAWLOR, J., *Piers Plowman: An Essay in Criticism,* London, 1962.

LECLERCQ, J. and J-P. BONNES, *Un maître de la vie spirituelle au* xie *siècle, Jean de Fécamp,* Paris, 1946.

LEWIS, C. S., *The Allegory of Love,* Oxford, 1936.

LIEBESCHÜTZ, H., *Fulgentius Metaforalis,* Leipzig, 1926.

Le livre des faicts du bon messire Jean le Maingre, dit Boucicaut, edited by J. F. Michaut and [J. J. F.] Poujoulat, Nouvelle collection des mémoires pour servir à l'histoire de France, II, Paris, 1836.

LUKÁCS, G., *Studies in European Realism*, translated by Edith Bone, London, 1950.

LYDGATE, JOHN, *The Minor Poems*, edited by H. N. MacCracken, E.E.T.S., 192 (1934).

— *Poems*, edited by J. Norton-Smith, Oxford, 1966.

— (?), *The Assembly of Gods*, edited by O. L. Triggs, E.E.T.S. (ES) 69 (1896).

MACROBIUS, *Commentarii in Somnium Scipionis*, edited by J. Willis, Leipzig, 1963.

MÂLE, E., *L'Art religieux de la fin du Moyen Âge en France*, 3rd edn., Paris, 1925.

MALORY, THOMAS, *Morte Darthur*, see *Works*, edited by E. Vinaver, 2nd edn., Oxford, 1967.

MANDEVILLE, *Travels*, edited by P. Hamelius, E.E.T.S., 153 (1919).

MARITAIN, J., *Art and Scholasticism*, London, 1930.

VAN MARLE, RAIMOND, *Iconographie de l'art profane: allégories et symboles*, The Hague, 1932.

MAXIMS, see *The Anglo-Saxon Minor Poems*.

MIKO, S. J., 'Malory and the Chivalric Order', *Medium Aevum*, xxxv (1966), 211–30.

Ovide Moralisé, edited by C. de Boer, M. G. de Boer and J. Th. van't Sant, Amsterdam, 1915–38.

OWINGS, M. A., *The Arts in the Middle English Romances*, New York, 1952.

The Oxford Book of Medieval Latin Verse, edited by F. J. E. Raby, 2nd edn., Oxford, 1959.

PANOFSKY, E., *Early Netherlandish Painting*, Cambridge, Mass., 1953.

Partonope of Blois, edited by A. Trampe Bødtker, E.E.T.S. (ES) 109 (1912).

Patterns of Language, edited by Angus McIntosh, and M. A. K. Halliday, London, 1966.

Patterns of Love and Courtesy; Essays in Memory of C. S. Lewis, edited by J. Lawlor, London, 1966.

PATTERSON, W. F., *Three Centuries of French Poetic Theory*, Parts I & II, Ann Arbor, 1935.

Pearl, edited by E. V. Gordon, Oxford, 1953.

PÉPIN, J., *Mythe et allégorie*, Paris, 1958.

PETER OF BLOIS, *De Amicitia Christiana et de Charitate Dei et Proximi*, PL, ccvii, cols. 871–95.

PETRARCH, FRANCESCO, *Africa*, edited by N. Festa, Firenze, 1926.

Piers Plowman: Critical Approaches, edited by S. S. Hussey, London, 1969.

PIKE, JOSEPH B., *Frivolities of Courtiers and Footprints of Philosophers: Being a translation of the First, Second and Third Books and Selections from the Seventh and Eighth Books of the 'Policraticus'*, Minneapolis, 1938.

Political Songs of England, edited by T. Wright, Camden Society (OS) 6, 1839.

Ponthus and Sidone, edited by F. J. Mather, *PMLA*, xii (1897), 1-150.

Prester John, edited by F. Zarncke, *Der Priester Johannes*, Abhandlungen der Phil.-hist. Classe d. K. Sächsischen Gesellschaft der Wissenschaften, VII (1879), 827-1030; VIII (1883), 1-186.

PRUDENTIUS, *Psychomachia*, edited by M. P. Cunningham, Corpus Christianorum, Series Latina, CXXVI, Turnholt, 1966.

PSEUDO-BONAVENTURA, *Meditations on the Life of Christ*, edited by I. Ragusa and R. B. Green, Princeton, 1961.

— *Meditaciones de Passione Christi*, edited by M. J. Stallings, The Catholic University of America: Studies in Medieval and Renaissance Latin Language and Literature, XXV, 1965.

Purity, edited by R. J. Menner, Yale Studies in English, 61 New Haven, 1920.

RABY, F. J. E., *Christian-Latin Poetry*, 2nd edn., Oxford, 1953.

Religious Lyrics of the Fourteenth Century, edited by Carleton Brown, 2nd edn., Oxford, 1952.

RENÉ, ROI, *Oeuvres Complètes*, II, edited by Le Comte Quatrebarbes, Angers, 1844.

RICHARD OF ST. VICTOR, *De Quatuor gradibus violentae caritatis*, edited by G. Dumeige, Textes philosophiques du moyen âge, III, Paris, 1955.

RIGG, A. G., *A Glastonbury Miscellany of the Fifteenth Century*, Oxford, 1968.

ROBERTSON, D. W., *A Preface to Chaucer*, Princeton, 1963.

— and B. F. Huppé, *Piers Plowman and Scriptural Tradition*, Princeton, 1951.

ROLLE, RICHARD, *The English Writings*, edited by H. E. Allen, Oxford, 1931.

The Romance of Guy of Warwick, edited by J. Zupitza, E.E.T.S. (ES) 42, 49 (1883-7).

RUSKIN, JOHN, *Complete Works*, edited by E. T. Cook and A. D. O. Wedderburn, London, 1903-12.

SALTER, E., *Piers Plowman*, Oxford, 1962.

— 'Medieval Poetry and the Visual Arts', *Essays and Studies*, 1969, 16–32.

SALZER, A., *Die Sinnbilder u. Beiworte Mariens in der deutschen Literatur u. lateinischen Hymnenpoesie des Mittelalters*, Darmstadt, 1967.

SANDOZ, E., 'Tourneys in the Arthurian Tradition', *Speculum*, xix (1944), 389–420.

SCHOFIELD, W. H., 'The Nature and Fabric of *The Pearl*', *PMLA*, xix (1904), 154–215.

The Seafarer, edited by I. L. Gordon, London, 1960.

SEZNEC, J., *The Survival of the Pagan Gods*, translated by Barbara F. Sessions, New York, 1953.

Sir Gawain and the Green Knight, edited by J. R. R. Tolkien and E. V. Gordon, revised by N. Davis, Oxford, 1968.

SMALLEY, B., *English Friars and Antiquity*, Oxford, 1960.

SOUTHERN, R. W., *Medieval Humanism and other Studies*, Oxford, 1970.

SPEARING, A. C., 'Symbolic and Dramatic development in *Pearl*', *MP*, lx (1962), 1–12.

— '*Patience* and the *Gawain*-Poet', *Anglia*, lxxxiv (1966), 305–29.

SPITZER, L., '*Explication de Texte* Applied to Three Great Middle English Poems', *Archivum Linguisticum*, iii (1951), 1–22, 137–65.

STAHL, W. H., *Macrobius, Commentary on the Dream of Scipio*, New York, 1952.

Stil-und Formprobleme in der Literatur, edited by P. Böckmann, Heidelberg, 1959.

STOCKTON, E. W., *The Major Latin Works of John Gower*, Seattle, 1962.

Style in Language, edited by T. A. Sebeok, New York, 1960.

SWEET, H., *Anglo-Saxon Reader*, 15th edn., revised by Dorothy Whitelock, Oxford, 1967.

Symposion für Walter F. Schirmer, edited by A. Esch, Tübingen, 1968.

DE TERVARENT, GUY, *Attributs et symboles dans l'art profane, 1450–1600*, Geneva, 1958–64.

THOMSON, H. J., *Prudentius*, London & Cambridge, Mass., 1949.

THORNTON, H. & A., and A. A. LIND, *Time and Style*, London, 1962.

Three Old English Elegies, edited by R. Leslie, Manchester, 1961.

TUVE, R., *Allegorical Imagery*, Princeton, 1966.

ULLMANN, S., *Language and Style*, Oxford, 1964.

URBAN, W. M., *Language and Reality*, London, New York, 1939.

VASTA, E., *The Spiritual Basis of 'Piers Plowman'*, The Hague, 1965.

VINAVER, E., *Form and Meaning in Medieval Romance*, The Presidential Address of the Modern Humanities Research Association, 1966.

DE VINCK, J., *The Works of Bonaventure*, Paterson, 1960.

The Wanderer, edited by T. P. Dunning and A. J. Bliss, London, 1969.

WEINBERG, B., *A History of Literary Criticism in the Italian Renaissance*, Chicago, 1961.

WHEELWRIGHT, P., *The Burning Fountain*, Bloomington, 1968.

WICKHAM, GLYNNE, *Early English Stages*, I, London, 1959.

The Wife's Lament, see *Three Old English Elegies*.

WILLIAMS, D. J., *A literary Study of the Middle English Poems 'Purity' and 'Patience'*, B. Litt. Thesis, Oxford, 1965.

WILMART, A., *Auteurs spirituels du Moyen Age latin*, Paris, 1932.

WIMSATT, J., *Chaucer and the French Love Poets*, Chapel Hill, 1968.

WIMSATT, W. K., *The Verbal Icon*, Lexington, 1954.

WÖLFFLIN, H., *Principles of Art History*, translated by M. D. Hottinger, London, 1932.

WOLFSON, H. A., *The Philosophy of the Church Fathers*, Cambridge, Mass., 1956 ff.

WOOLF, R., 'Some Non-Medieval Qualities of *Piers Plowman*', *Essays in Criticism*, xii (1962), 111–25.

— *The English Religious Lyric in the Middle Ages*, Oxford, 1968.

Glossary of Terms

ALLEGORY: a polysemous narrative.

ASPECT: the point of view from which something is seen. Note the following: (i) the consuetudinal aspect, *x does y; x is a bad man* (ii) the indicative aspect, *x is doing y; x is a fat man* (iii) deictic aspect, *look at x doing y.*

COLLOCABILITY: the statistical frequency with which words are conjoined; cp. *blind eyes, blind mouths, a lusty infant, a lusty sorrow.*

COMPLEXITY: complexity of associations.

CONGRUENCE: refers to the relationship between image and meaning.

EMBLEM: a static and pictorial device in allegory.

EPISODE: an action in which the characters are set in a limited and common context.

FICTIO: a fictitious story given a moralisation.

FIGURA: an historical or legendary person used to typify certain qualities in an allegory.

FIGURE: repetition of themes; cp. PATTERN.

FOCUS: effect of closeness to the object described or distance from it; but also sharpness of detail. This depends upon the kind of words used and the number of such words in the discourse.

FOREGROUNDING: bringing into prominence, by whatever devices, certain components of the image.

FRAME: the boundary between episodes.

IDOLON: classical god or goddess used in an allegorical context.

IMAGE: the object of apperception in a work of art; cp. MEANING.

IMPACT: the emotional intensity or semantic depth of a word.

INTELLECTUAL: a word whose meaning is not a matter of immediate sense perception; contrasted with INTUITIVE as in *fat: fatness.*

MEANING: the structure of the image; cp. IMAGE.

MIMETIC NARRATIVE: tells a story.

MODE: the form in which the *ruda materies* is realised.

MORALITY: an abstraction in action; dramatic rather than allegorical.

MYTHIC NARRATIVE: illustrates a theme.

PATTERN: thematic linking of repeated themes; cp. FIGURE.

PERSONIFICATION: an abstraction given concrete embodiment in an allegory. cp. MORALITY.

PERSPECTIVE: the composition of the literary picture.

PICTURE: the surface, literal level of an allegory.

PLOT: the creation of a narrative which exists within a space–time continuum.

REALISATION: CREATION OF THE IMAGE.

SEMANTIC DEPTH and SEMANTIC SHALLOWNESS; see IMPACT

SEMANTIC DENSITY; cp. TEXTURE.

SEMANTIC RANGE: the number of different concepts the vocabulary of a language expresses.

SYMBOL: sign + secondary meaning.

TEXTURE: the exploitation of lexical sets gives close texture or semantic density.

THEME: prose or deliberate meaning.